Frontispiece

ELIZABETH, COUNTESS OF FINGALL.

SEVENTY YEARS YOUNG

MEMORIES

of

ELIZABETH, COUNTESS OF FINGALL

Told to

PAMELA HINKSON

"Those whom the Gods love die young."
(They never grow old.)

THE LILLIPUT PRESS
in association with
CARTY/LYNCH
1991

First published by Collins of London in 1937
Paperback edition first published in 1991 by
THE LILLIPUT PRESS LTD
4 Rosemount Terrace, Arbour Hill,
Dublin 7, Ireland
in association with
Carty/Lynch, Dunsany, Co. Meath

A CIP record for this
title is available from
The British Library.

ISBN 0 946640 74 2

Cover design by Jole Bortoli
Offset from the original edition
and printed in Ireland by
Colour Books of Baldoyle

ILLUSTRATIONS

ACKNOWLEDGMENT

I wish to offer my most grateful thanks to my collaborator Miss Pamela Hinkson for her help in writing this book. I also thank Mr. Walter Callan, Mr. Gerald Heard, Countess Balfour, Dr. R. I. Best, Miss Charlotte Dease, Dr. Myles Dillon, Mrs. W. M. J. Starkie, Dr. George O'Brien, Mr. T. U. Sadleir and Mr. Robin Watson for their kind assistance and encouragement.

E. M. FINGALL.

FOREWORD

Lady Fingall ends her memoirs on a sombre note: a neighbour's house has been burned by republicans during the Irish civil war; a messenger has arrived at Killeen Castle with the grim news that it is next on the list; the Earl and Countess gather their most precious possessions, huddle up to the study fire with the shutters closed and await the dreaded knock, retiring eventually in the pale light of morning. Killeen escaped then. The knock came sixty years later, long after the castle had passed from family hands, when a wing was set on fire during the H-block protests of 1981.

Seventy Years Young is an important book. The Earl and Countess of Fingall were members of the *ancien régime* who, unlike many of their aristocratic contemporaries, did not pull up stakes and depart after independence, but chose to live on in what must sometimes have seemed to be an uncongenial, if not inhospitable, homeland. Lady Fingall was renowned for her ability to make friends and many of the influential figures of turn-of-the-century Ireland, and England, are quickly, if lightly, sketched in these pages. Her relationship with Horace Plunkett, one of the enigmatic personalities of the period, which remained central to all her extracurricular activity after her marriage, is more fully explored.

Lady Fingall was a Burke from Moycullen in Co. Galway. In 1883, after a whirlwind courtship, she married the eleventh earl, when she was seventeen and he twenty-four. Plunkett was the family name, and the Fingalls inherited a seat in the House of Lords. The Plunketts were heirs to the three peerages of Fingall, Louth and Dunsany. During the penal days the lords of Louth and Fingall remained Catholic, while the Dunsanys, in order to retain the family lands, became Protestant. When the necessity had passed the lands were returned to their Catholic kinsmen, but the religious distinction stayed in place.

Fingall, the 'somnolent Earl' (he regularly dozed off after dinner), was as dull as the Countess was lively. Vivacious rather than beautiful, with a quick intelligence and a gregarious nature, she longed for travel and society, while he confined himself to horses and the great hunting county of Meath. It was an unorthodox partnership which might not have lasted as it did had she not discovered a sympathetic companion, and one who would provide a ready outlet for her talents, in the neighbouring castle of Dunsany.

Lady Fingall's relationship with Horace Plunkett is the thread which holds this book together. It lasted (probably unconsummated – he was an exceptionally fastidious man) without ever rupturing the friendship with his cousin, the Earl. He remained a bachelor for the sake of Lady Fingall and was unquestionably in love with her. However, Bernard Shaw was to remark many years later, 'Yet I never felt convinced that he quite liked her.'

Plunkett is now remembered as the father of the co-operative movement in Irish agriculture. He is less well known as one of the leading moderates in that critical era between the fall of Parnell and the polarization of Irish politics during the first decade of the twentieth century. The third son of Lord Dunsany, he was threatened with tuberculosis, which swept away two members of his family, and spent almost ten years cattle-ranching on the high, dry plains of Wyoming. Returning to Ireland on his father's death in 1889, he mounted a campaign persuading Irish farmers to adopt co-operative methods of processing and marketing. A Protestant educated at Eton and Oxford, Plunkett was an unlikely campaigner among the farmers of the south and west of Ireland, but his sincerity and idealism were such that within five years a federation had been established (the Irish Agricultural Organization Society – now the Irish Co-operative Organization Society) with several hundred member societies (co-operative creameries) attached.

It was a staggering achievement, but represented only the first part of a larger strategy, for he united farmers and industrialists, north and south, Catholics and Protestants, in an ultimately successful attempt to extract from the British administration

4

Ireland's first independent government ministry, the Department of Agriculture and Technical Instruction (with himself as Vice President), supervising farming and vocational education in the whole island.

Lady Fingall was, of course, involved with these schemes. She acted as hostess at Plunkett's dinner-parties and as interior designer for Kilteragh, his house in Foxrock; she grew tobacco in her garden and cider apples in the orchard ('Bottle of the Boyne' was to be the slogan); and, in 1910, inspired by AE, in conjunction with the poet Emily Lawless (another Plunkett cousin), she became a founder-member of the United Irishwomen, which was a prototype for the Women's Institutes in Britain, and flourishes as the Irish Countrywomen's Association today.

Plunkett's position was, however, vulnerable (he had been an MP since 1892) for he had challenged the political *status quo*. Lady Fingall describes the attacks on him, and on his movement, which came from both sides of the political divide. Unionists, in 1900, drove Plunkett from his parliamentary seat in South Dublin; and seven years later the nationalists had him replaced as Vice President of DATI by the uninspiring T.W. Russell.

Lord Fingall died in 1929, and Horace Plunkett in England in 1932 (as a Free State senator he had been burned out by republicans during the civil war). Lady Fingall moved to a flat in Mespil Road, Dublin, where she entertained on Thursday afternoons. (Terence de Vere White has included a charming picture of these occasions, and of an ageing, fragile but still vivacious Lady Fingall, in his autobiography, *A Fretful Midge*.) She died in 1944. Her memoirs, commissioned by Collins and dictated to Pamela Hinkson (daughter of the poet Katharine Tynan) had appeared seven years earlier. One tantalizing feature is the collection of letters from distinguished acquaintances which are quoted verbatim, and which have since vanished. Lady Fingall herself discloses that she destroyed Earl Haig's letters – they described too many manoeuvres (not all, possibly, on the battlefield). Enquiries of her descendants produced only a typescript of the memoirs (now in the National Library of Ireland) and the guest-book from Kilteragh (now in Trinity College Library). The typescript quashed rumours, current in Dublin for some time, that the original version of *Seventy Years Young* contained racy passages, later omitted on the advice of George O'Brien, the cautious Professor of Economics at UCD. It remains, however, a fascinating book, none the less so for Lady Fingall's throwaway remark, made in later life to a much younger contemporary: 'My dear man, I never slept with either King Edward or Sir Horace Plunkett!'

Trinity College, Dublin   *Trevor West*
April 1991

CHAPTER ONE

MY memory is like one of those toy kaleidoscopes, into which children used to look long ago. (I am still thrilled by a glass paperweight containing a miniature cottage and a figure walking towards it, which you have only to shake, to see both lost in a most realistic and thrilling snowstorm.)

Into the kaleidoscope I looked as a child. A myriad colours moved before my wondering, delighted eyes. Blues, greens, reds, pinks and gold. They were never still. How should one catch them and put them into a pattern, making them as quiet, as beautiful as the scene in the paperweight when the snow lay on it again?

I have the same difficulty as I sit looking at this kaleidoscope of life. The colours move and dance. They are now bright, now dim, clear again, dazzling. But there were all the lovely shadowy moments, the half lights, the indefinable things. How should one recapture or convey the magic of these? The dim gold evenings when one walked or talked with a friend. The dreams we had, the visions we had, when we were young, with gallant, foolish hearts to put right the world, which had waited so long only for us to put it right! There is magic not to be caught or put down in cold print. What can one say of childhood, except that it was childhood? And that conveys everything. I begin at the beginning and cross so easily those long, full years. So safe and strong is the thread by which one finds one's way back to childhood. All that the years have held cannot make a wall to stop one's passing. Last year, the year before, ten years past, are farther away, harder to reach, than this enchanted country that lies just within a gate of which one has never lost the key. And, having said that, I am just in time to contradict myself. I shall contradict myself as often in this book, I warn my readers, as I have contradicted myself during life. How dull

7

life would be, indeed, if one were always to agree with oneself! "I am a multitude," A.E. said once, when confronted with two articles of his, one of which flatly contradicted the other. There was a year between them. But there might be only a minute, and I might change my mind as I have often changed it, before I come to the end of a sentence. And I am a multitude. I take A.E.'s phrase and shelter behind it. The Japanese, in their art, discovered how dull a thing regularity could be. There will be no rules in this book, no straight road with milestones beside it, heavy blocks of stone as dull as tombstones, to tell you how far you have come and how far you have yet to go. It will wander as pleasantly as a country road, of which there are still a few left ; a road made for travelling feet of men and women and children and animals, a road on which one may dawdle and go as one pleases, climbing the bank sometimes to look over the hedges if there is something beyond them to take one's fancy. The small things one passes on such a road are as important as the great, and they remain in memory, measured according to the eyes that saw them.

The Back Door of my childhood's home and the scenes at it, stand out clearly, when meetings with Kings and Queens and world-famous people are vague and half forgotten. The road is as one travels it, and many travellers might go the same way and, describing it to each other after, not discover it to be the same. There are stretches when the sun is on it and flowers growing on the banks (meadowsweet and wild roses in Ireland) and one lingers longer on such a piece of road. And there are miles that drop out altogether, and one does not know how one progressed from one village to the next, only that one arrived.

I have read somewhere that a memoir is a trap for egotism. Certainly one cannot avoid the use of the pronoun I, so I make no apology beforehand for the number of times that it will appear. It is quite impersonal to me in any case, for I have discovered that after all, although the gate opens, I cannot enter into that lost enchanted country. It is not that

8

the key turns rustily or that the hinges creak, as all the keys and all the hinges of garden gates that one knew in childhood, used to do. The gate is wide and someone moves inside. But it is not I. Someone else, someone I can see as impersonally, as detachedly as though I had never met her before, saw and did these things of which I am going to tell. She is the chief performer on this stage, but only—in the manner of Ruth Draper—so that she may bring other performers before you, and present, if she can, a picture of a life that is now quite done with, a world that is ended. A life and a world, which, perhaps, for all their disadvantages and injustices, had beauty in them for some people, and effort and music and glamour and romance and colour and many dreams. Now things are much more evened up and fair, which is right, but the streets in which we walk are also more uniformly grey. We were very, very busy in those days, and now we have almost nothing to do except to sit by the fire and tell our reminiscences, and wonder if we really could have seen and known the things of which we tell.

There is a gauze curtain over the stage, I discover, such as we used in the days when we did tableaux at the Chief Secretary's Lodge when Gerald and Betty Balfour ruled there—highbrow historical scenes of Irish history, with a view to improving our own minds and the minds of the audience. Seen through the gauze, the stage has the appearance of something in a dream. And it has a dream-like feeling to me, this stage on which someone I once knew is about to play showman. She will begin at the beginning and do her best. Be patient with her. She is no historian. Dates. They are as elusive as fireflies, as the little brilliant moths that flew before a child on the bogs of Connemara. One lays one's hand on this and that, as one used to close it over the exquisite trembling wings and then open it to find an empty palm. So one abandons many of the dates, with the milestones of the straight machine-made road, planned for motors. And turning back to a world in which motors were once not dreamed of—and into which they came then as strange, rare and

9

terrifying machines, there is the wandering country road on which one may do as one pleases.

The showman—or woman—can only give you the scene as she saw it, not explaining why this or that made an impression, or why so much was forgotten. Is a memoir a trap for an egotist? Certainly it cannot be written impersonally. If one were to try to keep the teller out of it, it would be like a room without a fire, a book without a heart. Because it is a life. I make no claim for it, or excuse for it ; but for those whom it interests, this is how we lived. And no one certainly will ever live like that again.

In a dream—or reality—I stand, a child again, in the light of a Connemara evening. The lake water, which I can hear moving softly against the stones, is black and mysterious. The light is on the mountains, but it passes the lakes by. There is long shadow under the blue beauty of the mountains, and the little cottages are lost in it as though they had shut their eyes and gone to sleep. And I am eight years old, a long, thin child, with spindly legs and hazel eyes—that is all I remember of myself. I was a little "fey," as I was told then, often.

"Don't be going after the fairies, Missie," an old man has just said to me. In his coat of white Galway *bainin*, and with his blue innocent eyes, he might have come, himself, from fairyland. "For if you once start going after them they will never let you alone."

For the moment I am safe by the edge of the lake, since the fairies do not come near water, of which they are afraid. So I will not linger here, because I have run away to look for fairies, leaving my small brother and sisters in the nursery, with our new genteel governess, recently imported from Dublin, and as miserable in the wilds of Connacht as any one might expect her to be. I have slipped out without any one noticing me. For quite a long time before I put this plan into action, I had sat in the nursery with the others, free already in spirit. While I appeared to be listening dutifully to whatever Miss Murphy was saying, my eyes were turned towards the window, through which I could see the bog with the sun lighting it after rain. I could smell the mixed scent of turf smoke and wet gorse, without indeed being aware of it. It was simply the smell of the country, of the world in which my small years were lived—a wide world, it appeared, with Lough Corrib bordering it and the bright blue crags of the Twelve Pins guarding it. So disembodied was I already, that I seemed able to slip through the old house and escape, without any danger of being seen or discovered, as though I had wrapped myself in a magic cloak.

The house is always a little dim even on a spring or summer day. It smells of old wood and the boards creak under a child's feet. In summer the many little moths from the bog and the lake's edge come to fly about the landing with vague beautiful flashes of colour; sometimes we find them, alas, dying against the dusty windows, having beaten their wings on them in an effort to get back to the sunlight. I pass, going on tiptoe, the door of my father's study, which is called the Magistrate's Room, and from which he rules the district as a firm and just autocrat. At this hour the door stands open. My father is out in the fields, sitting under a large cotton umbrella like a patriarchal figure, watching his men while they work; now and again talking to them in Irish. The umbrella is made of bright yellow cotton, lined with green, and Father sits under it because he is half blind and his eyes cannot stand the sun, even the intermittent sun of Western Ireland. That umbrella, however, protects him from rain as well.

Or, he is looking at his woods and loving them, or considering his land as though it were something alive, stooping over it, because of his half blind eyes. He is a good farmer, and he makes his men work. In that picture of him, he is like the Master in the Bible.

As I creep out of the house and through the shrubbery, I see my mother walking in the garden that is peculiarly hers. Sometimes she works in it, her beautiful hands, which are perhaps her one and only vanity, carefully gloved. She grows pansies and violas and primulas and such softly coloured, gentle flowers in a pattern about the roots of an old twisted thorn tree, which must not be cut down because the cutting of it would bring bad luck. We children can see the thorn tree from the window of the room in which we sleep. In the dusk, or clear on some night of full moon, it is like an evil old man—tortured, perhaps, by his own sins—and we are afraid of it.

My mother wears grey alpaca, which makes a small rustle as she walks with her full skirts, a little cap on her head and a shawl. She has a collection of shawls and we never see her without one.

She is dreaming, too among her flowers, the far-away look that we know, in her pale blue eyes. If one of us should be hurt—if I, running through the shrubbery, should stumble over one of the protruding roots, and fall at once into the soft earth and the hard despairing hurt of childhood, she would come back from her dreams. I should be picked up, washed and bandaged, comforted. A little absent, a little impersonal, my charming, aloof mother would be, rendering these services. And then, I think, I should be forgotten. And she would return to that world in which she lived as she walked between her flower beds.

If I had passed her by, instead of hiding in the dark, chill dampness of the laurels, she might say: "Daisy . . ." with her air of faint surprise. She is, I discover now, rather like a mother bird, who brings up her children, throws them out of the nest and is then done with them.

To-day my mother is not thinking of me, evidently. (We are all, she believes, safely in the schoolroom in the charge of the new governess, who, she hopes, will prove a success.) I get safely through the shrubbery, where a few months ago a carpet of snowdrops glimmered beautifully under the dark leaves. At the wicket gate that leads on to the road, I hesitate between temptations. There is the bog with the wind over it, the exquisite softness of the wet soil when I take off my shoes and run over it, barefoot, like all

12

the peasant children; and the little wood of Killerania where Spanish gold is buried, as every one knows, and where fairies play between the bluebells with the hidden gold under their feet. Or there is my Tree, a copper beech, growing against the wall, and spreading its great branches over the road, so that a climber, hidden in it, may see, herself unseen, the whole world come and go. It is my great hiding-place when I have run away from my nurse, or from the genteel governess, who is greatly to be pitied, I realise. Could she have known what she was coming to, when she turned her face towards this wild land and these half-savage children?

I see the world from the branches of my Tree. Not so far down the road is the small village of Moycullen, with its white rain-washed walls and the bright blue spirals of turf smoke rising above the yellow thatch. And now (I wander for a moment) it is a summer afternoon, with the bog and the lake lying glistening under the sun. (But somehow the sun never got into the cold lake water to warm or light it.) The white bog cotton is blown across the brown bog before the wind, like scattered snow. Hidden in the thick foliage of the copper beech, I am lost in delicious coolness. Then comes the trot, trot of horses' hoofs. It is Bianconi's Long Car, going from Galway to Clifden, carrying passengers and mails, our touch with the world. The road was one of those made by Nimmo in the previous century, when he discovered in his road building how well the Irish could work for themselves and how eager the people were to help in opening up the country. Anything, anybody, might arrive by Bianconi's Long Car, a vehicle which came and went, raising a cloud of gold dust of romance with its wheels. On this particular day, for some reason, it has no passengers, and the driver pulls up to rest his horses under the shade of my Tree. He and the conductor look up and admire it, quite unaware of my small peering face lost amid the leaves and my listening ears. I lean forward against one of the branches. (I can feel now the cool sweet smoothness of it against my hot little brow. It felt like the satin of my mother's best frock when a child's face touched it.) In my excitement I nearly fall. What a surprise the men would get if I were to tumble down on top of them!

Is there a rustle of the shining leaves? They do not hear it. And, presently, the horses are whipped up again, and with trot, trot, and the sound of wheels, I hear the car go on, on its immense journey by Oughterard, where horses are changed, to Clifden and the coast.

But now, on another day, after a moment's hesitation, I go through the wicket gate, passing my Tree. Across the road is the high grey wall of the garden. The trees had been planted and the garden made, before the road was cut through our property.

In the garden one is very young and lost, with the high wall made higher by the ferns and the red and white valerian that grow on top of it. Everything that will grow here at all, grows luxuriantly. There are red-hot pokers, tall enough to frighten a child, half their height! I can see them now, flaming beautifully through the mist of some late summer morning. There is an apricot tree against the wall on which yellow apricots grow, that are small and very sweet. We steal them when the gardener is not looking. If, for instance, being coachman as well, he has put on his faded green livery with its smell of many years of rain and turf smoke, and his old top-hat which has great dignity, although the silk of it is worn and rough, to drive our mother on one of her rare visits to our neighbours—the Comyns at Woodstock, or the Martins at Ross, where Violet Martin and her brother Bob are still in the schoolroom, and the immortal partnership of Somerville and Ross and the fame of Ballyhooly still undreamed of. Or, to Galway town to do her monthly shopping, from which expedition my mother will return with the parcels piled as high and wide as they will go on top of the old brougham and every available corner inside packed as well. So that it seems indeed as if she must have bought the whole of Galway.

But on these shopping expeditions we two older children,

14

Daisy and Florence, are often taken too, perhaps to keep us out of mischief, for I can think of no other reason for filling further a vehicle that was full enough already. And, from among the parcels piled round us and on top of us so that we are half-buried, our small, rather sick faces (the road was appalling and the brougham swung and rolled and pitched like a ship) must have looked out a little strangely at other travellers on the road as we passed them.

Sometimes clothes had to be bought for us, winter overcoats and shoes and such things, at Moon's, the big shop, which seemed a place of wonder and colour and enchantment to us. It is still there, and not so much changed from the shop I remember, when we climbed the narrow street to it, pushing our way through an endlessly exciting crowd of dark-haired fishermen and shawl-covered women, all talking Irish and busy and alive with their own affairs. The men who filled the Galway streets—not always fishermen—wore the wide black hats which they wear to-day and in which Jack Yeats has painted them.

At Moon's, in the room upstairs above the street, we were measured and our needs considered and then, going downstairs again, my mother bought needles and cotton and tapes and such things. Afterwards we would go out and buy fruit for ourselves at a stall in the Square. The stall was bright with oranges and russet apples and brown nuts and long bars of gaily-coloured sugar-stick, as it stood against the grey background of the Galway houses. The woman who kept it wore a gaily-striped skirt of many colours, with a little black shawl forming a bodice, and she had shining dark hair parted in the middle and twisted at the back of her head. Many years later I was to discover that she and her fruit-stall made a Goya picture. But, of course, I had never heard of Goya then. We called the woman of the fruit stall "the Lady Anne," and treated her with great respect, but I have no idea at all what was the origin of this grand title. She was part of the Spanish colour which Galway had then as now, a descendant, no doubt, of some Spaniard who had sailed his ship into the Bay in the

15

days when the Tribes of Galway lived within their walls and traded with France and Spain.

Our shopping over, it is time for us to turn homeward. The clock in the tower of St. Nicholas' Cathedral, built by an ancestor of mine, has just given Galway the time. We hear the hour strike beautifully as the brougham trundles heavily through the narrow streets, past the great Spanish houses with their carved heads and their courtyards, which the builders of Galway—Burkes and Blakes, Morrises and Martins and Lynches and so on—made for themselves when they came back from their travels, bringing with them more than the Spanish wine which filled the holds of their ships. We are too sleepy to glance at the carved plaque set in a ruined wall, which commemorates one of the famous deeds of Galway; the hanging, by Lynch, the Sheriff, from this very window, of his own son, for the murder of a Spanish guest who had aroused the young man's jealousy. The history of Galway records that Lynch, having performed this stupendous act of justice, since no one else would do it, never spoke again.

The brougham pitching as we get to the open sea of the Connemara road, I feel very sick and my seat is changed. Presently I fall asleep and continue in uneasy slumber with the parcels falling about me, half in dreams, half in reality, until we draw up before the lit, welcoming door of Danesfield.

When I ran away to look for fairies and my absence was discovered, my mother would forget her garden. I think the faint dust of anxiety that I knew, would come to her blue eyes: "Daisy. Why will you do such things?" And, at the moment of the search for me, she is interrupted, by the arrival at the back door, where she dispenses her charities and her medical supplies, of Mrs. O'Flaherty, whose child is ailing, for the very reason that he has gone after the fairies, the poor misguided boy. And the fairies would have taken him surely, if it hadn't been that he was dressed in petticoats, a wise precaution which careful mothers of Connemara adopted in those days. Apparently the fairies had little use for my sex,

16

which explains perhaps why I escaped. I wonder what my mother's prescription was? Castor oil, of which we had brought back an ample supply from Galway last week? Ipecacuanha wine, a thrilling-sounding medicine? Anything with such a name must be efficacious. Gregory's Powder?

Meanwhile I have a respite and the whole magic world is mine. It is my world and belongs to me and I to it. Any one who is born in Connemara and gives their heart to it, is never really quite happy anywhere else. I run over the bog, bare-footed, dancing with joy. From my earliest years I have danced as often as I have walked. It was good at eight years old to be alive and have the bog before one and the many-scented wind across it, in one's face. Now and again I stand still to press my toes into the soft springy soil, and see the brown water ooze between them. What a lovely sound it made! I often stood like this, watching my toes disappear at last, and I know that the bog soil and the bog water gave my feet something that they kept all through life. All my joy in dancing later, the wonderful service my feet have given me, I am sure I owe to my Connemara bog, and my early, barefooted walking on it.

I turn towards the wood of Killerania, where the fairies are. I am more interested in them, than in the Spanish gold which is hidden there, although my father and I have some-times talked seriously about that, wondering whether it could be found. And indeed it would have been useful at Danesfield. Once, at least, I saw a rainbow drop its arc of colour among the trees of Killerania. So the gold *was* there! And one had only to dig to find it. I thought, one of these days when I was older, I would take a spade and dig until I came to it. I was sure that I had marked the secret spot where the rainbow ended.

My father, who is watching his men work while I am with the fairies, is a big man with a long brown beard. In a later memory of him that beard is white. He is a Galway Burke. To any one acquainted with Irish history, that says everything that need be said about our family. And for those un-acquainted with that history, the story would, perhaps, have no interest.

I am tempted to dwell upon it, but I resist the temptation. I may mention just that the first of the family, a de Burgo, came to Ireland with Strongbow and received from Henry II. a grant of the lands of all Connacht. If neither William de Burgo, nor his descendants, were able ever to take possession of the property which was nominally theirs as the result of this generosity (!) they nevertheless asserted their leadership most forcibly and left their mark wherever they went. Two descend-ants of William de Burgo were those famous Normans who took off their English garb by the banks of the Shannon, renouncing, with it, English nationality and English speech, and, putting on such clothes as the Irish chiefs wore, became "more Irish than the Irish themselves." They and their descendants built castles about Ireland and particularly about Galway, which they made their own county; and held them in turn against the English King and the native Irish. One of those castles stands still, in ruins, at Oranmore, on the road to Galway—dreaming over the water that creeps in to its walls from the Atlantic, to lie there as still and quiet as a lake, reflecting the skies and the sunset. There was a period when the de Burgos, having defeated the Irish O'Conors at Athenry, ruled the entire province, from the Shannon to the sea. They built much of Galway town, including St. Nicholas' Church, in the vaults of which many of them were laid at the end of their vigorous and stormy lives, and the wall about Galway itself, which was designed to keep the wild Irish at bay, with its inscription over the West Gate: "From the ferocious O'Flaherties, good Lord deliver us!" That was O'Flaherty country into which I looked, when, as a child, my eyes turned towards Connemara. But the O'Flaherties had been driven farther even than the "Hell or Connaught," to which, in a later century, Cromwell consigned the Irish. From the Shannon to Galway Bay, the de Burgos ruled, but in the desolate land of Connemara, the "ferocious O'Flaherties" awaited their chance of cattle raiding, to take back some of their own. Hardy sheep or cattle may find a living on that bog or mountain, searching between the heather for a small stretch of sweet pasture, but it is of little use for anything else, although it held such riches for a child who loved it.

My father's land was almost the last stretch of good land on the Connemara road. His woods were the last woods too, and, in my memory, they seem to stand like outposts of an advancing army, looking across the wild Irish country, as my ancestors, who took the land, might have sat on their horses, looking towards Connemara, but going no farther.

The Burkes, like other great families, whether Irish or Danish or Norman, were constantly changing the side on which they fought. And there was a period during the great days of Galway, when a by-law decreed that neither O, nor Mac, nor Burke should "strutte" in the streets of the town. Nor should any citizen receive into their house or "feast else" one bearing any of these names. Galway then had a mint of its own and a Governor (several of Galway's Governors, at another time than that of this decree, were Burkes), and its own by-laws.

I do not know at what time my ancestors took possession of the land about Danesfield. It was a long white house with a rounded bow at either side, and steps up to the front door, built probably a hundred years or so before I was born. It was not beautiful without, and inside, the furniture was Victorian. We were mid-Victorian then as our furniture was. Queen Victoria had been on the throne for nearly thirty years when I came into the world. But, standing again in memory in that hall, or on the wide landing upstairs, outside the door of the little room that was used as a chapel and where Mass was sometimes said, with my father in his locally spun tweeds as server, I feel that indefinable thing that the house held. The smell of it, the faint mustiness, the dust, lit by a ray of sunlight coming through the window. The brooding peace and security within those four walls. It remains for me the house that held childhood. No other house in all the world can ever be the same.

Or—another memory—a child still, I am curled up in one of the big chairs in the Magistrate's Room, watching my father receive rents, interview his tenants, or administer justice. No one seems to have objected to a little girl's presence on these occasions. And sometimes I look on at exciting scenes indeed. There is a day when a lunatic is brought before the magistrate to be committed to an asylum. Poor thing! She comes in between two enormous policemen, a tiny little woman like a small brave bird. Suddenly, without warning, she springs at my father and catches him by his beard, holding on to it with superhuman strength. She has pulled him half-way round the room before the astonished policemen can capture her and release the magistrate.

I sit, holding my breath, in one of the shabby, comfortable leather chairs. There is a hole in the leather and my wandering fingers find it and dive into it, pulling out springs and stuffing for which I shall be scolded later. I can feel now the cold leather against my small fingers, the stuffing of horsehair, as they were lost in it.

The Magistrate's Room has high windows and the shrubbery is outside. There is a tall cupboard against one wall. My father goes to it, and, opening a drawer, takes out important-looking blue papers. When he is receiving rents, he sits in the middle of the room behind his big desk. Near him is the rent table, with its many drawers narrowing away to the middle like the slices of a cake. A rent table now is a valuable antiquity. Then it was a usual piece of furniture in an Irish country house. Each drawer had a name on it, and the rent, being received from that particular tenant, was put inside, and a note added to the name, of the amount paid.

Sometimes a man or woman would come in with a long story—and how long a story in the rich Irish tongue could be, and how expressive! The men wore cut-away coats and knee breeches and carried their low top hats in their hands. The women wore scarlet petticoats—of Galway flannel—and black or brown shawls which they drew over their faces, half-hiding them, mysteriously. My father, who knew all of them and all their affairs, knew who was speaking the truth when he or she declared their inability to pay. Rents were often forgiven or reduced. Frequently they were paid in kind and we adjourned to the yard to see a load of turf from the bog tipped out of its cart and measured.

Again, to the Magistrate's Room, they brought their disputes and quarrels, of which they had many, arguing them out before my father in Irish, which, with its ninety-five sounds to forty-five in English, is the language of all others in which to conduct a quarrel. They had the land hunger of the Irish and especially of the Western Irish, and often the quarrel was about land and mereing fences and such things. My father, who was known as "Blind Burke," sat at the table, looking at them with the glitter of the cataract in his eyes, listening. When he gave his judgment they hardly ever went against it. They had the Irish passion for litigation, a passion he shared with them and which was to cause us trouble and embarrassment later, on our travels abroad. So, probably he understood better and sympathised with them. Instead of going to the lawyers and the courts, they came to him, having complete trust in his justice and in his wisdom. In the same way they consulted him about all their business. Indeed, they took hardly any step without first asking his advice. He knew them all by name and they were all Paddy and Mary and Mick and Annie to him, as their children were. The troubles and joys of their lives—there were more of the former than the latter!—touched him as closely as his own. He was the Master to them, as my mother was the Mistress, and neither ever failed them in an hour of need.

My father spoke and understood Gaelic and we had an Irish-speaking nurse. She wore a white-frilled cap such as French peasant women wear, a petticoat of scarlet flannel and a checked apron with a little black shawl crossed over her bodice. She taught me to speak Irish, and family tradition has it that my first words were spoken in Irish. "Faugh Sin."

21

("Get out of that,") I am reputed to have said, clutching my mother by the skirt and pulling her out of my way, because I wanted to look at something and those voluminous skirts blocked my view. Otherwise I remember little of my nurse, except that she rubbed my face ferociously with soap and water, giving me a distaste for having my face washed or touched which I have kept ever since. She left my nose with an upward tilt which was straightened out later when I fell on it in one of my first falls out hunting, with greatly improved results to my appearance, I was told by my heartless friends! As a proof of psycho-analysts' theories it is a fact, that never, in a nursing home or elsewhere, have I ever allowed any one to wash my face, since I grew up and attained freedom in such things.

My memory of the drawing-room at Danesfield is that it was a shabby, rather faded room, and very little used. There was a table in the middle of it, on which a glass case, holding a bouquet of wax flowers, stood, with a crochet wool mat under it. Round this decoration books were arranged with an appalling regularity and tidiness, which forbade all thought of their ever being read. On the chimney-piece an old French clock ticked under its glass shade. By it, the minutes that we were allowed in this room were numbered, and when it struck a certain dim chime, like some sound coming from a world a long way away, it was time for us to go to bed. There were whatnots about the room, with bits of old china on them and shells and such things, and an ottoman, on which one might sit as uncomfortably as in a railway station waiting for a train. Sometimes my mother lay on the sofa in the bay window, to read. She could look up now and again and see, through the window, without moving, what her children were doing in the shrubbery and if they were at the work to which they had been set, weeding the flower beds. Sometimes she would put away her book, and a beautiful Rosary beads, which some one had brought her from Italy, would slip through her fingers. Was she praying, then? I do not know. She was religious, but not *dévote*, I think. She was passive as far as file would let her be. I think of her sometimes as a lovely slender ship, blown before the strong winds of my father's temperament. She would have been content to lie at anchor in some peaceful backwater, undisturbed by winds and storms. But, all her life, she will do what other people want her to do. Although—I realise—she surrenders her will to my father and later to us, it is only her body that we have. She slips into her own world, her own quiet, still waters, lying here on the sofa, her fingers playing with the Rosary. Or she is lost in a book. It may be a bound volume of *All the Year Round* in which a novel by Mr. Dickens appears as a serial. She will keep that serial to read aloud to my father, later.

Sometimes, for no apparent reason that I can discover, unless my mother has heard that such is the custom elsewhere—in England, for instance, from which distant country our neighbours at Ross have recently imported a new governess—the two eldest of us are dressed up in our best frocks and our most befrilled trousers, and we go down the wide stairs, hand in hand, to my mother in the drawing-room. And she, having evidently forgotten this arrangement, looks at us as we stand in the doorway, with the most charming surprise—and, after a moment's uncertainty—pleasure. It is on one of these occasions, that, gazing at me as though she saw me for the first time, my mother says: "You have a face like a wild flower . . . . like a daisy." That is how I come to my name, the name by which my friends are to know me always, although I have been christened Elizabeth.

There is an old musical-box which is a great treasure. It stands on a table in the drawing-room. On it is painted a picture of a lady and gentleman in the most lovely clothes, bowing to each other before they dance the minuet. What are the tunes that it plays? I cannot remember, although I can hear now the faint silvery notes that suited the atmosphere of the Danesfield drawing-room. I am allowed, as a great treat, to wind the musical-box.

Our mother had always an air of repose, in the intervals of her busy life. She was eternally occupied, yet never hurried,

23

coming and going on her feet that were beautiful like her hands. She was perfectly made in every way. And when she died many years later, the doctor said that he had never known a case in which the machinery of a body had worn out so perfectly and simultaneously, no one strength or limb failing before the other. There was no sad decline or maiming for her. All the machinery ran down together and the clock stopped.

Only now do I wonder about her. Children accept their parents, with their love, their charm, their peculiarities and whims, not considering them or wondering about them. They are as inevitable as life and the security of childhood, not to be considered dispassionately. Is my mother happy with her somewhat hard and tempestuous husband? Are they suited to each other? She seems to love him. "George," she says sometimes, helplessly, looking at him rather as she looks at us when we do something surprising. At the moment we are two perfectly-behaved children. Incredible! And how long will it last? And is this the effect of the new Dublin governess, who has spent quite a lot of time since her arrival, looking out at the rain-swept bog, her own face as tearful as the sky? She is at least as successful as the English importation of the Martins, who had stirred my mother's unusual envy until the afternoon when she took us, visiting to Ross, and, as we waited for our hostess, heard one of the girls call upstairs, "Mother. H'all the little Burkes are in the 'all." After that my mother ceased to be envious of her neighbours' ambitious acquisition.

CHAPTER TWO

My father remembered the last Famine, and the scenes at the door of Danesfield, when he had helped to lift sacks of flour and Indian meal on to the backs of men who staggered under the weight of them. Everything that the landlords had then, they shared with the people. I am speaking of the good landlords, of course, not of the absentees, whose sins were to be paid for by all of us. My father remembered the people dropping by the roadside on their way to the Big House for help, the "coffin ships" going out from Galway Bay. Those emigrants who reached America alive, were to establish a race sworn to implacable hatred of England. He remembered the smell in the air that foretold the blight, and sometimes when he stood looking at the land, without seeing it, he would lift his head, sniffing for a warning which he would understand if it were to come again.

In my childhood the people were terribly poor, and bore their poverty with apparently complete resignation. They were deeply religious, and accepted literally the teaching that this world was only a road to the next. What did it matter then, if it was hard to walk, when it led to such unimaginable bliss? We children used to visit them in their cottages on the bogs or in the village, where we were welcomed beautifully.

"God save all here!" we would say, standing in the doorway, blinking for a moment in the turf smoke and choking until we grew accustomed to it. "God save you kindly!" the answer would come.

Out of the obscurity their faces look at me as they looked then. Lined with suffering, but dignified and often beautiful. They received us like kings and queens, and frequently, unknown to our parents, of course, we sat with them to their meal of "Potatoes and Point," taking the good flowery potato in our small hands and dipping it into the herring dish in the middle of the table which was the "Point."

The young people went to America, leaving the old and the sick at home. And the old people stood on the quays until the ship was out of sight, wailed and keened as for the dead, and returned to the terrible quietness of a little house from which the young are gone. Sometimes, after years, they came back, having made a fortune. A returned American was one of the possible exciting fellow passengers beside whom someone might sit on Bianconi's car. I don't think that we ever travelled by that vehicle. In our lumbering brougham we were safe from the wind and rain on winter days when Bianconi's car swung past us, lifting its passengers to the mercy of the elements as only an outside car can lift them.

They were good sons and daughters, those Irish boys and girls, and the Mail carried in the "well" of the Long Car brought regular money home from America to make life easier for the old people. The Long Car carried many parcels in its "well" besides Her Majesty's Mail, and the conductor was a sort of general messenger for the people in the villages. He brought food supplies, an odd bit of bacon as a treat, tea and sugar, or the herring that was to be the point to the potatoes. He brought other things—cottons and sewing-materials for the women, tobacco for the men. The arrival of Bianconi's Long Car was the great event of the day in all the villages through which it passed. The whole population would turn out to receive it, and the conductor, bringing his flushed face out of the depths of the "well" after diving for the last package, still had time to tell the news or say a word about politics. Then the driver would whip up his horses and the Long Car would continue on its journey.

Leaving us, it went on into Connemara and the country that had once been the O'Flaherties', but, in my childhood was Martins' country, although that now only by name. The Martins were one of the Norman "tribes" of Galway and had lived like the other families of the "tribes" for a hundred years or so inside the walls of the town, trading with France and Spain

26

and building fortunes with their trade. Until, in the sixteenth century, there was a general moving out from within the walls and the Norman "tribes" discovered the country of Galway. The Martins cannot have been very good business men, for the land they took to themselves, 200,000 acres of it, was true Connemara country, bog and mountain and lake. They built on it, Ross, still the home of one branch of the Martins at the time of which I write, and Dangan and Ballinahinch Castle. It was at Ballinahinch that the most famous of that famous family lived—Richard Martin, the promotor of Martin's Act of 1822, the first Act to be passed in any parliament to protect animals ; and the man who, more than any other man, established the moral conscience of England with regard to the treatment of animals. This new conscience was proved by the act of 1835, protecting all domestic animals, which was passed a year after Martin's death.

Galways keeps its stories of Richard Martin and I heard them, naturally, as a child. He was a characteristic Galway gentleman, brave, violent, wildly generous, but also intensely pitiful. He lived in the great days of Galway duelling, when his neighbours were known as Blue-Blaze-Devil Bob, Nineteen-Duel Tom, and so on. He himself bore the name Hair-Trigger Dick. But it is as Humanity Martin, or Humanity Dick, that he is remembered.

The Long Car travelled through Oughterard and took the road that had once been Richard Martin's "avenue"—of which he had boasted to his friend George IV., when he called him to admire the Long Walk at Windsor, that it was forty miles long. And the travellers on it could look towards Ballinahinch. But the Castle had already passed from the Martins then and the last of that branch had gone to America. No wonder. For the stories were still fresh in my childhood of the wild and extravagant hospitality at Ballinahinch in Richard Martin's day and of the reckless giving to any one who asked or was in need, that had left the one time King of Connemara to die at last in poverty, an exile at Boulogne. I heard tales of the immense kitchen at Ballinahinch and the feasting in it when the whole countryside came to be fed; and of how, often, the beggars on their way there lined the avenue—an exaggeration, of course. Perhaps they lined one of the many miles of it.

Galway then was full of stories. Across the waters of Corrib Lake stood the Castle of Menlo, where Sir Val Blake's doings kept a countryside amused and delighted. They had splendid names, these Galway gentlemen, and the whole life was gay and rich and spacious, generous and wildly extravagant. No wonder that the crash came at last.

I don't think that I ever passed Ballinahinch in those days. Distance was still distance before the coming of motors, and the other side of the county was a long way away. Our life in our corner of it was very quiet, although we knew vaguely of the gaiety of the East side, where the Blazers hunted their incredible country of stone walls, so close together, bordering such small fields, that those who hunted there must have been in the air most of the time. It was that life that gave Galway the reputation it had then, of being the gayest county in Ireland. We had few neighbours and my father was unsociable and my mother, although she did so much, delicate. Or perhaps the delicacy was imposed upon her. I cannot believe that it would have been any great strain to her to put on that grey satin dinner dress—which, on the rare occasions when she wore it, rustled so beautifully to a child's ears, and touched with such magic and glamour a child's cheek—and go out to dinner. Sometimes, if rarely, this did happen. And, as rarely, people dined with us. The proof I have of this fact is a characteristic one. I remember two naughty children creeping down the stairs to loot whatever might be left on the tray, put down for a moment outside the dining-room door.

There was no great extravagance at Danesfield. For all of us, I suppose, it was the closing page of that chapter. I think the good wine that had been famous in Galway still filled many of the cellars—claret from Bordeaux and port from Portugal and Spain. Buttered claret was much drank by the

28

gentlemen, and I heard stories of the manner in which much of this wine had been brought in, not paying any duty.

When my mother read aloud to my father and to us, on long winter afternoons, beside the dining-room fire, I used to sit staring at an enormous sideboard against the opposite wall. It was decorated with heavy carved heads and there were strange marks defacing it, and here and there, the heads were damaged. That damage had been caused by bullets fired by intoxicated gentlemen, trying to prove their sobriety in this manner, before they collapsed to spend the rest of the night under the dining-room table. Had I heard that story from my parents, or in the nursery, where the servants and my nurse told stories over the fire and looked into the coals to read the future, or sought omens in teacups? I do not know. But there is somewhere, another picture, a thing seen, or a thing told—to an imaginative child the wall that keeps the two apart is very thin, and confusion easy—a gentleman being assisted on to an outside car in the early morning, at a hall door, and held there by a faithful servant as the car drives away.

I am sure I never saw that picture. We had no such revelry at Danesfield, although, evidently, there had been such scenes earlier and the older servants may have remembered them. Our rare entertainments were of the quietest and most decorous. And my memory of the front door is that hardly any one ever came to it. The front of the house seems to have had a blank look, the windows staring across the country, like blind eyes. It is a look that the windows of Irish country houses often have, as though indeed that was the spirit inside them, the spirit of the colonists and conquerors, looking out across the country which they possessed, but never owned.

But we were part of the country surely. To my father, Galway and his land held everything that he desired in life. Away from it, he was lost and only half alive. He spent his days out of doors, going off after breakfast and returning when it grew dark. He would take a sandwich for his lunch and eat it while his men rested at midday and ate the frugal meal they had brought with them. He had great simplicity, and seeing him among them, one could hardly have told master from men. His clothes were shabby and nearly as threadbare as theirs. I think the cleanliness of his, must have been almost the only mark of his superior rank.

There was much dancing at the Cross-roads then. A strange rather melancholy stately dancing, it was, two long lines of men and women facing each other, their arms folded, their bodies swaying. That is my memory of the Cross-road dancing as I must have seen it in some red and blue dusk of a Connemara evening. And there were "Patterns," somewhat similar to the *Pardons* in Brittany, for which fair booths were set up, with oranges and apples and sweets and gingerbread all mixed together gaily for sale. There were dancing competitions, and I think, as in Brittany, there was a religious association, or had been originally, and perhaps the religious part had lapsed and the "Pattern" had become a purely frivolous occasion, although there is little frivolity about that memory of mine. There was an old piper who used to play for the Cross-roads dancing or at a wedding, and other such occasions. His name was Burke and he was, I believe, a relative of ours, if an unacknowledged one. He was a beautiful old man with a long beard and uplifted, sightless eyes. For he was blind too. He had manners that any of us might have envied.

It must have been just before the Church began to wage war on the Cross-road dancing and other gaieties of Irish rural life. No doubt with the best intentions. But the dullness of country life that followed hastened the departure of the young for America.

The Back Door at Danesfield—I give it the capitals because of its dignity and importance in our lives—and the kitchens and the yard were so full of interest that we could be indifferent to the blankness of the front door. We had a modest and unpretentious staff of servants—all daughters of tenants on the estate—but we had also a great many unofficial servants, self-appointed, I think, who wandered through the house and through our lives, doing any work except their own, with a delightful enthusiasm.

I don't know if these vague figures who move through my memory—always ready to put down a brush or a duster (and indeed they might as well put them down for all the effect they had!) to play with a child or to tell us a story, whispering over it terrifyingly in the dusk of the nursery before the lamps were lit—received regular wages. I think probably they were content with their meals in the big kitchen—where, on a smaller scale, we were following the example of Ballinahinch, undaunted by that warning—and their lodging. The cook, who ruled the kitchen, was enormous—I see the firelight that filled the kitchen, on the wide expanse of her apron, making it rosy and kind. But she was bad tempered and we did not dare visit her except by special invitation, as on Hallowe'en, when we gathered round the fire to eat apples and roast nuts. How warm those memories are, lit by the wonderful fires of those days when coal was fifteen shillings a ton, or thereabouts, and turf unlimited for the cutting, on the bog! Chill economy of fires then was a thing undreamed of. Indeed, economy of any kind had not yet dawned upon us as a virtue to be practised. We had the Irish tradition which despised such a restraint, leaving it to our English and Scottish neighbours. One Irish servant, at least, defined as grand house a one "where as much was thrown away, as was used."

I don't believe that that kitchen fire ever went out. It seems to me, looking back, that there was always a rosy glow in the kitchen as there was in the turf ash on the cottage hearths. It was the life of the house. Now we have a thousand labour-saving devices, gas-cookers and electric fires and wonderful stoves that look the same, whether they are lit or not. It is all clean, economical, wonderfully practical. In an emergency one can have hot water at once. What convenience! But—I remember the glow in the kitchen at Danesfield. We have put out the fire of life with that fire.

But the turf smoke still rises in bright blue spirals above the Connemara cottages, to make lovely colour against the brown and purple bog. I believe some of those fires have never gone out since I was a child.

Growing up to turf fires, we accepted the wonder of them, how they might fade to grey ash, apparently cold and dead, and yet one had only to blow them to see the spark still there, pile fresh turf on it and have a fire again. I think now that those grey ashes were symbolic of the years of my childhood. Quietness had followed the Fenian Rising of '67 which had died tragically as soon as it was born, on a bitter March night when the Dublin mountains and all that they held, were hidden under the snow. The weather was always against the Irish, it seemed. Then or later, I heard of the winds holding off a French fleet in Bantry Bay that might have set Ireland free. I don't know where I listened to such tales, learning to be a small Rebel.

There was a period when the country lay quiet, exhausted by famine and poverty. But, as with the turf fires, the spark was still there in the ashes, waiting for the breath, the wind that should stir it again.

There were the usual Irish yards at Danesfield, made generously as to space, one opening out of the other, and surrounded by stables and farm buildings with grey weather-stained and mossy roofs. There were all the country delights for children, to make us rich. Ricks of hay and straw, round which we used to play hide and seek. Cattle and horses moved with mysterious, enchanting sounds within the dim doors. There was always life coming and going in the yard. Carts carrying hay and straw and turf, with apparently endless leisure for the drivers to stop and talk. It was a time of leisure. No hurrying and scurrying of the minutes racing past, before one can even put out one's hand to touch them, such as we have to-day. I thought that that was just an illusion of age, but my young friends tell me that they feel it too. No time, no time, is the song of the minutes as they go by. Then, they ticked as slowly, as peacefully, as the old clock under its glass shade in the drawing-room could tell them on a long summer afternoon. That clock had the wise, cautious face of an old nurse. And it was like an old nurse, marshalling the minutes as its charges.

32

I am afraid that one of our entertainments, provided by the yard, was the slaughter of poultry at which the domestic staff would look on, sometimes taking us to share the fun.

From the kitchen, the stone passage, a mysterious place full of shadows at evening, ran to the Back Door. One of the pantries off this passage was my mother's dispensary and the shelves of it were stocked with wonderful medicine bottles, bandages and ointments and such things, which were a great source of fascination to us. When my mother attended her amateur dispensary, Florence and I were allowed to assist. We would not have missed that treat for anything. We came and went between the dispensary and the Back Door, where the patients awaited their turn, sitting about the steps.

They had immense faith in my mother, far greater faith in her than in the doctor. A new energetic one had just come to the district full of the enthusiasm of the reformer. Poor young man! The women dismissed him simply from their superior feminine wisdom and experience. "He went about telling the mothers to wash the children, as if they hadn't enough to do. Sure, what was the use of washing them when they only got dirty again?"

All the gossip of the neighbourhood was spread and discussed while the women waited to see my mother. The rich, sonorous Irish tongue filled the air, which was warm with it. Florence and I acted as messengers, enjoying ourselves vastly. We go flying to our mamma who has an apron on over her grey alpaca, giving her a nun-like and heavenly appearance as she lifts a bottle and holds it against the light. We stare at the beautiful colour of the moving liquid, half-forgetting our tale of the mysterious sickness which has afflicted Mrs. Kirwan's second youngest child, aged three. (Can it be that he has gone after the fairies? I wonder, with a sudden strange feeling of guilt lying heavily on my small heart.)

Castor oil is a standard remedy which evidently cures a great many and varying illnesses. Carrying a small bottle of

33

it to Mrs. Kirwan, I tremble lest a like remedy should be prescribed for me.

Once there was such an unprecedented demand for this medicine that the supply—even the ample supply we had thought, brought from Galway on our last shopping expedition—ran out. What could have happened to make every woman in Moycullen and the district suddenly decide to dose herself and her family with castor oil? Had they been listening to the new doctor, after all?

We were illuminated as to the reason for the strange demand on my mother's resources, one Sunday in Moycullen Church, when we were almost overpowered by the sickening smell of castor oil. The women's side of the little Church—or Chapel as it was called, Church being then considered a Protestant word, and there was a rigid segregation of the sexes in Irish country churches—reeked of it. We could hardly sit through the long hour of the Mass and sermon in that atmosphere. Someone had heard that castor oil was the best of all tonics to promote luxuriant hair and the story had been passed on, in a way which the modern student of advertising and publicity, might envy. With the result that every woman in Moycullen had decided to test the truth of it and had drenched her head in the castor oil which my mother supplied.

At the end of the long thrilling day—and how long the days of childhood were—there is the hour already mentioned, when my mother reads aloud to us. She reads *The Times* newspaper to my father who cannot see to read for himself. His blindness has cut him off from a good many activities. He cannot hunt or ride. This is less of a deprivation because there is no hunting in our neighbourhood. We had our local race meeting, of course, for which my father once offered to present a prize. It should be called the "Danesfield Dish," he said, instead of the usual "Danesfield Plate." I do not know if the "Danesfield Dish" ever materialised.

The important news in *The Times* was presently done with, and my mother took up the bound volume of *All the Year Round* to read, *Our Mutual Friend* or *Dombey and Son*.

My father treated Dickens as though he were the Bible, and would cross-examine us later on the book we had heard, so we must listen carefully to my mother's clear sweet voice, or we shall be caught napping when we are asked, "What's the odds so long as you're 'appy?" and must supply the name of the book from which it is a quotation.

Only Florence and I, of course, are present at that reading. The other two, my youngest sister and the one boy, whom my father calls Burke Junior, are still in the nursery.

I have another clear picture which stands out on that dawdling misty road of childhood's memory, with nothing to link it with anything that went before, or came after. There is an election. It only concerns me because I see my father walk down to the poll at Moycullen, in the most patriarchal manner, at the head of his retainers and tenants. The days of the great Galway elections, when Richard Martin stood for Parliament and the Martin supporters—brought by sea to vote—and the supporters of the opposing candidate, fought each other on the quays of Galway, are over, and this is a peaceful scene. It was quite a usual scene at election time in Ireland before the power of the landlords was broken. That power lasted much longer in the West than elsewhere. Before railways came to open up the country, before motors were dreamed of, when no one had ever heard of telephones and wireless, new ideas travelled as slowly as any other traffic. So, in Western Ireland we remained feudal, even when the revolutionary wind had begun to stir elsewhere. We had an extra hour of time by our clocks—an hour and a half actually from Greenwich time—because we were nearer the setting sun; and we had an extra hour and a half of that chapter which I saw, and which Parnell was to end for ever.

I have just read Lady Gregory's life of her husband, Sir William Gregory, and find that when he stood for Parliament in 1857, "In the Western baronies, James Martin of Ross and George Burke of Danesfield took the lead in bringing up the voters." And "at Tuam the hussars were charging with drawn swords to enable my voters to come up."

35

The Galway landlords had their own rules of life and, many of them, left-handed families, to whom they were much attached. And there was still the custom of fosterage, which the English, trying to conquer Ireland, had endeavoured wisely to stamp out, knowing how much the young lord drank in with his foster-mother's milk beside that nourishment for his body. Many rebels were made of the Anglo-Irish in that way. And the tie of fosterage was often as strong a one—sometimes indeed stronger—than blood relationship.

I don't know how I came to see that picture which is so clear, of my father leading his people to the poll to vote as he told them. Perhaps I looked down on it from my Tree, high above such things as elections.

I know now that the election which I saw was that of 1874 in which Colonel Nolan was returned as a Home Ruler. Two years earlier the Ballot Act had been passed, and for the first time the Irish tenants could vote secretly, and not as their landlords bade them. I saw the last page of a chapter before it was turned over. Never again, if we had stayed at Danesfield, would my father have walked to the poll in such a way. Our neighbour, Mr. Martin, watched his tenants go to the poll at that election to vote against him for the first time. It broke his heart and he went back to Ross, a changed man, to die.

Meanwhile, in Wicklow, a young squire not long home from Cambridge was playing cricket, captaining his County Eleven, dreaming of Irish gold which might be found in his own hills, and listening, in some summer twilight, to the old lodge-keeper's stories of the '98 rebellion and the flogging of the rebels. With the purple of the Wicklow mountains, the sweet waters of the mountain rivers and the air of the Wicklow valleys, to make heady wine for him if he needed it.

The name of that young squire was Charles Stewart Parnell.

He ended that chapter of Irish history of which I saw the twilight. The good landlords and the bad went down together,

36

as was inevitable. They had no grievance. Nine out of ten of them had chosen to live as colonists. Lennox Robinson has said truly of them in his brilliant little life of Bryan Cooper: "They were merely a colony, and colonists have no rights, a theory which was to cost England America. Had the Irish planter been of the same religion as the native Irish, Ireland would have won independence before America. . . . But because of the monstrous injustice of the plantation, the two civilisations were to remain separate and antagonistic for nearly three hundred years." And separate and antagonistic they have remained, alas, to this day.

The Irish landlords continued to be colonists. The very building of their houses, the planting of their trees, the making of the high walls about their estates (raised by the incredibly cheap labour of the natives whom their ancestors had tried to exterminate) declared that intention. As the Norman "tribes" had lived within the walls of Galway, with the "ferocious O'Flaherties" outside, so the Irish landlords lived within their demesnes, making a world of their own, with Ireland outside the gates. They were English politically, anti-Irish politically, and still the country had laid some spell on them, so that many of them came to be more lost and homesick away from it, at last, than those whom they had dispossessed. Cheltenham and Bath might hold some, pleasantly and peacefully. They could spend their rack rents there, undisturbed by threats or danger to life. "Tell the people," wrote Clanricarde from London, to his agent in Ireland after an attempt on the agent's life—and he wrote it on a post-card, so that there was no need to tell the people, who probably had the message before the agent had it—"that they need not hope to intimidate me by shooting you."

But Cheltenham and Bath must have seemed airless at times after the space of the Irish bogs, the wide skies, the lakes, and the great winds over the mountains. A man who owned thirty thousand acres in Connacht might feel stifled and dispossessed and even unimportant walking slowly up

37

those steep Somerset hills, playing at the Pump Room, and drinking the waters; or walking the Promenade at Cheltenham and considering the beauty of the Cotswold Hills. In such a place he might remember the cry of the snipe over the bog, the calling of the wild geese in winter, and hear again the sound the lake water made when a young man pulled an oar through it ; or how it lapped in the reeds, growing darker and sharper on some winter evening as he sat waiting for the duck to come in.

But these had chosen to remain colonists; and colonists have no rights. Their children were to pay the price when they discovered themselves to belong to no country, the world their ancestors had built within their walls lying now in ashes. And England abandoned her colony, with her colonists, when it suited her.

I do not see my father in Bath or Cheltenham. He would have died at once in such a place, and he was never the same man away from Galway and all that it held for him. The blow that ended the life at Danesfield for us came earlier, and had nothing to do with politics. There had been, I know, a number of bad years, and his face, turned to his land, had been anxious. I fancy there were a good many material cares at Danesfield about this time, of which we children knew nothing. Then the small brother and sister fell ill with diphtheria, a dread disease in those days. Two doctors hurried out from Galway to consult with the local doctor—that same earnest young man who had advised the women to wash the children. We saw the outside car drive up the avenue through the rain to the front door, for once the centre of interest. Florence and I had been moved out of the nursery into the big spare-room, where we slept side by side in an enormous four-poster bed which quite swallowed even the two of us. We kept the windows unshuttered and, waking in the morning, I saw the copper leaves of my beloved tree against a pale early sky.

There was a period when people came and went, when we were often forgotten by elders busy with other things and speaking in hushed voices and whispers, and we wandered through the corridors and got under people's feet, in the way of dogs or children forgotten and neglected in a time of trouble. Until we were rounded up by someone and shut firmly in the schoolroom, from which, of course, we escaped again, to discover for ourselves, since no one would tell us, what was happening in the house. The doctors went back to Galway and returned with strange tubes which they drew out of their mysterious bags. They disappeared within the closed door of the sick-room. Presently my father appeared with a stricken face, and my mother in tears. They had been given the doctors' verdict. We never saw the little sister and brother again.

We left Danesfield when I was about nine years old. Only now do I wonder what that going meant to the people about, what they did without my father in the Magistrate's Room, my mother at the Back Door, where did they go for counsel, for medicine, for help of every kind. It was before the days of district nurses, and the village handy woman assisted babies into the world, unless her place was taken by the herd, as happened quite frequently.

Our departure from Danesfield is one of the things that slips into obscurity. I remember little between that closed sick-room door and the quay at Bordeaux where the sickest little girl in all the world is being carried ashore in a big sailor's arms. I can feel now the roughness of the blue jersey against my cheek and smell the salt on it. The sailor talks an unknown tongue. What strange tricks this kaleidoscope of memory plays! There had been a journey to Dublin, certainly—an endless journey—and we had waited a long time at Ballinasloe. I had read the name aloud. " It's well they didn't call it Ballinaquick," I had said wearily. And in Dublin I had run in sudden terror past a shop called Elephant House, lest it should trample on me. There are only these two faint pictures between Danesfield and Bordeaux.

We had gone abroad to get away from the sad associations.

39

My father's sight was now very bad indeed, and a pilgrimage to Lourdes, in the hope of a miracle, was decided on.

We had our adventures on the way. My father, without the width of his own fields in which to loose his rough winds, gave us a good deal of trouble. There were many stormy scenes with innkeepers, *cochers* and the like. We little girls suffered dreadfully over our father's behaviour, especially as we had often to act as interpreters for him. At one inn he was alleged to have damaged an article of bedroom china, not then generally mentioned in polite society. As we were leaving, the host presented a bill for it. The *diligence* in which we were to continue our journey was waiting, other passengers in it, our luggage stowed away, a little crowd about the door to see our departure. " *Je paie, mais je preng*," declared my father in appalling French. But his meaning was, alas, unmistakable, and he strode down the stairs and through the delighted crowd to the *diligence*, carrying the domestic article which was the cause of the trouble in his hand.

At Arcachon there were pine woods that reminded me of my beloved woods at home. I slipped away when no one was looking, to wander in them, and got lost. It was so easy to get lost in those woods where any space between the trees might be a path. It was summer and the pine woods were dark and warm and scented. I can hear now the resin running in the wood, the drip of it down the tree trunks to the ground. I had run over the dry pine needles as happily, as confidently as I had wandered in my own woods at home. Until the moment came when I thought of turning back and I stood still, looking for the way, and realised that I could not find it.

That adventure in the pine woods at Arcachon was one of the strangest and most terrifying of my life. The heavy silence of the forest came down upon me like a pall, oppressing me. I became paralysed. There was no sound at all except that endless running and dripping of the warm resin. The trees stood still in the summer heat with no breath of wind to stir their branches. Through them I could get just a glimpse of blue sky, but in the pine woods it was almost dark. My small running feet made no sound on the pine needles. When I called, no one answered. The dripping of the resin in the semi-darkness became as frightening a sound as the ticking of a clock in an empty house.

Then I had a strange illusion. It may have been fear and that paralysis. But I seemed to have left my body. I could only see, and I thought I saw trees growing into fantastic shapes, moving like weird living things in a sort of rhythm. My eyes followed them, until I had the sensation of moving, still outside my body, in some rhythm, too. I had become one of the forest spirits. Had the trees laid a spell on me? I do not know. But whatever the spell was, it saved me. For I was found by an anxious search-party, half unconscious, beside one of the tree trunks. Had I been able to run wildly on, I am sure I should have been lost for ever.

At Toulouse we are troubled, my mother and her two small daughters, about the state of my father's soul. There is something piquant and touching, I feel, looking back, about the consultation we held over this, and my father's acquiescence in our arrangements made for him to confess his sins. It was essential if a cure was to be hoped for at Lourdes that he should be in a state of grace. And surely, after these battles with innkeepers and car drivers and the rest and the magnificent flow of oaths he had poured out on such occasions, he could not be in a fit state for Lourdes! Again our limited knowledge of French had to be put to the test. But it was not so easy. One of the qualifications with which Miss Murphy had come to us was a knowledge of French and the ability to teach it. But she had not provided such French as we needed now. We got a dictionary and pored over it, searching for a translation of our father's oaths. No dictionary, of course, provided them! He was a splendid swearer in the best tradition of his time. I confess that even while we trembled and were shocked, we were also exhilarated by the magnificent volume of his curses.

We did our best—having learnt in our catechism that God was reasonable and did not ask the impossible of any of us.

And with our father properly coached (what an education for his small daughters!) we guided him to the door of the Confessional and knelt ourselves at a little distance in an agony of hope and apprehension.

Unfortunately, concentrating on the swear words, father mixed up the rest of his French and confused the tenses. Instead of " *J'ai dit*," he declared " *Je dis*," and a string of oaths followed. The astonished *curé* thought, of course, that he had an anti-clerical lunatic the other side of the grating. We saw him leap out of his box to have a look at the man who was threatening him. Fortunately he had a sense of humour, and he laughed heartily as he grasped the situation. Then he found an English-speaking priest to loose our father from his sins.

We were at Lourdes for a few days, which I spent in a state of exaltation.

Alas, there was no miracle for my father, in spite of all our prayers. We posted again through France in a *diligence*, crossing the great central plain with its immense cultivation. We looked out and saw the women working in the fields, bent double by long years of this labour. Many years later, during the Great War, I was to sit beside Lord Northcliffe at lunch in London, and hear him speak of the Frenchwoman as the strength of France. I had at once before my eyes that picture which I saw at nine years old from the *diligence*. While beside me, Lord Northcliffe was saying that the money which paid the enormous indemnity after the Franco-German War came out of the stockings of the peasant women.

From one grey French town to another we travelled, past Chartres and into Brittany.

My mother took an *appartement* at St. Servan, and we children went to the convent school there, while my father returned, I think very gladly, to Danesfield.

CHAPTER THREE

My next memory is of the convent at St. Leonards, where I was "finishing" my education, or being "finished," preparatory to my coming out.

I was very happy during my year there. I loved the atmosphere of the convent and the nuns, although I must often have been a trouble to them. I remember a despairing nun saying to me: "Daisy! You have a quite good brain if you could only hold hold on to it for a moment!" But that was just what I could not do.

It was not so many years later that Horace Plunkett was to say to me as despairingly as the nun: "You can't keep your mind long enough on anything to boil an egg." But I am one of those fortunate people who have always had their eggs boiled for them!

It was my inability to concentrate that filled my instructresses with despair. I have never been able to play Bridge for this reason. Nor have I ever been a needlewoman, except during those schooldays under compulsion.

I had a great phase of piety at St. Leonards. While my mood of religious exaltation lasted I became uplifted, indifferent to the material things of this earth. My feet now, whenever they were free, carried me to the Chapel. I have often thought since, that the Catholic religion, if consistently believed in and practised, is only really for priests and nuns. For how can one ever keep out of a Church when one believes that Our Lord is waiting there?

Then—was it in a sermon or in some pious reading or Christian Doctrine class?—we were told that God takes people to Him at the time when they are at their best. The words sounded in my ears with a terrible clearness, like a sentence of death. I saw myself—little Pharisee that I was—clearly in this mood of piety. Perhaps I was on the way to be a saint.

43

Certainly never before had I been, perhaps never again would I be, as fitted to enter Heaven.

I was not destined to enter Heaven then. I was terrified that God would take me, and I had no desire to go. I kept out of the Chapel. I even took serious, carefully planned steps to make sure that they should not want me in Heaven, to prove that I was *not* at my best. I planned crimes carefully and committed them. I scaled the wall and went into the town to buy food and even wine—in France every one drank wine—for a midnight feast. I stole apples from the convent orchard.

In spite of this disgraceful behaviour and my lack of concentration, I left St. Leonards with two prizes, one of which I certainly had not deserved.

I had been taken up to London from St. Leonards, to see Ellen Terry, then in her full glory, playing Portia. I had sat thrilled and rapt, in the dark theatre, listening to her wonderful voice: "The quality of mercy is not strained. . . ."

A little later they were doing *The Merchant of Venice* in the Elocution class. To my delight, I was given the part of Portia. I always adored acting, and I was imitative enough to catch something of what I had just seen and heard. At all events I received a prize for Elocution.

Then the Bishop came to examine us in Christian Doctrine. This was a serious matter for me, since I had never been able to make my scattered wits collect themselves together for long enough to learn the catechism off by heart. I trembled at the thought of being asked a question. Then, in despair, I had the brilliant idea of consulting the Bishop about a religious difficulty of mine—a genuine one. How could one reconcile the doctrine of Free Will, with the teaching that God knew everything that was going to happen before it happened? The Bishop evidently thought me an intelligent pupil and one worth converting, for he took a great deal of trouble to explain the doctrine.

I allowed myself to be converted, but slowly and cautiously, so that by the time we were done with Free Will, the hours

44

allotted for the examination were over, and I had not been asked a single question out of the catechism. To my astonishment and the astonishment, and not unnaturally, the indignation of my fellow-pupils who had learnt *their* catechism, I was awarded the prize for Christian Doctrine.

I am sure that no prize was ever less deserved than that one!

So with my two prizes, and my education "finished," and the convent a lovely memory, I return to Ireland with my father on the 6th May, 1882. My father has come and gone in the memories of the intervening years. He has been much at Danesfield, trying to save something out of the ruin that has followed the bad years. The day of the landlords is almost over. Even the greatest recluse among them, locked up within his strong walls or behind his high thick woods, must be aware of the battering on the gates. Parnell may be in Kilmainham, but he will not remain there, and there is the Land League outside. Some of the landlords who had tried to do their duty by the people and really loved the country, thought bitterly of this young man of English descent, American on his mother's side, at whose bidding the people were to turn against them. I had never seen Mr. Parnell then. But . . . had a schoolgirl already heard or felt something of his fascination? His picture had been in all the papers. He was no wild Irishman, no stage Irishman for the English to mock at. He was, like many Irish leaders, far more English than Irish in temperament. (Perhaps the love that Ireland wins from the stranger has some greater strength and magic than that which she wins from her own sons. There is enchantment in it, like the wonder of love at first sight that can never be touched by a slow falling in love, however good that may be.)

It is a fact that the majority of Irish leaders have been of Anglo-Irish or Norman-Irish descent. Lord Edward Fitzgerald, Robert Emmet, Wolfe Tone, Mitchel. Owen Roe O'Neill stands out almost alone when I search for an Irish

45

Catholic leader, and he died as tragically as other Irish leaders have died. None of these hated England as Parnell hated her. That came first from the American mother and was fostered by those tales of the '98 Rebellion that he had heard from the old lodge-keeper at Avondale in the Wicklow twilights. I suppose, at the time that my father and I returned to Ireland, he was at the very height of his fame, this young man, who had made his first appearance at a political meeting where he had stood up to speak and been so overcome with shyness that he had sat down again without saying a word. He was a figure to catch a girl's imagination, and I, at heart, was somewhat a rebel. There was a mystery about him which made him more fascinating, and he was handsome, extraordinarily distinguished, with a clear and cultured voice.

He had a certain haughtiness which made his followers always a little afraid of him, I believe. And the appearance of great coldness which belongs to men who have one great passion in their lives and one only. Perhaps the only person in the world who knew him really well was the woman he loved.

I only saw Parnell twice in my life. The first time, I was walking with T. P. Gill, and he came out of Morrison's Hotel in Dawson Street as we were passing it. Morrison's Hotel was his usual resting place in Dublin, and was famous in the ballads of the day, written about him. He had been arrested there, I think, more than once. There was an outside car waiting by the curb. T. P. Gill said quickly: "There is Mr. Parnell. Would you like to meet him?" Would I not!

He went forward and touched Mr. Parnell's arm. I remember that, as the Irish leader turned to see who had caught him, he looked cold and aloof.

T. P. Gill said: "I want to introduce a great admirer of yours, Mr. Parnell—Lady Fingall."

His face was still cold. I think his glance at me was unfriendly. Did I not belong to the class and people that were opposed to him and hated him, all the more because they had played cricket with him and entertained him a few

46

ELIZABETH, COUNTESS OF FINGALL.

THOMAS FITZGERALD.

years earlier, when he was a young man doing the things that they did?

He said something like: "I can hardly believe that . . . from one of Lady Fingall's class," looking down at me in that cold way.

I stammered out in a great hurry: "I know, Mr. Parnell, that you really love Ireland," and was overwhelmed, having said it. But he smiled suddenly, and the effect of his smile was wonderful. I understood then how his followers felt about him. He took my hand for a moment. Then, remembering that he was in a hurry, jumped up on the outside car that was waiting and drove away. As I looked after him, I remembered that Fingall's Uncle George had supported and worked for the candidate Parnell had defeated in Meath. Those were the days when there would be many meetings in country houses, gatherings of landlords, before an election. The defeat of Uncle George's candidate had affected him as much as though he himself, a Plunkett, had been beaten in his own county of Meath, and by a young man who was half American, and of English descent on the other side. Uncle George never recovered from that blow. He left Meath after it, and went to live in London, where he spent the rest of his days in a flat in Victoria Street with an old servant and a little dog. He, and his little dog on their daily walk, were familiar figures in the streets about Westminster, which were still quiet enough then to be pleasant to walk in. Or they made their way to St. James's Park, which, even at its best, must have been a poor exchange to a Plunkett for his own fields of Meath. But he never went back to Ireland again.

Several years after that meeting outside Morrison's Hotel, I was to see Parnell once more.

On that May day of our return, the ink was hardly dry on the Kilmainham Treaty. Parnell had been released. While he had been in Kilmainham, the Land League had gone on with its work, whether he liked it or not. I am told that he did not like it, that he said that he would never have taken off his coat for that, even while he used it, looking beyond it

47

to the real port of his dreams. When the leaders of the Land League were arrested and imprisoned, the Ladies' Land League sprang up under the leadership of Parnell's sister, Anna, who was so like him. There were outrages and arrests, evictions, assassinations. Many of the Irish landlords had police protection, and one agent at least was reputed to go about with a steel breastplate under his waistcoat, his appearance, I believe, certainly bearing out the story.

These things only reached me vaguely. History fills the history books more than the lives of those who are living it. Having seen so many eventful years, I realise now that, whatever is happening politically, the life of the ordinary person goes on much the same. It must have been so in the French Revolution as it was in our own wars and "Troubles." There were always quiet corners where people lived peacefully, almost unaware of the Terror a few miles away.

Even in my convent I had heard that there was to be a policy of conciliation. The omens indeed looked as fair as possible on that May morning, and the omens fitted in with my mood. For I had been almost as homesick as my father away from Ireland. Like most Irish people, I have always had some nostalgia away from my own country. In many years when I have received immense kindness in England, visiting my friends there, I have still kept that feeling that I did not belong to that country.

And now I was going back to Ireland—after seven years away. I was nearly seventeen, and before me lay the whole enchanted world. I looked from the deck at the Dublin Mountains, lying exquisitely, at that magic hour of early morning, under the sun. I think I must have known somehow then what those hills were to be in my life, and of how, through the years, I should look at them from one aspect or another, and they should be always changing and yet always the same.

It was a magical country that morning, a mystic isle. I had gone up on deck with my father to gaze upon Dublin Bay after the years of our exile. The boat slipped smoothly through the water. We were coming home. And it was good, that home-coming, as it has always been good.

My father drew my attention to a group of people at the end of the deck. There was a tall man among them, with a beard that stood out from his face.

It was the new Lord Lieutenant, Lord Spencer! I remember his vivid red beard as I saw it that morning, and that he looked cold and tired, almost a little dour, at that lovely hour. I believe the new Chief Secretary, Lord Frederick Cavendish, was also of the party. But I did not see him. These two were bringing with them a message of peace and conciliation for Ireland. Lord Spencer, like many Englishmen, had fallen under the spell of Ireland, during his earlier Vice-royalty, when he had been young and gay and popular and the Irish had shown their feeling for him, calling him "the Red Earl," and his lovely wife, "Spencer's Fairy Queen."

Something of this my father told me as we stood by the rail, with the water slipping away from the ship. It is in my memory of that morning, the feeling of hope, of a fair prospect for the country that lay shimmering so peacefully before us.

Then we were at Kingstown, and we saw the State reception. Always, in the crowd, that red beard was visible. Now it has a tragic association for me which I cannot forget. How could we have known that May morning what lay before the party—what would have happened by the end of that day!

We went to Dublin, by the slow old train to Westland Row, and stayed at Buswell's Hotel in Molesworth Street. I think there can have been no evening papers in those days, or perhaps they were slow with the news, for on Sunday morning I got up and dressed myself and went to Mass at the big gloomy church in Westland Row, with an untroubled heart. Is it a gloomy church, or is it only that it always seems so to me because I have many associations of funerals from it, and always the first association of that May morning, when I heard the wonderful voice of Father Tom Burke, the famous

49

Dominican preacher, thunder through the shadows his denunciation of the murderers of Mr. Burke and Lord Frederick Cavendish? That was how I learned of the terrible deed that had stained the green beauty of the Phœnix Park the evening before. I sat in my place, feeling stunned and sick. Every Irishman and woman, I think that day carried a heavy heart and a sense almost of personal guilt. There was no sound in the church except the rich voice of the preacher. It seemed impossible that we had ever laughed or would ever laugh again, to remember at such a moment that Father Tom Burke, like many men of his cloth, was a famous wit and had said of his own lineage that his father was Master of the Rolls because he was a baker in Galway.

That tragedy is ancient history now, with many packed pages of history lying between this day and that. I was glad to get away from Dublin and the gloom associated with my arrival in it—all the greater because of the lovely anticipation of my coming and the fair prospect that had been so terribly defiled. My next memory is of Loughlinstown House, between the Dublin Mountains and the sea, where I stayed that summer with my friends, the Fitzgeralds. I had been at school with one of the daughters, and they took pity on me, a forlorn little stranger, and asked me to spend the summer with them. I think my father and mother were down in Galway again and my sister still at school. There was a household of young people at Loughlinstown, and their cousins, sons and daughters of Lord Fitzgerald, came from Killiney, nearby, to join in our various pleasures; so it was a very gay and happy summer.

We walked or rode on ponies up the mountains, through the Bride's Glen, and along the slopes of Katty Golliher, a delicious small hill that lies like a great dog above the smiling country between it and the sea. We went picnicking, shooting later, over the heather-clad hills and into the darkness of the pine woods in Glendhu, "the Dark Valley," beyond. We ran races, and Wilfred Fitzgerald remembers to-day that I ran as fast as any of them and often won a race. He remembers

50

too, the stockings I wore on my thin legs with a pattern of stripes round them. I was trying to make my legs appear a little fatter!

I lost my heart for the first time that summer, to my host, old Tom Fitzgerald. I used to sit with him in the evenings while he made Punch from some special recipe of his own—treating the matter seriously as though it were a sacred rite. Then I would drink a small wine-glass of it with him, while he talked. "What is Father doing?" his sons and his daughters would ask. "Talking to D. D."—short for "Daisy Darling," their nickname for me—would be the answer.

His talk was worth listening to. He had known the '47 men when he was a young man, and remembered being taken to see O'Connell in prison. And he had the list of the guests at a dinner party which had taken place in the Richmond Bridewell in Dublin on December 5th, 1848. I remember the thrill with which I first read those names:

Thomas Meagher, Member of the Council of the Irish Confederation.
P. O'Donohue, Vice President, Dublin Grattan Club.
Terence Bellew McManus.
William Smith O'Brien.

Tom Fitzgerald had a beautiful face. There is a picture of him by Osborne which does justice to him. It was one of those faces to which the beauty comes from within and which increases with each year of age. An unusual face, I think, in his time, fine and sensitive, framed in the fine white hair which he had when I first knew him. He might have been a poet, a mystic saint. I gave him then as much of my heart as I wanted to give away. That has never been an organ that has troubled me very greatly. One needs concentration for affairs of the heart as for other affairs of life. I have never been able to concentrate on anything for more than one minute (even on this book that I am trying to make). So . . . if things ever began to look serious, I danced away lightly

51

after some new interest, as I had learned to dance with my fairies. And every one knows that no fairy ever carried so heavy a burden as a heart! Whatever I gave to Tom Fitzgerald was safe in his keeping. And as for Minnie and Wilfred Fitzgerald, they have been the dearest friends all my life.

While I was there, Tom Fitzgerald went over with his brother, Lord Fitzgerald, to the House of Lords, where a Committee was sitting, on the Rathmines Waterworks. He said to us all before he left: "What shall I bring you back?" I said: "A pair of black silk stockings," and gave him an odd one as a pattern. He thrust it into his pocket, forgot it, and, at the serious Committee, put his hand in to pull out some papers. He pulled out the silk stocking instead and stared at it in some surprise, greatly to the joy of the members of the Committee.

I must have paid a visit to the Martyns at Tulira early that autumn. I cannot establish the date of that first visit, but it appears to have been before my marriage. My impression is that my sister and I went down to County Galway together. Mrs. Martyn was a distant cousin of ours. I cannot be sure that it was then that Edward Martyn had just returned from Paris, where he had been with George Moore, and discovered the Impressionists. Perhaps it was later that he came back with at least one Monet picture and several Degas ballet girls. These last shocked Mrs. Martyn greatly and were strange ornaments to the walls of that old Norman Castle of the Martyns. I was at Tulira on several occasions later when W. B. Yeats was there—a dark-haired young man whose poetry was then stirring the Irish air—and Lady Gregory, a neighbour at Coole, and Sir William Geary, my future brother-in-law, and one time Governor of Nigeria. Yeats cannot have been a fellow-guest on that first visit of mine.

Of Tulira, I remember the plain living and the good wine and brilliant talk and thinking. That little corner of Galway was to become a centre of Irish culture. Enormous joints were put down before the host at meals; such joints as you might see on the table of an Irish parish priest. Edward Martyn

52

carved them as generously as a parish priest. He was very fat and a tremendous eater and very like a certain type of cleric. Indeed, the table to which he and his guests sat at Tulira, might, but for the wine and the conversation, have been spread in a parochial house. He gave his guests good claret to drink with the plain fare, and the talk was on a level with the wine. He had his own study at Tulira, furnished like a monk's cell. Afterwards, when I knew about such things, I thought of a picture by Albrecht Dürer. That was in strange contrast, too, to the ballet girls.

When Susan Mitchell was writing George Moore's life—this much later, of course—and she had put in a good bit, I used to say: "Come along, and read it to Edward Martyn." Once I said to him of George Moore: "Anyhow, he has made a lot of enemies."

"Oh, no," Edward Martyn said. "Moore has no enemies. But his friends don't like him."

Edward Martyn was one of the first men of his class and time to become a Nationalist and even a Sinn Feiner. He continued, however, to use the Kildare Street Club, the strong-hold of Conservatism in Ireland, as his Dublin residence. It was convenient, he said, and the excellent food and wine suited him. The Club tried to expel him, and he took an action against it and won his case. When he re-entered the Club dining-room at the end of the action, I believe every member there went up and shook hands with him.

These disjointed memories belong to a later mile of the road. I go back again to the year 1882. Quite suddenly, on that meandering road that is my memory, it is winter and I am at Buswell's Hotel again and going to my first Ball. The Dublin Castle Season, with its Levées and Drawing Rooms, at one of which I shall be Presented, does not begin until after Christmas. But there are already plenty of other dances in the houses of Fitzwilliam Square and Merrion Square. For that first Ball I wore, with my white frock, a wreath of scarlet mountain ash berries in my hair. I do not know what month it was, and the berries are no guide. It is December now as

53

I write this chapter in an Irish country house, and a tree of mountain ash berries flames beautifully outside my window. Beyond it, as a background for its colour, is the Bog of Allen, deep rich brown, stretching to a line of hills that are indigo. They are very busy on the bog with turf schemes and inventions for turning turf into coal so that we may burn it without having to replenish the fire all the time, lest with our backs turned for a moment it should die to grey ashes.

Here, to Bellair, come young men from Dublin—pleasant spoken officials of the new Government—and talk to my hostess about her bog and the question of leasing a strip of it for experiment. And we think of Lord Dunsany's "Curse of the Wise Woman," and wonder what will happen if they should burn away the heart of Ireland. And in this county, which was then called King's County and to-day is called Offaly, which is the Irish name it bore before the English King tried to conquer it, it seems only yesterday that there were other schemes for turning turf into a substitute for coal. And other serious young men came then from Dublin and examined the bogs, and money was sunk into them as deep as the bottom of the brown pools which no one has ever seen.

Count Hamon (the famous "Cheiro") lived near Bellair for some time, engaged in the fantastic project, which has ruined so many people, of endeavouring to turn turf into coal. He came later to Kilteragh to try to induce Horace Plunkett to back his scheme, and I remember thinking what a wonderful face he had, with hypnotic eyes. I was to meet him again, when, at the Catholic Church of St. James's, Spanish Place, London, he and I were god-parents to the little daughter of my friends, the Frank Taylors, and I often wonder what influence his strange power will have on the life of my lovely little god-daughter.

Meanwhile my fire of Turraun turf burns very pleasantly on this hearth at Bellair, and the Bog of Allen, which I can see from my table, seems so wide and endless that I think they will not, in my time—or in my children's—burn the

54

heart of Ireland away. And I wonder a little about their schemes, an onlooker now, who once was in the thick of many such schemes.

Our day and the day of our work is over, and there is not so much to show for all that effort. Have these earnest young men ever heard of our Co-operative movement, of an Irishman who dreamed, in America, a new dream for Ireland, that country of so many dreams? An entirely new one, this. Ireland might be saved and made happier and contented by Co-operation, by good butter and bacon and creameries. And beside my fire of Turraun turf, I think I can almost smell the scent of the blossom in the apple orchards we planted in obedience to him, and the tobacco flower in the garden at Killeen as it smelt on a summer evening; which we grew, too, to please him, as we did many other things of which I shall write later. And now there is left, of all that effort, nothing much more tangible than the smell of the fruit blossom and tobacco flower, floating over the years.

But I have wandered from my road, there being no hedges on a bog road, to keep me walking tidily between them. So my erratic mind has gone straying as it always does. I must return.

There are the flaming mountain-ash berries outside my window, such as I twisted into a wreath for my first dance. Although I had grown up to the country superstitition that they were unlucky because the mountain-ash belongs to the fairies and must not be touched by mortal hand. But, at seventeen, I cared nothing for such superstitions as I put them in my hair and liked the colour of them. Someone told me afterwards that as I danced, wearing them, I looked fey.

CHAPTER FOUR

MY frock had come home, and if one should possess in time the wardrobe of the princess in the fairy tale, no other frock would be the same as that first ball dress for one's first Ball. How deliciously the paper rustled as one disturbed it! I lifted the frock out reverently, and laid it on the bed. Just white tulle, yards and yards of it. What more could any girl want? The full skirt was made over a stiffened foundation to make it stand out. I had no difficulty about the waist. I had as many inches then to mine as I had years, and while my contemporaries were being laced by exhausted mothers and maids into torturing corsets, I was only troubled as to how to make myself seem a little fatter. When I was dressed, I looked in the long solemn mirror, and of course did not recognise myself. I stared at a stranger whom I saw for the first and last time. Never again can one see oneself in one's first ball dress. As impossible to recapture one's first vision of a place afterwards grown familiar.

A mirror was a more magic thing before the days of electric light. Someone held a pair of candles high, and they glimmered in the glass like little distant stars. One of them was caught in my hair.

My face was very solemn and serious, as well it might be on such an occasion. I was seventeen and grown up. And it was a very much more serious and sudden matter, growing up, in those days than it is now. One became, or one tried to become, a young lady. I must say good-bye now to my races over the Dublin Mountains for which I had lifted my full long skirt over my knees, to the riding ponies astride up the mountain paths and, perhaps, to the sweet thing that had stirred only so faintly between boy and girl in the summer dusk.

I go very solemnly to my first Ball, in my whispering

white tulle dress, with the scarlet berries in my hair. I had gone shopping deliciously beforehand in Grafton Street, buying long white gloves, open-work stockings, finest linen handkerchiefs with a little lace border, and other etceteras.

I did not always go to Grafton Street. Or perhaps I sometimes made a *détour*. For there was a bright autumn day when I walked back to Buswell's by way of Kildare Street. I wore a little fur jacket with the neatest of waists, and a tiny hat perched on the side of my hair, a little jaunty feather in it; altogether very like the hats that are worn to-day. I was quite unconscious and unaware of a young man who came out of the Kildare Street Club as I passed on the opposite side of the road, looked at me, and then, at a most discreet and courteous distance, followed me back to the hotel, into which I disappeared. That is how Fingall first saw me, and he declared afterwards that he fell in love with me at first sight.

My father was still down in Galway, and I was at Buswell's with my mother. But she did not accompany me to the Ball. I do not remember her ever taking me out. She was too delicate for the long, weary sitting up night after night, watching a daughter dance, and there were, fortunately, plenty of people ready enough to take me off her hands. I don't remember how I got to the Ball. Or home from it. Perhaps with the Fitzgeralds. I would not have gone alone, of course, even in the safety of a rumbling, musty-smelling Dublin cab. But that is a bit that drops out of my memory, although the Ball itself is perfectly clear.

The dance was just round the corner, in Merrion Square, and it was given by a great hostess of those days, known as "the Good Mrs. Browne." She was a charming Irishwoman of her time, combining religion with a lovely gaiety, and she was famous both for her hospitality and her charitable works. Every morning the steps of the fine Georgian house in Merrion Square resembled—with local differences—the scene at the Back Door in my childhood. When Mrs. Browne died, I believe all the beggars in Dublin followed her funeral. She had several tall, handsome nieces who helped her in her good

57

works and for whom she delighted to arrange gaieties. She loved to have young people about her and to see them enjoying themselves. So, often the steps that had been thronged with beggars in the morning, at evening were spread with red carpet and covered with awnings and a little crowd assembled—frequently of those who at the same door had received charity earlier in the day—to see the guests arrive.

Sometimes in those Dublin Squares, where many of the houses are now turned into flats, each one occupying a floor, and doctors and dentists examine their patients in the fine drawing-rooms which saw such gay entertainments, I half close my eyes and see them as they used to be.

It is the Season. There are Balls every night in one or other of the houses in the Square. Some of the old residents complain that they cannot sleep because of the carriages coming and going in the early hours of the morning, with a jingle of harness, a movement of sleepy horses.

But now it is ten o'clock, and the awnings are out. The music drifts into the blue dusk of the Square garden and is lost among the dim, dusty trees and bushes. The carriages come, put down their passengers, the horses are whipped up and move off. A coachman calls something to another. The skirts float up the steps and are lost in the warm, music-filled air.

They are playing waltz music. Why, I think those old trees of the Square must hold it still! Only the music and the very dimmest sound of voices coming through a window opened for a moment. For, of course, in those days we could not cross the road, even if it should be a Ball during Horse Show Week, and a hot summer night, to open the gate into the Square and walk on the grass between the trees. Such a thing would have been considered shocking beyond words, and a girl who did it might never have been asked again. In London, even during the Season of 1914, I remember the horror caused by a couple who, on a hot night, walked in the street between the dances.

So we sat out very properly in the small garden at the

back, or on the stairs, or in the rooms provided for the purpose, with little sitting-out places between palms and pots of flowers. Or in conservatories. There was great romance in the very feeling of those conservatories. You will discover it in the novels of the time.

The room was lit by many candles in a hanging glass chandelier. It was the usual lighting for a ballroom, and, of course, a most becoming light. But what cleaning bills the men must have had to pay for their evening clothes! For one saw them often with their black shoulders spattered with grease. Frocks were damaged, too, but the damage was more easily concealed. Looking back at the scene, I think there is no great originality in dress at that moment or much scope for it. White satin is greatly worn. One associates it with ball dresses. It is very thick and stiff and shining and beautiful. The bodices are rather elaborate, and mine stands out among them for its much greater simplicity. I always wore very simple clothes, because I liked them so and they suited me.

It was early during that evening at Mrs. Browne's, that my hostess, looking after every one—there were no wallflowers ever at her Balls—brought a young man up to me and introduced him: "Lord Fingall." I was not aware that I had ever seen him before, or that he had asked to be introduced to me. He was rather shy and a bad dancer. In spite of that, however, we danced more than once together, whether that was allowed or not. It was a lovely evening, and I enjoyed every moment of it.

When, in the early hours of the morning, I went to say good-bye to my hostess, she held my hand:

"Did you like Lord Fingall?"

I thought for a moment. The shy young man who danced so very badly?

"Oh! I loved them all!" I said.

Fingall told me afterwards that if he had not already fallen in love with me that day in Kildare Street, he would have done it at Mrs. Browne's Ball, when he saw me in my white frock with the scarlet berries in my hair.

Then . . . it is after Christmas, and my mother and I are still at Buswell's and I am to be Presented. My Presentation dress is being made by Mrs. Sims, the famous Dublin dressmaker. She has unrolled the gleaming white satin before my dazzled eyes. The dress is to be made with a regulation train, three yards long. And it is to cost the enormous sum of five pounds. I am wondering how I am ever to keep my hair up —already a difficult business—with the three white feathers in it and the long tulle lappets to add to the difficulty.

The position of Worth in Paris could not have been more firmly established and more magnificent than that of Mrs. Sims in the Dublin of those days. She had been grand already, but after she had been to London and Marlborough House, to fit and make a dress for Her Royal Highness, the Princess of Wales, she returned with a regal air, and fittings, with her, took on something of the solemnity of a Royal audience. She kept us in our places, and we were humble before her. Of course she was an artist, and we were so many canvases for her to work on. I remember the alarm with which I went to my fittings and the state of limp exhaustion in which I came away. I had stood for hours before the artist was satisfied. I hope the result was worth the suffering.

My summons to the Drawing Room came, delivered by a mounted orderly, clattering up Molesworth Street and swinging himself off his horse to hand in the large white envelope. It was very impressive with the stamp of the Chamberlain on it.

The Season opened officially with the Lord Lieutenant's Levée the day before the Ladies' Drawing Room. Dublin was very gay that day, the streets crowded with outside cars, the latter going at a reckless speed, it seemed, before one had dreamed of a motor carriage that might go at eighteen miles an hour! Dame Street, leading to the Castle, was packed from end to end, the day of His Excellency's Levée.

In the carriages rode the staider people: members of the nobility, generals and colonels and country gentlemen, bringing with them into the grey street something of the smell of the country, to which presently they would return with relief. There were Church dignitaries, too, in their carriages, suitably serious; learned professors, faintly dusty from their books, with a distinguished dustiness.

On the outside cars rode many of my future dance partners, soldiers and sailors, looking very gay in their uniforms. Sometimes they sat on the cars a trifle uncomfortably, being perhaps newly arrived in Ireland, and not yet having acquired the "seat" necessary for that vehicle, which seems to be as natural a gift to an Irishman or woman as the art of wearing a kilt is to a Scot. Those who had mastered the art sat with one leg thrown over the other, with an air of triumphant nonchalance.

The next day came the Ladies' Drawing Room.

I was Presented by my cousin, Madam MacDermot, wife of The MacDermot, whose Irish title is Prince of Coolavin. And one of her sons remembers to-day how, as a small boy, he peeped from his nursery and saw me go down the stairs in my Presentation dress. "Mother, do the angels look like that?" he asked. All the servants at the hotel had left their various duties to see me dressed for the great occasion. Several of the maids, who should have been doing something else, had assisted at my toilet. Buswell's of those days had a delightful atmosphere. It was an old-fashioned, friendly, family hotel, greatly frequented by the country gentry bringing their daughters to Dublin for the Season. And it had more the atmosphere of a private house than that of an hotel. I think Buswell's saw many romances in those days, and the delightful servants shared the pangs and thrills of them by proxy.

There was a crowd about the gates of the Castle. The Dublin poor always turned out to see any sight that there was. They shivered on the pavement in their thin, ragged clothes, waiting for hours sometimes, so that they might see the ladies in their silks and satins and furs step from their carriages into the warmth and light and gaiety that received them. The poor were incredibly patient. Even then I was dimly aware of that appalling contrast between their lives

61

and ours, and wondered how long they would remain patient.

We drove into the Castle Yard by the private entrance, The MacDermot having an official position which gave us this privilege, descended from our carriage and went in with crowds of other shivering débutantes and their sponsors. I remember the alarm in which, after we had divested ourselves of our cloaks, I followed Madam MacDermot up the red-carpeted stairs into one of the crowded ante-rooms where we waited until our names were called. That waiting was agony, as bad as later hunting mornings when we waited at Meets in a frozen trance, with other frozen, speechless figures, for the signal to move off that should release us. Supposing one's hair collapsed? How could it stand the weight of the feathers and long tulle lappets? And how should one ever manage one's train? Men came and went in gay uniforms. In ten minutes perhaps it would be over, and one would be still alive. (Would one be?) And one's curtsey? Could one be sure of it? Supposing one wobbled and fell at Their Excellencies' feet! Well. One could not practise it now!

An A.D.C. in the doorway. A name that sounded like one's own.

The Throne Room was picturesque on such an occasion. I saw it clearly later. Not then, when it swam before my frightened eyes. But there, unmistakably, was Lord Spencer with that long red beard again. In Court dress with glittering orders. But it is the beard that I remember. In those days the Lord Lieutenant kissed each of the débutantes as they were Presented—an ordeal for both. I can remember now the feeling of that long thick red beard against my cheek, tickling it. Then it is over, and now I curtsey to the lovely golden-haired, rose and white, but rather pompous-looking lady in her glittering jewels, beside Lord Spencer, and walk backwards a few steps as I have been taught to do ; without, I pray, falling over my train. An A.D.C. picks it up and replaces it on my arm, and the ceremony is over. In the long gallery, refreshments are served, and one meets one's friends as at an ordinary evening party.

I was present on later occasions when Lord Spencer's red beard turned white towards the end of the evening, so powder must have been coming into vogue then. For once, at least, he had to retire so that it might be removed, and his beard restored to its natural colour. And there were gay occasions during Lord Londonderry's Viceroyalty, when his brother, Lord Bertie Vane Tempest, who was very like him, used to stand beside him purposely so that shy and lovely débutantes mistook him for the Lord Lieutenant and offered him their rosy cheeks. He could not, of course, refrain from accepting such an invitation! And, having been kissed heartily by him, the débutantes discovered their mistake and retreated in shy confusion, their cheeks rosier than ever.

So now I am launched into my first Season, and every minute of it is packed with gaiety and delight. It is very short. The Dublin Season started after Christmas and ended with St. Patrick's Ball on St. Patrick's Night. Into that short space was crowded more gaiety than into many months elsewhere.

The mounted orderlies went riding through the streets of Dublin, delivering invitations for the Castle Balls and Parties. Such eagerly-awaited invitations. The messengers, carrying them, stopped before dignified houses in Fitzwilliam Square and Merrion Square, where the quiet curtained windows showed no sign of the fluttering hearts inside. In those days of little traffic, one could hear a horse at the other end of the Square. This was the day on which the invitations went out. Here he came. Would he pass by? Agony and ecstasy, as a horse was pulled up and his rider dismounted. Through a lace curtain a pair of quick, bright eyes could see the white envelope in the orderly's hand, a fitting message for such a messenger. No letter by post could ever be like that.

But sometimes, alas, the orderly rode by; and what a tragedy that was, and what woe and tears there were hidden then behind that quiet curtain that never stirred! I remember many years later Lady Cadogan pitying the young, with their inconsolable grief, their unbearable pain. "We can bear things," she said. "Every year that one grows older, one's endurance increases. But I am so sorry for the young. . . ." She was talking of her own sorrows, which perhaps she could not have borne if they had come in her youth.

An irrelevant memory. I think of pain when one faces it in the morning, and how hard it is to bear, and how with the mellowing light of afternoon the sharpness of it softens and it becomes endurable. And my heart aches, too, for the young, and for those tear-stained faces behind some lace curtain in Fitzwilliam or Merrion Square!

I think I had plenty of invitations. I do not remember that I ever wept in my room at Buswell's because the orderly had gone by. Probably Fingall saw to it. He was State Steward, and the Chamberlain, Colonel Dease, was his cousin. At Mrs. Browne's, Fingall had introduced me to his sisters, Lady Mary and Lady Henrietta Plunkett, who lived with him in the State Steward's house in a corner of the Castle Yard. They had been charming to me, and I went to many of my dances now with them. It seems to me that we danced almost every night, and I expect we did. So much had to be crowded into that short time.

On the day of a Ball one might receive delightful parcels, florists' boxes marked "With Care," and to be opened gently. They contained bouquets of flowers sent by one's *beaux* and admirers. And they took trouble, one's *beaux* of those days when indeed *beaux* were worth having. The thought that had gone to it made the gift the thrill that it was. One would be asked with apparent carelessness as one waltzed on Tuesday night: "What are you going to wear next Thursday?" And the bouquet was planned carefully to match one's dress. I do not know what happened when a young woman exercised her privilege of changing her mind! My answer was usually simple. I wore white with a coloured sash. The sash was green or blue. And every flower goes with green, and most flowers with blue. What they meant to a girl's heart, those bunches of flowers, chosen carefully! They were laid away in paper afterwards, dried and kept. Open the paper and you

64

will see only a yellowed dried skeleton of what was once a bunch of flowers. But nothing else can so bring back the memory of a night when one was young and went to a Ball, wearing these, knowing that someone waited for one's entry, to see if they would be worn or not. The whole world, perhaps, crashing or standing steady by the fact of a girl wearing a bunch of flowers, or not wearing them! I wonder if in some of the old Dublin houses there are still, pressed between paper leaves, the skeletons of those bouquets that went to dances when I was seventeen!

Sometimes a card came with them, bearing the sender's name. Or, sometimes, no card at all, and one could only guess, and the guessing, of course, was thrilling. And I know someone who found a note hidden in the heart of a tightly-packed nosegay, which contained a declaration of love and a proposal.

I had plenty of bouquets (although not with such notes in them!), and sometimes when several arrived before the same party it was difficult to know how to avoid hurting someone's feelings. I solved the problem by picking several bouquets to pieces and making a new one, with flowers chosen from each. Even then I had a passion for choosing flowers and putting them together. . . . ("You have," grumbles my maid, who has been with me for thirty-five years. "Sure you're always messing with those flowers!") And I would wear some at my waist, or in my hair, and carry the rest. And, as I went forth with my flowers, one of the hotel maids stood to gaze at me with rapture. "Sure, Miss Daisy," she said in a tone of personal pride, "it's what they say, you're mowing down the military!"

And on I went with my scythe, to mow down the military! But it was only a toy scythe, I think, and no permanent damage being done, they soon stood straight again after my mowing!

I go first to a gay dinner party of young people in the State Steward's house, where Fingall and his sisters live. It is in a corner of the Castle Yard. It is a wet night—Dublin knows how to rain, although there is so much sunlight between—and the reflection of the lamps shines on the wet pavement and in the gutters. What do we care for such things as weather, except that it may damage our frocks and our satin shoes! But the A.D.C.s who are dining with us have a plan and put it into action. There is an old Sedan chair which they bring to the door when it is time to go across to the Castle. The A.D.C.s are not those on duty to-night, and the ball is already beginning. We can hear the music as we put last touches to our hair and our frocks in one of the bedrooms upstairs. The windows of that room look out on an appalling slum, a fact characteristic of the life of those days. But the windows are curtained, and one need not lift the curtains and the wailing voice of a weary child only comes faintly through the glass.

There is the waltz music to drown it. We run downstairs in a hurry. It draws us. We cannot lose even one second of that ecstasy of waltzing.

The Sedan chair is at the door. I pick up my long skirts and step into it, over the wet pavement. I laugh as I am lifted and swung forward briskly. Evidently my weight gives no trouble to the bearers.

In the very middle of the yard, the chair is put down suddenly. I can hear the rain pattering on the roof. What has happened? I peer out of the window. Someone giggles. A voice says at either side: "You are a prisoner. How many dances do you give us as ransom?"

I shall scream for help, I threaten. Not a dance for such ruffians! The others are waiting to be carried across. We shall be late. I can hear that waltz music. I must go after it as often I went after the fairy music in Connemara.

"How many? Your ransom." I give them—under much protest!—all that they ask.

There is no finer room in Buckingham Palace than St. Patrick's Hall—I have been told, indeed, no room as fine. Now it is full of light and music and laughter and voices and the soft swish of skirts. The centre of light is the famous chandelier of Waterford glass which hangs from the ceiling in the middle of the hall, catching the light of all the candles to reflect in its blue-tinged loveliness. That chandelier had many strange adventures before it turned up in a Dublin curio shop a few years ago and was bought by Mr. Cosgrave's administration, with the idea, I think, that it should eventually hang in the Irish Parliament.

Then it lit the white and gold walls, the floating banners of the Knights of St. Patrick with their rich sombre colour and dim gold and silver, above our heads, the brilliant uniforms of the men and the gay dresses and wonderful jewels of the women who moved below.

I stand aside for a moment. I am a ghost at this scene, a ghost come back from what is still the future. I see it with my eyes of to-day, not with my eyes of that day that were as restless as my feet. One of the A.D.C.s, "Mary" Matthews —called so because of his pretty, girlish face—is begging me for a dance. Have I one left still, after all that those other villains wrung from me by force? One then, perhaps. My eyes and mind wander from him for a moment to where Colonel Frank Foster, the Master of the Horse, stands talking to Her Excellency. She looks beautiful to-night in her Court dress with her coronet and jewels. Her fair, very English beauty appealed particularly to the Irish, used as they were to the dark loveliness of their own women. And Colonel Foster. Well, we all adored him. He was not only extraordinarily handsome, but he had the most beautiful manners of any man I have ever met. And that is saying a great deal, for I have met many fine gentlemen in my life. None finer than he. He treated all women as queens, and if he were talking now to a charwoman, instead of to Lady Spencer, his manner would be exactly the same. He is the idol of the débutantes. No girl would ever feel hurt or neglected if he could help it. Presently, when he leaves Lady Spencer, he will be going about the room with a compliment for every woman. Then he will ask some shy girl to dance, and for a few minutes she will feel a princess. (One of the duties of the

A.D.C.s, incidentally, was to dance with plain girls who might otherwise be wallflowers.) And all the débutantes, of course, have their eye on Colonel Dease, who has in his hands the giving out of invitations. Those for the small intimate dances in the Throne Room are the most eagerly coveted. But the Chamberlain, alas, has the hard heart of the perfect official, and his head rules that heart, so that he performs his duty admirably. (He has, among other things, to tell the Lord Lieutenant what to do and see that he does it.) And the poor little débutantes with their languishing eyes are wasting their time. Fortunately there is Colonel Foster to comfort them with one of his charming compliments. They lift their heads when he has passed, like refreshed roses after a shower of rain.

The band is playing the waltz music that Strauss has sent us from Vienna.

I had no time then to stand by the wall looking on, or to see the game clearly as only an onlooker may see it, not one who is playing it, so absorbed in her part which takes all her time that she cannot notice how others are playing theirs, except when they send the ball perhaps her way, or fail to send it. One is naturally selfish when one is young, and the world clearly made only for oneself.

But I may look on now. It is one of the pleasant things of growing old that there is time to sit and look into the fire or into the kaleidoscope of life. It still moves and is always interesting. *Plus ça change, plus c'est la même chose.* I bring a boy and girl together and watch the first delicate stirring of love between them. They sit at my table in my small flat, high above this changed Dublin, and when it is time to go they leave together, and he sends me afterwards a note of gratitude which tells its own tale. And I am satisfied. That is the way to keep one's heart immortal. To be interested in people, and especially in the young.

There came to a Dublin Horse Show, during the Dudleys' Viceroyalty, a Count Haro, from Spain, and he asked to see me. We had met in Biarritz when Fingall and I were there many years earlier, and later a friend and I had visited Spain and

68

Count Haro had entertained us wonderfully. He was half Irish, his mother having been a daughter of Balfe, the composer. He had been so young and gay and handsome when I had known him first, and he was now a middle-aged man, saddened by his country's troubles. He declared that I had not changed at all. Men always say that; but I believe it is a fact that I change less than other people. "Whom the Gods love die young," means, I think, that they never grow old.

But now I must look back again. It is very warm, that fire of life which I see. No cold moments—the fire of life is within oneself like the Kingdom of Heaven—no grey ashes. In St. Patrick's Hall those days the wit and brilliance and beauty of the two kingdoms met and mingled. The State of the Viceregal Court was magnificent, especially in that Spencer Viceroyalty when I first saw it. In the winter Their Excellencies, with their staff, lived in the Castle, and in the summer they moved out to the Viceregal Lodge in the Phœnix Park, above which the flag flew in the Irish wind to show that they were in residence. Sometimes the Lord Lieutenant, representing his King at the Castle of Dublin, almost out-kinged his King. I have been told that for magnificence and brilliance only the Indian Viceregal Court, with its mingling colours of East and West, could compare with it. No other social life, I am sure, had such natural gaiety. That is something in which Ireland excels.

And, whatever was happening outside the walls—and things were happening, for Lord Spencer must ride with an escort when he went through the streets of Dublin—I think many of the visitors who moved and danced in St. Patrick's Hall those Seasons were under the spell of Ireland. Some were in love with her, and some were to be broken by her. For that is what Ireland gives to those who love her. I can hear John Redmond saying to me, many, many years later, during the Irish Convention in 1918: "Do not give your heart to Ireland, for if you do you will die of a broken heart." He spoke truly of himself, alas!

In St. Patrick's Hall now I am invisible. No one asks me

what I am doing here, a ghost from the future. It is Elizabeth Fingall, not Daisy Burke, who looks at the scene. The Ball has opened and they are dancing the State Quadrille behind the cord drawn across one end of the long room. The State Quadrille was a beautiful thing to dance or to watch. In those days we all had to know how to dance it. The very grand people are going through its movements, and we ordinary mortals stand behind the cord, looking on. I do not dream yet of a day quite close in the future, when I shall partner His Excellency in it, leading off the Ball with him. He is dancing with Lady Ormonde. Someone describes her to me in a word: "An enchantress." I can see her delicate, beautifully cut face under her dark lovely hair. She looked reserved and aristocratic, I thought, and her stiff dressing suited her. When she is not dancing she is talking in a very gentle way. And Lord Spencer is wearing his Court dress : blue coat and white knee breeches, his Star and Orders, the Garter round his knee. His legs in the silk stockings were the thinnest I have ever seen, and he had long thin feet sticking out from them. But most clearly of all I remember about him always, that flaming beard that was like a flag or a signal. It seems to have a sad association for me, as if from that first May day that I saw it.

Lady Spencer's partner is Lord Ormonde. He is good-looking and a commanding presence—a real Butler. They make a magnificent group, those four, as they move through the State Quadrille. Someone asks me if I have seen Kilkenny Castle. I had not then. But I saw it later, set like a Castle in Italy above the town of Kilkenny, a fitting background for Lilah Ormonde's loveliness. (And to-day, as I tell this story, they are selling off the furniture there and the house is to be closed up, ending another chapter.)

The State Quadrille ended, the cord is let down and dancing becomes general.

I look at the women passing me in this pageant of memory, and wonder if it was an age of beauty. Some of them were famous then, and the fame of their loveliness still remains. You will find pictures of them in the books of the period. But the still pictures do not do justice to their life and movement. Beauty had such glamour then. It was before the days of beauty parlours and make-up and the democratic similarity of dress—which is not to say that I do not admire the modern girl. I do. I like her walk, her bare head, with the wind in her hair. I like her make-up, too, which turns an ordinary girl into a goddess. Most of all, I like her splendid fearlessness.

Clothes always express the psychology of their time, and those women moved in a world of their own, within their elaborate, full-skirted dresses. They did not fight with the crowd, go into business, travel in trams or buses or tubes. They walked or rode or drove in carriages, and they did not often soil their lovely hands. A Dublin carman was still romantic enough to refuse a fare from the loveliest Duchess in the world, because he would pay more than that for the privilege of driving her. And someone—a woman now—is telling me to-day that she remembers walking the length of Dawson Street behind Hermione Leinster, for the delight of seeing her move. And there was a beautiful actress who was drawn through the streets by the young men of Dublin, who had taken the horses out of her carriage and harnessed themselves instead.

Beauty was not cheap then, and she was valued accordingly. She did not sell her face for an advertisement of face cream. Mystery (it was in those whispering skirts) makes for glamour. The known is so quickly dull in comparison with the unknown. So little now is hidden, so little rare and lovely, to be approached with reverence.

I have an old friend in a quiet French Château where the past is more real in the shadows than the present. He tells me, my charming Monsieur le Vicomte, that in his young days the sight of a lady's ankle as she descended from her carriage, caused him a grave disturbance of the heart.

"But *grave, Madame,*" he assures me, looking as though that disturbance troubled him again and he does not know

71

whether or not it is a pleasant thing. The quiet shadows in which he lives flutter and are lit for a moment.

I look round the room. What are we all doing? I am asked. Well: "Mary" Matthews is flirting—with me! (But presently he will be flirting with Aline Stewart, Lord Londonderry's daughter. We shared him quite amicably!) And another A.D.C., "Weazel" Orr Ewing, is certainly flirting. (Not with me!) In a corner the State Steward is having a moment's respite from his many responsibilities. He has used it to fall asleep. Already he has been christened "the somnolent Earl" for this habit of his. Given a chance, at any moment he will go to sleep, standing on his feet like a horse. He has good excuse, since he has little chance to sleep in bed these nights when he goes to bed late and rises in the dark to drive down to some Meet in Meath or Kildare. Because of the hunting next day, the Balls at the Castle ended early and, except on special occasions, such as St. Patrick's Night, "God Save the King" was played at one o'clock.

Fingall is not yet my responsibility—although there are already signs that he may be in the future—so I cannot send some one to wake him or make a desperate signal to an A.D.C. nearby: "Kick Fingall!" as I did once later, with disastrous results, for it was at a dinner table and the A.D.C. kicked Lady Spencer under the table by mistake.

I see a lovely head among the dancers—Titian red hair, a profile like a Greek cameo turned to me for a moment. The features are so perfect that they might be chiselled out of marble. It is Priscilla Armytage Moore, one of the famous beauties of her time, and now Priscilla, Countess Annesley. I cannot swear that it was during that Season, but some time about then and in that room I first saw Lady Warwick, then Lady Brooke, and someone said in my ear, pointing her out, that she was like her name, for she and her soft voice came into the room like a running brook.

There was Lady Listowel, another beauty, tall and fair and a little opulent. She looked very demure, but she had a gay little light in her eyes. I always thought her like the pictures

72

of Lady Blessington. Mrs. Cornwallis West I saw also in St. Patrick's Hall, brilliant and dark-eyed. Clare Castletown was another lovely creature. She had an exquisite figure and was the most beautifully dressed woman of the whole Court. Lord Spencer admired her greatly.

And there were the Irish beauties—plenty of them. The Lambarts of Beauparc in Meath. Seven sisters of them, all good lookers, and they had such slender waists, all of seventeen or eighteen inches, that some wit christened the white house on the Boyne, from which they came, Waistland. One of the younger ones—still then in the schoolroom—was afterwards Maid of Honour to Queen Victoria, and one day at Court she danced an Irish jig before the Queen. Her Majesty was so delighted with the performance that she asked Bertha Lambart to choose a royal gift in souvenir of the occasion.

"The head of Mr. Gladstone on a dish, Ma'am," said the witty Irish girl.

I saw Fa Conyngham about that time, newly married then and at the height of her beauty. I have a list of the beauties who were famous during those Seasons . . . Lady Power, Miss Dowse. All the Whites, my list says, so beauty then ran in families. And there was Lady Spencer's lovely niece, Lilah Agar Ellis, who married Luke White, later Lord Annaly. And the Miss Heads from Bray, one of whom inspired a famous jest of Father Healy's. She drove a little donkey trap, and one day her steed ran away with her. Meeting the Parish Priest of Bray immediately after, she said: "Oh, Father Healy. My donkey ran away with me!"

"Did he, now?" said Father Healy, looking at her brilliant, excited face. "Faith, then, he was no ass!"

I think it was in St. Patrick's Hall, too, that I first saw Evelyn de Vesci. A Scotswoman—her brother, then Lord Elcho, was to marry George Wyndham's sister that year—she had fallen in love with Ireland when she married Lord de Vesci and came to live at Abbey Leix.

She is not easy to describe. She was and is simply unlike any one else. She had something much more rare than beauty.

73

I think now that she was like a Rossetti picture with her deep-set eyes and her priestess look. Her way of dressing was absolutely her own. She wore very simple things, beautifully draped, which accentuated her height and slenderness. I thought that she dressed like an angel. She hardly ever wore any jewels.

I have later memories of her—one at Abbey Leix when it was late May and the woods were a sheet of bluebells under a roof of palest green and Evelyn walked in them, her feet deep in that heavenly carpet. The bluebells at Abbey Leix were famous. And Mary, her daughter, who was more like a young Joan of Arc than any child I have seen, ran ahead leaving a little trail where the flowers were bent, such as a small boat makes on a summer sea. I think we talked of Ireland—we were always talking of Ireland in those days— and even the Wyndhams, who were descended from Lord Edward Fitzgerald, did not love Ireland more, or perhaps as much as Evelyn de Vesci loved it. I remember her care to stop and talk to all the country people we met, and her anxiety lest she should omit the least degree of thought and courtesy for any one of them. How they adored her at Abbey Leix! I saw Mary Vesey later at a Castle Ball in Dublin when she had grown up and was just out, and, with her eagle face, like a splendid boy's, she looked more than ever a St. Joan. One wanted to give her a horse and a standard. She found a worthy mate when she married Aubrey Herbert, a knight and a Don Quixote.

That was my first vision of Evelyn de Vesci. In later years I stayed several times with her at Abbey Leix, and we were both fellow-guests on occasion at Carton, with the Leinsters. We met at other country houses, too, in those years when we were all busy with Ireland. She became a great friend of Horace Plunkett's, and used to come to Kilteragh, his house at Foxrock. I find her very early in the Kilteragh Visitors' Book, which was started in 1907. June, 1908, has the entries: Evelyn de Vesci. Mary Herbert.

Betty Balfour, talking of Evelyn de Vesci the other day,

compared her to a great Gothic Cathedral: "Where there is room for all to come for inspiration and peace and comfort, and where the sunlight streams in at times, lighting up the abiding solemnity. She gives one the feeling also of the air of dawn on a glorious summer morning, or the sea in a sunset glow, or of anything else that has a Divine origin and no self-consciousness. And her daughter is a youthful incarnation of herself." To make her perfect, she had the most lovely and rich sense of humour.

The other day I went to the Castle, and in the Herald's Office, that last survivor of a world which kept and treasured tradition and such things, we took down the Dinner Book and the Drawing Room Book of that time. The immense leather-covered records had remained undisturbed for years and had to have the dust wiped from them.

Dust over those names!

I found Lord and Lady Ormonde there, from Kilkenny Castle, and Lady Brooke, and the Duchess of Leinster of that day, and the Ladies Fitzgerald, from Carton. And the Marquis and Marchioness of Kildare, from Kilkea Castle—and many other names that I remembered. There was, surprisingly, Mr. George Moore, Moore Hall, Co. Mayo, staying at the Shelbourne Hotel, a young man up from the bogs and lakes of Mayo for the Dublin Season. And I find Madam MacDermot and myself, Miss Burke, Buswell's Hotel.

We put the records back for the dust to cover them again.

CHAPTER FIVE

THE splendour of the Castle Seasons was greatly increased by the fact that the Lord Lieutenants brought over their own pictures, much of their own furniture, and their own plate. This was often very magnificent. Only at Buckingham Palace and at the Viceregal Lodge have I eaten off gold plate. And very nasty and scratchy it is, too, to eat from. I prefer good china!

The success of a Viceroy, particularly from the social point of view, depended enormously on his staff. If he were well served in that way, his entertaining was a success, but if his staff served him badly, not all the splendour of his table could atone for that failure. Their positions were not easy ones. Fingall, who had to arrange about dinner invitations and the order of precedence at a dinner or banquet, had a job that was not at all enviable. The rule of precedence was very strict in those days. It was all according to " the Book." People went in according to their rank and the date of their creation. Once, after my marriage, an old country peer beside me at dinner asked me the date of my creation. I asked him what that had to do with him—for I thought he was asking me how old I was! The other question I could not have answered. Then the wives of officials, judges, etc., did not receive the precedence of their husbands, and a good deal of heartburning and feeling was caused by that fact. The Lord Chancellor took in the Viceroy's wife, but the Lord Chancellor's lady might sit in a very humble place. Fingall must have been relieved when they were all done with, assigned their places, and in them, whether they liked them or not, and he could sleep between the courses in peace, thinking of the fields that he would ride over to-morrow. (He liked fields at any time, better than drawing-rooms or dining-rooms.)

I was not troubled at all by such questions of precedence

during my first Season, when I was only Daisy Burke and seventeen. And it was certainly great fun then to be Daisy Burke and seventeen, and I envied none of the Duchesses or Marchionesses or Countesses who led off the Balls with His Excellency.

I went to most of my gaieties in the very best circumstances with Fingall and his two dear kind sisters, who had been so sweet to me from our first meeting. Fingall, who all his life hated society, had accepted the State Stewardship for the sake of his sisters.

He was then only in his twenty-fourth year, and had succeeded his father a couple of years earlier. He had already taken on his responsibilities and duties and taken them with a characteristic seriousness. He had opened the House of Lords a little while before, as a Liberal Peer, which he was then, although later he followed Lord Landsdowne. He had made a very good speech on that occasion. Rather unexpectedly he could always make a good speech when called upon to do so, although with occasional lapses of grammar, or into Gallicisms, a result of his French upbringing. He said he quite enjoyed speaking, as while he was on his legs no one could interrupt him. "Intewupt me," he said, for he could never manage his r's. In recognition of that opening of the House of Lords, he was offered the Knighthood of St. Patrick. He refused it, saying that he had done nothing to deserve it. It was the first of three such refusals during his life, and his reason for refusing was always the same. He would not accept an honour which he felt he had not personally earned.

He and his sisters had had a strange childhood. Their mother had died young. She was half French and half Welsh, her father being a French Academician, François Alexis Rio, her mother a Welsh Herbert. When she died at Pau—of consumption—the children were still only babies. Old Mrs. Jones, the housekeeper at Killeen, who had been Fingall's nurse, and remained at heart always his nurse, remembered that Lady Fingall had been beautiful, like all consumptives. She was very sweet and good, and it was sad for the children

77

who had to grow up without her. Their father, I gather, did not pay a great deal of attention to them. Mrs. Jones, then a young maid in the employment of the Herberts—Lady Fingall's cousins, and distant connections also by marriage of the Fingall family—first saw Fingall in Rome, where he was born, "as a red head on his mother's knee."

After Lady Fingall's death Lord Fingall lived in Paris and the children were largely brought up there. They lived in an old-fashioned hotel, the Hôtel des Deux Mondes in the Avenue de l'Opera. Because their mother had died of consumption, Lord Fingall was always anxious about the children's health, so they were never sent to school. Fingall was educated first by his sisters' governess, a stern martinet, and later by an old priest, Father Macnamara, whom he loved. Father Macnamara came from Meath too, actually from a small mill near Killeen where his people still lived. They were quite simple, but the young priest had been sent abroad for his education, as was still a frequent custom with Irish priests in those days. He had been at Douai and in Rome and spoke several languages. Fingall was devoted to his tutor, as his tutor was to him. But the Paris he saw with Father Macnamara was a monk's Paris indeed—he knew all the churches and had visited the Morgue!—and very different from the Paris known by other young men of his class.

From this upbringing he brought the slight French accent with which he always spoke. He used to go back alone to Killeen sometimes for hunting in the winter holidays and live by himself with a couple of servants in the big house. The little room, as simple and bare as he could make it, which he chose then, was the room that he kept as his own all his life. He hunted, with such horses as his very limited money could provide for him, or on borrowed horses. He was always a good rider, so in that friendly and hospitable country he did not lack these. The neighbours were very good to the lonely boy. Some people who hunted in Meath at that time remember him, up to his knees in a muddy ditch, trying to pull out the mare who had fallen with him.

"Can't you stwuggle, Mawia?" he was saying. "Mawia. Can't you stwuggle?" Evidently Maria had had enough of it and preferred to lie where she had fallen.

I don't think he was ever conscious of loneliness during those holidays. The servants loved him and the country about was full of his friends, gentle and simple. And he had the companionship of animals which, all his life, was to please him, I believe, better than the companionship of many humans. Hunting, he learnt to know the country, the mystery and wisdom of it as it must be learnt in boyhood or girlhood if it is ever to be fully possessed.

The Plunketts seem to have been born riders, for the girls took to riding and hunting as eagerly, as fearlessly as their brother, and I do not believe that they had ever been on a horse until they came to Meath.

Fingall himself was always hardy, absolutely indifferent to material comfort—indeed he went further and, for himself, positively disliked comfort or any suggestion of luxury. It was nothing to him to rise in the dark, have a cup of tea if he could get it—or, if not, breakfast sparsely on an apple and a glass of water, and, on that chilly meal, ride away in the cold grey light to a distant Meet.

Never having been to a public school, he had missed that association with other boys. And if he lost something by it, he gained something also. He was never put through any machine or turned out in any mould. He was himself, always. And he remained himself through all his life. In the ordinary sense he was never educated. But he had good Father Macnamara's teaching. He could not spell either English or French—to the end of his days he spelt both *boath*—and he wrote such an atrocious hand that I had great difficulty in reading the letter in which he proposed to me! Yet he made that fine speech opening the House of Lords, to which older, experienced and accomplished men listened. Perhaps he had the most distinguished gift of all—simplicity. He always said that if his life had not been settled for him by his circumstances of birth and by his early succession, and he could have

79

chosen a profession, he would have liked to have been a doctor first and a soldier afterwards. He was born, however, to be a country gentleman. And a very good country gentleman he was.

He was at Killeen for his coming of age, when the butler, preparing the great celebrations, got gloriously drunk and set the dining-room on fire, damaging the only good pictures we had at Killeen, including two Vandycks of King Charles I. and Queen Henrietta Maria. Years later Hugh Lane looked at the damaged collection sadly, even when the best that could be done had been done with them, and said: "They are not pictures. But they will make good furniture." The Vandycks alas, were damaged past repair. Fingall, on his way home, breakfasted at the Shelbourne Hotel and read in the morning paper: "Fire at Killeen Castle," and thought that the house had been burnt. But, fortunately, the fire had not gone beyond the dining-room.

He persuaded his father, who had lived abroad for so long, to return to Killeen for the last year or so of his life. He broke the entail on this condition, so that the old Lord Fingall might meet an obligation and also provide for his two daughters. One of the results of the breaking of the entail was that the family diamonds were set free, and Fingall gave them to me on our marriage.

His father died at Killeen, as was right, and was buried in the family graveyard between the walls of the ruined chapel that was the old Abbey Church.

Fingall had always the most beautiful manners and his French upbringing added to them a little stiffness. He was not really shy, because he was too unconscious of himself for that. He had the gift of silence to a supreme degree, having a theory that people should not talk unless they had something worth saying. As he was very seldom certain that he had anything worth saying, he remained silent. His silence was perfectly courteous always. Indeed, in after years, many times I found it soothing to fly from some chattering party to Fingall's study, to be rested by his silence. He would slip away to be alone there after lunch or dinner, when it was possible without discourtesy to his guests. He never objected to my parties although they must often have wearied him, and he was so courteous and affable a host that his guests, finding him so, would hardly have believed it if they had been told that he was waiting to fly from them as soon as he could do so without being rude.

His sisters also spoke with that slight French accent, and after their conventual life with the stern governess in Paris, and their visiting also of many churches, with picture galleries and museums as a light relief, they had a quaint stiffness of manner, too. They wore old-fashioned clothes that suited them, high plain bodices and full flared skirts and they had rather a nun-like look in the gay world in which they moved. I think of them always with love and gratitude. For they might have been so very different to me. Fingall, of course, should have married money. And what had I to bring him, but a pretty face? Such a face as might be found in any field of daisies. I have always said that I did not deserve him. I say it now. And I am terrified to think of the power that is given just to a pretty face. That I should have had so much because Fingall looked at me once, as I passed in the street, and loved me! And there were so many prettier faces.

But when I talk of this to-day to my friend, Tom Case, he says that I am wrong and that the beauty of English women made the greatness of England. For beauty, he says, and goodness, must go together. And what is the expression of a face but the soul behind it? Is he right and is that true? Or is it a man's point of view? Surely, there have been many wicked women who have also been lovely.

Sometime that Season I went out hunting for the first time, in a borrowed habit, belonging to Henrietta Plunkett, which hung round me in folds. Alas, that I could not borrow, with it, some of the Plunkett courage and fearlessness! It simply did not occur to any of them that one could be frightened.

We drove down to my first Meet on a winter morning, I,

sitting beside Fingall on his coach, frozen inside my borrowed clothes, for all the thick folds of them. Fingall was a wonderful whip and negotiated the narrow gate of the Castle Yard with great skill. Then the leaders danced on their hind legs down the street to the great joy of a small crowd watching. By the time we got into Meath and reached the cross-roads where our hunters were waiting, I was stiff with cold and fright. But how should I acknowledge it to all those alarming people, sitting fresh bucking horses as calmly as though they were the red and gold chairs in St. Patrick's Hall? Or walking their horses up and down under the trees, brushing the hedges, talking to them now and again, twisting themselves in the saddle to settle a girth or a stirrup. I was swung up on to an enormous horse, guaranteed wise and confidential enough to carry even a complete ignoramus across country. My only experience of riding had been those rides over the Dublin mountains with Wilfred and Minnie Fitzgerald. And that country, as I saw it through Lifeboat's ears (a good reassuring name at least), looked, on the whole, even bigger and more terrifying than it had looked when I saw it from my feet! How cold it was! People spoke in low voices mysteriously and with an air of saying as little as possible, and their voices seemed as frozen as the air, in which the horses' breath rose slowly, making a white mist.

My wise and confidential mount must be in the fashion, so he goes curvetting sideways with a great show of impatience. I hold the reins with small, incompetent, cold fingers. Sitting here by the fire talking, I can feel that coldness of a hunting morning, my first hunting morning, and of many such mornings to follow. Fingall has obviously forgotten me. Even his face looks chilly above his red coat. We move off slowly, down a lane, squelching in the mud, through a gate. Lifeboat, in his hurry, knocks me against the post. Has he broken my leg? No. I am still whole. But, of course, I shall be killed and no one will mind at all! There is nothing like going out hunting with your best friends, to teach you how little you matter to them.

Then we are galloping. Over the field, up the hill. I have ceased to be cold. How good the feeling of the ground under a horse's feet is! Lifeboat and I are warming to each other. Soon we shall be friends. The terrible coldness that froze all of us apart, making us lonely strangers, is over. Someone passing me calls something back and laughs. I have jumped a bank and a ditch and am still there. How did it happen? Lifeboat is going like a wave. Oh, this is ecstasy! Almost better than the Blue Danube last night.

Although I had never hunted before that day, the trusty Lifeboat carried me safely over the most alarming country, until, taking a jump, he jerked up his head and hit me on the nose. I dropped the reins and fell off in agony. Fingall came galloping back. (After all I do matter to someone!) "Are you hurt?" "He has broken my nose," I sobbed. And indeed I believe always that that accident did alter the shape of it. My fierce Irish-speaking nurse with her scrubbing had made it turn upwards. My friends assured me that the change was an improvement.

I spent that night with a large raw beefsteak over my nose to keep it from turning black. The remedy was evidently successful for I appeared at the Ball the following night apparently quite undamaged by my first hunting accident.

CHAPTER SIX

AND at the Ball one heard such scraps of conversation as: "If you're riding the grey to-morrow, it's only the tail of you I'll see." Or, "Will you be walking in Grafton Street to-morrow morning?"

Well, one might be, having shopping to do. Shopping greatly enlivened by the possibility of a meeting with some-one—an entirely chance meeting, of course!

Or presently it was: "Will you be skating on the Viceregal Pond to-morrow afternoon?" For there was a spell of frost which put a temporary end to hunting, and those who lived chiefly for that occupation wailed over it. We went out in parties to the Park, to skate, instead. The Viceregal Pond was really within the Zoo grounds with a private gate leading to it from the grounds of the Viceregal Lodge. I suppose it was a special privilege to skate there. I remember performing strange movements on the ice with the assistance of a chair. My skating was as elementary as my hunting. But the frosty air was lovely and the return home through the winter dusk, in time to dress and go dancing again at night.

We must have danced like the Congress of Vienna for those six weeks. I wonder the red and gilt chairs in St. Patrick's Hall did not get up at last and move to the Strauss music. Live, Laugh and Love. Well, we lived, laughed and loved.

It was a friendly world. Irish society was too small to have the circles and cliques of London. Every one knew every one else. The girls had a wonderful time. There were plenty of men and they, being numerically superior, used to "cut in" on our dances. Of course it was fun when they surrounded us, begging for a dance. A Colonel did not disdain to share a dance with his subaltern. Men were much less spoilt then than they are now. It was a romantic time. Many an English heart was lost to Ireland for ever and ever during those Dublin Seasons. The Irish girls were lovely, gay and simple

84

and unspoilt. I can hear their soft voices and their laughter. No wonder the slower Englishmen were bewildered and caught into that bewilderment which is a maze out of which a man may not find the way. There was a great deal of humour. One Dublin lady came regularly to Court with one of her own drawing-room curtains fastened to her shoulders as a train. It was unmistakably a curtain. But she made a most regal entrance with it sweeping behind her. It might have been said of her as it was said of an English Duchess, whose mother was reputed to have been a cook, that "she made a very good entrée." And there were the mistakes made by Mr. Gaston Monsell, the Gentleman Usher, who had the most unfortunate failing for his position, that he could not get names clearly or remember them. Once, at a Levée, he announced Mr. Sclater Booth as "Mr. Scatter Boots." Or so the story was told. I expect we told a good many stories. There was a later occasion, when the bearer of an ancient Irish title arrived at a Castle Ball intoxicated and tried to draw his toy sword upon some-one. In an inquiry about that happening later, Fingall was asked if he had noticed anything out of the ordinary about the Irish prince on that night.

"No," said Fingall in his slow voice, "nothing out of the ordinary."

The Chamberlain, Colonel Dease, afterwards Sir Gerald Dease, was Fingall's cousin and mentor. He lived at Celbridge Abbey where Vanessa lived and died, after a terrible occasion when Swift visited her there. I was sure when I stayed at Celbridge Abbey that I saw and heard Vanessa's ghost crying in the garden by the waters of the Liffey. But that is a later memory.

Lord Charlemont was the Comptroller. The Comptroller's house was in the opposite corner of the Yard from the State Steward's, and Lord Charlemont was the only person who knew all the mysteries of the Castle kitchens. Then there was the Gentleman-Usher, already mentioned. And Colonel Frank Foster, Master of the Horse, Colonel Alfred Turner, Military Secretary. And—enchanting title—there are two Gentlemen-at-Large, Colonels Donaldson and Kearney. What, I am asked, are the duties of Gentlemen-at-Large? Well, I suppose, they are just at large! It suggests that they are very dangerous people. And there were five A.D.C.s as well. So we were well provided with young men and dance partners.

Meanwhile things were progressing in a most interesting way for me. Sometimes, during that Season, Fingall and his sisters gave a big Ball at Killeen Castle. It was the first Ball they had given and, I think, the first that there had been at Killeen for a long time. That occasion, too, is all rather dream-like in my mind as though I saw it behind a gauze curtain. I went down to stay at Killeen for it, with the Fitzgeralds. Fingall met us at Drumree station, driving his coach. I sat up beside him and so we travelled along the Meath roads. It was almost dark when we turned in at the gate and drove up the avenue. But there was enough light still to show the walls of the old Castle, dark against the evening sky, and to outline the towers and make the whole picture impressive and beautiful. All the windows were lit up and I thought it looked like a fairy palace. That was my first sight of Killeen.

I remember feeling very shy at the Ball and aware that a lot of people were looking at me—criticising me. For the Ball had a significance of which I was aware, of course. All the county people were there. In the background were some alarming old ladies, Fingall's relatives, examining and considering me.

And I must have looked very young and inadequate in my simple white tulle frock against that background. I had never stayed in such a large house before, and it was all very frightening, especially as I was conscious of so many eyes on me, and not all of them friendly. The Ball lasted the whole night and was magnificently done in every way. Killeen, lit up with many lamps and candles, roaring fires in the old fire-places—and even then it was cold, I think—with the music in it and the tables in the great dining-room spread for supper, seemed to me more than ever like a fairy palace. And I felt very like Cinderella.

Fingall introduced me to every one and danced a great many dances with me, himself. Alas! How badly he danced

86

and how little attention he paid to time or music! I had not discovered then that he did not know one note or one tune from another. I longed for another partner, but there seemed to be a conspiracy to leave me to my host. Presently he introduced his cousin, Horace Plunkett, to me. He seemed to know that I was very shy and was kind, trying to put me at my ease. We danced together. But, alas, he danced as badly as Fingall! So we sat out instead and talked and he told me about his ranching in America, where he had been sent for his health. He was then about twenty-eight, very pleasant looking and gay, with blue eyes and that quick wonderful smile, of which Sir Frederick Moore was to say long after when Horace was his chief at the Department of Agriculture: "When Sir Horace smiles, a man would do anything for that smile." It was much more frequent in those days of Horace's youth than it was in later years, after Ireland had made him serious. But he had, even then, the stoop of ill health without which I never remember him. My impression that night was that he was taking stock of me too, but in a kindly and sympathetic way. I felt him a friendly presence. He told me about the life that he had lived at Wyoming with his friends Alexis Roche and Beau Watson, who were ranching with him, and about the riding and the rounding up of the cattle. He had been a real cowboy and worn the shaggy cowboy trousers, the loose shirt and the wide hat that were to become familiar to us afterwards on the cinema. It was such talk as one would think of to amuse someone very young, almost a child. If his dreams for Ireland had already stirred in him—I know now, of course, that they had stirred—he did not speak of them that night. My first impression of him is just of someone gay and kind and charming.

We left Killeen the following afternoon. But before that I had to spend a rather uncomfortable morning. I see a very sleepy little person, sitting in the big chilly drawing-room with a terrifying old aunt of Fingall's, Lady Henrietta Riddell. She is cross-examining and interrogating me and considering me with her bright, curious old eyes. It is all

87

vitally important, of course, to the family. Where have I lived? What of my father and mother? Whom do I know? I answered politely and tried hard not to yawn with overwhelming sleepiness. I watched the door, praying that it would open and that someone would come through it, to rescue me from this terrifying dragon. Fingall—the Knight. Or one of his sisters . . .

Then, after lunch, the coach came round to the door and I got up beside Fingall again, and good-byes were said and he drove us back to the station.

There, as he assisted me down, he slipped a note into my hand. "Will you read this when you are alone?" he said. "And give me your answer to-morrow night at the Castle."

I don't remember that I was so tremendously excited. I suppose I had known for some time what was coming. I only nodded and thrust the note into my bag. I had more sense than to read it in the train under my companions' eyes. So I waited until I got back to Buswell's and was alone in my own room. I dare say that it was not the first time that the Victorian pictures had looked down upon such a scene.

It was a stiff, formal little letter, written in a scrawling, schoolboy's hand. We always told Fingall that his writing was like a trapped fly running over the paper, spreading ink behind it. But the gist of it was that he asked me if I would do him the very great honour of marrying him and allowing him to do everything in his power to make me happy.

I ran upstairs at once to my mother, who did not receive the news at all in the conventional manner. She was terribly surprised and overcome, wept, and said, through her tears, that I was much too young to be married, and in any case not fit at all to take the position of Fingall's wife. Instructed by her, I wrote a letter in reply, thanking him, but asking him to give me a little time before I answered. My mother wanted my father's advice and he was still down in Galway. My father, when he did arrive, was as unworldly as my mother, and said also that I was not fitted for the position, and that Fingall should marry someone with money. However,

Fingall didn't see it that way. He had made up his mind that first day when he saw me in the street. And once he had done that no one in world could be more obstinate. "As obstinate as a pig or a Plunkett," was a later saying of mine, which applied not only to him, but to other Plunketts I have known. (I added—of the pigs, or the Plunketts! "The more yon pull them one way, the more they go the other." For I had learnt then that you could lead them but never drive them.) At the next Ball as we danced together, he begged me not to keep him waiting any longer but to say that I would marry him and again he assured me that he would do everything in his power to make me happy. I thought how nice he was and what fun it would be to live at Killeen. And I probably thought that it would be fun to marry an Earl, too. And, of course, it was exciting to get engaged in one's very first Season. So I said, "I think I would like to, awfully!"

I wonder which of us, entering upon that great adventure, was the greatest babe, he at twenty-four, or I at seventeen!

My father still thought that we were both too young and that Fingall with his old name and impoverished estate should look for a richer bride. But as Fingall was determined and there were no serious objections, we became engaged and our engagement, which, of course, did not surprise any one, was the great excitement of the Season. Every one told me how lucky I was and how lovely I would look in the family diamonds, and naturally I enjoyed it all immensely.

My next memories are blurred because I was too tired to remember anything clearly. I had to get a trousseau as fine as my parents could afford, A dozen of everything, and fine embroidered linen. People spent far more on underthings then and had fewer dresses. I always wore less clothes than other people but even I had three petticoats under my skirts in those days. Mrs. Sims was making my wedding dress and my other trousseau frocks and I had to stand for hours while she fitted me, until at last I almost fainted. My wedding dress, of course, had to be of white satin. That, or brocade, or a thick, stiff moiré which was called tabinet, was the only wear for formal occasions. The dress was beautifully cut with a simple, almost nun-like severity. That is all I remember of it. We were already, I think, wearing Princess dresses in those days, called after the lovely Princess of Wales, whose beauty had thrilled England and captured the people's hearts. My brides-maids were all in white too—full-frilled dresses of tulle which they wore with very wide hats.

The wedding itself was quiet. We were married in the Archbishop of Dublin's private chapel in Rutland Square, which could not hold many people. But my uncle, Sir Patrick Keenan, gave the reception for us afterwards at Delville where he was then living. I could not have had a more charming setting for my wedding reception. It was May, —the 15th of that lovely month and my friends had not failed to warn me that, by tradition, May was an unlucky month to choose for a wedding. I only laughed and my defiance of the superstition was well justified, for my married life was to be extraordinarily happy. I might have said with Mrs. Delany, who wrote this, at Delville, a century earlier: "A moderate share of health and wealth but a vast quantity of love and friendship, I shall not envy any one's estate while I have that." She wrote that in one of the rooms at Delville which were flung open for my wedding reception. She had left her charming spirit in those rooms, a fragrance which lingered, so that you were aware of it when you pushed open the high red gate in the wall above Glasnevin village and stepped into that tranquil atmosphere of another age. As for her philosophy—"A vast quantity of love and friendship," that is the riches of the world and I have had it in full.

My uncle treasured all the memories of Delville, a historic house as well as a beautiful one. Swift had been a constant visitor there and his famous Drapier letters, which no Dublin printer dared handle, were set up in a secret underground printing press under the temple in the garden. There is an inscription over the temple composed by Swift, *Hinc Despicis Vestigia Urbis.* ("Hence you look down on traces of the town.") It had two meanings, but in the simple one, Delville did indeed look down from its hill on to the town. In those days before the houses grew up about it and with Glasnevin only a country village below the gates, there was a clear view of the sea and the hill of Howth from the upper windows.

Not only did Swift visit Delville, but Stella also. Before Dr. Delany's marriage to Mrs. Pendarves, Stella was the only woman present at his dinners and parties, being considered sufficiently clever to be there. I have been told that at the dinners she and Swift and Dean Delany used to compete, writing verses, and that there is one poem in Swift's published works which is said to have been written in part by her and in part by Swift and by the Dean. There was a fig tree in the garden, which she was supposed to have planted. We took a cutting from it and it grew in due course against one of the garden walls at Killeen.

The house was beautiful, with carved marble chimney-pieces and Italian decorations on the walls and ceilings. Dean Delany was justified in writing to Mrs. Pendarves in the letter in which he proposed marriage: "I have . . . a good house (as houses go in this part of the world) moderately furnished, a good many books, a pleasant garden (better, I believe, than when you saw it). Would to God I might have leave to lay them at your feet." Mrs. Delany was evidently enchanted with it. She collected sea shells from the silver shore which she could see from her windows and decorated the walls and ceilings and cornice with them to look like a stucco, in the dining-room where our wedding feast was spread.

I wish I could find the photograph that was taken on the steps at Delville of the wedding group. But alas, it has disappeared. The Viceroy and Lady Spencer and all the Viceregal Court, of course, were there. And an enormous number of guests. All Fingall's relatives and friends and my relatives and friends. I remember Judge Morris making jokes in an exaggerated brogue as usual, Father Healy capping him. Our going-away carriage came to the door drawn by the traditional white horses of the Plunketts. Someone remembered that an old shoe must be thrown after it for luck.

"Get Morris to throw *his* brogue," said Father Healy.

CHAPTER SEVEN

WE went to Paris for our honeymoon. May played us false in the matter of weather and I was terribly ill on the journey. The stewardess on the boat prophesied gloomily, "There'll be music in the pans to-night." And music there was. I was so ill afterwards that we had to get out of the London train at Bangor, where we spent two or three dismal days and nights at the George Hotel. I remember the gloom of the vast Victorian room and the enormous bed in which I lay sick and miserable. I had a queer maid, provided for me by my aunt, and I think chosen for her piety rather than for her efficiency. Dowling's strange ways and sayings were to amuse me later, but her ministrations at the George Hotel at Bangor fit in with my depressing associations of those days.

In due course I recovered and we proceeded to Paris, where we must have been a quaint pair indeed. We exchanged the gloom of the George Hotel for the solemnity of the old family hotel—the Hôtel des Deux Mondes in the Avenue de l'Opera, where Fingall had lived as a boy with his father and sisters. We then proceeded to see the Paris that Fingall knew—a monk's Paris! We visited many churches—I remember Notre Dame and Saint Sulpice and an expedition to the Morgue, which seems a strange choice for a honeymoon! We went to Longchamps once, but racing and horse talk were still Greek to me and I was bored. There were a few carefully chosen, very proper plays, and one or two visits to elderly people. Fingall only knew elderly people and priests in Paris.

I remember walking with Fingall along a street—a wide street with trees bordering it—was it the Champs Elysées?—wearing one of my trousseau frocks with a bustle to it that rustled behind me, a hat tied under my chin with strings and a little beaded cape. There the memory breaks off.

Fingall was soon homesick for Killeen. When—away from

92

it—was he not homesick for Killeen? And when he was ready to turn his face that'way I was glad enough to agree with him.

London was better. We stayed a few days at Fleming's Hotel in Half-Moon Street and went shopping. I had to buy riding clothes. For now, of course, that I was married to Fingall, there was no escape and I must take to riding and hunting in earnest. The clothes were fun. Whatever terror I went through in my hunting days, I always adored my hunting clothes. To Busvine I went for a riding habit and much admired my own figure as I turned before the mirror while it was being fitted. No garment in the world showed off or gave away a figure like the riding habit of those days. I had no grievance about my waist, having then not as many inches to it as I had years. And to Peal and Bartley for boots which must fit perfectly, not showing a wrinkle anywhere. Such bootmakers were geniuses, born, not made, and Peal's genius was for the leg of a boot, Bartley's for the foot. The result might well be the work of art that it was. Those hunting clothes must be perfect to satisfy Fingall. They were the only clothes of mine that he really ever noticed. I was to discover that very soon. He would say of a dress after I had worn it for five years or so and when I was about to discard it: "I like that thing you are wearing. Is it new?" But my hunting clothes were another matter. If they had fallen short of his high standard he would not have allowed me to come out in them.

After Busvine and Peal and Bartley, we went to Mr. Lock, the famous hatter in St. James's Street. It might be only yesterday that Fingall and I walked down the sunlit street to it and stopped before the low little shop with diamond-paned windows and Mr. Lock himself came to the door to receive us. He had the appearance and manners of a very grand and distinguished butler. He always received one himself and arranging to have a hat made by him was an important ceremonial. There was no such thing as hurry—had one heard the word then, or dreamed of the hurry in which the world might yet be in our time?

93

The shop is still there—unchanged from that May day of 1883. It had the atmosphere of a shop connected with hunting and horses, country gentlemen and country ladies.

Mr. Lock was *the* maker of hunting hats—shining tall hats for gentlemen, bowlers, tall hats, just as shining for ladies. I was to have tall hats for hunting, bowlers for cubbing and schooling days yet to be. Mr. Lock measured my head carefully. I expect the measurements are still there to-day. He had those of all the great riders of his time who came to him for their hats. No doubt they too are still there, although many of the distinguished and lovely heads, for which Mr. Lock made hats, have fallen long since.

Various models were tried on my head and, after careful consideration, it was decided that a slight wave in the brim was softer and more becoming to me than the hard straight line. So my tall hats and bowlers were made for me with a little curly brim and I always kept to that pattern.

Then to Hodgkinson's in the Piccadilly Arcade for ties and handkerchiefs and stocks. Hodgkinson's, too, is still there.

Our shopping done, we turned our faces homeward, stopping on the way for a few days at Llanarth in Monmouthshire, to visit Fingall's cousin Mrs. Herbert, only daughter of Lord and Lady Llanover. One of the Herberts who had been standard bearer to Henry VIII. had changed his name to Jones, but, in a later century, when Fingall's great-aunt Harriet was married to Mr. Jones of Llanarth, the family reverted to their original name of Herbert. All, except Lady Harriet and her husband. She had married a Jones and Jones she would remain, declared this strong-minded lady. Lord Llanover, as Sir Benjamin Hall and Minister for the Board of Works, had put up the Westminster clock Big Ben, that makes time for England, and was called after him. He was a great Liberal in every sense of the word.

At Llanarth, Fingall's father and mother had become engaged. Lady Fingall was, of course, also connected with the Herberts on her mother's side. We went to Llanover one day from Llanarth and I was greatly impressed and rather alarmed

94

by old Lady Llanover, then a widow, who had been called "the Queen of Wales." She drove about the place in a little donkey chaise and always spoke Welsh to the people on the estate. I was told that she would employ no servant who was not a Welsh speaker, and that that was the language of the household. On Sundays she went to church, wearing the Welsh national dress with the high peaked hat, and all the women of her village had to wear it too. When she entered the church, every one stood up. Lady Llanover hated men, I believe, and was determined to leave everything that she could to the women of her family.

After this, we went home to Killeen, arriving on a June evening when the County of Meath was green and white and gold. There is no other green in the world like it, and the High Kings of Ireland knew what they were doing when they lifted their palaces on the Hill of Tara over that fat land. And the Norse and Norman barons—Plunketts and others who followed them, knew too what they were doing.

We drove from Drumree again. At the boundary of the Killeen property the tenants took the horses out of the carriage and drew us up the avenue and I saw Killeen for the second time—with different eyes now, since it was to be my home. It was towering and dark that summer evening, amid its quiet fields. Often in those years when I lived there I was to look at it and think what a lovely ruin it would make. The green light of Meath seemed to be in the windows, still unlit at that hour. I was a little frightened of it and of all the tradition that it held. As the carriage was swung by willing hands round to the steps of the hall door, I heard a man's voice in the crowd say disparagingly: "Sure, she's only a little slip of a thing."

He expressed exactly what I felt. Of course it was a disappointment to them all that Fingall had not married some great and rich lady to bring money to the Castle and estate which so badly needed it. And I must have looked as I felt, a quite absurd and inadequate child to become chatelaine of one of the greatest and oldest Norman Castles in Ireland, one that had been suggested as a possible Royal residence; and to be the wife of the eleventh Earl.

My two kind sisters-in-law were at the door, and how glad I was of their welcome and reassuring presence. I was very tired and it was lovely to slip away from the cheering crowd and go upstairs with them to the rooms prepared for us.

Mary and Henrietta were the best of friends to me from the hour of our first meeting until they died. Their marriages took them only a short distance away, still within the borders of Meath, so that they were always there when I wanted them. They loved their brother and said that any one he loved they would love. They meant it and they took me into their generous hearts, on a fortunate day for me.

That night of our arrival there was a tenants' party in the big Servants' Hall and it overflowed into a marquee that had been put up on the lawn. The tenants had come to welcome us, not only from the Killeen estate, but from the property which Fingall still owned at the other end of the county. There were speeches and presentations. And then it was all over and I was left the mistress of Killeen and feeling as frightened as the little girl at Arcachon who had got lost in the pine woods. Fortunately not much was expected of me with regard to the duties of mistress. My sisters-in-law, who had their own rooms upstairs so that we only met at meals or when we wanted to, ran the house, with the assistance of Mrs. Jones, the housekeeper. I fancy that Mrs. Jones was the real ruler. She kept me in my place severely.

"You little know, my lady," she would say darkly, shaking her head which had already a natural shake from a nervous complaint. I felt as though I had been told to run away and play with my toys which was, in effect, what I did. I believe at the end of that first year I hardly knew my cook by sight and there were many parts of the castle to which I had still never penetrated.

It seems, looking back, to have been a very long summer, that first summer after my marriage, at Killeen. Fingall and I must have looked a quaint pair of children when we walked about the place, hand in hand. He and his sisters treated me as something to be laughed at and spoilt and petted. I must learn to ride properly before the hunting season, and teaching me to ride was the occupation and amusement of those summer mornings. Only I knew how terrified I was. And the horse I rode. I used to see it later in the eyes of Bootles, one of my hunters. In the stable he would turn a weary eye on me. "Here she is again!" Out hunting I would try to hold him, in vain. He would shake his head. "Look at this baggage!" And be off. He knew that it was quite another matter when he was brought out for Fingall. He became a different horse then. Fingall took him out regularly when I was hunting him, for fear he would get the habit of funking from me.

But those hunting days were all in the future, those summer mornings when we did schooling in the Arlintown fields over by Dunsany. There were natural jumps there, representing, although on a smaller scale, the country I should have to face later; ditches, banks and doubles. Schooling was almost worse than hunting, for one did it in cold blood. Fortunately the horses knew all about it and I was just a passenger.

"Her ladyship is in rather a funk," Fingall would say, but he did not really believe it. It was a sensation he had never known, so how could he imagine it? And I was too proud to say that I was terrified. Or, perhaps speechless with terror. Anyhow I went through it, sitting grim and cold on Lifeboat or Bootles or some other wise horse and hoping that they would do it all for me. There were those terrifying moments before I mounted, when Lifeboat seemed as tall as a house, and he stood with his ears pricked, blowing out steam through his nostrils, his eye on the distant horizon as though he only waited for me to be up to carry me over the edge of the world. And he did carry me over those jumps. And I sat there somehow. It seems that I spent most of that summer learning to ride. The grass grew higher in Meath, deepened in green colour, the trees became heavier and darker, until at last I felt that the lush growth of everything was sending me asleep. It must have been in an effort to keep awake that I used to dance by myself under the beech trees those summer evenings. "I am alive," I would cry joyously. "I am alive! And no one can take that from me! "

We seem to have had few visitors. I had soon learnt how unsociable Fingall was. "I love my friends and detest my acquaintances," he used to say. And we became so unaccustomed to the society of our fellow creatures that there was a day that summer when he and I, sitting under one of the trees near the house beside the pond and seeing a carriage drive up the avenue, lay flat, hiding ourselves in the long grass that covered us, like truant children; until we saw the carriage turn from the door and drive away again, when we breathed a sigh of relief and lifted our heads. Later, someone was to ask me this question: "What do you do in Meath in the Summer?" I answered sadly: "We just wait for the Winter."

So I was obliged to hunt, however little heart I had for it. Because if you didn't hunt in Meath you might as well be dead. The whole life of the country centred round that occupation. During the hunting season no one talked of anything else. And I think, having had years of it, that, to the non-hunting person, hunting jargon is the most boring in the world. Even fishing and golf stories are not as bad, or so I think. But I did not live with fishermen or golfers or I might have a different opinion.

Meanwhile Fingall looked at his horses and at his fields— a fence must be mended there, a cottage improved here—we walked over the estate, considering these things, and then he looked at his horses again or at his stables and he had everything in the world he wanted at Killeen, as he was to have always. In later years during his rare absences—at the South African War, in America, his letters written home to me all show that same longing to be back, the same concentration of his mind and heart on that little world of his—Killeen.

I still found the Castle frightening, and, looking up at it, wondered sometimes if I had dreamed it all, or if I could be mistress of such a place. There were summer afternoons when the shadows of the trees were lengthening over the fields outside and the green light and the shadows too were in the house and I thought I heard footsteps following me in the long passages. I would look over my shoulder and find nothing there. Once I was sure that I felt a strange cold wind chilling me and freezing my heart. One of the ghosts of Killeen? I fled from it out into the sunshine. There were ghosts. I cannot say that I ever saw them, but I felt them. Were they asking me, in those early days, who I was, and how I came there, examining me, as curiously as the old Aunt Henrietta had examined me the morning after the Ball? I became accustomed to them in time as one does to one's own ghosts. I never saw them but I felt their presence. Fortunately for me, the Clammy Hand never moved over my face as I slept. Nor were the bedclothes pulled off me as happened to somebody sleeping in one of the rooms.

When we had turned the old library upstairs, where we used to sit in my early married days, back to its original use as a bedroom, people sleeping in the smaller room off it used to see in the early morning a man come out of the powdering closet and stand at the foot of the bed. He wore a blue suit and had powdered hair and one of the guests took him for a footman, calling him at that early hour. An officious footman, the guest said a little irritably at breakfast, and he had evidently mistaken the time. And then, as a thought struck him: "I did not know that you had such a grand powdered footman at Killeen."

"We have no powdered footmen," I said. "You know Fingall's views. It would offend his idea of human dignity to dress up his servants in such clothes. He would never want any of them to wear anything that he would not wear himself."

"But," our guest insisted, staring at me, "this morning I was certainly called by a footman wearing a blue coat with a powdered wig. He stood at the end of my bed, but he did not

99

say anything. I thought he had made a mistake about the time and went away when he discovered it."

"Look over your head," I said. We looked together at one of the portraits on the wall—one of those that had escaped the disastrous fire. This gentleman in a quiet blue coat with a dim braid edging it and smoothly-powdered hair, might easily, in a dim light, by a person half-awake, be taken for a footman. It was not the first time such a thing had happened, nor was it to be the last.

That was the 4th Earl, coming back to the rooms that had once been his. He did not always walk, or I suppose we should not have put our guests in those rooms. The 4th Earl, Peter, had been loyal to James II. whom he had followed on his wanderings, and had been with him when he died. (His wife and daughters were the only ladies who accompanied Catherine of Braganza to Portugal.) There was an account of the life and wars of that ill-fated Stuart monarch at Killeen, written beautifully on parchment and called "Light to the Blind." It is now in the National Library in Dublin. We have no certainty as to who wrote it, but we have always believed the hand to be that of the 4th Earl who was outlawed for his loyalty.

There are lovely stories in the history of the Plunkett family, but if I were to write them they would fill a book of their own. The family is so old that Debrett confesses itself beaten by its antiquity and does not delve farther into its history than its establishment in Meath in the eleventh century. Debrett says: "This noble family is of Danish origin, but its settlement in Ireland is so remote that nothing can be ascertained as to the precise period."

I learnt the legends of the house haphazardly in those early days after my marriage. Fingall and his sisters cared and knew little of such things. I liked the story of the first Plunketts coming to Ireland with one Rollo the Dane, bringing with them their white jennets from which they were called Blanc jenet, and in time Planc jenet and so, Plunkett. Their motto is *Festina Lente* (as is that of the Onslows, appropriately). According to this charming legend, the Plunketts, arriving in Ireland, ambled slowly and surely on their white jennets through the green land of Meath, and took possession of as many acres of that rich land as they could hold. One settled down under the Hill of Tara at Killeen, another at Dunsany, nearby. One at Rathmore, one at Dunshaughlin. Another went over the border into Louth and founded the family of the present Lord Louth. By the end of the sixteenth century, the manuscript roll of the Gentry of Meath recorded the existence of fifteen Plunketts, all estated men and all relatives. And in the present century at Dublin Castle King Edward VII. said to me: "Lady Fingall, I never seem to get away from the Plunketts in this country. There is Lord Plunket. And Sir Horace Plunkett. And Bishop Plunket, Colonel Plunkett and Count Plunkett." He paused and glanced across the room at my small son who was a Court page. "And there is that horrid little boy of yours treading on the Queen's train"!

I have always marvelled at the power of survival of the Plunketts. The family Tree which disposes of the Danish legend brings the founder of the family, Allaine, a descendant of the 1st Duke of Normandy, to the Battle of Hastings with a troop of horsemen, riding white horses. His son, Christopher, came to Ireland in 1170 and married the daughter of Hugh de Laci, Lord Justice of Ireland, who built the Castle of Killeen. From now on the Plunketts intermarried with other Meath families, with Cruises, Prestons, Nettervilles, Maguinesses, Nugents, and Flemings of Slane. They went farther afield and mingled their blood with that of Irish O'Briens—Kings of Munster—Norman de la Poers, and MacDonells of Antrim. By the twentieth century there was hardly an important family in Ireland with which they were not somehow connected.

Although they produced one martyr, Blessed Oliver Plunkett, there were plenty who were no saints among them. Meath still remembers the saying, "Travellers in Meath should beware. For if they are not robbed by the Lord of

Killeen, they are sure to be robbed by the Lord "of Dunsane.

Like other Irish and Norman Irish families, through Irish history they were to be found on either side—now outlawed by the English Crown, now serving it. I have marvelled at their power of survival, but indeed all the Irish must have had great staying powers or the conquest and repopulation of the country would have been complete. Naturally, as Norman lords who had come to Ireland, as my Burke ancestors had come, with Henry II. and Strongbow, the Plunketts tended to support the government which had originally established them, rather than the native Irish. But their religion drove them, as it drove other Norman families, into alliance with the Irish chiefs of the same Faith, as in Sir Phelim O'Neill's rebellion of 1641 and during Cromwell's terrible months in Ireland.

Here is just one story I may tell briefly, because it has a bearing on future history. It was in 1641 that Robert Plunket, Lord of Rathmore, was accused on the word of an informer of having been responsible for the death of five English soldiers stationed at Athboy. The historian says that Plunket's name was against him. The rolls of the Irish Confederation were crowded with Plunketts. In Meath alone they numbered: Plunkett of Dunsany, of Killeen, Balrath, of Tara, Gilstown, Castlekieran, of Derrypatrick, of Flenelstown; all of whom lost their properties in the confiscations that followed.

The historian tells how a warning was carried to Robert Plunket by "a young boy; one of those stunted, sullen, keen-featured 'gossoons' peculiar to Ireland, with weasel eyes, hair in elf locks and a countenance twenty years in advance of his real age; looking like a fairy changeling, shrewd, inquisitive, nimble, stealthy; such a boy as this had heard the order given to arrest Mr. Plunket and had sped on his thin bare legs right across country, over bog, stream, ditches and field, straight as the crow flies to Rathmore, and, reaching the Castle, called, hallooed and flung up stones at Mr. Plunket's window till that gentleman awakened, opened it and asked what was the matter."

Another warning was to be carried in a strangely similar way by a strangely similar messenger, over the hill of Tara to Killeen on an autumn night, nearly three centuries later.

I have not space to tell the whole story of the same Robert Plunket, some years later, riding out to meet Oliver Cromwell (who had demanded that he should come to him with all his treasure) with his tall sons and his one precious daughter riding behind him in the order of their age. These were his treasures, and he produced them, hoping perhaps to soften even Cromwell's heart by such a sight. In vain, alas. Robert Plunket and all his sons were killed by Cromwell's soldiers, only the girl escaping with her life.

Nor have I space to tell in full the earlier charming story of Mary Cruys, who married a younger son of the first Baron of Killeen and brought Rathmore into the Plunkett possession. A romantic story of a dispossessed heiress washing clothes humbly on the river bank in London and singing an Irish song about her own fields of Meath, which caught the ear of a successful Irish lawyer, Sir Thomas Plunkett, as he walked through the Temple gardens one summer morning. There is a sculptured stone in the park at Killeen with the names:

THOMAS PLUNKETT
MARY CRUYS

and no date. But the stone was a memorial left by the newly-married couple after their first visit to Killeen, the lady's estates having now been restored to her by Sir Thomas's efforts, and her husband, helped no doubt by her riches, on his way to becoming Lord Chancellor of Ireland.

When, in 1895, David Plunket, then M.P. for Dublin University, and a son of Lord Plunket—his maternal grandfather being Kendal Bushe, the famous Lord Chief Justice of Ireland—was given a peerage, he wrote to Fingall, asking if he had any objection to his taking the title of Rathmore. Fingall, of course, replied that it would be an honour to have such a man to represent the old name. So there was again a

Plunket of Rathmore, but the new peer lived mostly in London and the estate was never his.

A Plunkett of Dunsany was outlawed also for loyalty to James. But he was named in the Treaty of Limerick and the estates were restored to his grandson. The 12th Baron became a Protestant in the Penal Days. I have heard his descendant say that it was in order to keep his horse, at a time when no Catholic might keep a horse of more value than £5, and any Protestant offering him £5 for the horse could take it at that price. He kept, for his branch of the family, more than his horse. As with other families in Ireland, the Protestant branch remained rich and grew richer, while the Catholic branch was left poor and became poorer. It was at this time that an old lady, changing her religion to guard the family estates, said, " What is an old woman worth compared to the future of a great family?"

The Dunsanys, having turned Protestant, were secure in their property, and, as in many other cases, they became "holders" for their Catholic cousins of Killeen. That is to say that they swore that the Killeen property was theirs, holding it, every inch and every penny, in name. Each year Lord Dunsany had to swear afresh that the lands and property of Killeen were his. This was at a time when any member of a family turning Protestant could take the property of all his Catholic relatives, a son robbing a father, a brother a brother and so on. There were "holders"—i.e. Protestants who held land in this way for their Catholic neighbours—in every county, sometimes quite simple and poor men themselves.

I have seen a touching letter from the Lord Dunsany of that day, written to his cousin at Killeen. "My dear Fingall," he says, "I am now an old man and shall soon have to meet my Maker. I do not want to go to Him with a lie upon my soul. Could you not get someone else to swear that the land and property are theirs?"

With the ending of the Penal Days, the property was handed back. When I wrote to the present Lord Dunsany about something connected with these things, and reminded him that his ancestors—or one of them—gave up the Faith to keep his house and land, he wrote me this letter. It is dated March 11, but no year is given. I believe, however, that it was about 1929.

"DEAR LADY FINGALL,—You are evidently right. But my ancestor neglected to avail himself of the Treaty of Limerick by signing something by a certain date, so he went on the run and died on the run and lost everything. The estates were only restored to his grandson, Randal, in 1732. I have just consulted the documents of the case which are in this room.

"Yours ever,

"DUNSANY."

As with most Irish families, there were many Plunketts who went abroad to become soldiers of fortune and to fall in foreign service. There were plenty of them among the Wild Geese, as those Irish were called who went away to take service under foreign kings in the days when it was impossible for an Irish Catholic gentleman to live in Ireland. Of the Plunketts of Killeen, one, Luke, a Captain in the Austrian service, was killed in Italy in 1794. His brother, who survived the wars, was a Colonel in the same service. They were the sons of the 7th Earl, who had married an English heiress—Henrietta Maria Wollascott, only daughter and heiress of William Wollascott of Woolhampton Court in Berks. She brought to Killeen a library, mostly of religious and medical books, some beautifully bound and very old, much beautiful Queen Anne furniture and silver, and some lovely lace, all of which I was to discover, by degrees, during my time there, hidden away in some chest, or left to moulder in some empty room. Fingall sat in the House of Lords as Baron Fingall of Woolhampton Court. It was in the priest's hiding-hole at Woolhampton that the missing numbers of the Charters of Reading Abbey were discovered, which were at Killeen until the troubled days of 1921-22, when I took them for safety

105

to London, and, with Lord Coventry's help sold them to the British Museum, where they are now.

I have marvelled too at the capacity the Plunketts had for returning. Killeen might stand without a roof for years, with the wind crying about it and the rain pouring into it. Perhaps the thick walls that had been built for a Pale fortress stood secure, knowing that the owner would return. And he did return.

Of course, the Catholic Plunketts suffered for their religion. One of the possessions of the house was a chest of drawers, which appears as much as possible like such a piece of furniture as you would find in a servant's room. It was of the plainest wood and had china handles to it. The top lifted up and revealed inside an altar perfectly arranged for saying Mass. It was a relic of the Penal Days, when Mass might only be said secretly at Killeen as elsewhere, with scouts posted to watch for any danger. A hurried warning and the lid could be closed down, the priest hidden, the congregation scattered. The emissaries of the law coming, would find nothing more suspicious than a very plain chest of drawers against the wall—so plain and ugly that they would hardly notice it.

King James, fleeing from the Battle of the Boyne, through Meath, stopped at Lismullen, Sir John Dillon's place, and dropped there his gloves—true Stewart gloves with their pearl-sewn gauntlets. The Meath gentry, who had fought for him must flee too. We had King James's Army List at Killeen. There are only three families named in it, surviving in Meath now—Plunketts, Taaffes and Barnewalls. Many Meath Castles were left deserted after the Boyne battle and fell into the hands of the conquerors. Lord Slane was killed, and from Slane Castle, standing above the Boyne River—where, during other history Hugh O'Neill had slept his last night in Ireland—Lady Slane fled with her children to Dublin and threw herself on the mercy of William of Orange, who gave her a safe conduct to France where the Slanes had a French estate and also a French title; on condition that she renounced all claim to the lands and properties of Slane. She left her pedigree at Killeen on the way. They were not the first Flemings of Slane to be outlawed, and, although the title became extinct, I have been told that one family of Flemings at least, living in France, and otherwise French, continue to call themselves by the Irish title—Lords of Slane. And not so many years ago—since the War—a very strange thing happened.

I had gone down for a few days to join my sisters-in-law, who were staying at Tunbridge Wells. They said to me: "Do you know that someone called Lord Slane has died here? There is to be a Requiem at the Catholic Church to-morrow." They showed me the announcement in the local paper. Lord Slane! If it was true he must be a relative, for the Plunketts and Flemings had been much intermarried. I went to the church the next day and saw the coffin and the mourners, a tall, very foreign, distinguished lady in black, with a pretty daughter who looked much more English than her mother. In the local paper the girl was referred to as the Hon. —— Fleming.

After the Mass I went up and spoke to the lady, expressing my sympathy, telling her who I was, and mentioning the kinship of the Plunketts and the Flemings. I asked where and when Lord Slane was going to be buried and said that I would like to attend the funeral. Lady Slane answered me politely but distantly. She spoke English with a foreign accent. The funeral was to be quite private, she said, and politely but firmly froze me off. I went back to my sisters-in-law and reported: "Well, I got snubbed for my pains." I never saw Lady Slane again.

A night or two later, a Meath gentleman, Mr. Blackburne, who lived at Tankardstown near Slane, was driving home from Dublin. His way led up the hill over Slane and the river valley. There is a beautiful view from that road of the Castle and the river and a glimpse, at a little distance, of Beauparc in its woods. Among the trees is the old ruined Plunkett Castle, Carrick Dexter, inhabited before Slane was built.

Mr. Blackburne walked his horse up the hill, as every good man does. Beside the road there is the Croppies' Stone, erected after '98, to mark the place where the "Croppies" or rebels were buried. Below it there is a little old burial ground where the Flemings of Slane used to be laid at the end of their days. On this night Mr. Blackburne was surprised to see lights in the graveyard and to hear sounds of digging. Who could be engaged on a burial at such an hour, and apparently with some need for secrecy? I think the graveyard had been unused for years. Mr. Blackburne was curious enough to come back the next day to examine the place, when he found unmistakable signs that the vault of the Flemings, Lords of Slane, had been opened and closed again. We never knew any more than that, or which Fleming it was, that, dying in France, had expressed a desire to be buried in his own earth, or how the burial had been carried out with such secrecy.

The Castles of the Pale held Ireland for the English. In 1798, that romantic and tragic rebellion, led largely by Protestant Anglo-Irishmen, we see Lord Fingall at the head of his Catholic Yeomanry, fighting the rebels on the hill of Tara. This, the same Lord Fingall, who, as the Premier Catholic Peer of Ireland, was to take the Chair of the Catholic Committee in 1812 and be forcibly removed from it by a Police Magistrate, on the ground that this Committee to consider Catholic grievances and disabilities and petition for the removal of them, was an illegal assembly! At the fight on Tara hill, the rebels, according to Lecky, numbered 4000 men and they were totally routed by a much smaller number of yeomanry.

The family tradition tells the story, that on that night Lord Fingall was seeing home his cousin, Dunsany, who had been dining with him, when they saw a light on Tara hill. They called out the yeomen and galloped up the hill, Fingall jumping a wall on the way, and coming upon the rebels, engaged with them. Lord Dunsany followed more slowly, since his horse could not clear the wall. A Scottish regiment from Dunshauglin joined forces with them and the rebels were beaten.

Irish history has left its stain on the country. A stain of blood in time sinks into the earth and becomes part of it. There is still, from that night, the Croppies' grave on Tara Hill which is supposed to be bloodstained for ever, like the stone floor of the little room at Holyrood where Rizzio was murdered. And there is the Haunted Ash tree between Killeen and Dunsany, on which the rebels were hanged. They said in Meath that from the turf beside the road, under which they had laid the dead rebels, there grew tall green spears of corn —as tall, tradition says, as the corn we tried to grow in that too rich land during Horace Plunkett's schemes, many years afterwards—and crops of beans, from the handfuls of wheat and beans which the ill-provided Croppies had thrust into their pockets as provender. After the battle of Tara, George Lambart of Beauparc wrote, "The roads this day were covered with dead bodies and green cockades, together with pikes and horses." And another account says that among the spoils taken were a general's uniform and a side-saddle. A woman had been noticed prominent among the rebels in the fight.

The following night a butcher from Kilmessan came to Lord Fingall and told him that he knew where the flying and exhausted rebels were sleeping, in a shed. They could all be killed as they slept. "Butcher," said Lord Fingall. "It may be your trade, but it is not the trade of a Plunkett to kill sleeping men!"

This informer must have betrayed the men, nevertheless— perhaps to the English soldiers. For the story says that some time later a lame man appeared in the country and presently set upon that informer and killed him with a hammer, after which he jumped over the hedge and ran, with no trace of lameness, and was never seen again.

CHAPTER EIGHT

I DELVED into these things those winter days when the others were all out hunting. I was too delicate for hunting every day in the week and so must be left at home, like a horse in the stable, for one day at least between hunts. It was on such a day that I found a room upstairs—room fifteen—shut up and sealed—like Bluebeard's chamber! And when it was broken open, discovered in it an enormous hair trunk, studded with nails, which contained a treasure store of lovely clothes, embroidered waistcoats and beautiful period dresses, Coronation robes, a coronet and a store of lace. Many other treasures, including a sword of a Knight of St. Patrick, belonging no doubt to the 8th Earl. Some of the lace in due course went to Court with me, and to Ascot, and danced with me in St. Patrick's Hall. The Coronation robes belonged to Fingall's grandfather, the 9th Earl, who was Lord-in-Waiting to Queen Victoria. He was a pompous old gentleman, as he looks in his pictures, and I believe the Queen held him in some alarm. He married a daughter of his neighbour, Elias Corbally of Corbalton Hall, Tara—a saintly gentle creature, as her face, between the hanging ringlets, suggests. At Queen Victoria's Coronation, Lord Fingall managed to secure the canopy which is now in a glass case in the library at Killeen, leaving the other Irish and Meath Lord—Conyngham —to take the chair. The English and Scottish Lords had to make the best of whatever was left.

Then, in an old Chinese chest in the empty drawing-room, I found more lace and a collection of miniatures and the little embroidered cases containing the letters of Fanny Killeen, who had been Fanny Donelan, of Bally Donelan in Galway before she married the 8th Earl. They were such beautiful cases, tooled and embroidered, one worked in silk, one in the finest design in a woman's hair! The last was a wreath of flowers encircling two hearts pierced with an arrow. It had a spirit, that design, and a fineness, that no silken embroidery could emulate. . . . I have thought of Fanny Killeen—whom I came to know from her letters—doing it, perhaps in those days at Geneva, when she awaited the arrival referred to in the letters of "un Petit Suisse." One could not have imagined the "Petit Suisse" growing into that pompous gentleman, the 9th Earl!

Among the papers was a charming mock certificate, by which a French regiment at Nancy, in the last days of the King's rule, made Fanny an honorary Maréchal de Camps, "*pour son assurance et experience à l'art de plaire.*" There are long letters from an evidently devoted admirer, the Marquis de Molans. One reads of the mutiny at Nancy, of the "*petite societé*" there, which includes many Irish names. The Countess O'Donnell writes and asks that her title should not be used in future "*d'après les nouvelles ordonnances,*" and mentions that this province, "*que jusqu'à present avait été si tranquille, commence à se troubler. On a pillé deux châteaux dernièrement.*

It was the first year of the Revolution, with the National Assembly established in Paris, and the King still nominal ruler of France. But the wind, that was to become a storm and then a hurricane, was already troubling the air. One feels the trembling of it, and before it, these exiles—Jacobites or Wild Geese—are moving south or east to Switzerland, to Germany, or Italy where Lord Killeen's brother, Luke Plunkett, was to die in the Austrian service four years later. Lady Killeen, crossing the frontier to Switzerland, is suspected of being of the suite of Madame D'Artois.

An enchanting person, evidently, my Lady Killeen, who had such charming letters written to her and poems, and left so many delicious and fragrant souvenirs. My crayon drawing of her shows a lady dressed in Marie Antoinette style, with a mignonne face, bright eyes, a head of lovely curls. More is shown of her in the letters to her than she reveals in the one of hers, which is brief and unrevealing.

111

Discreet, perhaps? Had she need for discretion? None of these letters to her, written always so respectfully, always with messages to Lord Killeen, suggest that she had any such need. She was just a flirt, perhaps. And she must have been very well equipped indeed for that rôle, judging by the things that fell out of the case embroidered with someone's hair!

But I have stayed long enough forgetting the present and the future for the past, as I sat forgetting it, in some winter twilight at Killeen. I must leave Fanny and get on with my own story, even though I think hers, if we knew it all, might be one better worth telling and hearing! I put away these papers and come back to the day on which I found them.

The others are all out hunting. Fingall and my indefatigable sisters-in-law hunted cheerfully six days a week. Naturally, then, during the hunting season, they had not much energy of mind or body for anything else. But I was a rather delicate little thing, and it was all I could do to manage two days a week.

I grew for quite a long time after my marriage, and presently discovered that my skirts were becoming too short! Full of shame, I made the similar discovery about all my clothes. I was growing out of them! I took my trousseau frocks back to Mrs. Sims who, vastly amused, naturally, let down the hems. My sisters-in-law were in the guilty secret, but I implored them to keep it and never to tell any one. It was too good a joke, however, to keep to themselves, and very soon the whole hunting field knew it and was roaring with laughter at the idea of her ladyship "being let down." I had to face much teasing about it.

My sisters-in-law still had their own rooms at the top of the house; and their rooms were like themselves—stiff and Victorian, yet with a certain charm, altogether their own, which suited the charming old-fashioned ladies who lived in them. They used to retire there in the evening to read and sew. They were great workers and they mended Fingall's socks and made waistcoats for him—hunting waistcoats of corduroy, with braid let in, of quite appalling ugliness. I began a similar waistcoat in the early years of my marriage in a mood of wifely duty, but it is still unfinished.

I never was any good at my needle. I can pull a frock about, finding the line in it, give the little personal touch, which it must have before it belongs to the wearer. But someone else must do the sewing for me. I have been so fortunate all my life in getting other people to do things for me! I would have got someone to do my riding for me if I could. I should have been only too willing to pay a proxy! The only thing I would not have asked or wanted any one to do for me was to dance.

During those first years of my married life most things were done for me and decided for me. Mrs. Jones was respectful but firm. "You little know, my lady," with that shake of her head. Having been Fingall's nurse, she had still the nurse's attitude towards her children.

Mrs. Jones was a great old lady. She died at Killeen in 1911 in the bosom of the family she loved and who loved her. She had spent her life with and for them. She had become housekeeper when her services were no longer required as nurse. What a burden those frail shoulders carried! I have often marvelled at the way in which a housekeeper or a butler will carry the whole weight of some big house on their shoulders—not the house only, but the people who live in it as well. When Mrs. Jones died, Miss Devereux, who is now my maid, took up her duties and fulfilled them as competently and bravely. I remember a day in those early years when Mrs. Jones was recovering from 'flu and Fingall visited her after dinner and found her rather depressed.

"Would a little champagne do you good, Mrs. Jones?" he asked.

Her head shook more violently than ever. "A little wouldn't do me much good, my lord." We opened a bottle hastily.

Killeen, when I went to it first, was monstrously ugly in its furnishing and extraordinarily uncomfortable. Fingall's grandfather—the 9th Earl—had pulled down a part of the

Castle and rebuilt it in imitation of Windsor. He hardly ever lived at Killeen, being in attendance on the Queen in London or at Brighton. The result of that rebuilding was a strange grafting of the architectural style of Windsor on to the old Norman castle of Hugh de Lacy—which had nearby the ruins of the old Abbey of St. Mary of Killeen, with the Crusaders and their ladies carved in stone, and the Norman tower, from which the fighting monks used to look out across the countryside. Somebody, once asked to describe Killeen, said: "Have you seen Windsor Castle?"

Unfortunately the Fingalls had a bit of money at that moment so they could do their worst to the house.

But I was always so glad that they stopped their building with the house and raised no walls about it such as there are about so many Irish country houses, keeping Ireland and the people outside. Round Killeen we had only hedges or low fences which you could look over, or climb through, and the gates were the simplest possible, quite unsuitable, probably, for a castle. They were never shut, except to keep the cattle in! I remember the parish priest, Father Morrissey, commenting on that, one day when he came to call during my early married life.

"Isn't it a grand thing," he said, "to think that any one who likes, can come up to this castle and never be refused admission, with the gate always open!"

I always remembered that saying of Father Morrissey's. And I was glad then—as I am now—to think of that open gate, and inside, about our house and our lives, the green peaceful stretch of fields, open to the sky.

When I went to Killeen first, the big drawing-room was shut up and all the lovely Catherine of Braganza ebony furniture and Henrietta Maria Wollascott's treasures were shrouded away, with a ghostly effect, so that one opened the door and fled before the chill of the great room inhabited only by phantoms. The drawing-room that we used was as ugly as possible. We used to sit in the evenings (no one ever sat at any other time in the hunting season) in the old library,

KILLEEN CASTLE, CO. MEATH, IRELAND.

THE EARL OF FINGALL, M.F.H.

until I found it too haunted. Things used to move in it and ghosts come and go—although I myself never saw the 4th Earl in his blue coat and powdered hair. But all those rooms had powdering closets, and the ghosts came out of them. The house was difficult, of course, to light and heat in those days, when we had only oil lamps and candles. There were two boys to do the lamps and keep the fires of wood and turf going, and carry enormous cans of hot water for baths. I believe it took nearly a hundred lamps to light the house, and even then there were many dim corners. All the bedrooms were lit by candlelight. Nothing, of course, could have been more becoming than that lamplight and candlelight. Fourteen candles were an average to light a large bedroom, and Kate Devereux remembers that when you passed an open door and glanced in, the dressing-table looked "like an altar."

It was a good description of my room when I was dressing for dinner, with six candles on the dressing-table alone. A three-fold mirror reflected them, making twelve. There would be two large candlesticks, one on either side of the mirror and two more, smaller ones, each side. Then two on the writing-table and several more on the chimney piece. A wood fire in the grate and a lamp as well. Imagine the labour involved! It used to be someone's special duty to go round, putting out the candles after we had gone down to dinner.

Then every drop of bath water was carried, and we all had our baths in front of the fire, the big bath laid on enormous mats, with large cans of hot water to fill them and big towels ready to dry us. In later days of bathrooms, one of my guests expressed regret and hankering after those other baths. "Oh, I do miss my lovely bath before the fire!" he said. You could sit there as long as you liked and then get out and toast yourself delightfully. And if a draught blew down the chimney or in through the crevices of the windows, one did not notice it, turning oneself before the fire, with the warmth of the candles and the lamp as well in the room. I remember being told that there was only one bathroom in the whole of Dublin Castle, and so it remained until King

George's visit in 1911. I don't know who used that one
—the Lord Lieutenant, I suppose. But in the days when a
bathroom to each house was becoming a general idea, old
Mr. Ponsonby, Lady Mayo's father, declared that it was quite
the most disgusting and insanitary idea he had ever known,
and that he would not share his bath with any one—not even
his wife or daughter! We had no bathroom at Killeen until
after the War. Once we were entertaining a cricketing party,
and I said after tea: "You would like baths, I expect."

My schoolboy son Gerald looked at the long cricketers, as
if measuring them and all the water that they would take.

"*One each?*" he said incredulously, thinking of the already
used bath water with which the youngest of the family had
to be content.

The staff at Killeen in those days—and I dare say it was
always an inadequate one—consisted of twelve servants in
addition to my own maid. The housekeeper, butler, footman
and three housemaids saw to the house. There were the two
lamp and fire boys; in the vast kitchen a cook with a kitchen-
maid under her, and, as well, a laundrymaid and a dairymaid.

The servants' quarters were big and airy, but they had
stone floors until I put in a wooden floor for a rheumatic
butler. There were what I called "catacombs" underneath the
house, in the way of cellars, and, for all the fires and lamps
and candles the house was always cold. There were two other
big staircases in addition to the great stone one out of the
entrance hall, and I used to say that I never knew down which
staircase I should be blown when I came out of my room.
When Mr. Collier, the rich American, took Killeen for a
winter, he declared that he burnt a ton of coal a day heating
it. You could have roasted an ox at the enormous open fire
in the kitchen.

There was a good story told of the coldness of country
house visiting in those days. Lord Clonmel arrived to stay
at Moore Abbey in Kildare, with one particularly heavy trunk.
As the footmen staggered up the stairs under the burden,
they dropped it and it burst open. It was full of coal! The

guest was making sure at least of the adequacy of his bedroom fire!

Mr. Collier had taken Killeen for the hunting season during one of our brief and necessary and, I think, usually ineffectual periods of retrenchment. He told us afterwards that one night that winter he was having a dinner party. He had come in rather late, and, as he was hurrying through the hall to receive his guests, he saw a man coming towards him wearing a snuff-coloured suit and a white wig. Strange clothes to wear for a country dinner party in Meath in this century. The thought floated across the host's mind as he went forward to meet his guest, who moved with a strange gliding walk. As Mr. Collier held out his hand, the stranger slipped away towards Fingall's study. That study, with its vaulted roof, was the oldest room in the house. It had been the banqueting hall, in which sometimes a hundred people had sat down to eat, family, guests and retainers, in order of precedence, sitting above and below the salt. I don't suppose there is an older inhabited room in Ireland. And Killeen is probably the oldest inhabited castle.

I do not know who the snuff-coloured gentleman was. We never saw him. There are several snuff-coloured gentlemen among the family portraits. Mr. Collier had not seen the face of his guest clearly, and could not identify him by any of the portraits.

It was no wonder that our fortunes—or what was left of them—went blazing up the chimney cheerfully with the enormous fires in those days. As cheerfully as they were being eaten up also by the horses in the stables, and by the endless grooms and retainers outside, including what Fingall called with the sudden acid wit that was as unexpected a thing in him as it was in Horace Plunkett, "the hereditary pipe smokers." The stables were the best part of Killeen, and there was room in them for thirty or forty horses. When Fingall had the Hounds and we stabled some of the Hunt horses, every one of the boxes would be filled. They were very good stables, with beautiful boxes and an overhanging roof to the stable buildings, beneath which we used to stand to watch the horses being trotted round the yard or walked or examined. Then would come the consideration, with much passing of wise hands over shoulders and fetlocks and so on, and much mysterious thought and watching, and again the horse would be walked, and again he would be trotted and then pulled up. Why was this one dropping his hind leg, and was it from the hock it was that he was lame, or from the shoulder? "I had my suspicions, my lord, and presently my suspicions were justified," from the groom, who could not have been anything else but a groom. I spent hours with Fingall and his sisters at those parades. We lived always as much in the stables as in the house. Although I was never to be a great rider, I came in time to have quite a good eye for a horse, and Fingall used to consult me often before he bought one, trusting to that eye and some instinct that I had. Instinct in the human race is a feminine gift, I think, and I seldom made a mistake about a horse, as, I flatter myself, I have rarely been mistaken about people.

Later, when Fingall was Master, the yard used to be the scene of weekly assemblies of the people coming for compensation for damage done by the fox to their property, bringing often the gory remains of the said property (if the fox had left any remains) in the shape of lambs' tails, or a head or a leg of a fowl or a duck.

Fingall, of course, was easy enough to manage, and although he appeared to weigh the evidence and the claim carefully, the compensation demanded was paid—pretty well always, I think—and on a generous scale.

I had my first regular hunting that autumn and winter. I had let Fingall and his sisters go cubbing without me, not being enthusiastic enough to rise in the dark and share their chilly breakfast and ride out in the blue-black light of the dawn to some covert where cubs were being stirred up and young hounds taught their business. Afterwards I was to discover that those glimpses of the early morning country as it was in September—always one of the best of all months

118

in Ireland—were worth a good deal, and the ride home through a golden world, with everything fresh and shining, and then, if one would, another breakfast, with a good appetite for it.

My hunting began, in late October or early November, with the day when I put on my new habit; and I acknowledge I enjoyed that part of it. How beautifully cut it was, tight about my small waist, the cut-away coat showing the white waistcoat in front! The tying of my stock—from Hodgkinson's—was a dream, but often the stiffened part round my neck cut me horribly. My hat had been made so carefully and was put on so tightly that it was almost impossible to lose it —an important thing if one should fall on one's head—to be sure of that protection! The putting on of my hat was so important that I often did it before I did anything else, and was discovered once by Mrs. Jones sitting in my bath with nothing on at all except my top hat over my carefully netted hair. There was not a wrinkle in the legs of my boots. There were none of the soft boots that you see now, in those days. You had to put powder inside them before you could get them on, and they were torture to walk in, or when one was getting on or off a horse. My hair, of course, under my top hat must be irreproachable. If one had appeared in curls in those days as people appear now, one would have looked like a chorus girl, and if I had dared to do such a thing Fingall would have sent me home at once.

But I think I must have done him credit when I emerged dressed for the fray, even if I felt more as if I were dressed for the sacrifice! My heart was always in my boots then, as later. Very pretty boots, fortunately, but still that was no place for my heart to be! I loved meeting my friends, of course, and trotting all together along some bright sunlit road, talking, with the cheerful accompaniment of the horses' hoofs, which no other sound can equal. I have always said that there is no place in the world for getting to know people to be compared to the hunting field. Above all, I think that is true when it is a case of one's future husband or wife.

You can see, out hunting, whether a man is selfish or considerate, whether he is a braggart or has courage. And there are so many moments when people can be alone together, easily and naturally, with the country about them, and talk and knowledge of each other come so quickly and are so real in those surroundings. At a covert side waiting, in some moment when the hunt is lost temporarily and two people try together to find it again. (Or, if they are tired of each other, they can always ride away!) And there are the long friendly rides home at the end of the day. There is—I repeat it, as I have often repeated it—no better test of the man you consider as a husband than to spend a day hunting with him. The other alternative (less easy) is to go on a journey with him. For, after all, what is life, but a journey?

CHAPTER TEN

AFTER Christmas we were back in the State Steward's House in the Castle Yard, and poor Fingall was busy with his official duties again. How he hated them, and what a business all that question of precedence was, and what heart-burning there was over it! It was as bad in the Servants' Hall and the Housekeepers' Room (where the ladies' maids had their meals), for the servants used to go in, in order of their masters' and mistress' ranks. Several times I had to comfort my tearful maid, who had been pulled back by a Marchioness' or Duchess' lady: "That's not your place, my dear," and reminded that her mistress was only a Countess! Upstairs, the Countess had to sit by some pompous old bore when she would much have preferred the company of people of her own generation.

The meals were endless. If we had eaten half that was offered to us, we should have died of apoplexy. Dinners were ceremonial occasions in those days. As Lady Londonderry said later: "Breakfast and lunch are informal occasions, but dinner is a parade, and you must not be late for it." And I remember when I stayed with them at Wynyard, a footman, who was called "the Whipper-in," used to go round to all the guests' doors, knocking at them, five minutes before dinner was served—the signal to come down at once. Any one who was late must walk in alone and face the music—which required some facing, when it was C and Theresa Londonderry!

Dinner at the Castle during the Spencer Viceroyalty was a magnificent parade. For a State dinner, the State Steward and other officials, carrying wands, led the procession to the banquet hall; the household, their Excellencies' guests and their Excellencies followed. The table was laden with plate and wonderful Waterford glass. The footmen wore powdered wigs and scarlet and gold livery. This was a background for the women's dresses and jewels and the men's uniforms. At the end of the dinner the King's health was drunk, standing, and for many years it was the custom to pledge him in Port Wine, because the King of Portugal was the oldest Ally of the English Crown.

During those long dinners you had your listener certainly at your mercy, where he or she could not escape. I think it must have been in that spacious time that the great story tellers, the wits who are a tradition in Dublin, made their fame. There were wits then in both countries. They were witty without being nasty. Now they are often nasty without being witty. When I first went to dinner parties there was such a thing as conversation. People vied with each other in telling good stories. There are no good stories now, because people don't listen to them. I think conversation has been ruined by the restaurant habit more than by anything else. In these days when people hardly ever ask you to private houses, but only to restaurants, wit has gone out and been replaced by jazz. A blaring band makes it impossible to hear one's own voice, much less any one else's. And one has hardly sat down before one must be up again and rushing on somewhere else. It is a sacrilege to tell a story in such circumstances, not even being sure that one will be allowed to finish it. I think of great story tellers I have known and wonder what would have happened to them if they had lived in these days. There was Percy La Touche, who amused us all, but himself more than any of us, all his life. When he could no longer amuse himself, he died. He had a wonderful store of stories which used to delight King Edward. There were two Percies, both of whom the King liked: Percy Chubb, the American, and Percy La Touche, the Irishman. "The two old men," he called them, and would ask for them to be included in the Jamesons' party at Stowlangtoft when he was going there. Percy's stories took ages to tell. There were long and inimitable conversations, told with a sly look in the teller's eye. No one would listen to Percy now. He said one or two very witty things, which I have always remembered.

Once we must have been discussing marriage, for he said: "It doesn't much matter who you marry, my lady, for at the end of a week you will find you have married someone else." And on another occasion he assured me: "Believe me, little lady, you'll find out some day that the pain of regret is far worse than that of remorse, for though you may be sorry for what you have done, you can never get back what you have missed." That last saying of his makes a good subject for argument. Which is the worse? To know what you have done and have remorse for it, or not to have looked over the fence, and so never to have known what was the other side? I always said that I was no good at fences anyhow. I always wanted to know what was the other side before I jumped!

Percy could have done almost anything he chose to do. He had a brilliant brain, but he just amused himself and others. He was such an asset to a party and such a good sportsman, riding well and shooting well, that he could have lived for ever in other people's houses. He was very poor, and he was untidy and careless in his dress, and his nails were often unkempt. I used to say that he washed one ear twice and forgot the other. But no one minded these things. He helped to run Punchestown very efficiently, and otherwise he just shot and hunted. I have sometimes thought about him, remembering Father Finlay and Horace Plunkett: "Do you really believe, Sir Horace, that you will get a higher place in Heaven if you can put Irish butter up a penny a pound?" and Sir Horace, after a pause, answering solemnly: "I do," that Percy perhaps got a higher place for having amused so many people. Perhaps he got a better mark for his laughter than Horace for his butter! He certainly amused more people than Horace did.

Alexis Roche, Horace Plunkett's great friend, was also a story teller. And David Plunket—afterwards Lord Rathmore. Both had alluring stutters which helped a story enormously. I cannot count the wits and story tellers of those days. You used to see men buttonholing each other at the

123

street corners in Dublin, to tell stories, roaring with laughter over them. And there was brilliant talk and wit over the tables of the Judges in Fitzwilliam Square, of the Doctors in Merrion Square. There were the Trinity College Dons, Tyrrell and Mahaffy, both famous wits. There was Father Healy's parish priest's house out at Bray, with his simple and excellent meals of boiled chicken and apple tart and the good wine and the sparkling wit to drink with it. Many famous and distinguished people went to Bray to sit at that table in those days. I believe, probably, the last stronghold of story telling will be an Irish priest's dinner table.

Once I was walking in Grafton Street with a lady who was a famous bore and we met Father Healy. "Oh, Father Healy!" said my companion. "Do say something funny!"

"Well," said Father Healy, smiling at her. "I am delighted to see you. Now, isn't that funny?"

During the Zetlands' Viceroyalty, their daughter, Hilda, married Lord Southampton, in St. Patrick's Cathedral. It was then forbidden for Catholics to enter a Protestant Church while a service was going on. So we and the Kenmares, the Granards and other Catholics, including Father Healy, waited outside the Cathedral and went on afterwards to the breakfast at the Viceregal Lodge. There Lady Dorothy Neville called across the table:

"Father Healy, is it a fact that if you had gone into the Cathedral to-day, you would have been unfrocked?"

There was a moment's suspense, while we waited for a controversy to start. Then came Father Healy's answer: "Is it unfrocked, my dear lady? Sure, it isn't a stitch of clothes at all, at all, they'd have left on me!"

Father Healy's circle of friends was wide and inclusive. One, a Protestant Bishop, said to him: "You know, Father Healy, there is really very little difference between us."

Father Healy said: "Faith, you won't be dead ten minutes before you'll *know* the difference."

He stayed about in many great houses in England. Mrs. Bischoffsheim was a friend of his, and he often visited her.

The story was that he was converting her. Someone said to him once: "Have you nearly converted her, Father Healy?"

"Sure, amn't I doing all I can to *delay* her conversion!" he answered. For, once she was converted, he would have no further excuse for enjoying her hospitality!

This famous Father Healy was still the simplest man alive, a good parish priest, much beloved by his parishioners, especially the poor. He had his flock in great order, but he ruled them more by affection than by fear. God had given him the gift of wit, and he used it to enrich the world.

The system of precedence at the Castle made it dull for the young marrieds. In those very youthful days of mine I would sit beside some elderly peer, if I did not have the position of honour beside the Lord Lieutenant. But sometimes I had luck indeed with my dinner partners. It was on a night during that first Season after my marriage that Lord Coventry took me in to dinner, the beginning of a rich friendship that was to last until the day of his death. I have a letter from him dated January 25, 1925, the sixtieth anniversary of his wedding, when his many friends were congratulating him and Lady Coventry.

"My earliest recollection of you is when the 'Red Earl' at the Viceregal Lodge, who was an old and dear friend, looking over the list of those bidden to a banquet, said to me: 'You are to take in a young lady just married, whom you will admire.' And this was you; and I am proud to think that our friendship has continued without a break, and I feel sure will always last."

Lord Coventry was about forty-six at the time that I first met him. He looked then, what he always was, a real English Squire. We became friends at once. Dear "Covey," how much I owe to him. No friendship of many proud friendships made made me as proud as his. I think he must have come, soon after that, to stay with us at Killeen. He used to visit Ireland often to buy cattle, and he was a familiar figure at big country fairs such as Ballinasloe and later, of course, at the Horse Show, when he came to judge. He was always a country gentleman, and so he looked in his tweeds and leggings with the low high hat he wore, whether in town or country, pushing his way between the cattle or looking at them with a considering eye, or talking to farmers and countrymen of all classes. At Killeen he looked at our fields and said:

"My lady"—in that pretty way he always addressed me—"this land is a gold mine for horse breeders. With the lime in the soil that makes bone, and the two months' early grass."

He was to repeat that saying many times, that for young horses there was no country in the world like the Meath country. Later, perhaps, they did better in England, he said, where the oats were of superior quality and their general care and feeding was probably better, too. But nowhere was there such lime for bone-making, or such early grass as in Meath or Kildare or in the Golden Vale of Tipperary, another great horse-breeding ground.

Lord Coventry loved Irish life. He enjoyed driving on outside cars, and so we drove together in Dublin one Horse Show week. He said humorously as we passed through some street of high houses: "The people of this city must be very sober, my lady, for I notice all the houses have high steps up to their front doors."

I go back to the Castle Season as I first saw it. There was a Guard-room, I remember, where, during their time on guard, two artistic young officers, Captain Swinton and Jack Leslie, painted frescoes on the walls, of well-known people of the Court. There was one of Lord Spencer—accentuating the red beard, which was a delight, of course, to any artist with caricaturist tendencies; and one of Liddell, the famous Band Master who played for our Balls. We thought it great fun to be invited to ladies' tea-parties with the officers on guard.

I used to go driving with Lady Spencer during that Season—sometimes in state with outriders, sometimes more simply. The carriage swayed like a ship, and I often felt seasick. Also, Lady Spencer was rather pompous and alarming and I did not know what to say to her. I remember driving up

126

the Wicklow Mountains to visit the Milltowns at Russborough, one of the loveliest houses in Ireland, and feeling too sick to enjoy any of the beauty that we passed. Or we drove to St. Helen's, where Lord Gough was then living. Or across the Park to Luttrellstown, which the Annalys had bought from the wicked Lord Carhampton. Luke White, who was to succeed his father as Lord Annaly a few years later, was an A.D.C. to the Spencers and married Lady Spencer's niece, Lilah Agar Ellis.

Luttrellstown, looking over the Liffey, was a very pleasant drive from Dublin, and I could survive that without feeling sick.

I remember hearing the terrible tales of the things that had been done there earlier: of Lord Carhampton's ill-treatment of the people during the '98 rebellion, of nights of horror when children were made to dance barefoot on red-hot trays, and so on.

Our own times were troubled, I realise, and Lord Spencer, who had been so gay and beloved in his previous Viceroyalty, rode sadly through the streets of Dublin with his escort about him for protection.

People's nerves were evidently on edge, since once, as we drove in state, this time down Grafton Street, a canary in a cage fell with a crash from an upper window right under the leading horses' feet. Poor little canary! It was trampled to death in the moment's panic that followed. The horses shied and bolted. Every one, of course, thought that it was a bomb, and the drivers let the horses go as quickly as possible for a few minutes. Fortunately no one was hurt, and we returned to the Castle in safety.

We used to drive in a landau with an escort. And I remember our taking devious routes and returning by the South Circular Road to avoid being ambushed. Lord Spencer used to drive his own coach often with a beautiful team of blue roans that had come from Dick Oswald. Since the Phœnix Park murders, of course, there was always great alarm about the safety of the Lord Lieutenant.

I had a little carriage of my own in which I used to drive

about Dublin. It was an open carriage (was it called a Sociable?), and it was painted blue and yellow, and looked so like something out of Cinderella that I should not have been surprised at any moment if it had turned into a pumpkin. I had an enchanting little boy footman—a "Tiger" was the name for such little boy grooms, for some reason. This one was so small that he had to lift himself out of his long top boots when he stood on a step to knock at a door. Presently it would open, for a large butler to stand staring down at the "tiger" in some surprise.

Once I went calling with him at the Viceregal Lodge, and when the grand footman in his livery opened the door, the little "tiger" whipped off his hat and stood trembling in alarm before this wonderful apparition, convinced that it was the Lord Lieutenant himself! I noticed, after I had paid a good many calls with my little "tiger," that the butlers who opened the doors to his knock always smiled and appeared amused when they answered his question as to whether the lady of the house was at home. At last I asked a butler, who was a particular friend of mine, what had amused him. He told me that the question was always put in the same way: "Is *she* in?"

Now, as the wife of the State Steward, I used to dance the State Quadrille with His Excellency, and often led off the ball with him. On St. Patrick's night we danced a dance called the Country Dance, "Up and down the middle again." I think it was the same as Sir Roger de Coverley, which I danced the other night with Sir George Franks at a Country-women's Association dance, during Horse Show Week, and enjoyed it just as much as those Country Dances in St. Patrick's Hall which we both remembered. After the State Quadrille there was general dancing. Waltzes to the Strauss music which Liddell's Band played so divinely. I can hear the "Blue Danube" now, as it sounded in St. Patrick's Hall then. If you were in your grave and Liddell played beside you, you would have to get up and dance. I believe he used to have a supply of champagne beside him as he played.

With my satin and brocade ball dresses I wore the family diamonds which Fingall had given me as a wedding present. Since the breaking of the entail had set them free, they were now my own property. He gave me also a string of pearls for which he paid £300, an enormous sum, it seemed to me. The diamonds were beautiful. Fingall's grandmother had got them when she was in waiting on the Queen and had to be a little magnificent. There was a bandeau for my hair, a necklace, with a lovely leaf design, and a stomacher with three great falling drops.

I sold the necklace and the stomacher during the War, when we wanted money for various Red Cross activities.

I hardly ever wore the bandeau on my head. I confess that I had two vanities: the shape of my head and my feet. George Wyndham said to me once: "You are quite right not to wear a tiara. You have a head like a swallow, with the same little movements."

Dancing was life to me. It has always been that. It expresses for me, more than any art, feeling of mind and heart and body. If I could be born again and choose what I would like to be, I would be a dancer and ask for the physical strength for it.

The men danced beautifully in those days when I first went to Balls. They had learnt to dance and took trouble about it, not trampling on you cheerfully as they do now, and of course they were always introduced and never thought of not doing their duty dances. There was a good deal of sitting out and of romance in hidden corners among the young people. I would sit out an interval, but nothing would ever induce me to sit out a dance. The dances began at nine and ended at twelve, often, because of the hunting next day. Sometimes the big general balls that were for all the world, the Colonel's lady and Mrs. O'Grady, lasted longer. The small dances were of course the nicest. They were so intimate and friendly and had all the gaiety of a Hunt Ball. We used to have dinner parties of young people at the State Steward's house before the dances, and the Sedan chair was brought out

129

again to carry us across the Yard. With the intimacy and friendliness there was always the grandeur. (Though I believe that there was never any grandeur in the world to compare with Vienna, where Fingall's uncle, Sir Francis Plunkett, was later to be Ambassador and a friend of the Emperor's. I have always regretted that we never went to stay with him, when we were invited.) But we were almost as magnificent as Buckingham Palace at our toy Court, and much more amusing, those days and nights, when we danced until "God Save the Queen" was played, and then went home across the Yard to the State Steward's House, while the carriages were still driving away. And in the morning we went hunting across Kildare or Meath country, with the waltz music played by Liddell's Band still in our ears.

The military bands used to play in the Castle Yard in the morning with a most cheerful sound, and there was changing of the guard and such ceremonies. And, on St. Patrick's Day, trooping of the Colour. It is hard to realise in these sombre days all the music and elaborate toy shows that that Yard held. To-day it is so grey and quiet, with no colour at all, that that might all have been a dream. And the portraits of the Lords Lieutenant—bad portraits, most of them—look down strangely on the empty State-rooms which I remember so crowded and so gay.

We drove down to our Meets in Meath or Kildare. Sometimes I went with Fingall in a dog-cart with a tandem, and I was very frightened when Gertrude, one of the hunt horses, put as leader in the tandem, performed some of her most terrifying tricks, such as twisting herself round a lamp post and looking back at us; or, out in the country, suddenly thinking that she was hunting, would try to take the ditch!

Sometimes I went more safely in the Viceregal covered brake, in which one could finish one's dressing on the journey, modestly hidden from the view of the passers-by. They were long drives, of course, however one made them. Now they would seem interminable, and one would think twice or many times before one undertook such a journey. Then our standards of time were different, and I suppose we had not, anyhow, very much to do except amuse ourselves. I only hunted once a week, I think, from the Castle. Sometimes I drove down to a Meet with Lord Spencer. Once we went to Bellinter when the Meet was there. A beautiful setting for such a scene, Bellinter made. It was one of the loveliest of old Meath houses, and, like most of them, full of beautiful things. It stands on the banks of the Boyne, with its back to the water, and the long avenue to it runs through the trees, parallel with the river. It is one of the usual Georgian houses, with a centre block and high windows looking over its own fields, and two side wings and high steps up to the hall door. Our host—old Mr. Preston, who could have claimed the title of Lord Tara if he had chosen to do so—stood at the door waiting to receive the Lord Lieutenant. He wore an old-fashioned frock coat and check waistcoat with grey trousers, well strapped down under his boots, and had a white top hat held in his hand. While the horses about the door champed and bucked and were ridden about by their owners or walked by their grooms, we climbed the steps and went in with Mr. Preston to the Hunt breakfast that was set in the dining-room. The hall and the wide staircase leading up to a gallery were panelled. There was a Bossi chimney-piece in the dining-room, and the table and the chairs on which we sat were Chippendale. The china and silver were in keeping. Lord Spencer picked up one of the spoons and looked at it. "Queen Anne! By Jove!"

"Oh, Sir," said I. "She's dead!"

How I used to pray secretly, as we trotted gaily down the road, that they might not find! I dreaded the note of the horn which meant that we must leave the pleasant harbour between the hedges for the terrifying open sea of the country. The call "Gone away," would send my poor heart, that had been so cheerful a minute ago, to the very bottom of Mr. Peal's boots, there to remain, with brief lifting intervals, for the rest of the day!

It was terrifying country, of course. When Lord Zetland, who was very short-sighted, hunted in Meath later during his Viceroyalty, he said of it: "This is a terrible country. You are galloping along, and suddenly the earth opens and swallows you!"

That must have been the Fairyhouse Drain, I think, that he was describing. And there were those days when the fox would take the way across Bush Farm with its series of awful fences. The horse did it all for me, and I was just a passenger. Yet I came to look very well on a horse, I believe, in spite of my secret terror—not so very secret, either—and I sometimes went rather wildly on the fine horses Fingall gave me, so that people said: "That little woman will kill herself." I had some bad falls. Fingall had said often: "Bootles doesn't know how to fall." It was true, for the only time he did come down, off a slippery double, he was so surprised that he could not get up. The pommel of the saddle against the ground prevented him from crushing me. As he was an enormous horse, but for this there would not have been much left of me. Another time when the horse fell I was hung up by my habit and had to be released. Lord Spencer was near when I got up.

"That's right," he said. "If you hadn't got up at once you would have lost your nerve and perhaps never ridden again." I did not tell him, as I might have, that I never had any nerve to lose!

Well, you had to go in Meath or stick to the roads. There was no hope of that pleasant course with Bootles. Later, after I had had a few bad falls, I got a pony guaranteed not to jump anything, and we hugged the roads comfortably together. Bootles meantime had been sold to Lord Howth, who jumped him at Pau and at the Dublin Horse Show, where I watched him go over the bank and the stone wall and the fences, thanking Heaven that I was not on his back.

The Empress of Austria and her hunting in Meath were still a vivid tradition in the country then. She had hunted from Summerhill, Lord Langford's house, a few years earlier,

when Fingall had come second in a race for the Empress'
Cup. She had taken Summerhill for two seasons, after having
stayed with Lord Spencer during his first Viceroyalty and
discovered the delight of Irish hunting then. I believe she said
afterwards that those hunting days in Meath were the happiest
of her life. Poor woman, she had not many happy days.
Tradition frames a figure and makes it stand out clearly, so
that I could picture that lovely one, when people talked of her,
and she was still "th' Empress" to the countrymen and
women. I think in time we forgot that we had never seen
her going across country on the wonderful horses which that
great rider, Bay Middleton, provided her with.

The legend which framed her against the best background
in the world, that of the country, told of her beauty, her
wonderful hair—such masses of it that it gave her a headache
and the first thing she always did when she entered a house
was to take off her hat. Mrs. Kearney at Culmullen remembered that. The Empress used to leave her carriage there
and her ladies-in-waiting while she hunted. The ladies-in-
waiting stood in awe of her.

" We love our Empress," one of them said to Mrs. Kearney.
" But she always makes us remember that she *is* our Empress."

People in Meath still tell stories of her, of the little fan
that she used to carry out hunting, hiding her face behind it
when people stared at her, and the wonderful habits she wore
which looked as if she had been poured into them, and the
tiny handkerchiefs with which she used to wipe her face
when she got hot, and then throw them away, used once, and
how they would be picked up eagerly and kept by someone
as souvenirs.

Bay Middleton was the best pilot in the world, they said,
and he stood no nonsense, Empress or no Empress. If she
hesitated at a jump, " Come on, Ma'am," he would call, " if
you are coming," and she would obey, so that she was always
at the top of the hunt.

I saw the Empress only once, many years later, at Nauheim, not long before her assassination. An old woman now,

who kept a parasol before her face, still hiding from any one who would look at her.

Our own hunting days were interesting enough. Lord Spencer, who hunted regularly, used to come out with an escort. (We were in the years that were to be known afterwards as "the black eighties," although we seem to have been so little aware of that shadow which only threw itself by such signs—the Lord Lieutenant's escort, an occasional sight of mounted police in the streets, rumours of political trouble.) There was a tall red-bearded A.D.C., Captain Hammond by name, who hunted, and was so like Lord Spencer as to be almost his double. There was undoubtedly an idea that his presence made the Lord Lieutenant safer; but I imagine Captain Hammond could hardly have had an official position, such as is held by the doubles of some Eastern potentates, who keep near their prince or emperor to receive an assassin's bullet if possible!

There have been great changes, of course. People ask at once: What are the greatest changes that have come about in the hunting field since I first saw it? I think immediately of the position and numbers of women. Then, in Meath, there were only ten or fifteen women who hunted regularly, and of those, five or six hardly ever missed a meet. Later I remember some of them who were privileged to wear a red coat, and how grand they looked in their shining top hats and waistcoats and their little bunches of violets, which were all the ornamentation allowed. Mrs. Sammy Garnett, afterwards Lady Winchester and première Marchioness of England, was one of these. Jock Trotter was Master then, and once we saw the two in such deep and confidential conversation that some of us were vulgar enough to creep up behind them and see if we could overhear what she was saying in such a mysterious whisper. We strained our ears and heard:

"I always had suspicions of his hocks . . . !"

The next change I note is the size of the field. Larger now? I am asked. The days are more democratic and the horse is

134

still the interest that every man and woman and child in Ireland sees eye to eye on.

No. The fields are smaller now, in spite of the fact that there are more women than men. The garrison, in those other days, of course, swelled the numbers enormously. And there was the Viceregal Staff as well and the Lord Lieutenant's house-party. And there were the visitors at various country houses. General Sir Charles Fraser lived at Bective and had parties there to which came many lovely ladies, sporting or otherwise. He used to hunt with one arm strapped to his side, the result of some injury. When I first saw him I asked someone why his arm was like that, and a "wag" told me that it was to prevent him putting it round ladies' waists, which he was inclined to do. I think I was simple enough almost to believe this story. At all events, I kept at a safe distance!

The Willie Jamesons hunted from Athlumney (she was one of the first women I remember wearing a red coat) and the Conynghams from Slane and the Headforts, and many others. There was much more money, I suppose, then than there is now.

Of course one of the greatest changes of all has been made by the coming of motors. We used to hack to the Meets when we did not drive. No one of this generation can imagine how energetic we were. A carriage could not follow us round as a motor can, to pick us up when we were tired, and the horses of those days had not dreamed of those that were to come after them, and travel in strange wooden boxes that would move of their own accord!

Another great change, of course. No woman ever rode astride then.

I was fortunate in my pilots. I had at one time "Ould Johnny Roberts," a well-known figure in the hunting world. He sold me a horse, Charlie, as wise as himself. Charlie never refused in his life or fell at a fence. But when he was getting old he fell with me on the flat, and very disconcerting it was. We put him out to grass after that, and he died after a peaceful old age.

They said of Johnny Roberts that he not only knew every inch of the country, but that he knew the mind of a fóx, and which way it would go. He had a jolly red face which matched his coat, and delightful manners, and was more like a hound than a fox, with rather weeping eyes, like a hound's. I have seen that hound look often in other hunting men. "Come on, my lady!" he would say to me, like Bay Middleton, and, like the Empress, I obeyed. He never jumped an unnecessary fence or shirked a necessary one, however big. So we went over anything we came to, and often we arrived before the Master, and had to hide, lest our iniquity be discovered. I derived great reflected courage and confidence from "Ould Johnny Roberts."

It was in my early hunting days that a lady hunted regularly, wearing, instead of breeches, a red flannel petticoat under her habit skirt, a glimpse of which was given to us on occasion. Fortunately she had changed her apparel before a day when she had a bad fall into a ditch and was entangled with her habit and her saddle, so that it was necessary to cut her free. As a young man stood over her, rather nervously, wondering where to begin, she called up to him: "You may cut away! I have trousers on."

In another ditch a Meath gentleman fell one day at the head of the hunt and lay, while thirty others or more went over him. Patrick Thunder of Lagore was his magnificent sounding name and address. Every time he lifted his head, "Duck, Pat!" called another rider, high in the air. "Duck Pat!" cried another, coming after him. Thirty times Pat Thunder of Lagore ducked his head and lived to tell the tale.

Many hunting days ended for us at the Black Bull Inn or at the Spencer Arms at Drumree, where we would find the carriages waiting to take us back to Dublin, and a hunter's tea spread for us. I don't think any meals were ever as good as those. Bacon and eggs and scones and potato cakes and home-made bread, and many cups of strong tea poured from comfortable brown teapots, with the fire crackling cheerfully and lamplight and hunting talk. We went over all our

136

jumps again (how comfortably and safely, sitting at the tea-table in this warm room!). We were busy making excuses as to why we hadn't taken that one, and why we had gone round that way instead of the other, until the tea was over, and, feeling exquisitely weary and sleepy, we stumbled out into the yard, put on our warm coats and got into our various vehicles for the return journey to Dublin. I think the horses were often stabled at the Black Bull. Or if they travelled in those days they did it by train. Sometimes by the time we drove through the Park and approached the lights of Dublin I was fast asleep in my corner of the carriage and already dreaming of the dance that night.

CHAPTER TEN

At the end of the following Season Fingall resigned the State Stewardship with a deep sigh of relief on his part, but to my great sorrow. Once released from social duties, he hardly went near the Castle again if he could help it until, under the Dudleys, many years later, he became Master of the Horse. Now he could settle down to the life he loved at Killeen. No more visiting for him—except when hunting made it necessary to spend the night at Headfort, or at Loughcrew or Beauparc or some other house in the county. He "loved his friends, but he hated his acquaintances," and the State Steward had had to endure many acquaintances. As for me, I was now a married lady, and Fingall thought that married ladies should settle down at home and wear a cap. Even a poor little married lady who was still growing out of her frocks should not be exempt from that fate. Since we had given up the State Steward's house, we had no Dublin residence, and, understand, that in those motorless days Dublin was twenty, full, long miles away. The Fingalls had had, like other Irish families, their Dublin house "Killeen House" in Great Denmark Street—next door to Belvedere House belonging to the Jesuits —in which the Lady Fingall of the day, the charming Fanny Killeen, had heard the news of the '98 rebellion. But some time in our very early married days the Jesuits made an offer for Killeen House. Sir Gerald Dease, as our agent, sent the offer on to Fingall. I forget what the offer was; but just at that moment Fingall had his eye on a couple of horses, and it would enable him to buy those. So Killeen House passed into the keeping of the Jesuits, thus escaping the fate of most of the other town houses of the nobility and gentry—of being turned into tenements. I think the Jesuits must have got a good bargain, for some time later, when I had begun to take an interest in such things, I was in a furniture shop in Dublin and saw two very fine marble chimney-pieces. I admired them and asked where they came from. The owner of the shop looked at me in surprise. "You ought to know, my lady. They came from Killeen House." I asked the price, and it was a good deal more than had been paid for the whole house, with them included in it. But Fingall had his hunters!

In those quiet days at Killeen I came to know Fingall better. He was at his most charming with young shy people, simple people, and animals. The children remember him as such a good comrade and father, getting their ponies ready for them before they came back from school and full of hunting plans for the holidays..

He belonged in a sense to another age. Once a discussion arose at a dinner party at Killeen as to what constituted a gentleman. When every one else had spoken, Fingall, who was never first except in the hunting field, came in. "I think," he said slowly, "that any man is a gentleman who tells the truth and takes a bath every day."

But it was an inadequate definition indeed, compared to the high standard he exacted from himself. Like most good people, it was only for himself that he was rigid, and for others he had a wonderful tolerance and capacity for forgiveness. We had a footman once who stole a considerable quantity of silver. When he came out of jail, it was Fingall who insisted on taking him back and giving him another chance. "Poor thing," he said, and that was a phrase that was often on his lips. I heard him use it of a friend of his who could not tell the truth, and that must have been one of the hardest things for him to forgive, for he was fanatically truthful. Often my wild tongue used to distress him and he would protest: "I think your ladyship exaggerates." But no more than that gentle reproof.

I used to tease him sometimes, telling him that his rigid standard for himself, with that tolerance for others, was a form of conceit. I told him, too, that the threadbare clothes he wore might also be a form of vanity. He saw himself as

139

a *Grand Seigneur*, I said, above such things as clothes. Of course these accusations were not true. He was the simplest soul alive. And he was proud, not vain. I remember Lord Langford saying to me once: "I do envy Fingall his family history." But family history and pride of race meant nothing to Fingall except the responsibilities they carried with them. In that sense he was proud. He spent all his life trying to atone for the fact that he had been born with possessions when other people had none. Wages were terribly low in those days, and although of course money bought more, a labourer with many children was passing poor on a wage of nine or ten shillings a week. Fingall worried about these things before many people of his class had begun to think of them. It was not so easy to put right. If he were to raise wages at once he would make it difficult for his friends and neighbours. But he could make it up with kind—milk, firewood, home-killed meat and such things; and he did make it up.

There was a strike of farm labourers in those early years, and a number of Meath landlords, meeting together, proposed to put more of their land to pasture—an admirable way of making money for them with no effort, for they had only to put their cattle on the rich land and see them fatten—and so be done with many labourers and their wages and the possibility of strikes. Fingall got up at the meeting.

"God did not give me possessions so that I might oppress my fellow-men," he said, and would have none of the proposals.

He had the most extraordinary respect for the dignity of his fellow-men. He expected the people to come to him for help and counsel and his boundless charity, which they did. But he never went into their houses without being asked. He would have considered that an impertinence. And he never rang a bell in his life. He did not think it consistent with the dignity of a human being to summon one in that way. (I told this to an Irish friend the other day, and she thought for a moment: "I don't think I ever rang a bell in my life; but, then, I never had one that rang!")

He had this feeling also to a very large extent about his animals, considering that they too had their own lives and their own dignity. So he never shouted or whistled to his dogs unnecessarily, and he very rarely caressed them. He hated to see a dog handled or pulled about.

I remember once that someone spoke to him about Russell, the carpenter at Killeen, whose family had been there for several generations. Russell looked like another carpenter —St. Joseph—and, thinking of him, I put him beside Lord Coventry and other fine gentlemen I have known. "What would you do," someone said, "if you wanted to dismiss Russell?"

"Dismiss Russell?" Fingall said. "He might as well dismiss me!"

And he was patient with those he called the "hereditary pipe smokers," employees with unspecified duties, self-appointed, perhaps, who dragged brooms or spades about the place happily, hardly ever using them apparently, only now and again chasing an odd leaf blown before the wind. "Innocent Johnnie" was one of these, a half-wit. We never knew his history. He had come to us from the workhouse, and they did not know his parentage even there. But there was a story that his mother had been a governess in some Irish country house, and that he was her illegitimate son.

Innocent Johnnie was devoted to the family. He always referred to them in the royal manner as: "We." "We were very grand in those days, Miss Devereux," he would say to Kate. And: "When *we* went to the Crusades."

Once I asked him if he had seen "the girls," and he rebuked me with his answer:

"Your ladyship means the lady offsprings."

Fingall was a wonderfully loyal friend. After someone whom he had put up for the Kildare Street Club had been pilled, he never entered the doors of the Club again. He said that if his friends were not good enough for it, it was not good enough for him. And he was incredibly generous.

No Earl ever went more threadbare, although he was always so neat and clean.

The people in the little country church at Killeen used to stare at the "Earl's patches" and giggle over them. But when he gave them away—which he did if someone needed a garment, just as he would take a blanket off his bed for a beggar asking for one—the recipients were deeply touched. "Would you ever think," one of them said, "that the Earl would have such clothes?"

There was an occasion when a poor man went begging clothes from an English neighbour at the Glebe. I may observe here that the Irish gardeners and hangers-on have an insatiable appetite for "an ould pair of trousers." I do not know what the precise garment was that was sought at the Glebe and not found. "Why don't you go over to the Castle and ask his Lordship?" our neighbour suggested.

The answer was given in pious horror:

"Sure, haven't I a character to keep up!"

When Fingall went visiting, which he did as infrequently as possible, his luggage was of the simplest. He used to carry his studs in a small empty jujube tin. Once, at Headfort, I overheard the footman in the next room unpacking for him, unaware of my presence near:

"Look at that, for a blooming h'Earl!"

Evidently, from the rattling sound, the jujube box had been discovered.

I thought something should be done about it, and went off and bought the "blooming h'Earl" a dressing-case of suitable dignity and simplicity. But it was never used, and I forgot to pay for it, and the bill for my gift to him reached Fingall in due course. He preferred his jujube box.

There is a moment, before sunset, when one sees the world clearly, the line of the last hill, the last field, sharpened against the sky, before it vanishes. With people there is one moment, of all others, when one sees them clearly as never before and never again. All barriers gone, all confusion of vision and the mist we set up between ourselves and others, with conven-

142

tions, the heavy burden of things we have become unable to say, and so must carry through life unsaid. That time of complete simplicity and reality comes for people, in the hour after the earthly light has gone out. While it lasts, we can see them and speak of them as never before and never again.

In that hour, some who knew him gave me their vision of Fingall. I give it now, although I write here of the dawn when we had not thought of the evening.

Maurice Healy, who served as a young officer under him in 1915: "I held him in the warmest affection. I think he would have been surprised as well as gratified if he had known how often I have spoken of him since then. And I think he must be feeling that sort of surprise now, on finding how much higher is the place allotted to him in Heaven than he would have ventured to choose for himself. . . ."

And the Galway priest who as a young curate had attended my father at his death, and who said the Requiem Mass which Fingall served then, meeting him many years later, when he—the priest—was chaplain to the Connaught Rangers, wrote of him: "Your unassuming and genial husband."

"He was always straight, true, kind and wise in everything I knew of him," wrote Sir Philip Hanson.

"A great Irish gentleman," wrote Colonel Maurice Moore. "There was no man in Ireland for whom I had so great a respect. I have not forgotten that when Ireland had great need of help he did not hesitate to come to her aid and risk the loss of friends and position. He was a good Irishman."

The young curate, preaching on the sin of vanity in our little country church, had nothing to teach Fingall, however much his sermons might apply to Fingall's wife! We had our own private chapel at Killeen, but we went to the parish church to set a good example. In the days of bustles and fringes, the new young curate began his sermon thus:

"I have not been four weeks in the parish, and I have already discovered that the besetting sin of this parish is vanity—above all among the women. Now take notice once for all, that I refuse absolution to any female wearing curls in front or wires behind."

I had no fringe in front, but I felt a guilty waggle of my little piece of whalebone behind! I am sure I was as guilty of that sin of vanity as any of my sex there, and my mind often wandered during the sermon to the question of my next new frock, or my next party.

It must have been the Puritanical period just then in Ireland, when all dancing and company keeping was frowned upon by the Church, and denounced under threat of terrible punishment in the next world. We had a Sergeant of Police in the village, who was as stern a moralist as any parish priest or curate. Woe betide a young man and woman who were found kissing in a country lane! Between all these authorities there was not much chance for the natural impulses of the young. Sergeant Kirwan used to come to Fingall as a magistrate, sometimes.

"I have my suspicions," he would say darkly, looking gloomy over those suspicions.

However, as Mary, Duchess of Abercorn, once said to me: "My dear, we none of us know what we will do until we die."

And Sergeant Kirwan was no exception to this truth! Being generally regarded as "settled" in the expressive Irish phrase, into single blessedness, he sprang it on all of us that he was going to be married to the schoolmistress. Miss Moriarty was no longer very young, and was also regarded in the Irish phrase as "a settled girl." (You may be a "settled girl" at any age from thirty to seventy.) I wonder where they did their courting, the sergeant having made such an occupation almost impossible in his district, and how he proposed! Anyhow the news of the impending marriage was conveyed to us with suitable dignity and solemnity by the sergeant himself. Fingall, of course, gave the wedding breakfast, and gave it with his usual generosity. There was enough champagne to make certain of the gaiety, which lasted, I believe, far into the night, after which the sergeant and his bride retired to the married quarters of the barracks, which had

144

been for so long wasted. Most people slept late the next morning, but a sleepy constable, passing the closed door of the bridal chamber round about ten o'clock or so, was in time to hear the sergeant's familiar voice crying in startled tones:

"In the name of God, Miss Moriarty, what brings you there!"

There was all the pious horror in his voice which the constable knew so well, as Sergeant Kirwan having—the result of Fingall's champagne—completely forgotten the events of the previous day, regarded the astonishing and shocking sight of Miss Moriarty's head beside him on the pillow!

CHAPTER ELEVEN

I HAD first seen Horace Plunkett at the Ball given at Killeen before my marriage, and after that one glimpse of him he goes out of the picture for a time. He was in America again, on his ranch at Wyoming, or perhaps, alas, at Battle Creek, on one of his many visits to Sanatoriums. Even when I first knew him he had the stoop of ill-health. I don't believe that he ever had one day's perfect health in his life.

But that summer—it must have been 1885 or thereabouts—when he was back at Dunsany and we saw so much of him, he was gay. People who only knew him in after years, when Ireland had laid her heavy burden on his already stooping shoulders, would have been astonished if they could have known how gay he had once been. I remember my sister saying at Kilteragh in those later years: "How Ireland has changed that man!" ("Lord," wrote Edmund Spenser of Ireland. "How quickly doth that country alter men's natures!")

Betty Balfour said of Horace: "He came young, gay, rich, to Ireland. He lost it all." Yes, I think that is the way with that Old Woman, the Shan Van Vocht! She sucks you dry. But if you are born Irish, you will never get away from her, so it is no use trying. I used to say that if Horace had ever married, his wife would only have got the leavings of Ireland. And Ireland doesn't leave much.

Like many men who have loved Ireland and given their lives to her, he was more English than Irish in temperament. He had a patient, cold determination, and he went on, undaunted by failure. The Irish can't work in that way. It is not their temperament. They must do whatever they do in fierce heat, and are bad stayers. When Horace was organising his Co-operative Societies (which were to save Ireland by milk, butter, fowl and bacon!) he would travel the country,

146

organising meetings, and often, arriving at the meeting-place would find one old man. He would laugh and go on, and at the next meeting he might find fifteen. So he progressed slowly, patient and indomitable. *Festina Lente!*

But Ireland was still only a dream in those summer days and evenings when he came to Killeen or we went to Dunsany each day.

He was living alone in the old Norman castle, with his inadequate and quaint staff of servants. His father and his erratic and amusing elder brother, an M.P., who was to succeed to the title, lived then in England. There was a time when the House of Commons used to fill at the news that Johnnie Plunkett (later Lord Dunsany and father of the present Lord Dunsany) was to speak.

It was on Horace that the responsibilities of the family fell, and fell early. I think his childhood had been gloomy. His parents were very Low Church, and in his own extreme youth he had been under the influence of Moody and Sankey. After he had escaped from that rather grim and terrible religion in which he had been brought up, I think he discarded definite religion, although few men lived more closely to the Christian ideal and at the end of his days, as his secretary, Gerald Heard, wrote: "He liked to think that if there was a future life, he had so lived in this world as to have proved worthy of it." And Dr. Kelly, the Catholic Bishop of Ross, wrote to him: "You seem to me to have all the heroic virtues."

His dreams for Ireland had first stirred in him at Wyoming when he was riding as a cowboy over his ranch, rounding up the cattle. It was a new dream in one sense. There was no political thought in it. Horace was never a politician. But Ireland, prosperous, would be (or might be) Ireland contented. Coming back to Europe, he went travelling again: to Denmark, to Sweden, Belgium and Holland and studied farming methods there—with always in his mind that country where there was no method about anything—and Co-operation.

He loved slogans and presently he found one for Ireland. "Better farming, better business, better living." Another saying of his was: "The more business there is in politics and the less politics there is in business, the better for both." And another wise one, "Irish history is for all England to remember and all Ireland to forget."

That first summer that I came to know him well, his dreams were still vague and formless. He was always a little abstract, a man who made plans on paper, or in committees, not a farmer like my father, looking at his land and loving it. He said once, half-humorously, looking up at the ivied walls of Dunsany and the high-turreted windows gazing over the countryside, that anything he could do for Ireland was only a small, just restitution for the robbery of the old Plunkett barons when travellers through Meath had had to beware of them. He was very happy those days, living in a rather ramshackle way. Undeterred by the inadequacy of his domestic staff and indeed, apparently unaware of it, he entertained a great deal, and invited his grandest friends from England to stay with him. They came, of course, and adored it. The carelessness of the household was only an added Irish charm. The Duchess of Hamilton came to stay with him for the hunting, with other guests. When her visit was imminent, I went across and did my best to make the house and her room fit for a Duchess. I did the flowers, arranged writing-tables and so on. Horace would have been unaware of such things. He was always absolutely indifferent to comfort, and any luxury he afforded himself in later days was only in order that his strength might be preserved for Ireland and for that work for Ireland to which he had given himself. The Duchess was enchanted with the house and the life and loved the hunting. She got at Dunsany good fires and good food and she spent all her days out on a horse. So what more did she want? Horace had constant visitors. His men friends, Beau Watson who had been ranching with him, and Cyril Coleridge and Alexis Roche, were frequently there. We had some very gay parties at Dunsany. I even remember Horace as a practical

148

joker. The treasure of his domestic staff was Reid, his man-servant—what is called in Ireland, expressively, "an up-with-the-kettle, round-with-the-car, man." Reid was a black Northern Protestant who used to curse the Papists with terrible curses and live with them in perfect amity. He waited at dinner with the ends of his trousers tucked into his boots, and when he thought the guests had stayed too long he would open the door and thrust his head round it: "Does any of yez want your yokes?" There was no mistaking that hint. Once, as he handed champagne which he had discovered to be corked, he leaned over my shoulder and whispered in my ear:

"Don't touch it, me lady. It'd sicken your stomach."

Horace was often gay then. Even when he had grown most solemn, if he smiled, his face lit up. And when he had time to laugh, I never heard any one laugh better than he did. A good laugh is a wonderful asset to any man or woman in life.

I had been finding it not very gay at Killeen those long summer evenings. My sisters-in-law would go away up to their own rooms to mend Fingall's socks and sew his waist-coats, and Fingall would fall asleep and snore. Sometimes Horace had come to dine and fallen asleep too, and I said that they made a duet with their snores, one on a high note, one on a low note, and it was not at all amusing for me!

But sometimes Fingall slept and Horace stayed awake and talked. It may be summer or early autumn, but there is a wood and turf fire in these memories. Horace is talking and I am listening a little abstractedly. His dream grew, absorbing him by degrees, until he belonged to it. These are only the first faint stirrings.

Ireland again. More dreams for Ireland. It seems that, for most of my life, people talked of nothing else. And now one rarely talks of Ireland at all and a long dream seems to be ended in a rather chilly and grey dawn of awakening.

Well, Horace talked, and sometimes I listened, and some-times my mind wandered off. Then a portion of it got caught and pulled back to this room and Fingall's snores and Horace's talk, almost, I think, against my will. Ireland was to be

149

saved by Co-operation. It was a new idea, a dream. And I
have always loved new ideas and dreams. It was more interesting to me than hunting and much safer!

Sometimes Fingall woke up and listened and joined in the
discussion. He was prepared to support Horace loyally in his
work—as he did support him, to his great financial loss. But
he never believed in those dreams. I think, perhaps, he knew
his own people better than we did. You should not give the
Irish anything they had not asked for, he told Horace—that is
what the English are always doing—and it almost seems to
me now that he must have looked down the years and seen
the end of all our work, our labour, and our dreams, and how
little substantial result there was to be to show for any of
them. Nor did he approve of going into other people's houses
and interfering in their affairs. It was against his ideas of
human dignity and the natural respect that men and women
should have for each other and for the privacy of each other's
lives.

"If the people want anything that I can give them," he
said, "they know the way to my study door." And, with that,
I think he fell asleep again. But Horace knew, as I knew, that
Fingall would support him, if he considered it his duty to do
so, whether he believed the effort to be doomed to failure or
not.

Four years were still to pass before Horace actually began
his work, in a tentative way. He goes out of the picture for
periods. He is at Wyoming again; or at Battle Creek Sana-
torium for treatment; or in hospital having an operation. I
think he must have had more operations than any man alive.
He had the extraordinary energy and vitality that frequently
goes with a delicate body. The spirit is often stronger in a frail
body, and so frequently it is sick men and women who leave
most behind them when they go.

Horace hunted from Dunsany in the winter and enjoyed
it, although he never became a hunting man in the ordinary
and narrow sense. I can see him now against the Meath
country, stooping a little always, riding his big, wise horses

150

which would carry him reasonably and safely over the ditches and banks. Cyril Coleridge bought his horses for him. He had one who was called Tripod, because he had three sound legs and made such excellent use of them that one did not notice the absence of a fourth. A rough bay, well named Biscay. Cyclops was blind in one eye, but made such good use of the other that it did not matter. I don't know who bought Fitzgerald for him, but he said of him, "I hope Gerald gets him for he fits no one else."

He had that capacity for sarcasm which Fingall had also. Their common ancestor was so many centuries away that it is strange that they should have had certain Plunkett characteristics in common; even that little difficulty with their r's which each shared. Horace once described someone: "If that man is not a villain he ought to take an action against his face!"

Horace was no "thruster" out hunting so I liked to follow him. "Look after her ladyship," Fingall would call back, going off. I had not the courage to follow him. Sometimes a groom boy used to be sent out with me with orders to whip my horse on if I funked. "Gentleman Joe," the groom was called, because he dressed himself so smartly. He kept so close to me that someone asked me once: "Is he in charge of your soul as well as your body?"

I used to play tricks, making my horse refuse. I would call out, "He won't jump!"

Gentleman Joe settled that for me, "Give him a skelp," he would say, not waiting for me to give him one.

Sometimes my pilot Johnny Roberts inspired me with momentary courage. "Come on now, me lady, and ride for your life, and we'll be in at the death!" And I would ride blindly after him, letting my horse take the fences as he liked, thinking that each one would be my last.

I am sure that people who are born cowards, and do the things they fear, are far more brave than those who do not know what fear is. Horace went well, but reasonably and safely, not doing wild things, or jumping impossible places.

I dare say even out hunting, Ireland was somewhere in his thoughts. She is not a lover to be content with half a man's mind for long. She takes everything and Horace gave her everything in the end.

If he had guests at Dunsany it was the usual thing for them to walk over to Killeen on Sunday afternoons, or for dinner, if we did not go to Dunsany. Somewhere about this time I established myself in my tower-room which was to be such a joy to me. It was just the top of a turret, and, from its narrow window, I could survey the countryside as the fighting monks of the old abbey had surveyed it. There was room inside my tower for a desk and a chair—only for one chair. So I could be Queen of my Castle, mistress of my soul, and hermit if I chose. Any one who came to speak to me had to do so from outside the door. Even Fingall could not enter my fortress. And Mrs. Jones or my cook, coming to interview me in the morning about household matters, did so through the doorway. I loved my tower and the security of soul that it gave me. I think every one needs some such fortress of their own into which no one else may enter. The French have a saying that most of our troubles come from not being sufficiently alone. They can come from being too much alone, of course, also. But my tower-room gave me the sense of isolation and security that one may derive from the secret and impregnable places of one's soul.

I used to look from the window—not to see an enemy approaching—but for our guests crossing the fields from Dunsany. Then I would jump up and run down the turret stairs and across the grass to meet them. I have always been a person who ran to meet my guests and friends. One is a giver-out or a taker, as one is made. (Or—and I pity them—there are those who live in their own prison house, not giving out or taking in.) Givers enrich the world in which they live. My advice to the young who come (sometimes) asking wisdom from the old, who should be wise, is, "Give, give and give again, and it will be given to you a thousandfold. (Not perhaps by those to whom you give it. But surely and certainly it will be given.) Cast your bread on the waters, and it will return to you."

My collaborator says: "Yes. You have always been a great bread-slinger."

This is a side track. I return to my tower where I was young and, I dare say, not so very wise. When I ran down the steep stairs from it, and out through the door to meet the party coming across the fields, we met often by the stone of Mary Cruys; or, sometimes, at the gate leading from the field. It seems usually to have been summer, but memory plays such tricks and one summer day in it obscures many days of winter. Certainly there were green evenings when I looked from my tower and saw the heavy brooding beauty of the beech and chestnut trees and the long dark shadows on the grass. And everything in Meath then had gone to sleep to wait for the winter. And, as I sit at my desk, I hear voices in the still evening air. Sometimes it is spring. I have a letter of Horace's before me, written in May, 1922. It is chiefly about the sad Irish politics of that day. But I must have written to him from Killeen in May, for he says:

"Your fine day, and the memories it recalled, pleased me. It is quite true: this is the only time of the year that Killeen and Dunsany are climatically enjoyable. The blossom on the May trees is the chief beauty of the year there . . . it was by far the happiest time of my life, that Spring."

He ends on a sad note about his Irish Agricultural Organisation Society, into which he was still pouring money and strength. "I suppose it will only add a dark chapter to the biography which I shall write in exile, if at all."

It seems only yesterday that I sat at my desk, high above the Meath fields, and heard the gate swing and creak, and there was Horace with his dreams.

We must have broken the green monotony of the life at Killeen, by a visit to London during those first years after my marriage. For I remember going with Fingall first to 9 Great Stanhope Street, a house where I was later to know great kindness, to visit Mrs. Herbert with whom we had stayed at

Llanarth on our honeymoon. It was then that I saw old Lady Llanover for the second time. To my nineteen years she seemed immortally aged—and she had been married in 1823 and died in 1896. The clothes she wore made her seem more so. She had a white frilled cap such as Madame du Deffand wears in the picture of her that is a frontispiece to her *Letters*. Her face between the white frills made me think of a witch.

She sat in regal state in the drawing-room of the Stanhope Street house, with two, apparently ladies-in-waiting, either side of her. They were poor relatives, I think, who acted as her companions. She was a terrifying old lady and I pitied them.

Opposite the windows was the famous corner house that Barney Barnato had built, with the statues that some one christened "the petrified shareholders" on top. Old Lady Llanover had sat, I believe, just as I saw her, in her drawing-room, watching the house go up, storey by storey, blotting out the light from her windows. I suppose she could not have sat there always, since the house took years to build, but when I heard the tale I had that picture of her and I cannot change it. Anyhow she watched and the house opposite grew higher and the light dimmer in the room at 9 Great Stanhope Street as Barney Barnato flung his walls between Lady Llanover and the sun. When it was all done, even to the statues on the roof, Lady Llanover moved. Not until then. And then she moved with a vengeance. Mr. Barnato had forgotten her "antient lites," which forbade him to build more than a certain height opposite her house. I forget how many storeys had to come down, but down they had to come.

I only remember that one vision of Lady Llanover at Great Stanhope Street, although she lived until 1896. She was not there when I paid a visit to Mrs. Herbert and her daughter, Poppy, who had kindly asked their little Irish cousin by marriage to stay with them and see something of London. Poppy Herbert, who married later, Walter Maxwell, uncle of the Duchess of Norfolk, was to be one of my life-long friends.

That was my first visit on my own. I expect Fingall wondered why any one should want to see anything of London, but when the invitation came, his sisters at once said that I must be allowed to accept. They pointed out to Fingall that it was very dull at Killeen for anything so young and gay as I was, and Fingall, who was always reasonable and so generous, consented. So I went to London for a portion of the Season.

It was May and London of the eighties. All the houses had bright newly-watered window-boxes. There were flowers everywhere and sunshine and jingling hansoms. It was great fun to be alive and to be young. There were the Sunday Parades in the Park, where people walked up and down after church, met their friends and talked with them. The women were beautifully dressed. It was the time of big hats and full rustling silk dresses. The men wore top hats and frock coats and gay buttonholes. The Achilles Statue was the great meeting-place. There you found your friends—by appointment—and walked with them. Usually you went on to lunch somewhere or you brought someone back to lunch. There were always Sunday lunch parties at 9 Great Stanhope Street. I met Lord Coventry at the Achilles Statue and was proud to walk with the great English gentleman that he was. There had been no failing in our friendship since that night when we sat beside each other at dinner at Dublin Castle. Or I met Charlie Burn, one of the best looking young men I have ever seen. He was stationed in Dublin and must have been on leave. Or it was Horace, who enjoyed showing his country cousin the sights of London. Or Alexis Roche, or both of them. Or Denis Lawless. Or many other friends.

On week-days people rode in the Park, beautifully turned out, and riding beautifully. Very different from the sights one sees in the Row nowadays. No astride women, no appalling coloured jumpers. The women rode side-saddle and had an undressed smartness. Not hunting clothes. A covert coat and white waistcoat perhaps. Some people wore alpaca coats and some top hats. (Obviously made by Mr. Lock.) Those early summer mornings we collected in groups on the rails to talk to our friends who were riding. The trees above us were pale green. The air smelt of dust and that indefinable smell of London summer which I associate with the scene. There was no petrol then to defile the air. Only the breath and sweat of horses.

No country cousin ever saw London more delightfully than I saw it during that first season. The Herberts were much connected with the diplomatic world and they had grand and dignified parties to which many foreign diplomats and their wives came.

I went coaching with Baron Deichmann who lived in the same street; and we drove down to Richmond through the summer air, and Richmond was quite country then and the chestnuts were out. Past Knightsbridge we drove, and Princes Gate, where Tom Hare told me once, he remembered shooting snipe from Kingston House when Knightsbridge was a swamp; and through Old Kensington, and so to Hammersmith and across the river.

I went driving too with Lord Coventry, over Kingston Hill to Richmond again. He told me that twenty-five years or so earlier, he had gone that way to stay with the Duc and Duchesse d'Aumale at Orleans House and had hunted from there with the Duc's Harriers!

Lord Coventry had plenty of history to tell me. At the age of seven he had walked to church hand in hand with the great Duke of Wellington, from Apsley House. He lived then with his grandmother, Lady Cockerell, next door to the Duke. He had succeeded—poor little Earl—at the age of five. Both his parents had died young and he and his sister Maria, afterwards Lady Maria Ponsonby and mother of Geraldine, Lady Mayo, were brought up by their grandmother, chiefly at Sezincote in Gloucestershire. The boy went to school at Cheltenham at the age of six and a half! And to Eton when he was thirteen. He was certainly an advertisement for this Spartan treatment. He remembered, as a child, going to lunch with Lord and Lady Palmerston who both liked young people; and being patted on the head by "Pam." And, in those days Lord Palmerston always rode to the Derby and was cheered by the populace as he went. He used to ride sucking a piece of straw, to give him a sporting appearance!

After Lady Cockerell's death, young Coventry spent his holidays with his uncle, General Lygon, or with his aunt at Holland House, that wonderful country house in the heart of Kensington, with its rose gardens and water gardens and bluebell woods and even pheasants; and the statue of Charles James Fox in the garden and its historical memories. Those gardens then were still untouched by the encroaching of London, that monster that eats up everything in its path.

"Covey" had seen many of the great political figures of the time at Holland House. He said it made him ashamed to see these great men often so fuddled with wine that they were unable to join the ladies after dinner. That early sight had a great effect on him, and he said that it was one of the reasons why he determined never to drink to excess, and he never did. Nor did he play cards. He said that card-playing bored him. But I believe his real reason was the one he gave King Edward when he asked him why he never played Bridge: "Sir, I don't much care to win other people's money, and, still less, like losing my own!"

I believe the King considered him a prig, but when there was any question of honour to be decided, he was always sent for. He was a great gentleman and his integrity was undoubted. He was at Tranby Croft on the famous occasion when one of the guests was caught cheating at cards, and he was called out of bed at once to be consulted as to what should be done. I believe his advice was taken.

Lord Coventry, who was a great connoisseur, taught me much about beautiful things. From now on, his friendship was to enrich my life. I saw many treasures with him when I went to London. There, too, he looked what he always was, the Squire farmer, and he was most at home in his own county of Worcestershire where I walked with him about the country and visited the farmers, all of whom were his friends. But

157

that was later. In London he took me to Soanes' to see the Adam books. And he taught me at once:

"Adam, my lady, never say Adams."

I remembered my lesson.

I went too with him to Dulwich to see the picture gallery there, and on the way he pointed out the River Waddle where he used to fish when he was a boy. It was already half-hidden under the crowded suburb of Wandsworth.

He had his own way of dressing, whether in London or the country. A low high hat, a special tie—bird's eye, I think it was called—blue with white spots, tied round his old-fashioned collar, a check waistcoat and a cut-away coat. He was something of a dandy and I usually remember him with a button-hole. He always wore square-toed boots made for him by Mr. Thomas of St. James's Street. I was at Newmarket with him once and he said: "My lady, you are always perfectly dressed but, if I may say so, your shoes are not sufficiently business-like." The next time I was in London he took me to Mr. Thomas and had a pair of Newmarket shoes made for me: laced shoes, with low heels, and perfectly fitting—a gift from Lord Coventry. For many Christmases after I received a similar gift.

Wertheimer and other famous dealers often wrote to Lord Coventry when they had something particularly beautiful to show. It was Wertheimer who told me that I had a *flair* for things and that he would be quite ready to employ me as a buyer for him. But that was later when Coventry and Hugh Lane had educated me, and I had discovered a Franz Hals in an old house in Ireland.

There was a charming butler at Great Stanhope Street, a Welshman and a Welsh speaker, like all Lady Llanover's servants, who came from the Llanarth and Llanover estates. Lord Coventry, coming to see me there one day, after an occasion when he had called and found me out, said: "My lady, what very charming people these must be! I always judge a house and the people who own it by the servants, and these people must be very nice indeed to have such a delightful butler." He added thoughtfully, "But perhaps it would be as well if he were not to give quite so much information to a caller. When I called the other day, he said: ' Her ladyship has gone out with a very tall gentleman and I think she won't be back for some time '!"

Lord Coventry was right, judging people by their servants. Countries get the governments, and people the servants they deserve.

Horace Plunkett came a great deal to the house, being a cousin, also. He enjoyed showing me London and I made many expeditions with him and Denis Lawless. They were great friends and had rooms together at this time in Park Lane. They took me down the river some of those summer afternoons. The river was at its loveliest then, before motor traffic came to crowd it. We drifted in some backwater. Horace, I think, talked even then of Ireland and Co-operation. But he was gay too and we laughed a lot and were very young and happy, and presently it was time to think of dinner, so we slipped back to Maidenhead, and dined on the terrace in a green twilight over the river, with the lit hotel windows behind us. Or, another night, we dined at the Star and Garter at Richmond, or we ate whitebait for lunch at Greenwich. Or we went bowling down to Ranelagh or Hurlingham to watch the polo and dine at the Club there and drive back in the cool of the evening—or we went to the Gaiety to see Kate Vaughan dance or Connie Gilchrist. Oh! It was a gay time. Horace and Denis Lawless, being eligible young men, were much sought after. But they seemed to have plenty of time to take a country cousin about.

With my return to Killeen drawing near, I had shopping to do. The London shops were thrilling to a girl of nineteen. I drove in hansoms by myself, much enjoying this emancipation. One morning, when I was going on to lunch with Charlie Burn and "Mary" Matthews and other hunting friends at the Berkeley, I took a hansom, driven by a charming and good-looking young man. He was a paragon among hansom drivers. Such courtesy, such delight in rendering me service! I could not part from him at the door of the first shop and told him to wait for me. And when I said Busvine (for an alteration to my habit) he needed no address. Nor for Hodgkinson's to buy hunting ties and silk handkerchiefs. Nor for the dressmaker to whom we all went in those days, in Dover Street. He seemed indeed to know where one wanted to go, almost before one knew oneself. So I kept him for the morning, recklessly. And when all the shopping was done, it was time for lunch and we drove to the Berkeley. As I paid him I said, "I would have liked very much to have kept you, but I'm afraid I can't afford it."

He took off his hat with a low bow:

"That's just what I was thinking about *you*, miss."

I fled into the Berkeley, scarlet. Charlie Burn, waiting for me, asked: "What has happened?" I told the story to the lunch party, pledging them to secrecy, with the usual result of such pledges that it was all over London the next day.

I don't seem to have wasted any of that month. I made many new friends and strengthened the bonds of friendship with some already made. Certainly Mrs. Delany's wish for herself, "a moderate share of wealth . . . but a vast store of love and friendship . . ." came true for me. No one has ever been richer in friendship than I have been.

Lord Rowton—then Monty Corry—was a new friend that I made during that visit. He came to see me one day at Great Stanhope Street and I received him in the drawing-room where old Lady Llanover had sat, watching the building of the Barnato house. Having shaken hands, he stood still for a moment and looked about him. "Where have I seen this room before—this paper?" The paper was unforgettable, being of the brightest blue-bag blue, with gold oak leaves and acorns on it. Appalling, but no doubt thought beautiful at the time. The curtains at the windows matched it.

"Have I been here before?" my guest asked. How could I tell? The name of my hostess—Mrs. Herbert—meant nothing to him. But when I mentioned that the house belonged to Lady Llanover, it was another matter. Of course he had been there, with Disraeli, when he was his secretary and Disraeli had often visited the Llanovers. They were great friends in spite of their different political opinions, and it was at Llanover, I believe, that Dizzy met the lady he married.

After that summer month in London there is another green interval at Killeen. Those green intervals, all my life, were to be much longer than my expeditions abroad. I went out into the world for brief periods but always returned to the quietness of Killeen, which opened and received me. I think it was something of an effort to pull up my roots again each time I went away. But perhaps that made it more imperative that I should go, before the grass covered me altogether. So I made these occasional dashes to England to stay at grand houses in London and later at Wynyard with the Londonderrys, or at Elveden with the Iveaghs, or Culford with the Cadogans and at many other houses as I made more and more friends. But much as I valued the kind and lovely hospitality of my hosts, I was always conscious of something in me drawing back during those visits. I did not belong to that country or that life.

As for Fingall. To all Plunketts of that branch, I have just said, the world began and ended with that gloomy study at Killeen which I have already described. Have I said that it was built on the ground without foundations, which made it low and dark and chilly? But, for Fingall, it was near to the courtyard door, so that the people who wanted him could come to him easily without troubling the rest of the house. And Oliver, the present Fingall, is the same. It was he who drew this exclamation from me, only the other day.

Mrs. Willie Jameson was a friend I made about this time while she and Willie Jameson were hunting from Athlumney and our friendship was to be a life-long one. We often went to the Castle together, during the time that the Londonderrys were there. They were always very kind to me and they were both extremely fond of Mrs. Willie, whom they called "Soft Eyes." A good name for her. She was charming and so full of sweetness and with a very good brain. Willie Jameson

161

—who was one of the greatest yachtsmen of his day—and Lady Londonderry had a common interest in yachting. He was an all-round sportsman. He sailed the *Britannia* for the King and we had such good times on the *Magdalena*, his own luxurious yacht. Willie Jameson was the kindest of men in spite of a somewhat rough tongue. We always fought but I was very fond of him, as I believe and hope he was of me, although I have always said that it is not possible to be equal friends with a husband and wife, and it was she who was my friend.

When Lord Londonderry came to the Castle he hurried up the dinners. He hated food and he instituted short meals instead of the immensely long ones to which we had been accustomed. I believe half an hour was the time allowed for dinner and the occasion would have been a poor one for a gourmet. A footman stood behind nearly every chair and plates were often whipped away from the guests before they had finished. If you stopped to talk you would get nothing to eat at all. Lord Londonderry must have cut down the number of dishes. He also instituted cold entrées and it was a new idea to be offered cold ham at dinner.

One night I sat beside a Lord Mayor at a State Banquet. The Lord Mayor, who, no doubt, had been looking forward to his Viceregal meal, was a slow eater and talker and while he had his head turned towards me the footman took away his plate and he was left looking at the empty one put before him for the next course, in some surprise. When he was offered cold ham his endurance gave out and he expressed his feelings to me. "I don't call this a dinner at all," he said. "I call it a rush," and, eyeing the ham disdainfully, "cheap, too!"

Lord Londonderry, during his Viceroyalty, was busy fighting Parnell, a fight that death was to decide in the end. His secretary was Johnny Mulhall, suave and cautious. Lord Londonderry, writing an angry letter after some outrage, referred to Parnell as a murderer. Johnny Mulhall corrected him, "It would be better, your Excellency, to say that he *connived* at murder."

From the Portrait by Sargent

THERESA, MARCHIONESS OF LONDONDERRY

FIELD-MARSHAL EARL HAIG.

I have often wondered why the Londonderrys should have been so good to me, rebel and Papist as I was. Sometimes I thought that they asked me first to prove their broadminded-ness. Anyhow their friendship was never failing and it made no difference to it that we often fought on politics and it was fun, I expect, at those parties at Mount Stewart where I was alone, with all that I represented, to see me flare up in angry defence of my side. Their Viceroyalty was very magnificent. She was most beautiful then, although not in her first youth. If she had had a little more height she would have been wonderful to look at, but she was too short for her regal beauty and rather square in figure. Hers was a most dominant personality. She had the proudest face I have ever seen, with a short upper lip and a beautifully-shaped, determined chin. She had the mind of a man with the temperament of a woman. At one time she was supposed to rule England and statesmen used to quail before her. She was "Theresa Londonderry" when she wrote a stern letter, "Nellie" to her friends. I remember George Wyndham saying half-humorously but in genuine alarm: "I have just had a letter signed ' Theresa ' and am looking out for squalls."

She was a wonderful friend if she was your friend, and it was a very good thing indeed to be Lady Londonderry's friend in those days. She had an all-powerful position both in politics and society. If you were Lady Londonderry's friend or the Duchess of Devonshire's, no one would dare to say a word against you. It was an equally bad thing to be the enemy of either.

Lady Londonderry was a great hostess at the Viceregal Lodge or at Mount Stewart or at Wynyard, their place in the north of England, from which most of the Londonderry money came. The people there adored her and she lived and ruled at Wynyard like a very benevolent monarch, knowing all the people and their affairs. Once, from there, I went to Stockton Races with my hosts and our reception as we drove on to the course was such as might be given to Royalty. At the Viceregal Lodge, as at her own houses, she or her daughter

Birdie, afterwards Lady Ilchester, always went round the visitors' rooms when they had been prepared for guests, putting those last touches that mean everything of welcome and hospitality, seeing to the writing-tables, the choice of books for each guest and so on. I remember Birdie Ilchester often fulfilling this duty. At Mount Stewart and at Wynyard Lady Londonderry did this herself. When they were at the Castle they had a special chair for Fingall—"the somnolent Earl" with sides to it, because if he sat on an ordinary gold one, he would fall off.

In Ireland Lady Londonderry was interested in fostering industries. Irish tweed factories and Irish lace-making received a stimulus during her time at the Viceregal Lodge. Each Lord Lieutenant's wife had her own particular and pet charity. Lady Londonderry's was Irish Industries. Lady Dudley's, a scheme for providing nurses for the poor, throughout Ireland. Lady Aberdeen's, the war against Tuberculosis. She did succeed in making the Irish open their windows, and that is something tangible that remains, when so much of the work of those years of effort has vanished as completely as though we only built a house of cards with all our labour!

Perhaps Fingall was right when he said to Horace that you should not give the Irish anything that they did not ask for. For certainly, at one touch of a harsh wind, most of what we had made came tumbling down, as if it were indeed a house of cards, with no roots or foundations in the Irish earth on which it was built.

CHAPTER TWELVE

THROUGH my friendship with Mrs. Willie Jameson I came to my friendship with her brother, Douglas Haig. He was a great deal younger than she was and their mother had died when he was still a child so that she had brought him up and mothered him. She adored him and he was a most devoted brother. His first affection for me came because I was " Retta's " friend. That was his name for her. He was known to his family as " Dockie,"—" short for Doctor "—because he was inclined to be a little hypochondriacal and to fuss about things that were good or bad to eat.

Once you were his friend he never forgot you. He had, among many qualities from his Scottish blood, that of fidelity. Scottish men and women, in my experience, make the most faithful friends.

When I knew him first, he was a newly-joined subaltern of the 7th Hussars, and spending his leave hunting from Athlumney, where his brother-in-law kept open house and a stable full of splendid horses. Douglas was then about twenty-four or twenty-five, and very good looking, with blue eyes, a square chin, and an expression that was rather shy and serious. He had a good, if rather slow, sense of humour, and could take a joke well.

He was always somewhat inarticulate and, when at a loss for words, would make gestures with his hands as though he were trying to capture that elusive word that he could not find, to express his meaning. In my earlier memories of him he was usually silent, but, on occasion, would burst forth and talk a good deal.

His religion was of the rigid and dour Scottish kind. And he was always rather shy. He was a tremendously keen soldier and his letters to me were usually full of military tactics and such things, which I did not in the least understand. Napoleon was his hero.

He had a room of his own at the Jamesons' flat, 45 Albert Gate—the simplest possible soldier's room, which was walled with military books, histories of campaigns, tactics and so on. Here he used to sit up late at night, reading and studying. At their house in Princes Gate, later, he also had a room of his own, which I sometimes occupied when he was not there. We called it humorously "our room." Often Douglas went out of it just before I went in, and vice versa.

We became great friends first, out hunting, the best place of all, as I have said, for getting to know people. Douglas rode well in a military way, and he was a great polo player. Out hunting he, like Horace, was no thruster, but was always there at the end of a run. I don't think he talked much but he was a pleasant companion to be with. He called me "Countess"—the name deriving from a humorous nickname someone had given me, "the Countess of Constantinople," the origin of which I have quite forgotten—and his family always said that I was his first love. A very safe and good love it was and ours was a long and delightful friendship.

He was serious, even then. His Scottish forebears showed in that, and in his strong religious feeling. We did not dream then, of course, of what the future held, or of the burden that was to be laid on his shoulders. He did not change essentially with the years from the Douglas I had first known. All through the War he sought for and believed in Divine guidance. And his last, "back to the wall," proclamation of 1918, shows him, as I knew him, inarticulate, struggling for words, in that moment when any words would have been inadequate. But all that was a long way down the years that first winter that we hunted together over the Meath country.

Sometimes he was disconcerting. Henrietta and I were amazed a good many years later, when he came to tell us that he was engaged. We had had no warning of such a thing impending. He had met Dorothy Vivian, as she then was, at Windsor Castle during an Ascot week. She was one of the lovely Vivian twins and a Maid of Honour. He sat opposite to her at dinner one night and, as he looked across the table

166

made up his mind that he would marry her. (A characteristic masculine decision! He doesn't appear to have thought of the lady's feelings!) Henrietta said: "But how did you make up your mind so quickly, Dockie?"

"Oh!" he said. "I have often had to make up my mind in a shorter time on much more important matters."

He had an extraordinarily charming smile and when he laughed it was a very good sound. He did it wholeheartedly, throwing back his head and showing his good teeth. He was rather a self-contained young man, even then. Like Horace —whom he resembled in other ways, also—he was absorbed in his dreams. But Douglas' dreams were of soldiering and campaigns.

I had a great many of his letters but I burnt them all before I left Killeen. He wrote to me from the South African War, and from the French manœuvres. They were dull, impersonal letters, all about tactics and such things of which I knew nothing at all. The sort of letters through which a woman looks despairingly, seeking a mention of herself. I sought in vain! There was nothing personal about me or about him and I got bored with them. I remember being at Princes Gate and hearing Haig and French discussing the South African War before they went to it. I remember also a discussion between them as to which was the best training for soldiers —polo or hunting. French was in favour of hunting, which taught a man all about the country and light and wind and shadow, and the use of trees and hedges as cover and camouflage, a word we had never used in those days. Haig was for polo, which taught team work, he said. And he maintained that hunting had a certain selfishness in the training it gave. Still French insisted that hunting demanded more initiative from a man and more acting for himself, which was good.

Earlier, when we were both quite young, there were lovely visits to the Jamesons at Blairfindie, their shooting lodge, in Banffshire, and Douglas was often there.

I remember arriving at the little Scottish station and

Douglas coming to meet me. Once he must have been a minute or two late, for I had time to weigh myself on the station weighing-machine, or to try to. I put in my penny and nothing happened.

"Is it automatic?" I asked the one and only porter on the platform.

"Automatic? It's a' to hell, lang syne," he answered.

Then Douglas arrived, driving a dog-cart, eager and welcoming. Blairfindie is a lovely memory. It was a white-washed, simple shooting-lodge and we lived largely on what we fished and shot. There was a very good cook who turned this provender into delicious dishes. The country about was all heather with rough shooting and there was a little brown trout stream. An old gillie, such as only Scotland could produce, came fishing with us. When I caught tiny little fish I wanted to throw them back into the water, feeling sorry for them, but the gillie would take them from me, firmly.

"It's aye a fush," he would say.

Douglas was a charming companion, so boyish and young and gay and we had such fun. The Scottish air, of course, was like champagne. We used to run over the moors through the heather. How I could run then!

One day we were going shooting. Douglas and his brother Bee Haig were there, both in kilts, with bare knees. The van, in which the dogs were waiting, ran away from the door down the hill and the dogs escaped and in their excitement ran into the beehives and upset one of them. Of course the bees attacked us and the two men with their bare knees got the worst of it. I can see them now, the future Field Marshal and his brother, running away across the heather, pursued by the bees.

Most of all I remember the lovely summer nights at Blair-findie before we went to bed by candlelight. There was a wonderful harvest moon during one visit, so bright that we read *The Times* by it, sitting out on the steps at midnight. I think I can smell those pines and the wind coming across the moors with the smell of heather on it. And there is a river running somewhere. And Rosie Anstruther Thompson, a charming girl, who was also a guest, is singing as she used to sing for us those nights, sitting on the steps in the moonlight:

"There's aye a slippy stone at ichabody's door."

It has the moonlight in it, that memory of Blairfindie and the white walls are silver edged.

There was a day in June, 1907, when I was staying at Princes Gate with the Jamesons. Douglas was also there and very busy with his military duties at the War Office. On a lovely June morning he said to me at breakfast: "Countess, would you like to run down with me in time to see the Derby run and then come straight back?" I said I would love to do that. It would suit me admirably, for a whole day's racing always tired me. So we took a good hansom and as there was little or no traffic on the road at that hour, we got down in a very short time. We went straight to the paddock where the horses were being led round. I saw Orby at once and kept my eyes on him. I had last seen him in a rough field at the foot of the Three Rock Mountain in Co. Dublin, when he was being trained by Dr. McCabe for Boss Croker, who had built himself a mansion not far from Horace Plunkett's house, Kilteragh. The Boss of Tammany used often to come over and talk politics with Horace, for whose work he had a great admiration.

Orby looked well that day in the Paddock, cool and business-like; but I was torn, too, by my liking for my friend, Harry Greer's great horse, Slieve Gallion, who had won the Craven Stakes. Two Thousand Guineas! Whereas Orby had not even won a selling plate in Ireland. However, it was odds on Slieve Gallion, so, thinking of Kilteragh and the Three Rock Mountain, I put five pounds at 100 to 9 on Orby—really for the sake of the Three Rock Mountain—and went back to the stand. No race ever thrilled me as much as that, except one—the Cambridgeshire after the War, when Verdict won it for Lord Coventry.

Reiff rode a great race and Orby won the Derby from Slieve Gallion by two lengths. We just waited to see Croker lead him in, with little Reiff up, and then ran back to our hansom and drove back to London for tea.

Killeen was on Douglas' staff for a time in France during the War. The Commander-in-Chief used to ride every day. He had a liver, and always thought a good deal about his health. He was absent-minded then, the War filling his thoughts, and Killeen's job was to ride ahead of him and make sure of the road, and that the Commander-in-Chief did not ride into a shell hole without seeing it. He hardly spoke, except to say Good-morning or Good-evening, his A.D.C. said. Just occasionally he would break his heavy silence to ask: "How is your mother? Is she well?" Or it might be some question about the hunting in Meath and a covert there that he remembered. Then he would ride again in silence, with the War on his shoulders. It must have seemed to him another world in which he had hunted in Meath, or shot and fished at Blairfindie when we were both young.

I used to stay with the Jamesons a good deal during the War, at 21 Princes Gate, where Douglas and I had joked about "our" room in pre-War days and he had sat up late at night in that bare simple little soldier's room, studying. He had a wonderful collection of maps there which he used to show us. Lady Haig had a house down on Kingston Hill those War years (their son was born during the War) and Princes Gate was always the first place that Douglas came to when he arrived in London from France.

There was a day after Passchendaele when I sat in the study which was in the front of the house, reading the appalling casualty list. I was waiting to go to lunch with the Pagets at 35 Belgrave Square. Lady Paget's War-time lunches were famous. Every one who came back from the War went to them and you met at that table most of the important soldiers and statesmen of the time. I remember the Asquiths being there and the Duchess of Westminster, back from her hospital in France and Colonel House, and Walter Page, the American Ambassador, among others. It was the time of rationing, of course, and I believe the luncheon dish was usually the same—macaroni with eggs on top was often the *pièce de résistance*, but it was so beautifully cooked. The tablecloth and the table-napkins were of paper. Minnie Paget was always very kind to me. We had seen a lot of each other at the Iveaghs and at the Viceregal Lodge, when Sir Arthur Paget was Commander-in-Chief in Ireland.

I was dressed and ready to go to lunch and was just waiting until it was time to start. Willie and Henrietta were both out.

Suddenly the door opened and Douglas came in. For a minute I thought he was a ghost. I had been absorbed in that appalling casualty list and had not heard a taxi drive up to the door. His face was terrible, a ravaged, harrowed face, and his eyes were bloodshot. His clothes were travel stained. My impression was almost that they had the French mud on them. I looked up suddenly to see him there. For fully a minute I was not sure if he was a living man, or a dead one come back from the company of those others whose names I had been reading. I could not recognise the braw Scots lad I had once known.

Then I found my voice.

"Douglas," I said. "What has brought you back? Has something awful happened?"

He made that familiar gesture with his hands. It was the gesture of a man in agony.

"They've sent for me to heckle me."

He was on his way to the War Council. I said, "But, Douglas, you are not fit to go." I rang the bell for Plowes, the butler. When he came I said, "Get something for the Field Marshal." Plowes brought whisky and soda but Douglas did not touch it.

"I haven't time for anything, Countess," he said. "Is Retta in?"

No, I told him. She and Willie were both out.

He left almost immediately to go to the War Council. I had to go on to my lunch party although I felt little like it. I could think of nothing except Douglas' tortured face. All through lunch that was before my eyes. There was a vacant

171

place beside me at the table. I was too absorbed in my thoughts of Douglas, to wonder who should have occupied it. Lunch was nearly over when Arthur Balfour came in with his usual impenetrable face and sat down beside me.

Minnie Paget turned to him at once.

"Well, Arthur. Did you get anything out of him?"

Arthur Balfour made a despairing gesture.

"The man is inarticulate," he said.

I saw red. I know I behaved like a tiger cat. With that vision of Douglas as I had seen him, before me, I turned on Arthur Balfour.

I said something like, "Can't you believe in anything but talk? Can't you understand a man who isn't a talker and leave him alone to do his work when that is all that he wants to do?"

I was near tears when I broke off. No one spoke a word. Luckily it was near the end of lunch. I jumped up then and ran out of the room and out of the house. I got a taxi and drove home. On the way I said to myself: "Well, I'll never be asked there again."

Arthur Paget and Douglas Haig had been enemies since the Curragh incident just before the War, when Paget had been in command at the Royal Hospital. He was responsible for offering the officers at the Curragh their choice of going to fight the North if necessary, or resigning, which some of them did. The story goes that the Connaught Rangers said that if their officers would not go, they would go and fight without them. Haig spoke his mind openly about the affair, taking a soldier's view of soldiers being asked if they would do their duty, when it was:

> "Theirs not to make reply,
> Theirs not to reason why," etc.

This made Arthur Paget his bitter enemy ever after. I had felt that in the air, I suppose, all through lunch.

Douglas came to Princes Gate that night, for an hour or so on his way back to the Front.

"They don't trust me," he said.

A few days later, someone who knew Arthur Balfour very well wrote to me: "What did you say to Arthur the other day? He said you turned on him like a tiger cat. But that a great deal of what you said was true."

And my hostess was very forgiving and I was asked again.

There was another day in the years following the War, when again I was sitting reading in that same room at Princes Gate, and the door opened and Douglas, in full Field Marshal's uniform, came in. The tears were rolling down his face.

I said, "Douglas! What has happened? Not something to one of the children?" What else could make him look like that?

He said, "They have killed Wilson."

Wilson had been his enemy, yet he wept for him. He told me then that Wilson had been shot on his own doorstep, coming from the unveiling of the War Memorial at Baker Street station which they had both attended. Douglas was in full uniform for the occasion.

Later I was told another chapter of that story by Robin Watson, who had a flat in Ebury Street. He was looking out of his window that day and he saw a small crowd in the street. A lorry was going by and a man, sitting on it, was trying to pull up another man who was obviously lame. The crowd came up with the lorry and pulled the lame man down. When this happened the other jumped off too and joined his friend. The crowd seemed to be trying to lynch the lame man and the other fought wildly to defend him. Then the crowd closed in and Robin Watson saw no more.

But someone else told me that the lame man—one of the two who had shot Sir Henry Wilson on his doorstep—was a lift-man at the War Office. He had lost one leg in the War. Both the men were ex-soldiers. The one-legged lift-man, I was told by my friend in the War Office, was the gayest of the gay, always so cheerful and happy, going up and down in his lift. Until one day he became suddenly dark and gloomy. After that it was impossible to make him smile. No one knew what had happened to change him so completely.

Evidently he had received his orders from whatever organisation he belonged to, to shoot Sir Henry Wilson.

Douglas Haig was always a tremendous worker. A one-idea'd man like Horace Plunkett. Lord Osborne Beauclerk, talking to me of him the other day, said he got on by work, where other men took short-cuts, which I think was true. There was a cabal against him, and he had no words to meet them to express what was in his mind. They had words and nothing in their minds.

Douglas was very unjealous and he handed over the supreme command to Foch readily and loyally. I never heard him talk much about the War. I think it hurt too much. But he thought about it all the time. He felt the casualties terribly, though he knew they were an inevitable part of war. I remember going to the House of Lords after the War to see him made a Peer.

CHAPTER THIRTEEN

IT was sometime in the late eighties that I first met Hermione
Leinster who was to become one of my greatest friends. Her
beauty has become a legend.

I met her for the first time at Lyons, the Cloncurrys' place
in Co. Kildare, when I was staying there for a few days.
Emily Lawless, Lord Cloncurry's daughter, was Hermione's
greatest friend and there could not have been two people
more unlike. Emily Lawless wrote *Maelcho* and other Irish
books and poetry that startled us all, not only by their power,
but by their intensity of national feeling. The most passionate
lovers of Ireland, the most passionate fighters for her, have
always been the converts from the conquering race. And
Emily Lawless was a staunch Unionist although so full of
romance about Ireland. She loved the Burren of Clare, that
barren wild land, which is a background for some of her work.
I remember hearing later that Gladstone spoke of her *With
Essex In Ireland* with immense admiration, saying that it was
an amazing *tour de force* and that he wondered if the author
had had access to some hitherto unpublished documents for
her information. She wrote, too, those stirring and heart-
breaking ballads of Clare's Brigade, and the Wild Geese. No
one was ever less like her work than Emily Lawless. She gave
one no idea of the passion and power within her. She was
pale and flaccid, with half-closed, near-sighted eyes and limp
white hands. Her speech was slow and she was very delicate
and rather hypochondriachal and untidy in her dressing.

The old Duke of Leinster had died in 1887 and the young
Duke and Duchess had then just come to Carton from Kilkea
Castle, where they had lived as Lord and Lady Kildare and
where Hermione had once, in a mood of rebellion, composed
the verse:

"Kilkea Castle and Lord Kildare
Are more than any woman can bear."

175

Emily Lawless was constantly at Carton and a little later if Hermione was bored and Emily were not there, she was sending for me. I think we two, Emily and I—so unlike—were her greatest friends.

I drove over to Lyons for that visit, which was to become memorable because of the meeting with her. Horace Plunkett was of the party—Denis Lawless being one of his great friends—and we drove together from Meath on an outside car, leaning across the "well" to talk to each other. That little trick and glimpse of memory is as clear as though we drove yesterday. It must have been spring or summer I think, or, hardy as we were, we should have chosen a vehicle that gave more protection. I pause for a moment, thinking of outside cars. They seem to me typical of Irish character. Two people can drive on one through the same country and yet each see quite a different view. One looks one side, one the other. The only person who can see the whole truth of the landscape, is the jarvey who sits in the middle. And if he sits in the middle, he says nothing. Although, if he were to sit on the other side and lean across to you, he would have plenty to say. I remember many good journeys on outside cars, enlivened and made short by the pleasant conversation as one leant towards one's companion across the "well." For a really nice chat give me an outside car. It would be hard to remain silent in such an attitude. Although I *have* known silent drivers.

I have just that glimpse of memory. And then I remember the drawing-room at Lyons and Hermione Leinster coming into it. I thought her the most beautiful creature that I had ever seen.

I think that she did not stay long on that occasion. She had visitors coming and had to go back to Carton to receive them. We met again at Adare, but perhaps before that I visited her at Carton. I cannot remember the sequence. Only that we were in each other's lives now for the brief years that remained of her lovely and tragic one.

First, of her beauty. It has not in any way been exagger-

HERMIONE, DUCHESS OF LEINSTER.

"THE OLD MASTER"

(Robert Watson, M.F.H.)

ated by tradition and time, which have that power of making loveliness lovelier each year as it recedes into memory. She was "divinely tall," with an Angelica Kauffmann figure. Looking at the portrait of her by Hughes that hangs at the foot of the stairs at Carton, in which she is all in brown and painted with Cymru—the Chow that Dunraven gave her—I realise that, according to the standards of to-day, she might seem a little too fat. It is extraordinary how women's figures change according to the fashion of the times. Then, hers seemed to be absolutely perfect. She had that wonderful long neck, and a skin so delicate and transparent that, like Mary Queen of Scots, when she swallowed, you could almost see the passage of the wine through her throat. I have never seen such a skin or such flesh. She had beautiful feet and hands. I don't think she ever used her hands except for her music and sculpturing. She was a tremendous gardener but I don't believe she did any of the actual work herself. She only planned and directed. When I stayed at Carton, which was often, during those brief years of our friendship, she used to come to my room at night, with her lovely brown hair loose about her shoulders and sit talking by the fire, turning her feet up to the flames. That is how I know that she had beautiful feet. It was in those hours that I came to know her really well. She told me many things then that I may not speak of.

Her face was lovely, with soft brown eyes, a delicately formed, slightly retroussé nose, and brilliant, pouting lips. It was before the days of make-up and her wonderful colour was her own. Alas! That colour told its own tragic story. It was the beauty of the consumptive. I think I only once saw Hermione at a disadvantage and that was when, looking across the House of Lords, I saw her sitting beside Queen Alexandra. The Queen looked like a Greek statue with her absolutely perfect features. Beside her — incredibly — Hermione's brilliant beauty seemed almost too highly coloured.

I may say now that Hermione's life was a sad one. And it must have seemed so beautiful to any one looking on from outside. How little we know of the life beyond other people's walls, whether those walls are the material ones, or the walls we build about ourselves so that we may hide within them! Those evenings at Carton when she came to my room and sat, turning her feet to the fire and talking, she opened a gate in her wall and I went through. But when I came back I closed the gate again and so it must stay.

The Duke was good and kind. But not the man for her. She wanted a man whom she could look up to and fear a little, as well as love. The Duke used to sit in his library at Carton, cataloguing his books and tidying them. She would go to him, with a plan perhaps, of which he did not approve. He would argue.

"But Kildare . . . " she would begin in that lovely voice of hers that would call the birds off the trees, as the Irish say.

"Hermione, I have settled it." And he would walk out of the room, leaving her looking after him.

I did not know her when she lived at the older Fitzgerald Castle of Kilkea in South Kildare. She had the ghosts of the Fitzgeralds about her there, even more than she had at Carton. Kilkea had the rich green plains of Kildare on one side, on another the blue and purple hills of Wicklow. There was a haunted room in the Castle where the silver was stored for safety. For no one would be interfering with it there, to risk a meeting with the Enchanted Earl, revisiting his Castle of Kilkea. The Enchanted Earl of Kildare lies buried on the Curragh, surrounded by a number of his followers who fell asleep with him. People thought that they had died. But they are only sleeping. And once, every eleven years, the Earl comes awake for so many hours, and, wasting none of them, he rides from the Curragh to Kilkea and goes up to that room which was his Countess's. The horse he rides, enchanted too, is shod with silver, and when the silver is quite worn through the spell will be broken, and the Earl will rise from sleep for ever, with his followers, and he will rule all Ireland. So the story says. And he was seen by an old countryman when he rode last—how many years ago?—and the silver then on the horse's hoofs as they flashed by (and he galloping like the wind) was no thicker than that of a threepenny bit!

So—in my lifetime, shall I yet see him rise and rule all Ireland, as a Fitzgerald should? On the Curragh of Kildare, on some green summer evening, or in an amethyst valley of the Wicklow Hills, I think that I should believe it. But I think he goes across country, keeping to the fields, avoiding the cold horror of modern tarred roads which must astonish him. So the silver would be longer wearing through!

Much of the history of Ireland looked down at Hermione from the walls of Carton, with the great Earls of Kildare and later Dukes of Leinster. In the dining-room hung the portrait of Lord Edward, the beloved rebel, who died of wounds received resisting an arrest upon a charge of high treason, on June 4, 1798. And from another frame looked out the charming face of his wife, Pamela.

Hermione had been Hermione Duncombe, Lord Feversham's eldest daughter, and she married Lord Kildare, as he then was, in 1884. (I had seen her sisters ride with their father in the Row a few years earlier.) Her name was in the Dublin Castle Drawing Room Book at which I looked the other day—as Lady Kildare, come up with Lord Kildare from the Castle of Kilkea. But she did not go very much to the Vice-regal Court.

At Carton she had her music and her garden and her parties of friends. She had very small parties, just of the people she liked. Of course, occasionally, as on the occasion of the Nuncio's visit to Ireland, she had to entertain large parties officially, with the Lord Lieutenant and other important people. We had wonderful musical evenings in that white and gold music-room which is one of the settings in which I remember her best. I would have received a summons from her and would have driven over the flat Meath roads from Killeen, in a high dog-cart, with a "tiger" and a maid clutching my suitcase behind. I would be shown into the music-room with its white gold-tooled walls, its white and gold organ and the white carved marble fireplace. Or, she would have

179

been sitting at her grand piano perhaps, playing, and would take her lovely hands from the keys as I came in, and smile, that smile of hers that always seemed to light a room. The windows of that room looked out over the formal garden to the park and the Dublin and Wicklow mountains were always blue against the sky.

I would find her there, perhaps. Or sometimes I would be shown upstairs to her own boudoir which had the same view over the park to the mountains. Next door was her bedroom —a small white room with a narrow bed like a girl's.

There were lovely things in her boudoir. I remember the Chippendale furniture, cabinets of beautiful china, many books. There was a beautiful chimney-piece with a Chippendale mirror over it, and a picture that she loved, but I think that was in her bedroom. It showed a monk leaning on a balustrading looking at a sunrise. Underneath was the inscription: "If love be dead, why dost thou rise, Oh, Sun?"

Her own portrait hung in her boudoir. It was there then. And it is the only thing left in the room now. Everything else was taken out to be sold that tragic day when fourteen pantechnicons took away most of the treasures of Carton that were not entailed. Her grand piano, at which I remember her sitting, was one of the things taken. And the music-room now is as bare as her own boudoir, with all the lovely furniture gone from it. The house is stripped of its greatest treasures. Even many of the precious books had to go. But it is still beautiful. Hermione, in that picture, was painted in a white frock of embroidered muslin and lace, the simplest thing in the world, with a sash of soft creamy yellow. Such a frock as a girl might wear to her first party. That portrait used to look down on the room when she was occupying it, and there were in it all the traces of her occupation. When they took everything else, they left the portrait, so that Hermione in her white dress and yellow sash looks down now on the empty room. And I never saw her look more beautiful!

I cannot recall many things that she said in ordinary conversation. She was rather still and dumb, I think. I remember her sitting at dinner almost silent and looking wonderfully beautiful. She said to me once:

"You have far more admirers than I have." Which was not true. If I had admirers, she had worshippers. She was like a goddess, up above them all the time. But I think she looked down on them all, although unconsciously. She was, I imagine, fully aware of her own gifts, apart from that one of her great beauty. She was very talented. Later she studied sculpture and painting—the last, under Watts.

She made at Carton the first pergola that was ever made in Ireland. When the sun shone on its red brick and the roses growing over it, it seemed to bring Italy to that Irish garden. Her initials, H.L., and the date, are worked into the paving at the entrance to the pergola. She planted snowdrops everywhere, giant snowdrops that make the grounds of Carton white and beautiful each year, as though someone had strewn snow under the trees for pleasure. There was a gardener—an elderly man now, a gardener's boy then—who was her particular assistant.

"The Duchess's boy I was called," he says. He did the work for her while she directed it. I don't think she ever put her own hands to the earth. The gardener remembers that they planted more snowdrops each year, and that every year they increased. There is a wood of silver birch, where there is a sheet of them in January, white, under the slender silver trees. Someone has tried to paint it, but such ethereal beauty is not to be caught by any paintbrush. She planted other things, blue scylla, and wild violets and many daffodils about the lake. I remember summer afternoons with her in a boat on that lake when the pink water-lilies were out, turning their solemn little faces up to us.

She adored her sister Helen, who married Sir Edgar Vincent—now Lord d'Abernon—and had much of Hermione's beauty. Someone thought of the name for the newly-married pair: "Swan and Edgar."

But Hermione said to me once that all the people she loved had been taken away from her. Helen and Edgar

Vincent were staying at Carton when they were engaged. They went out together one day towards the lake and Hermione stood looking after them. She made a little movement with her hands.

"There go two of the people I love best in the world and they have taken each other away from me," she said.

Again I remember her receiving Lord Houghton, who was not having a very easy time in Ireland during his years as a Liberal Viceroy. Not knowing the thorny pathway before him in a thorny country, he had at the very beginning done something which had set the Unionists, who represented the majority of the nobility and gentry then, against him, and there was a boycott of the Castle so far as they were concerned. He was Hermione's cousin so she must ask him to Carton. But—"I receive you as cousin, not as Viceroy," I remember her saying as he came in. And I don't think he got a curtsey from her.

They had various big parties at Carton during those years. King Edward and Queen Alexandra, then Prince and Princess of Wales, had been there during their Irish visit of 1885, although not to stay. And the Visitors' Book is full of important and interesting names. But I often stayed there when they were alone or when there were only two or three of her particular friends. Emily Lawless and her brother Freddie, who used to play the organ, Arthur Paget, Lord Elcho, whom we called "Count Hugo," Dunraven, Bully Oliphant, Bee Cloncurry, Lady Eva Bourke, now Lady Dunraven, are some of those I remember.

The Duke was always very kind to me and we got on extremely well together. One night, coming from Killeen and having been delayed on the way, I arrived late, and was shown straight into my room. It was the Chinese Bedroom which I often had, a very beautiful room on the ground floor, with an old Chinese paper on the walls and wonderful blue and gold rococo decorations. Thomas Creevey, visiting Carton, had slept in this room and praised the great canopy bed which was hung with rich Chinese embroidered curtains.

There were painted panels on the walls and much gilding. I believe the people whose business it was to strip the house later, tried to take the paper off the walls of the Chinese Bedroom. But fortunately it was not possible.

There was a Queen Anne mirror on the dressing-table. It was too small for me to see my face easily and I propped it up at the back in order to see better. Someone came in to tell me that I was late, and—already fussed—I turned quickly to speak. Something caught—the mirror crashed and was broken in pieces. I was greatly upset. I went in to dinner— they had gone on without me—and sat down beside the Duke.

I said: "Something terrible has happened."

"Nothing to the children, I hope?" he said at once in his kind way.

"Oh, no." I told him about the mirror. "It means seven years' misfortune for me, doesn't it?"

"Not for you, Lady Fingall," he assured me, smiling. "The misfortune is for the house in which it happens."

This did not make me feel any happier. I cried out against such an idea, even while he smiled and took it lightly. Within seven years he and Hermione were both dead and much trouble was to come on the house in the following years.

I used to have my breakfast in bed in that wonderful Chinese room. Sometimes some of the other guests would collect at the window and talk to me through the glass while I enjoyed my breakfast. Standing in that room the other day, I thought I could see their faces—so many of them dead now—at the window.

I saw Hermione in London, too, when we were both there. But I always thought that the Leinster town house in Hertford Street was quite unworthy of her. It was narrow and rather dark and gloomy, not such a house as Hermione needed for her setting. Perhaps partly because of the inadequacy of that house, I do not remember her taking much part in London life. But she had so little time.

I have to go on a few years to finish her story. In the winter of 1894-95 I had a flat in South Audley Street. It was before the birth of one of my children, and I was feeling rather wretched and sick. Fingall was away, and London, even with such good friends as I had, could be lonely. I remember Mrs. Jones, who was with us in London, coming in from a walk in the Park and saying:

"You can be terribly alone in London, my lady."

I felt it, looking down from my window at the street below. Carriages were passing. Sometimes people I knew. Would they stop? Occasionally they did. But often only, alas, to leave cards and go away again, unaware of the sad little face up there at the window, watching them.

One of those winter days, unexpectedly, the butler announced: "The Duchess of Leinster."

And Hermione came into the little drawing-room, which seemed so much too small for her. She was still wearing black—the Duke had died a year and a half before—and nothing ever became her beauty better. She had a bright colour in her cheeks and she was panting as if she had run up the stairs, being in such a hurry with the news she had to tell me. I never saw her colour more brilliant, but she was very thin.

"'Mione!" I jumped up. "Where have you come from?"

She had been staying with Emily Lawless and Lady Sarah Spencer at their cottage in the country outside London. She had been with them a great deal since the Duke's death, doing her sculpturing and studying painting under Watts, who lived close by.

"I must tell you," she said, as excited as a girl who has received a proposal. "You won't believe it! The Doctors have just told me that I have only a year to live; and even to live that year I must go abroad at once."

I stared at her, struck to silence. My heart was heavy, for I knew only too well that they were right.

She was crossing that night to Dublin to speak to the girls at the Alexandra School, where she had founded the Hermione Lectures.

"Only a year to live," she repeated, and that wonderful

184

smile of hers lit my wintry room as though spring had suddenly come to it. "I think I must tell the girls. Wouldn't they think it a joke?"

"'Mione," I said, "for goodness' sake don't! They might *not* think it a joke."

She could not stay, having so much to do. I never saw her again. When she had gone—leaving me for ever with that picture of her, even more brilliant and lovely in her black than I had ever seen her before—I wrote to Emily Lawless. Was it true? The answer came back. It was quite true. Indeed I had known that it was. Hermione had always had the seeds of consumption in her lovely body. They made her go abroad and then to Mentone, where she died. She did not even live the year. She died in the following March—two months before my baby was born—in the prime of her youth and beauty, for she was only thirty-one. One of her sons, Desmond, whom we all loved, was killed in the War—alas, accidentally, I believe. An unexploded bomb had fallen near him. A chaplain picked it up. It exploded and blew off the priest's hand and killed Desmond, who was standing beside him.

They brought Hermione back from Mentone and buried her in the little graveyard at Carton—a lovely place in which to lie at last. It is a blue glade in spring, with the birds singing like a choir above the graves. Hers is under a beech tree, and her own words are carved on the stone cross at her head:

"My God, I know all that Thou ordainest is for the best, and I am content."

Beside her is the Duke's grave with the stone Cross which she had designed. It has another similar Cross, laid flat on the grave, as the shadow of the standing Cross falls, when the sun shines behind it. So that there is always the shadow of the Cross over the grave.

CHAPTER FOURTEEN

In 1888 Fingall took over the Meath Hounds from Jock Trotter, and was Master until 1891, when he retired, a good deal poorer. Having the Hounds twice—he was Master again from 1908-1911—nearly ruined him.

The winters were busy for him now. He sat for hours on Sundays in that gloomy study, with the map of the cou .try before him, planning Meets, and how many hours I spent with him, moving pieces of paper on the map! He was, for all the world, like a Commander-in-Chief organising a campaign. Always with the most careful consideration for one-horse and two-horsemen, before those days of horse-boxes. Oldcastle, this Wednesday. Loughcrew, Friday. He moved his pins, altered them, remembered this one-horse man who must be thought of, and began again. So much else had to be considered. New grass, races, coursing. He tried to draw all coverts and hunt all the country. It was like working out an international complication.

I might be Mistress of Hounds by reflected rank, but I knew well I had no hope ever of attaining the distinction of the red coat, and that the most I could hope for was not to disgrace the Master. A charming wearer of it at this time was Flora Hesketh, who had been Flora Sharon from California. She and her husband had taken Somerville for the hunting. Later they took Killeen from us for a winter, and Flora declared that it was the coldest house she had ever been in, in her life.

Flora looked very well on a horse, with her neat figure and charming face. She was most attractive and had all the young men after her. She used to entertain greatly in London later at their house, 111 Piccadilly, and often entertained King Edward there. On one occasion Flora told Lady Annette La Touche that she was to meet the Prince of Wales—as King Edward was then—at dinner, and Lady Annette thought that Flora was making fun of her. And, being introduced to His Royal Highness, refused flatly to curtsey, saying, "Oh, I know you are *not* the Prince of Wales!"

I talked of Flora the other day to Sir Seymour Fortescue. He said: "What I liked was Flora's independence. If she liked you, she liked you, no matter who you were. If she didn't like you, she didn't like you, no matter who you were."

In those early hunting days in Meath she went with more courage than knowledge, and couldn't hold her horses, so that they carried her rather wildly across the country. Once, pulling hard, but unable to stop her mount, she landed on top of Harry Bourke—Lord Mayo's brother, and a great hunting man—at a double. When they were disentangled on the other side he asked her, with much good language, what the devil she thought she was doing. Flora smiled at him enchantingly.

"Well," she said. "If you will sit roo-oosting on those doubles."

It was Flora's victory.

I remember Meets at Slane and the pink coats gay against the grey old Castle walls and the brown waters of the Boyne. Galloping again in memory over the wonderful turf of Meath —even forgetting my terror for a while in that ecstasy of movement—or trotting along a road, or waiting at a covert side, I hear voices and see faces. Horace Plunkett came back from America in 1889 and started his Co-operative work tentatively, but still had time to hunt occasionally. Douglas Haig was often out those winters when he was on leave, going well and seriously, but not wildly. "He was looking after you," Olive Guthrie says. But I contradict her at once. He was too good a sportsman to lose a hunt for the sake of a woman. Hunts and battles are things that no man worthy of the name should lose for any woman.

Harry Bourke, who lived at Hayes, was a great supporter of Fingall's, and a help to him. I can't remember when it was that he said to me: "I have a friend coming to stay for hunting, and I would be most grateful if you would be nice to him. He is not good looking, but when you know him you will like him. And he is extremely clever and a great financier. His name is Sir Ernest Cassel."

I said, "Of course I will be nice to any friend of yours, Harry."

He introduced me to his friend the next day, a stout, Teutonic gentleman in a pink coat, looking rather uncomfortable in it and on his horse. But he had kind eyes, a rich voice, and was extremely charming and witty to talk to. He spoke with a very German accent. It was no effort to be nice to Sir Ernest Cassel, for he was so extraordinarily interesting —much more interesting than most of the young men. I was well rewarded for any little kindness I showed him in those hunting days by his friendship. He used to stay with the Iveaghs in Ireland, and I remember a day at Punchestown when I walked with him across the course and stood talking to him on the hill by the Big Double. He told me a lot about his life, and spoke of his great devotion to and affection for the King. He talked to me a great deal during the years of our friendship which ended only in that year when Lord Coventry and I passed Brooke House, the great house Sir Ernest had built for himself in London, and saw a doctor's car outside the door. And Coventry said: "My lady, there's no doubt the Lord is a damned good Handicapper!"

I think Sir Ernest Cassel would have agreed with him. I remember sitting beside him at dinner at his house, Moulton Paddocks, when we were staying there for the Races at Newmarket, and he told me about his life. He said to me: "Lady Fingall, I have had everything in the world that I did not want and nothing that I did."

He told me then about his marriage to the wife he had adored. He had become a Catholic for her sake. He said: "I did everything that your Church told me. I obeyed all the rules of the Church. I subscribed to their charities. But when she died"—he had had only three years—"I said, ' The Lord has not treated me fairly.'"

I said: "Oh, Sir Ernest, you cannot bargain with the Lord. You will have to come back without bargaining."

Someone told me that, at the end of Sir Ernest's life, his little brougham used to be seen outside a London convent in the mornings. So he had learnt not to bargain with the Lord, or perhaps found a better way of bargaining. He did come back, on the Lord's terms. He died a Catholic, and was buried by the Farm Street priests, with all the rites of the Church.

Sir Ernest was one of the kindest people I have ever met. Having been poor himself, he never forgot what that meant, and he was so careful that none of his guests should be allowed to pay for anything for themselves.

He was always wanting to invest money for me. If I had accepted his offers I should be very rich to-day. But finance, like other gambling, never attracted me at all.

At Moulton Paddocks he provided wonderful food for his guests which he could never eat himself. He was a hopeless dyspeptic. But he used to enjoy watching other people eating good things, and would heap their plates while he himself ate a piece of toast.

I was lunching with him one day at his house in Grosvenor Square, where he lived before he built Brooke House. It was a hot summer day, and we were offered, somewhat unsuitably, roast pork. I said tactlessly:

"Oh, Sir Ernest! *You* shouldn't touch this."

Wilfred Ashley, his son-in-law, kicked me under the table violently, and Sir Ernest said:

"And, pray, why not?"

I replied hastily: "Because it is very indigestible." But of course I had meant because he was a Jew.

His life was a sad one in many ways. During the War he, like many others, was looked upon with suspicion, and some people refused to meet him. He had a magnificent hospital, and even about that people told stories. I saw him often during the War years, as he was a great friend of my friend, Olive Guthrie, who used to ask me to lunch to meet him.

Certainly his whole feeling was for England in the War, although he had been born a German. Just after it, I was talking to him at Newmarket, and he said a strange thing. I think I was lamenting the old days and grumbling about the changes and about the weather that day. He said, putting up his hand:

"Don't grumble, Lady Fingall. Has it ever occurred to you what it would have been like here if Germany had won the War?"

"No," I said.

"Well," he said, "*I* know."

Of course he was a German Jew, and he did know.

I don't believe I needed Sir Ernest Cassel's lesson to teach me the wisdom of how little money can buy of happiness. I have always had enough and never wanted more than that. I think if there is any truth in the theory of a previous existence that I must have been very poor in my last sphere of life. For I never lie down at night without thanking Heaven for my comfortable bed and my clean sheets. Yet I have never lacked a bed, and I have always had clean sheets in this life!

Lord Zetland followed Lord Londonderry as Viceroy. The Zetlands were very kind to me, too. They were both short-sighted, and she used to give you a rather vague hand, and then, discovering you, "Why, Daisy. . . ." Once I walked over the course at Punchestown with Lord Zetland, and he fell into a ditch and emerged all covered with dust and mud. We had to slip into the enclosure by a quiet entrance before he could be brushed and cleaned, and we had some difficulty in getting past the men at the gate, who did not recognise the Lord Lieutenant. I think they accepted him in the end on my word.

Fingall liked the Zetlands, and broke, for them, his resolve of never visiting. We went to stay with them at Aske for Christmas.

"This place must be lovely in the spring," I said to Lady Zetland.

"Oh, my dear," she said, "I am sure it is. But we never see it in the spring. We have to be in London then. And then in the summer, Scotland, and in winter, South for shooting. We only get just this glimpse of Aske."

Poor prisoners of their many possessions! There were many people like them then, who were never free, and never saw their country houses at the loveliest time.

I took Constance Gore Booth to parties during the Zetland Viceroyalty. Her mother, Lady Gore Booth, was a cousin of Lady Zetland's. Constance then was a wild, beautiful girl, and all the young men wanted to dance with her. She was lovely and gay in her youth at Lissadell, hunting and dancing, and she was the life and soul of any party. She was much loved as well as admired. I remember her being at Adare, and often at the Castle. Then she went like other young ladies of her class to parties at Dublin Castle, and sometimes I chaperoned her and stayed the night with her and her mother. They had a house in Harcourt Terrace, known to an older Dublin as Joly's Buildings.

The houses of Harcourt Terrace—as it is now—were built by a French refugee named Dr. Joly, and they have a French air. The little road is like a corner of old Paris, rather shabby old Paris. Behind the one in which Constance and her mother lived—that which had been Dr. Joly's—there is an old dried-up well in the garden. Over the garden wall was a field belonging to what was once a country house, Peter Place. In that field the gentlemen of the eighteenth century used to fight their duels in the early morning.

In 1798 Lord Edward Fitzgerald, "on his keeping," was sheltered by Dr. Joly, a friend and compatriot of Lord Edward's wife, Pamela. When pursuit came near, he was hidden in the dried-up well in the garden. But the noise of the search must have reached Lord Edward there, and seemed too close to be healthy, for he left his hiding-place and climbed the wall on to the canal bank. A slow-moving canal barge was just passing. Lord Edward jumped from the bank on to it and hid himself among the cargo it carried. In this

191

manner he travelled some of the way to Thomas Street, his last hiding-place, where he was arrested and resisting, received mortal wounds.

There was a night when Constance Gore Booth and I returned to the house in Harcourt Terrace from a Castle Ball. Lady Gore Booth was in bad health at the time, and we were very careful to return quietly, not to disturb her rest. It was a little disconcerting then to find, just as the Viceregal carriage dropped us, a very intoxicated soldier in uniform clutching one of the gateposts. Constance said: "You must not make that noise. You will wake my mother." To me she said briskly: "I can always manage drunkards." And she took him by the arm and led him down to the gate, put him outside it and shut it. She had sympathy with him, even then. For he must be out without leave, and would get into trouble.

We closed the door behind us and tiptoed upstairs. We had just got into our dressing-gowns when the peace of the quiet terrace was rudely disturbed by drunken singing. Our friend had returned.

Constance never hesitated. And I could do nothing but follow her. We just stopped to throw coats hastily over our dressing-gowns, otherwise we must have died of cold, then went downstairs and out again.

"Now we'll have to take him to the canal," said Constance. She took the man by one arm and I by the other, and we walked him down to the canal bank and set him on his way to the barracks. We returned then to the house in Harcourt Terrace. Only when, upstairs again, we saw ourselves in a mirror, did the full humour of our appearance reach us. I was still wearing my tiara—which for once I had put on for that official party—and with it my dressing-gown and bedroom slippers! Constance seized paper and pencil at once, to make a sketch of me in this strange attire.

That was before she went to Paris on a small legacy left her by an aunt, to study art and live in the *Quartier Latin*. There she met her Polish Count, Casimir Markievicz, whom she married. He is in the Golden Book of Russian Nobility

192

(a lovely name for such a record!). She and Casimir came to Killeen on their honeymoon, and when they arrived, Casimir sat down at the piano in the hall and thumped the keys and roared a song to his own accompaniment.

"Con. She is mad!" He used to say in his great booming voice.

Constance was a stormy petrel from the beginning to the end. She was to command the Rebels in the Dublin College of Surgeons, during the Rebellion of 1916, and to be sentenced to death by court-martial afterwards, a sentence that was only commuted on account of her sex. Even in her last illness after the War, a Republican doctor came to fight with a Unionist doctor over her dying body.

The last time I ever saw Casimir Markievicz was at her funeral. I watched the procession pass, from the Arnotts' house in Merrion Square, where we had all had such good times in other days when that house was a centre of hospitality in Dublin; and where I remembered often Con and her husband singing and playing the piano, while the daughters of the house, Mary and Vicky, played the violin and 'cello, Casimir and his son walked immediately behind the coffin, which was carried by the Fianna Scouts, so many of whom Constance had trained. Casimir looked up and waved sadly as the tragic little cortège passed the house.

CHAPTER FIFTEEN

I FIND that in 1889 Horace Plunkett had already started his Co-operative Store in Dunsany. It was destined to be the only one in Meath. For Horace's own county was the county in which Co-operation seemed to have least success.

I was still an amateur worker in those days, although I was becoming infected by Horace's enthusiasm. It was not possible to be his neighbour and friend without becoming infected. I think I was won, almost unwillingly, to the cause by the man. This was in direct contrast to Horace, who more and more judged and chose people according to their usefulness to his work.

It is true that each year from the time I knew him first people mattered to him less and the cause more. He was a man travelling a road to a goal, his eyes and mind so fixed on the end that he had very little time to look at the hedges either side of him, or over them—unless he were likely to see something there that would help him towards the goal. Such travellers tend to become, at last, dull companions for their fellow-passengers on the journey of life.

He was in a hurry always along that road, and one felt that in him. He never walked, but always ran, and it was sometimes hard to keep up with him. When we walked at Killeen together, I used to run after him, calling: "Whoa," and hooking him with my umbrella. Certainly, as I have often said, if he had ever married, sooner or later his unfortunate wife would have been left, like a forgotten parcel, at some railway station, Horace having gone off after something that might help Co-operation! His mind kept pace with his body in that quick impatience.

Trying to consider Horace's character, I find that he is still too near. Looking at a person is like looking at a moun-

194

tain. You must have perspective. And again, like a mountain, it is the little things that you see when you are close, but in distance it is the effect of the whole, and the little things are too far away to be clear. Horace was bad about little things. For instance he never gave his friends presents. Now—this is wisdom for any man who wants it and will learn—every woman loves to get a present, just as she loves to have nice things said to her. These make the sunshine in life for her, without which she wilts like a flower in a grey sunless garden. Horace, only once, in all the years of our friendship, gave me a present. He had been in Spain with Lennox Robinson, and he brought me back the most beautiful black silk Spanish shawl, with pink and red roses embroidered on it. I wear it still on state occasions.

I said, greatly touched by this unusual thoughtfulness: "Horace, how nice of you. . . ."

He cut my thanks short, rather shamefacedly.

"I am afraid it was Lynx who thought of it!"

He was wildly generous to his causes, and every penny he had went into his schemes. A little inhuman in that, perhaps. I used to say that he would almost have taken a bottle out of a baby's mouth to put it into his creameries!

He was a difficult man to work with, but he was so attractive that those who worked with him and for him forgave him everything. He was not thinking of mere material prosperity for the Irish farmer. If his movement had been only that, he would not have got the Jesuit, Father Finlay, into it, heart and soul, or Lord Monteagle, the high-minded gentleman, or the poet and visionary A. E., who put his poetry and art into Horace's work for Ireland. Better farming, better business were only the first steps on the road. The goal, better living, . was to be spiritual as well as material. He wanted to help the Irish farmers to help themselves. But, Father Finlay said the other day, the Irish farmers did not deserve Horace. He had a wonderful way of bringing men together widely opposed in views and character. Sinclair and Andrews, the hard Northern business men, worked side by side with poets and visionaries. It was a remarkable company, at last, of business men, poets, dreamers and clerics.

I think it is true that he gave his personal affection grudgingly. I believe he gave nothing willingly except to his work, and to that he gave everything. In a sense he was a miser of his strength and affections, not hoarding them for himself, but lest he should take them from his work.

He shared another characteristic with Fingall—an absolute indifference to beauty. Neither of them had any feeling for art or for any of the loveliness of life. I believe the only thing they both admired was me—and me not often! It was no use wearing a pretty frock ever for either of them. You might wear it for ten years before they noticed it. Once Horace did notice a pretty thing I was wearing which I had often worn before. He said: "That's a lovely frock. . . ." And, all in one breath, before I had had time to be pleased at this rare triumph: "Go away, little woman. You are disturbing us!"

Nor had they any feeling for music, and Fingall, I think, positively disliked flowers, while there was only one flower that I ever knew Horace to notice—heliotrope.

"If I come to the garden with you," Fingall used to say, "will you promise not to pick, or weed?"

My collaborator, who knows me, comments:

"Well, he might be excused that."

When Fingall was ill, and people brought him flowers, he would wait politely until they had gone, and then ask for the flowers to be removed. He did not know one tune from another, and once in London when I took him to hear Patti sing, he slept through the whole performance, only waking up at the end when she was singing: "Home Sweet Home."

"That's ' God Save the Queen,'" he said with great relief.

There was one song that Horace liked: "Way Down by the Swanee River." But he liked it because it reminded him of his days in America and the negroes singing in the evening. I only remember one verse of poetry that he ever quoted; and that he liked, too, for a reason:

"Ah, Love! could thou and I with Fate conspire
To grasp this sorry Scheme of Things entire,
Would not we shatter it to bits—and then
Re-mould it nearer to the Heart's Desire!"

He applied it to his Co-operation, and so it pleased him. But that had nothing to do with the quality of the poetry.

We sat in the old library upstairs those evenings with the ghosts whispering about us, and we talked Co-operation. And I dare say the 4th Earl, in his blue coat, stood sometimes in the shadows to listen to us.

Fingall stuck to his original view, although he was prepared loyally to help Horace in every way. I suppose I had begun tentatively trying to do things for the cottage people, to improve their breed of fowl, and give them plants and seeds for their gardens, and so on. For Fingall disapproved of that, although he did not interfere with me. "How would you like it if Mrs. ——"—he mentioned a lady, famous in Meath for her interfering habits—"told you that your delphiniums were the wrong colour, or that your fowl were not the right kind, and that you ought to have Wyandottes instead of Sussex?"

It was fine of Fingall, thinking like that, to support Horace as he did. He gave up his best paddock to be an orchard. But what with caterpillars and pests and early frosts in May, though we sprayed and painted and dug as the Department directed, we had no luck with our orchards. I grew tobacco, too, in the garden. It smelt lovely in the evening, but that was all I got out of it.

All the time Fingall was shaking his head over our efforts. "You should not give the Irish anything that they do not ask for."

I think now that Fingall was right, probably. He always was right, I believe.

CHAPTER SIXTEEN

WHEN Fingall gave up the Hounds in 1891, it was to the famous John Watson. Now, while it was his horses that Fingall loved best, John Watson adored his Hounds. All the Watsons were great Hound men. There is a portrait in the possession of the family, of John Watson's father, Robert Watson, "The Old Master," with a hound on his knee. The hound is looking up at his god with adoring eyes. The deep-set eyes, the expression of dog and man are amazingly similar. Men who live in sympathy with horses or hounds for a great part of their lives usually come to look like them. The breed of hounds sent out into the world by old Robert Watson made the Quorn and the Pytchely, and all the famous English packs.

Fingall was always saving his horses. He was a rider who rode absolutely in sympathy with the living flesh and nerve between his knees, and always aware of it. But I saw John Watson handling his horses ruthlessly, almost savagely. He was the cruellest man with a horse that I have ever seen; and I have never seen a man so strong. He had a way of wrapping his great legs round his horse as he rode it at a fence or a bank, seeming almost able to lift a tired horse over. He would ride a horse till it dropped, to get to his hounds. A lame horse or a tired horse, he would always get them there. Out hunting he was a dour, silent, unsociable man. He hated women in the hunting field, and hardly ever spoke to them, although sometimes he glared at one if she got in his way. "I wish they'd go home and do their knitting," he used to mutter. . . .

John Watson's language in the hunting field was notorious. A man who hunted in Warwickshire after Meath and got cursed by the Master, Lord Willoughby de Broke, said to him: "You may save yourself the trouble, my lord. I have just been hunting in Meath with John Watson. And anything you could say sounds to me only like the twittering of a bird on the bough!"

Once I rode some way home with John Watson at the end of a hunting day. It was an evening of grey spring twilight, the quietness unbroken except for the singing of birds and the sound of the horses' hoofs on the white road. I think John Watson only spoke once on that ride, and then he pointed with his whip over a low hedge, beyond which there was a field with young lambs playing in it.

"Look at those damned lambs," he said.

To him that sight only meant that hunting was over.

Yet summer had its compensations for him. For he was mad about polo. And his language at polo was appalling. He introduced the game to America, and I have seen at Meadowbrook, Long Island, photographs of John Watson and the ponies he took out with him. But whereas in England polo had been an amusement, a game played by poor soldiers on such ponies as they could afford, the Americans made a business of it, and a rich man's business. John Watson had taken out a number of ponies with him, and they were all bought from him at good prices and remained in America.

The Watsons came from Ballydarton in Carlow where "the Old Master" kept his own pack of hounds and lived for his hunting. They were distant cousins of the Earls of Rockingham, a title now extinct. But when the last Earl died, it was discovered that a possible claim to the Castle might be put forward by the Irish Watsons. (Oliver Cromwell had besieged Rockingham Castle and failed to take it.) A neat young lawyer travelled to Ballydarton to acquaint Mr. Watson with this fact. He travelled by night, *via* Dublin, and so arrived at Ballydarton in Carlow in the middle of the morning. It was a spring morning (or so I have imagined it, seeing the picture as the story was told to me), such a day as only Ireland can show—a blue sky with floating white clouds, green, softly curving hills lying against it, early gorse lighting the landscape like many lamps and fires. Ballydarton was the usual Irish country house of some dignity, with pillars in front and a long, straggling, rather untidy avenue. The house probably would have needed some painting and repairing. There had been great hospitality there—open housekeeping, which must have reduced the family fortunes. The big table in the dining-room was often spread with cold meats for hunt breakfasts, and Mrs. Watson had a special and very secret recipe for corned beef, which was famous. She never imparted it to any one, and it died with her.

That day there were horses and hounds on the gravel sweep in front of the house. And the "Old Master" was getting up on to his horse (he was rather heavy now, and it was a bit of a heave) when the young lawyer drove up. The Master's coat was old and faded from much good service. He looked surprised at this unexpected visitor as the car turned round before the door.

The lawyer had to hurry, realising that the business of hunting might not wait for any one. He had almost to hold the Master while he explained. He had come to tell him that, Lord Rockingham, being dead, Mr. Watson might put in a claim for Rockingham Castle in Leicestershire, one of the loveliest places in England, and one which Cromwell couldn't take.

When he had finished speaking there was a moment's silence. The "Old Master" was looking at his hounds and at his horses and beyond, to his own fields and the lovely colour of the country unrolling to the hills.

"Young man, what would I be wanting," he asked presently, bringing his gaze back to the puzzled face of the lawyer, "with an English Castle, when I have Ballydarton and the best Hounds in Ireland?"

And he rode off with his hounds, leaving the lawyer staring after him.

Tradition lingers in a life that does not greatly change. The essentials of Irish hunting life are the same—even though women ride astride and a curl may be seen under a bowler hat, and horse boxes and cars wait in the villages to

BALLYDARTON.

SIR HORACE PLUNKETT IN HIS DE DION BOUTON

The first motor car ever brought to Ireland.

carry hunting men and women and their horses home swiftly to the hot baths and warm stables that await them. But there are still in Ireland many people who hunt in the old-fashioned way—having very little money to spend and getting more enjoyment, perhaps, than those who spend a great deal— hacking their horses to a Meet and home after the day, in twilight, or under a moon, with the country for company or another rider like themselves.

In such a way someone I know rode home the other day, with a groom who had once served John Watson. No one keeps the atmosphere of the past and can re-create it better than those men who have talked and listened all their lives— in stables, where the soft warm breath of the horses filling the air makes talking easy, or at some cross-roads where they wait with other grooms to give up second horses or take tired horses home.

My friend, riding quietly in semi-twilight, content after the hard day, listened.

"A terrible man," the groom said of John Watson, and after a pause: "But you could *live* with him." So expressive a phrase that there is nothing more to say, for, after all, the world is divided into those people with whom one may live, and those with whom it is impossible to live at all! He told his stories of John Watson. He liked his horses wise, he said, and wouldn't have one under ten years old. "And my heels were worn out pushing them along the road. But Mr. Watson had only to come into sight and to call them, and they were all leppin' on their hind legs, like two-year-olds."

I think I was probably relieved when Fingall gave up the Hounds, although I had enjoyed being "Mistress," and the position it gave me. I knew every one in the hunting field now, and in after years, in the most surprising circumstances and places, many many miles from Meath, I met people who had hunted over our country, and were kind enough to remember that I had been pleasant to them.

I was in London for most of the winter of 1890-91. The

Jamesons then had a flat in Albert Gate, and I stayed with them first and later had a flat of my own. It must have been summer when I had my own flat, for I used to ride Douglas Haig's Arab ponies with him in the Park. And I remember the charm and gaiety of the Row those early summer mornings. The ponies would be brought round to the back of Albert Gate, and one got up in the passage and rode straight into the Park, without going through the streets. The ponies were often very fresh. Douglas' friends and brother officers used to come, too, sometimes. John Vaughan and "Stodger" Carew and others. Often I had a whole cavalry brigade with me on those morning rides. It used to be great fun to frighten me by galloping up behind me, when the ponies, thinking they were playing polo, would dash off, and I would have no chance at all of holding mine. A joke for them, but not for me. I remember going round and round the Park on the fresh ponies. Once or twice I saw a runaway horse, a much more serious and dangerous thing in the Row, with its limited space, than in any fields.

In March, 1891, Mrs. Willie and I were in Paris. We were staying at the Hotel Brighton, where the wife of the proprietor was an Irishwoman who had been born at Drumree. Because of this association she treated us like royalty and was always ready to advise us where to go and what to see and so on. I don't know why she sent us to a fortune teller. But she knew a wonderful woman who was supposed really to tell you the future. I expect we went for the fun of it. We were to take with us, she told us, a hair of a living person in whom we were interested. Not so easy, unless one was in the habit of carrying about a collection of hair! But we were hurrying back to England to see Willie's horse, Come Away, run in the Grand National. And Mrs. Willie had some hairs from Come Away's tail which she was going to have put in a locket if he won. I also had an interest in Cloister, who was running in the same race. We had bred him at Killeen, by Ascetic out of Grace II.

Henrietta produced the hairs in the room where the

fortune-teller sat, with the usual paraphernalia of crystals and curtains and semi-darkness.

The woman took them in her hands.

"*Mais mon Dieu!*" she said, staring at them. "*Ces ne sont pas les cheveux d'une personne.*" Then she looked into the crystal. "*Ah! C'est un cheval!*" She proceeded to describe Come Away minutely, even to the white hairs in his tail. "But," she said, "he has his legs in buckets. They are rubbing them." After a pause: "*Mais il gagnera tout le même.*"

We returned to the hotel, certainly greatly intrigued. There we found the afternoon post and a letter from Willie. Come Away had almost broken down. But they had been rubbing his legs with whisky and hoped to run him all the same. We hurried back to see the Grand National. Remembering the fortune teller, "He will win," I put a moderate bet on him and backed Cloister as well. That was the year when Come Away won the Grand National on three legs, with Harry Beasley up, and with twenty-one starters and the odds 4-1 against. I wished afterwards that I had had more confidence in the crystal and had risked a larger bet! Cloister, who was to win the National in 1893, ran in the same race and was second. He belonged to Lord Dudley then. When he won in 1894 it was in the shortest time and with the heaviest weight—12 stone, 7 pounds—in the National, up to date. We had bred him at Killeen in 1884, and he was sold as a foal at foot with his dam, for thirty guineas. He was twice second in the Grand National, and won many other races.

CHAPTER SEVENTEEN

SOME time in 1891 I had the only quarrel that I can remember with Fingall. The occasion of it was a Meeting at Navan to which Parnell came to speak. I insisted on going to hear him, which I did—from the upper window of the tailor's shop of Mr. Cooney, who made clothes for the Hunt servants. It was the second and last time that I ever saw the Irish leader. My memory of Parnell that day is that he looked like a sick eagle. I have never forgotten his tragic face while he was speaking, with obvious effort, for over an hour. It poured with rain, and the wet street of the grey country town made a sad background for the scene. The people seemed to me very apathetic.

There was another day in the autumn of that year, when it rained again and the wind howled about the walls of Killeen, and I sat in the dark study, hardly able to bear it. It was a terrible day, with thunder and lightning, and heartbreak in the air, as though the sky were weeping. The next day I heard that Parnell had died at Brighton. What an unfitting place for the death of the Uncrowned King of Ireland!

He had crossed to England against the wishes of his doctor, as he had gone to the Meeting at Creggs that Sunday before he died.

"If I do not go they will say that I am dead."

He had held his last meeting in the National League Rooms in Dublin on the Monday and had taken the boat afterwards. He was a sick man and wanted to be with the woman he loved. A week later, on the 6th of October, he died in her arms.

Fingall at this time was in America with Horace, and homesick as always to get back to Killeen. "I can't tell you how glad I am to get back," he writes on October 9th, 1891, from Omaha, telling me that they were sailing on the 21st on the *Teutonic*, "the best boat afloat. . . . As to the usefulness of our expedition, we have of course seen many people and learnt much. Horace, I think, sees his way to some plan of operations. Personally I can't say that I am so favourably impressed with the overwhelming advantages to Patrick that this country offers, as to induce me to take a very active part in promoting his transplantation. Horace is most energetic and never happy unless at a fever pitch. I shall be in no hurry to start upon another expedition with him."

He refers to their being "pestered with reporters" at St. Paul's.

"I sent you a couple of papers from there, and I dare say you were able to imagine what we had actually told them and what they took out of their own heads. I now enclose a slip from yesterday's Omaha paper and have asked the man there to enclose you another that appeared *before* I had ever got there."

The paragraph said: "The Earl was a sandy-complected under-sized gent, in a pair of check pants. (He never possessed such things!) There was a Ball, and the Earl danced. He paid no attention to time or music; but he was an Earl!"

On the same visit, a small American girl, being told that "the Lord" was coming to stay, asked: "Do we say our prayers to him?"

From now on we were very busy with a lot of things. The Congested Districts Board had been established. Arthur Balfour had started the Light Railways to open up the inland parts of Ireland. Harbours were being built and new bridges, roads that often led nowhere, and piers that were of no earthly use.

Lord Zetland, the Viceroy, opened a new road from Galway to Carna, and my sister and I went to stay with a Connemara priest, Father Tom Flannery, for the occasion. It was Father Flannery's road, given by the Government in response to his eloquent representations. Father Tom was full of schemes. He was the typical Irish priest of his day—a benevolent tyrant, inspired with zeal for his people, the director, temporal and spiritual, of his flock.

During that visit, as I went for a walk by a mountain road, suddenly out of a little cabin that seemed part of the rock a young man came forth, dressed in the white flannel they made in the district. He rather frightened me—he was so tall to have come out of such a tiny house.

I said, "Good-morning," to him, and he said, "Good-morning, Miss."

I went on then, looking round: "This is a very poor country."

It was, he agreed.

"But you have a good priest," I said.

He answered: "Yes, God be praised. And he never turned any man into a goat on *this* mountain!"

I was so amazed that I had nothing to say.

We went on to Carna by the newly-made road, where I opened a knitting industry started by some good young women from Liverpool. I said to the carman who was to drive us, when ordering him the night before, "You won't be late?"

"I'll be there, Miss, when the night kisses the dawn," he answered.

I paid some visits during those years. I drove over to Carton to stay with Hermione Leinster. I went to London once or twice to the Jamesons at Princes Gate, and up to the North to the Londonderrys at Mount Stewart.

It was on one of my first visits to Mount Stewart that I arrived early and was sitting with Lady Londonderry in the hall while she gave me the list of my fellow-guests.

"Amongst others," she told me, "there is a clever lawyer from Dublin, whom C. thinks may be useful." Presently the door at the end of the hall opened and a face appeared. I said under my breath, "Oh, my dear, what an awful face!"

Lady Londonderry went to the door and shook hands with her guest and brought him back to introduce him. "Mr.

Carson. . . . Lady Fingall says you have an awful face," she told him.

Ever after, whenever we met, Carson reminded me: "She says I have an awful face." I believe if we ever meet in the next world he will say the same thing!

Carson, "the clever young lawyer from Dublin," *was* useful, and we were often asked to meet him. He never lost his brogue—he could not cast that off as easily as he did his native part of Ireland—and I was at Mount Stewart when the news came that the Londonderrys had succeeded in having him made Solicitor General. He was in England, and Lady Londonderry wanted to let him know at once, so we discussed how she could convey the news in a telegram without making it public while it was still officially secret.

Another guest, Mrs. Mulhall, wife of Lord Londonderry's Private Secretary, Johnny Mulhall, said: "Why not wire ' Wan Solicitor'?" Which was done. And Mr. Carson understood.

Mount Stewart was a delightful place to meet people. It held space, peace and tranquillity, and it was possible to meet great men—and even Royalty—much more simply and easily there, than anywhere else. Kind Edward and Queen Alexandra paid a Royal visit in 1903, when there was such a large party that some of the guests had to be put up in tents. Queen Alexandra wrote in the Visitors' Book: "Beautiful place, but very damp."

At one time England was ruled largely from the quiet and dignified rooms at Mount Stewart. All the great statesmen of the time came there, and Lady Londonderry was a wonderful hostess.

The drawing-room was very Victorian, with antimacassars on the chairs, and there were tall screens and palms and chairs arranged tête-à-tête, or in groups, so that you could talk intimately and have good conversation. There was such good talk then and wit.

Lady Londonderry had not much taste or feeling for beauty in the furnishing of a house or in dress. She usually wore black or white herself. "It takes so much less trouble," she said. But she loved books and flowers, and there were always masses of them in her rooms. At Wynyard, their house in the North of England, she had a "Garden of Friendship." It was as beautiful and peaceful as its name. The flowers there—Rosemary, Pansies, Love-in-a-Mist, Violas and such things—had each been planted by her friends.

My maid, Miss Devereux, has interesting memories of the way in which big houses were run in those days. There was a most strict etiquette for the staff. People like the Londonderrys lived "like Royalty," she says. The House Steward at Mount Stewart she described as "like something out of an old picture." And there was a stately Housekeeper, who wore grey alpaca in the morning and black silk in the evening. She was a widow with two children, and was allowed to bring them up in the house with her. The housemaids seemed to have been kept somewhat like novices in a convent! They were not allowed to go out alone, and every Sunday evening they must put on their bonnets and go to Service in the Chapel. The visiting ladies' maids, as in every other grand house, took the rank of their mistresses. They dined in the Steward's Room with the Housekeeper, waited on by a footman. There was a very large bedroom, divided up into cubicles, for visiting ladies' maids.

Miss Devereux describes Theresa, Lady Londonderry, as "Very pompous," but her daughter, Lady Helen, "every one loved."

I came to know the Londonderrys better at their own home. Lord Londonderry was a great gentleman. He was not very clever, but did the right thing by instinct, and after all, that is the best way to do it. Lady Londonderry was a wonderful woman, with her masculine brain and warm feminine temperament. The best and staunchest friend in the world, she would back you up through thick and thin. In love with Love, she was deeply interested in the love affairs of her friends, and very disappointed if they did not take advantage of the opportunities she put in their way. She used to say of herself: "I am a Pirate. All is fair in Love and War," and woe betide any one who crossed her in either of these! Like a Queen of France, she had a private understanding with the Almighty as to what people in her position could or could not do!

She was very handsome. If she had been a shade taller, she would have been quite perfect. Somebody told me that when the Shah of Persia came to England and saw Lady Londonderry, he wanted to buy her. I don't know if he inquired about her price! But I think if he had carried through the purchase he would have found that he had met his match!

She had wonderful jewellery and looked magnificent when she wore it for her parties at Londonderry House, and stood at the top of the great staircase to receive her guests. Sometimes I was allowed to stand behind my host and hostess on these occasions and watch the procession of "fair ladies and great men" coming up the stairs, the men in uniform for an official reception, the women beautifully dressed and wearing their jewels. It was a pageant to remember.

Whenever I went to London, for many years, I always "reported" at Londonderry House soon after my arrival, and was asked to some of their smaller parties. At Mount Stewart I met most interesting people. I remember, among others, Sir Michael Hicks Beach (Black Michael, as he was called then) Chancellor of the Exchequer and afterwards Lord St. Aldwyn, one-time Chief Secretary of Ireland—a dark man, who loved Ireland in his cold way; Ronald McNeill, afterwards Lord Cushendun, a political follower of Lady Londonderry's; Edmund Gosse, a great friend of mine later on, who wrote the Life of his father, which somebody called "Gosse and Gossoon." Lord Charles Beresford and his wife I met there, too. We were also fellow-guests on another occasion, at Wynyard, where one night Lady Charles as usual, came down to dinner very late and rather decolletée and painted. Lord Charles exclaimed: "Here comes my little clipper with her decks cleared and a fresh coat of paint!"

Another fellow-guest at Mount Stewart was Lord Chief Justice O'Brien—"Peter the Packer"—who later took Castletown in Kildare and hunted from there. There is a good story told of him, that, being knocked out in a hunting accident, he woke to find his head on the knees of the beautiful Mary Greer, and exclaimed: "Tell my dear wife that I begged her forgiveness!"

Arthur Balfour was at Mount Stewart, too, on some visit of mine. I never knew him well and was afraid of him, but admired him from a distance. He seemed cold and aloof, and was, I think, more philosopher than politician. He always saw both sides of every question and so was rarely absolutely convinced, seeing the other side too much to be bigoted about his own. In politics you must be bigoted if you wish to make others follow you. I don't think he ever liked the Irish or understood them.

Lady Londonderry had not the name of being politically broad-minded; but I always thought she was, because she frequently chose for her friends those who were in the opposite camp. For instance—myself, whom she knew to be a " Rebel " and a Papist, and Horace Plunkett, for whom she had a real affection, although she disliked all his working schemes for Ireland; and George Wyndham, to whom she was always attached, although they could not have agreed politically.

She was a great yachtswoman, and Willie Jameson and his charming wife were frequently at Mount Stewart, Willie helping Theresa to sail her little boat on the very dangerous Strangford Lough, where afterwards a number of the Mount Stewart servants were drowned on a disastrous boating trip.

I had been there just before that tragedy, and my maid of those days was very much annoyed when I told her that I had to go away the day before this yachting expedition which had been arranged for the household. Seeing the disappointment in her face, I told her that if she liked she could remain behind and follow me. But—still nursing her grievance a little—she preferred to come. Fortunately for her, as all the others were drowned.

Londonderry and I were both bad sailors and used to feel sick even going across that short strip of water to Bangor.

Once, going to Mount Stewart, I travelled to the North, *via* Carlingford Lough and Newry, and as I drove through the town I noticed the great number of churches in it, and said to the jarvey:

"What a religious people they must be here!"

"God bless your soul, ma'am," he answered. "Sure, it's not religion at all—it's shpite!"

Another time I arrived at Mount Stewart before my host and hostess, who had left the housekeeper and governess to receive me. I was met by the grandchildren, who gave me a warm welcome. We became good friends, but somehow it transpired that I was a Roman Catholic. We had a pillow fight then, between Papists and Heretics. I think I won. The next morning the children rushed in to their grandparents and said: "Oh, Pa " (as they always called him), "there's such a nice lady staying here. We think her name is Mrs. Fingle, but they *do* say she is a Roman Catholic, and we never thought we would see one in *this* house."

I was always called "Mrs. Fingle" ever after, and Lord Londonderry thought this a great joke.

My hosts were most particular to send me and my maid on Sundays to Mass at the beautiful little Chapel at Newtownards, built by a Catholic Lady Londonderry. And great care was taken to give me abstinence fare on Fridays, which I often secretly regretted, as I had no excuse to avoid abstaining!

At Dublin Castle once, I remember on a Friday night sitting beside Lord Beauchamp, who was very High Church and *would* discuss religion with me. I said: "Why don't you come over to us? At present you are neither fish, flesh nor good red herring." He looked at me, eating a very uninteresting egg, while he was enjoying a quail.

"No," he said thoughtfully. "I could never be a Catholic. There is too much to swallow and too little to eat!"

I went again lately to Mount Stewart on a lovely autumn day, to visit the charming younger generation; but alas! to me the place was changed. Even apart from one's arrival. We used to come, driving from Newtownards in a leisurely carriage. Now one flies in a car along the motor road from Belfast. I came a little early and was left for some time alone in the big drawing-room, where the splendid picture of Castlereagh in his magnificent robes seemed to dominate the place. So alive seemed his fine profile that I began to feel that he could speak and that presently he would, and would tell me the truth about his tragic end.

The room had been changed. All the screens and little cosy nooks had disappeared, and you saw the full length of it now with its pillars and beautiful pictures and the rather austere furnishing. But there could be no opportunity of conversation in such a room that every one could not hear.

When my hostess came, I turned to her: "Did Nellie ever see this?"

"Oh," she said, "she did. She arrived unexpectedly after we had altered it."

"What did she say?"

"She looked round the room. Then she said: ' Some people like to live in a Barrack! *I* don't! '"

I could hear Theresa saying it.

We went out into the garden. There had been, I seemed to remember, very little garden about the house—just the terrace and the wide lawns and then woods that had been full of bluebells and primroses in spring. Now there were many statues and rare plants with crazy paths between. They had cut down some of the trees, which were probably too close to the house. It is only the mind of another generation. Mine found so much to look at in the new garden that it grew tired. I missed the peace and beauty of those velvet lawns and the woods with the silver Lough water showing between the trees, and the great cedar trees beneath which big men talked about big things in peace and intimacy. Are there any to replace them now?

We went in to tea, where presently Lord Clydesdale joined us in flying clothes and goggles, having just landed close by in his plane. And the following day the whole party went off, by air, to Germany.

We went to London in the winter of 1893, because our agent had again ordered us to economise. So Killeen was let and we took a flat in Ashley Gardens, consisting of a first-floor and basement. Maude Valerie White, who lived next door, called it "Fingall's Cave."

We had most interesting people above us—Mr. and Mrs. Henry Lucy. He was the famous "Toby, M.P.," of *Punch*, and as the Lucys and Horace Plunkett had stayed together with Cecil Rhodes at Groote Schuur, we soon came to know each other. They gave wonderful dinner-parties, to which many distinguished and interesting people came. People said that no M.P. dared refuse one of Toby's invitations, for fear of being pilloried in *Punch*. The guests at those dinners used to be asked to write their names on the tablecloth, and afterwards Mrs. Lucy would go over the signatures in red embroidery and make them permanent. I wonder what has happened to those historic tablecloths.

One night I was sitting beside Arthur Balfour, when in the middle of dinner a curious-looking little man suddenly appeared the other side of the table, facing me. His hair was combed over his forehead and he looked like a French *voyou*. I said to my neighbour: "Who on earth is that?"

He told me: "That is Phil May, a wonderful artist, and if you are nice to him he may draw you a picture on the back of your fan."

I was. And he did draw a picture for me—not in his usual style—of ladies dancing a minuet on the white satin of my fan. Alas! I lost the fan.

Another night Horace gave a dinner at his flat in Mount Street and asked Flora Hesketh and the Lucys. When Flora came into the room, Toby M.P. was standing with his back to the fire. He had wonderful white hair which stood up from his forehead, rather like a coxcomb. Flora ran at him in her impulsive way: "I must, I must!" We wondered what

213

she was going to do. She ran her fingers through his hair. "It is so soft!" she explained. "Not your head—your hair!"

While we were at Ashley Gardens, Fingall hunted fairly regularly with the Whaddon Chase. Then he had a very bad hunting accident which left him unconscious for quite a long time. He had hurt the base of his skull, and the doctor said that he must have a long sea voyage before he could recover. So he went to Australia with my cousin Norbert Keenan, and I was left alone at Ashley Gardens.

The Lucys were very good to me during this time, and I was often at their parties. One day a message came down asking if I would like to come up and meet a very interesting man. When I went into their drawing-room, there were two men standing beside the fireplace, one tall, with a face like a mastiff, the other small, and rather like a little Irish terrier. He was gazing up at the bigger one, exactly like a small dog admiring a great one. They hardly noticed me at all when we were introduced and went on talking. The word I heard was "Empire, Empire, Empire." They also talked about King Solomon's Mines, and where they were located—a thrilling subject for me.

These two were Cecil Rhodes and "Dr. Jim."

It struck me then and on other occasions—I was to meet Cecil Rhodes also at the Rothschilds—that he was more interested in the old gold of King Solomon and the possibility of discovering this than in the new gold mines. He wanted money, not for its own sake, but because it meant power. He was tremendously interested in Ireland, and at this time, in the Irish Party, which he wanted to back his South African schemes.

Again at the Lucys I sat beside Sir Francis Jeune, the famous Divorce Judge. I felt rather shy of him and, trying to make conversation, stuttered:

"Sir Francis, you must see a lot of the seamy side of life?"

"Oh, yes, my dear lady," he said. "But not half as much as they see in the Probate Court! People don't break their hearts nearly as much for love as they do for money!"

It was a very interesting time for me. Horace was now in the House of Commons, representing South Dublin. I often listened to the Debates, had tea on the Terrace and dined at the House. One day in the Ladies' Gallery, I was introduced by Lady Londonderry to a charming old lady sitting beside me—Mrs. Gladstone.

She said as we talked and she discovered that I was Irish: "Of course, Lady Fingall, you are a Home Ruler!"

"Oh, no, Mrs. Gladstone," I answered. "You see, I *live* in Ireland!"

I heard Gladstone speak on the Home Rule Bill. His words came like a torrent. He never hesitated, and the fire that was behind his speech showed in his eyes. You could not help being carried away by him, no matter what your convictions were. Then I heard David Plunket—later Lord Rathmore—making some of his witty speeches, the effect greatly helped by his stutter. While he was Commissioner of Works, a Labour M.P., looking a little dishevelled and dirty, got up to protest about people bathing naked in the Serpentine (that was long before the days of Mr. Lansbury's Lidos!) and invited the Commissioner to come with him and see the disgraceful sight for himself. David Plunket replied: "I must b-b-beg to be excused from g-g-going on a b-b-bathing expedition with the Honourable Member."

I sat next Joe Chamberlain at one of Horace's dinners at the House. He hated the Irish, ever since he had been let down by O'Shea in the Parnell days. There had been a stormy debate that evening, with the Irish very noisy and Tim Healy in his best form of vitriolic wit.

I said laughingly as we talked about it: "After all, Mr. Chamberlain, we Irish are the salt of the earth."

He replied acidly: "Yes, and should be in the same quantity as the garlic in a salad."

My countryman, Bob Martin of Ross, was also in the House. He always wore a monocle and spoke with a perfect English accent. When—being poor—he had married a rich widow, he had said that he preferred "the Union to the workhouse." One day some wild man got up and proposed that every Irish Member should in future prefix his name by "O" or "Mac." Bob Martin came in to dinner afterwards and called loudly: "Waiter, bring me some *MA*Caroni *O'*Gratin."

I came to know Baroness Burdett-Coutts—a very old lady now—during this time, and she was very kind to me. She was a great friend of Cardinal Manning's and "the poor man's Cardinal" helped her with her work amongst the poor Irish on her East End property. Her husband, who was much younger than she and had been her secretary, was devoted to her and never failed in his attentions. He also was most kind, and often drove me out to their country villa, Holly Lodge, at Highgate. He always drove hackneys, which he and Frederick Wrench had introduced into the North of Ireland, thereby ruining the breed of thoroughbred horses there. I hated hackneys, as they seemed to put their feet down where they took them up, and shook one's liver horribly. I christened this pair "Podopphlin" and "Carter."

The Baroness entertained a great deal in her fine house at the corner of Stratton Street and Piccadilly, which was full of beautiful things. The big drawing-room was walled with cases of wonderful china. I remember the Baroness herself as a small, thin old lady who wore black and a good deal of lace and heavy, good jewellery. She used to entertain the Duchess of Teck and Princess May often, and I met the Duchess there. She was so charming and simple and talked to me about the Catholic religion, in which she was much interested. She told me that she was most proud of the Stuart side of her ancestry. She was very fat and so good humoured. Once she visited Andrew Carnegie, the great philanthropist, at Skibo Castle, and wanting to see the view from the roof, went up the spiral staircase inside one of the towers. The staircase grew narrower as it ascended and the little girl of the house, standing at the foot, watching anxiously, whispered to someone, not realising the unusual accoustic properties of the tower: "Fat Moll will *stick*."

216

A cheerful voice called back, "Fat Moll *has* stuck!"

The Baroness was the first great English hostess to entertain actors and actresses. In her drawing-room I met Henry Irving, looking like Hamlet off the stage. He had a beautiful voice and always talked as if he were still acting. W. B. Yeats' way of talking reminds me of him. I also met Ellen Terry. She had a charming mobile face, beautiful gestures and a wonderful voice. And the great Sarah, with her green, deep-set eyes and shock of red-gold hair, I met there too. With her slim figure and the long, clinging garments she wore, she was really like a Garbo of her time. Only her voice was more beautiful. It was a deep golden voice and so clear, although it had not the softness and feeling of Ellen Terry's which could make you cry.

Another friend I made at this Ashley Gardens period was Pearl Mary Craigie, who wrote as "John Oliver Hobbes." I met her first at the Lucys when she was collaborating with George Moore. She was most attractive, without being beautiful, and very clever. A little later she and George Curzon became great friends and I saw a good deal of them both when I was in South Audley Street the following year. He was one of the rising young men of the day and was well described as "George Nathaniel Curzon, a most superior person." We all thought at one time that Curzon was going to marry Pearl Craigie. If he had, I believe he would have been Prime Minister. Soon after, he did marry—the lovely American, Mary Leiter, who made such a beautiful Vicereine of India. When I met them both at a dinner party given for them by Mrs. Craigie, I thought Lady Curzon one of the most beautiful women I had ever seen in an age of beauty. I remember especially her fine forehead and wonderful eyes.

That winter I moved into a flat in South Audley Street. It was on the third floor and from my back windows I had a view of the trees in the Park. I had various great friends including the Coventrys and Horace Plunkett, living close by. In the same street lived Mrs. Winslow and her lovely daughters, who were, I believe, the first exponents of Christian Science in London. They had a charming flat and gave wonderful food at their parties. The peach-fed hams attracted me—and some other people—rather more than the Christian Science, I fear! Arthur Balfour used to go there and Lord Dunraven, the last, I think, disbelieving. And there I first met Mrs. George Keppel. She was very clever and good looking and always so pleasant to every one, which was one of her great assets.

Many of my friends afterwards joined that comfortable and happy faith, and there are now eleven or twelve churches in London alone. I, too, tried to believe that there was no sickness or death, but found that when pain and unhappiness came to the door, Christian Science fled out of the window!

Lord Rowton was also a very good friend. He used to take me to see his Rowton Houses. I wanted very much to spend a night in one of them, dressed, of course, in my housemaid's clothes, but he would not let me. He said, "You will see things that you will never forget and bring away a great deal more than you take!"

Mrs. Craigie was very anxious to meet him and I invited them both to lunch one day. They got on extremely well—so well that for some time I never saw either of them and felt rather neglected.

I discovered afterwards that Pearl Craigie was writing a novel about Disraeli, and that she was getting all the information she could from Rowton about his ex-chief, which she used for the book. When next he did come to see me, he was very bitter about this and I gave him no sympathy.

"Serve you right!" I said.

One of those days I was walking with Lord Coventry through the gardens of Mount Street, when he drew my attention to a spruce little lady just ahead of us. He whispered to me:

"Do you know who that is?"

"No."

He told me. It was a very celebrated lady called "Skittles";

one of the few of her profession in England who had a position as such ladies had in France. She had a salon and insisted on the gentlemen who attended it, appearing *en grande tenue* as to a diplomatic party.

While we were talking I caught a glimpse of her face, which was neither young nor beautiful. Then she went in through the door of Farm Street Church.

Coventry continued: "A very serious situation has arisen —that lady has a number of compromising letters from some very important men. It is urgent that they should be destroyed before they can get into dangerous hands."

"Is she a Catholic?" I asked, remembering that she had gone into the church.

"Yes. I believe a convert, and very devout."

I said, "Then we must find out who is her Father Confessor and he will get the letters and see that they are destroyed." And so it was done.

Skittles was a famous character in her day. She had a wonderful figure and beautiful feet and hands. She rode to hounds, going extremely well, I believe.

The incident reminded me of a story I had been told at Dublin Castle one night by my dinner partner, a most distinguished statesman. A very handsome and charming person, he was a little deaf and used to tell me stories in a rather loud voice, while his saintly wife watched us across the table, anxiously. He had been saying that the French and English "pretty ladies" were quite different—that the English were "good fellows" and did not desire to rook or ruin their men. Then he told me this story.

He had been in Paris as a young man and had met there a beautiful lady of that profession, a queen in her own world. He was a poor young man and had little to bring her. She had the position of the French women of her kind and took that position seriously. It was a trade union and she could not let it down. But she softened to him and said, "Bring me what you can."

So he raised all the money that he could and took it to her

219

one night in notes. She arranged the notes, one beside the other, round a plate like a fan. Then she struck a match and lit one.

"I am yours for as long as these take to burn," she said as they flared up. She had kept her bond with her profession. And she made that gesture like a queen.

While I was in South Audley Street I first went to the famous dressmaker, Sarah Monteith Fullerton Young. She lived next door, which was very convenient, for I could hammer on the wall when my dress had not come for a party, which I frequently did!

Mrs. Young was a real artist and a great character. She was very proud of her connection with the Monteiths and was also connected with the Herberts. She liked me, first because of this association, and also because I was a little "different." She liked my way of wearing my hair flat on my head with a little bun at the back, in contrast to the fringes and puffed-out hair of the day.

She made clothes for the "Souls," and for many of the beauties of the time—Lady Granby, amongst others, whom she sent to Ascot once in a white frock and large hat, with a pink rose on the brim and tied under the chin with a narrow string which looked like a boot-lace.

She herself was an ugly little woman and wore a dress that you would be ashamed to see on your cook, but she was an artist and studied her subject as an artist would. She never had any models but frequently copied old pictures. She would take pieces of lovely material, put them up against you and study their effect, saying, "No, no, that won't do!" When she had made up her mind, she would make the dress and never tell you in the least what it was going to be like, until it was finished. Even then, if it did not satisfy her, she would get into a rage and tear the beautiful silk to pieces. No wonder that, like all artists, she died very poor.

Elspeth Phelps, the great dressmaker, told me once that nearly everything she knew about her art, she had learnt from Mrs. Young. There was such glamour about the frocks that

she made. She never sent you anywhere without a rose somewhere in your dress. Rather faded pink roses usually. Oh,
those pink roses! Soft, floppy things. Cabbage roses. Cottage
roses. They suited the simple muslin frocks in which she liked
to dress me—with a blue sash, or a sash of faded pink to match
the rose. They were not in the least like the roses produced
for Rose Shows. Whenever I see them now, in an old-fashioned
garden, I think of Sarah Young pinning one into the bosom
of a dress, or thrusting two or three into a sash as if they had
just been plucked from a garden wall, or putting one on the
brim of a hat, or underneath the leaf, against a lovely face.
Sometimes it was yellow, sometimes crimson. But there was
always a rose. And it is the pink roses that I remember, as one
remembers the lost enchanted country of youth in some
magic moment of romance. So I stand still in a garden when
I see a bush of them, or even in a department of a London
shop where they are selling artificial flowers and I see again
those roses of yesterday.

Mrs. Young made me a dress of midnight blue satin, very
full at the waist, the skirt covered with beautiful black
Brussels lace, looped up in flounces round the feet, and caught
with pink and yellow roses; a black lace fichu to the bodice,
caught also by a pink and yellow rose. She had taken the
design from an old Spanish picture.

One of my difficulties with day dress was to get a hat to
stay on my head without hair. The hats of those days sat up
on top of piles of hair. In many cases it was a great advantage
to a face to have all that hair framing it. The shapes of most
people's heads were never shown in those days. And foreheads
were hidden as if they were indecent. I tried the piled hair
once with a pad put under my own in order to have something to pin my hat to. I looked quite awful. So Sarah took
to making my hats too.

Mrs. Young adored lace and took a lot of old Point that
had come back from Portugal with the 4th Earl's wife, and
made it into a lovely Court dress. She was the first to ally
fine dainty embroidery with serge and cotton, and she had

some of my old Marie Antoinette embroideries copied. I have several cuffs and collars and jabots of them now.

I *did* love clothes and I may sound extravagant. But, of course, clothes, like everything else, cost much less in those days. I believe I paid from £10 to £15 for some of my best dresses.

Meanwhile Fingall had arrived in Australia. On the boat he had met and made friends with a financier named Myring. They went together to Western Australia where Fingall had always wanted to go. When they arrived at Perth, a mine had just been discovered at Coolgardie by two Irishmen from Londonderry. Fingall and his friend went to prospect the mine. The discoverers had apparently driven down at every angle and always met gold. There was one spot which seemed so rich that it was called "The Golden Hole." Fingall and his new friend determined to acquire an option on this mine. Fingall wrote to Lord Londonderry asking if he had any objection to it being called after him as it had been discovered by Londonderry men. He had no objection and they *did* acquire an option and brought it back to London to be put on the market by the great financier of the day, Colonel North, who, I believe, put the biggest capital on it that had ever been put on a gold mine up to that time.

Fingall's nominees on the board of directors were: Colonel Dease, Lord de Grey, Horace Plunkett. The other directors were Colonel North, Sir George Irwin and T. H. Myring. Presently there were large lumps of quartz, pure gold, in the windows of a London goldsmith. We were all to make our fortune and there was a frantic rush for shares. Even the Prince of Wales wanted them. My flat was crowded with visitors—all my friends trying to get in—as they said, "On the ground floor."

"How can you get in on the ground floor, when we live on the third!" I asked. Personally I never believed in that fortune and never even bought a hat on the strength of it.

In due course Fingall was asked to go out again and open up the mine. I was in Paris with Mrs. Willie Jameson when I received a telegram from Coolgardie: "See Horace Plunkett and de Grey and get them to publish my telegram of April 1st."

The telegram of April 1st had been sent to Colonel North: "Practically nothing in The Golden Hole." Of course they thought this was a hoax. (It was All Fools' Day, and also by a coincidence, Fingall's birthday.) In the city they were not used to this devastating truthfulness. They would have understood "Mine not up to expectations," or something similar. The Gold Bubble had burst!

I went back to London where practically all the gold of The Golden Hole was in the goldsmith's window. It was a great shock but less of one to me, because I had been right. I had always felt that my luck was not to come in money. It might have ruined Fingall as he gave back all he could. Colonel North did the same. And so ended our dream of wealth! Luckily the widows and orphans, who are usually the victims of these dangerous speculations, lost very little over it.

After this, Fingall had many offers to go on City Boards and could have earned quite a large income by taking director-ships. He had established his name as an honest man! Only the other day Lady Athlumney, who had just returned from visiting her native Perth, said to me, "You should hear how they still speak of your husband there. They say he was the most honest Englishman that ever came to Perth."

"But," I said, "he was not an Englishman. He was Irish. And, with all our faults, love of money is not one of them."

Fingall refused these offers. "City honour is not my honour," he said. "I don't know anything about business."

I upbraided him at first, but was glad afterwards when I saw how many other fine names were tarnished by joining those dangerous companies. Fingall was right to keep to his own ways of life which he understood.

Just after the bursting of his gold bubble, an event occurred which was very much more important to us. Oliver was born.

It had been a very hot summer waiting for him. Fingall had had to be away again winding up the mine and, with his long absences, I associate the South Audley Street flat with great loneliness. London can be the loneliest place in the world as Mrs. Jones had discovered.

Of course I had, fortunately, some very good friends. Mary Gwynn Holford, a great friend of mine, lived in Grosvenor Square; Sir Thomas and Lady Troubridge opposite; besides Horace Plunkett and the Coventrys. I knew plenty of people in London now. But many of them were grand and busy and when you are ill or in trouble, these acquaintances just fade out of the picture. And it is your real friends who come closer and clearer than ever before, as things appear in a winter landscape that have been hidden by the soft foliage of summer. I remember a sad little person who often sat at the window during those long hot afternoons, looking down into the street, wistfully. Great carriages jingled by. Sometimes they stopped. Then I would hope that someone —anyone—was coming in to see me. But often, instead, a fine footman would get down and leave cards. Sometimes I had the greatest desire to drop something on the heads of those acquaintances as they drove on!

Then in June, while Fingall was still away, Oliver was born. On the hottest day it seemed of all that summer. I had Dr. Gibbons, the famous obstetrician for the event. He was rather pompous, and for all my agony I nearly giggled at the sight of the grande "Gibbie," as we called him, very hot, assisting in his shirt sleeves.

Oliver was taken to his Christening at the small parish church, wrapped in a white Indian shawl that had been given to his Great-Grandmother by Queen Victoria. And he wore a family Christening robe, several centuries old, covered with fine Point d'Argentan that had been made under a microscope. He was christened Oliver James Horace. Oliver, after Blessed Oliver Plunkett; James, after our friend, Sir James Talbot Power; Horace, after Horace Plunkett. The Blessed Oliver has certainly had his hand over him through life.

Then Fingall came back, having wound up his part of the Londonderry Mine, and as soon as I could be moved we gave up the flat and came back to the wide open spaces of Meath, taking with us our treasure, more precious than any gold mine. We had a wonderful reception from the people, who welcomed the heir with all the love that the Irish keep for "th' ould stock." However Republican they may declare themselves, no race is less truly democratic.

It was a very hot summer, even in Meath—the only cool place being the house, within its thick walls. I lay on the sofa in the library, with Fingall and the dogs running in and out. And how glad I was, at evening, to slip into my big four-post bed, and lie there, listening to the lovely sound of silence, broken now and again by the bleating of the sheep and the cawing of the rooks.

CHAPTER EIGHTEEN

Now that we were back at Killeen, poorer but honest, since our gold mine had proved empty, Ireland took possession of us. Horace had started his Irish Agricultural Organisation Society. Here are the names of the first Committee, because they are interesting for the Ireland of those days where differences of politics and religion kept men so sternly apart. President: The Hon. Horace Plunkett, M.P.; Vice-President: The Rt. Hon. C. T. Redington; Committee: Rev. T. A. Finlay, M.A., S.J.; Christopher Digges La Touche (Managing Director of Guinness' Brewery); Lord Monteagle, K.P.; Thomas Sexton, M.P.; Major John Alexander, D.L.; The Most Rev. Patrick O'Donnell, D.D., Bishop of Raphoe; Colonel Gerald Dease, D.L.; Coroner James Byrne, J.P.; James Musgrave, D.L.; John E. Redmond, M.P.; Count Arthur Moore, D.L.; George F. Stewart, D.L.: R. A. Anderson, who was secretary to the I.A.O.S., has written: "Nobody other than Horace Plunkett could have attracted to himself such a remarkable body of men, and, what is more, infused into them such a measure of his own fine enthusiasm as to hold them together through so many years of strain, vicissitude and conflict."

I have heard many people say that Dr. O'Donnell had the biggest brains of his Church, and even outside it, in Ireland. Christopher La Touche was a first-rate business man, a brilliant talker, with all the wit and fine manners of his Huguenot origin. Then—Father Tom Finlay—Horace's greatest adherent. When Horace Plunkett first met Father Finlay, he told me that he had at last found a man who had been thinking on the same lines as himself, long before they met. It was like the meeting of two fires. In those days it was still a brave thing for the Jesuit to join the Protestant Unionist M.P.

Father Finlay brought varied gifts to the work. An extremely good business man, he had the deep knowledge of human nature which belongs to the best type of Catholic priest. He had the wisdom of the serpent and the gentleness of the dove. Also a rich sense of humour—perhaps that the greatest gift of all.

Speaking at a Northern Co-operative Meeting once, he remarked that he could not see why we should be troubled about an ancient quarrel between a Dutchman and a Scotsman, and that, anyhow, their quarrel must have been long since settled in some other place. His popularity was so great in the North that some of the Southerners said: "Sure he can't be a priest at all!"

This pioneer work had been going on while we were in London.

Horace had introduced into Ireland the very first motor-car to be seen in the country, and he drove about the quiet lanes at the terrifying speed of ten or twelve miles an hour, being frequently stopped for furious driving by an apologetic R.I.C. man. I have some old photographs of this first motor-car—and very uncomfortable it looks—one of Horace in it, and one with myself, Lady Mayo and Father Finlay as passengers. Our hats, including Father Finlay's clerical one, are tied on with enormous veils! We are all just about to start on one of our expeditions. We shall rattle over the bad roads, terrifying the donkeys and cows who graze on the strip of grass by the roadside and who have never before seen such a contraption as ours. Hens and chickens and ducks will fly before us and we shall have a sensation of moving at desperate speed through space. We are going (at twelve miles an hour!) to wake up the Irish countryside, to visit some budding industry or to try to start others. What adventures we had on those tours of ours! Once, in a hotel at Mullingar, we looked rather doubtfully at our beds and decided to sleep in our dressing-gowns. The windows could not be kept open unless propped up by the water-jug. However, we were tired, and quickly fell asleep, to be rudely awakened

227

about midnight, by the most frantic knocking on the hall door. After a long time we heard the landlord going downstairs grumbling. The front door was opened, evidently to let in a very noisy and apparently intoxicated individual, who staggered up to the room next ours and whose stentorian snores kept us awake the rest of the night. In the morning we complained to the landlord.

"Ah, sure me heart is scalded!" he agreed. "That's the new American dentist who comes in - drunk every night!"

So pleasant for the patients next day!

One of our expeditions was to Foxford in the County Mayo, for the Connacht Exhibition, organised by that great woman and wonderful Sister of Charity, Mother Morrogh Bernard. She had built up at Foxford, within a few years, an industry that, with its many offshoots and wide embracing roof of Christian Charity, was like a Guild of the Middle Ages. The Exhibition was designed primarily to advertise the woollen goods being produced at the Foxford mills. But the side sections indicated the width and imagination of Mother Morrogh Bernard's work in her district for the better living, towards which we were all, in our different ways, trying to help the people. There were prizes for gardening, domestic science, poultry, dairy products, even for the most humble and necessary trade of mending. The great business woman, who was responsible for all this, forgot nothing, organised everything. And then, when the grand party of influential people whom she had collected to assist her travelled to the County Mayo for the Exhibition, she hid herself away as she always did on such occasions.

The net of this great little nun was as wide as her charity and the most surprising people got caught in it and were safely landed on the Foxford shore—where they might sometimes have been surprised to find themselves!

When she had first thought of establishing the Providence Woollen Mills on the Moy River, which should work under the Eye of God and by direction of the Sisters of Charity, she had written to the man who, she was told, could help her more than any other man in Ireland, for his advice. That man happened to be Mr. Smith of the Caledon Mills, Tyrone, who replied to her letter:

"Madam! Are you aware that you have written to a Protestant and a Freemason?"

I do not know Mother Morrogh Bernard's answer. But in due course the Protestant and Freemason travelled at his own expense to Foxford, was met at the station by the parish priest and his curate and accompanied to the convent. Having surveyed the proposed site and gone into other details, he advised Mother Morrogh Bernard to abandon her scheme. When that had no effect he placed himself "and his twenty years' experience at her disposal." He kept his word. And what a good alliance—the Protestant Freemason from the North and the Southern Catholic nun, both filled with the same spirit of charity.

Her courage was unwavering—"always a wonderful champion of the poor and outcast," writes one of her sister nuns—her justice absolute. There had been an incident during the height of the fever following the Parnell Divorce Case and split. Some employees of the Woollen Mills had hissed the local priests at a political demonstration, and the Bishop's orders were conveyed to the Reverend Mother. The men were to be dismissed. She refused. She could not excuse the men for what they had done, she said. But neither could she dismiss them. She gave her reasons to her own superior authority. Politics had no place in their industry. The Sisters of Charity had no politics. She had left all that in the world. If she allowed the men to be dismissed it would mean—that like so many other things in Ireland—politics would enter the mills disastrously. It would come in time that only those of a certain way of thinking need apply. She stood firm. A second request came from the Bishop. She refused. But she guaranteed an apology from the men and read it herself in public on a Sunday morning, standing between the two priests who had been insulted. Her first and last public appearance.   The following Sunday, the Bishop came and said Mass at the convent.

Fingall and I went down to the Exhibition with the Talbot Powers, on their coach. Miss Minnie Fitzgerald and Horace Plunkett were also of the party. The other guests—among them Lord and Lady Lucan, the Lord Chancellor and Lady Ashbourne, the Lord Mayor of Dublin (a strong Parnellite who sat happily beside the Unionist Lord Chancellor), Father Denis O'Hara, the famous Land League Priest—prove the width of Mother Morrogh Bernard's net.

Our expedition by coach was a pleasant leisurely one, stopping here and there for the night. We had taken bicycles with us, then new and strange sights in the Irish countryside, and we rode them about, sight-seeing, at our various resting-places. We women were still pleased with our bicycles and ourselves in our neat tweed suits, specially designed for that occupation, and little jaunty felt hats planned not to catch the wind. In the vicinity of Foxford, an old man stood still and stared, then crossed himself solemnly as I flew by!

In the summer of 1895 the Cadogans came to the Viceregal Lodge and Gerald Balfour to the Chief Secretary's Lodge; each full of schemes for Ireland. The new Lord Lieutenant was very earnest and bent on doing his best for the country and the people, while Lady Cadogan was quite the most perfect hostess of all those whom I knew at the Viceregal Lodge. She never thought of herself but always of her guests. And she was very jolly. She hunted and took part in all the interests of our life in Ireland and was friendly with every one. She would often stop to talk to the old women in their cottages and ask about their families, for which they loved her. Her daughter Tiny Cadogan, afterwards Lady Lurgan, was one of the most beautiful riders I have ever seen. She had a wonderful seat and figure and after the longest hunt she would be as neat and tidy as when she started.

As a hostess Lady Cadogan was always careful to make all her guests feel at home and she was ably helped in this by her niece, Lady Dorothy Coventry. She would take particular

230

THE RIGHT HON. GERALD BALFOUR.

Chief Secretary for Ireland, 1895-1900. Now Earl Balfour.

"THE COUNTESS CATHLEEN."

The Nurse—Lady Constance Lytton; The Countess Cathleen—Lady Fingall; with Miss Armstrong and Miss Porter.

trouble about some simple old lady up from the country, making sure that she did not feel lost and shy in that gay assembly.

The Cadogans vied with the Londonderrys in the magnificence of the Viceroyalty and their entertaining. It was a wonderful moment. Ireland was in the very air. From being a problem she had entered into her Golden Age, and as Dark Rosaleen, come into her own.

The Balfours soon opened their hearts and their home to me—why, I could never quite understand—and I stayed a great deal with them at the Chief Secretary's Lodge. Their friendship is still one of the treasures that enrich my life. During their Irish years they entertained many people who would not, or could not have gone to the Viceregal Lodge, and theirs was a far more interesting milieu, naturally. Politically, I believe the Chief Secretary, who was in the Cabinet, was more important than the Lord Lieutenant.

Unlike other Englishmen and Scotsmen who came to Ireland in one capacity or other, Arthur and Gerald Balfour never fell in love with Ireland. Fortunate and wise men! They kept their heads and their hearts and their vision clear, where men in love lose all these faculties. Gerald did not give his heart to Ireland. He gave his brain instead and he left her, for his service, more I believe, than any other Chief Secretary. His Land Act, the Department of Agriculture, the Local Government Act, which replaced the old Grand Juries by County Councils.

Gerald would always take and back another man's idea. With Horace Plunkett it had to be *his* Ireland, but Gerald would take any man's Ireland so long as he found it good. He took Horace's idea of the Department of Agriculture which grew out of the Recess Committee. Horace laid the foundation stone of the Department of Agriculture and it was so well and truly laid that it is one of the few stones left unmoved in the making of the new Ireland. Also, Gerald never became a one-idea'd man. He was interested in other things besides the job he was doing at that moment. I think his attitude to

Horace's work was rather like Fingall's. He took it with a grain of salt, perhaps not fully believing, but content to let Horace have his way and get all the credit too. He would always listen and he listened to other people besides Horace. Sir Henry Robinson for instance and Lord Atkinson. Certainly Gerald was a wonderful person to work with.

Like all the Balfours, he saw round corners and the other side of the question and could work even with his opponents. It was an unexpected and pleasant thing to discover of recent years that Tim Healy had almost an adoration for Gerald Balfour, seeing him as an English gentleman on whose word you could absolutely depend. Gerald had, too, an absolutely logical mind and could not understand the want of it in others. He would say, " But it is not logical."

I answered once, " Do you expect to find the Irish logical?"

Sometimes he was very withering. During the South African War I was staying at the Chief Secretary's when Gerald went over to London for a Cabinet Meeting. Betty and I got up early the morning of his return to welcome him and hear the latest from the War, which he must bring from his London meeting. As he came into the hall we said breathlessly, " Gerald, what news?"

He turned the cold face of an early morning traveller to us. His voice was as bleak as his face. " Any news that I am at liberty to give you, you will find in the morning papers."

I wanted to slap him!

If Gerald viewed us somewhat aloofly and as a problem to be solved, Betty gave us her heart. She did fall in love with Ireland. " A country one comes to love like a person," she wrote of it. She was thrilled with Yeats' poetry and A.E. and Irish music and art and drama and the fairies.

Gerald had to face the unpopularity of all reformers, especially with the Irish landlords who considered that he had cheated them out of their properties. Lord Ardilaun said, when asked to meet him, " that he would not meet a common thief, therefore he would not meet Gerald Balfour."

Now, Gerald looked as if he ought to have been one of the

232

Knights of the Round Table. Someone who had seen him in his blue robes at an investiture of the Knights of St. Patrick had called him "Sir Galahad." Betty commented, hearing Lord Ardilaun's remark, "You cannot be Galahad and Lucifer, too!"

She was an enthusiast. And she had come to Ireland at just the right time. A letter to her from T. P. Gill, all otherwise about Agriculture and the Department, begins with a note of reminder that *The Heather Field* is being played at the Abbey. The new Irish drama was in the air, too. Yeats was giving us his poetry; A.E. poetry, philosophy and strange-coloured dreams. Lady Gregory, Yeats and Edward Martyn had founded the Irish theatre. A.E. had joined Horace's Co-operative Movement and was editing the *Irish Homestead* and putting his best writing into wisdom about creameries and pigs and potatoes and such things.

I think Betty came out to Ireland, while Gerald stayed rather austerely at the Chief Secretary's Lodge, and Ireland must go to him. Many interesting visitors came there from both sides of the Channel. Lord Salisbury, I remember as one who was deeply interested in the Irish question. Then, Betty's brother, Lytton, "Brer Vic" as we called him. Ireland was laying her spell on him too. He was to come again as George Wyndham's secretary, with his lovely wife, Pamela, of whom A. E. said, that she was, "more like a flower than any woman he had seen." I remember warning Lytton not to give his heart to Dark Rosaleen, and perhaps it was just the warning he was waiting for and my words broke that spell while it was just no more than a silver web and easily broken.

At the Chief Secretary's Lodge, too, in those days, I first met Constance Lytton—one of the few real saints I have known. She was then a lovely young girl, with blue eyes, fair curly hair, and a delicious sense of humour, with the fascinating Lytton twist to her mouth when she laughed. The Balfour children adored Aunt Con. One of my memories of her is of a golden head bent among a group of children at the end of the room and the laughter of which she was the centre.

Later she was to become one of the leaders of the Suffragette movement under Mrs. Pankhurst. She was a natural martyr and would give herself completely in a cause. And she *did* give herself. Her cause was the cause of women—much more than just the struggle for the vote. It was the uplifting and freeing of women all over the world. She was so essentially feminine and sensitive, and only we who knew her could guess what it must have cost her to be wholeheartedly in that movement. To be associated with such acts as women chaining themselves to railings, flinging themselves before Derby horses, destroying letter-boxes, defacing pictures, and so on. She did whatever she had to do heroically, as heroically as earlier she had given up the musical career she had desired, to remain with her mother. When the call came, even her mother was set aside.

During the Suffragette agitation she was arrested and sent to prison at Newcastle as Lady Constance Lytton. She went on hunger strike and her heart was examined. It being discovered that she had slight heart disease, she was not forcibly fed, but released after two days. Later she assumed a false name and disguise—over the hideousness of which she suffered considerably—and as "Jane Warton" went to prison again. There was no heart test for Jane Warton and she was forcibly fed eight times before she was released. She never recovered from that prison treatment which hastened the illness that killed her.

At the Chief Secretary's Lodge, where Constance was someone whom one always liked to be with, she and I acted together in tableaux of Yeats' *Countess Cathleen*, when Betty produced them at one of her parties for a Dublin audience that would much have preferred a dance.

This was Betty uplifting us. Catching the Irish movement in the air and making us appreciate it to the full. I was the Countess Cathleen, and I am sure I enjoyed it, although I look my wistful part in the photographs of the tableaux which I have. I was not well at the time and I mentioned this fact to Mr. Yeats, who coached us himself. He only said, unfeelingly:

"You can't look too thin or too miserable for this part!"

Constance was the nurse; and T. W. Rolleston and Dr. Coffey, the Keeper of Irish Antiquities at the Dublin Museum, were the two very handsome merchants who bargained for my soul. I was dressed in a white classical robe with long sleeves, and had borrowed Celtic gold ornaments from the Museum for my hair and waist. Deena Hanson, then Deena Tyrrell, remembers the occasion: "A dismal affair," she says, and sighs for the girl who was cheated of a dance and given, instead, melancholy Irish tableaux!

As I lay dead, a voice from the back of the room exclaimed: "Doesn't she make an elegant corpse!"

Another of Betty's enthusiasms was the discovery of strange vegetarian dishes. She gave us black potatoes to eat which were not a great success; and nettles, having read that they made a good vegetable, but she forgot to boil them. Gerald complained that they burnt his throat! No wonder!

I tried to take Betty's dressing in hand for she was very careless about such things. "And," she said, "what is the use, when Gerald would not notice if I came down in my dressing-gown?"

Gerald was rather slow to notice everyday things. There was an occasion when Mrs. Patrick Campbell was invited to dine and was unable to come, at the last moment. A girl, staying at the Lodge, dressed herself up and was announced as Mrs. Patrick Campbell. Gerald took her in to dinner. She talked to him in a deep voice, flattering him outrageously. We were all giggling, but it was not until the end of dinner that he discovered that he was the object of a hoax.

I was there one night when Professor and Mrs. Tyrrell were dining. Betty said something and then corrected herself, exclaiming, "How stupid of me!"

Mrs. Tyrrell leaned across the table:

"Isn't it a queer thing, Lady Betty, how clever men like your husband and mine, always marry stupid women!"

The schemes and dreams for Ireland gave us some lovely moments to make up for our hard work. I do not know if Horace had already christened me "the honey-pot." I don't think that it was at all a suitable name for me. I think I was much more of a scold! But the honey-pot was there to attract the bees, and my job, then or later, was to coax people into doing things we wanted them to do (for Ireland) and collect money. I have some amusing correspondence, which I cannot publish, concerning a title that we created and the substantial sum given to the I.A.O.S. in return.

We went about the country—to Achill Island, where, after a terrible ferry disaster in the narrow strip of water between the island and the mainland, in Arthur Balfour's day, Michael Davitt had agitated for and got a bridge built by the Conservative Government. And we went to the Aran Islands from Spiddal, where a party of us—the Balfours, Horace Plunkett and I—were staying with Lord and Lady Morris. The talk and the wit were good at Spiddal. Of course Lord Morris gave us his best brogue, of which Lady Dorothy Neville had said to him at the Castle, "Lord Morris, how beautifully you imitate the brogue!" and he had answered, "Me dear ma'am, isn't it doing all in my power to smother it, I am!"

Lady Morris was a Protestant, although he and the children were Catholics. He said, explaining this, "In my family we have reduced our salvation to a certainty. My wife goes to Church and I go to Chapel. And my God! we can't both be wrong!"

These stories of our host at Spiddal are digressions. We went to Aran on the Congested District Board's boat, the *Granuaile*, on which I could have made many expeditions if I had been a better sailor. But though the *Granuaile* was good and sea-worthy, she rolled terribly on those Atlantic waves and I was often ill.

It was a lovely September morning when we sailed across

Galway Bay, with the islands of Inishmaan and Inisheer and Inishmore lying between us and America, and the Clare hills blue in the south. We landed at Inishmore, the largest island, from which the priest and doctor must go across by boat to Inishmaan and Inisheer when they were wanted, whatever the weather.

We drove round the island on an outside car behind a rather lame and miserable horse, which, we were told, was the only horse on Inishmore. I remember the island as being arid and stony and shadeless, but that day it looked its best with a cloudless blue Italian sky above. There were small patches of rich soil between the stone walls, our carman told us; and certainly, the people in their Sunday clothes looked surprisinly well fed and dressed. They walked erect like kings and queens, and it was explained to us that they had to carry their loads of turf on their heads. Some of the girls were beautiful. We passed a group of them, coming from Mass. Our driver leaned forward and drew his whip gently across the shawl of the prettiest. She flung back the shawl with an extraordinarily graceful movement and looked up indignantly. Then her face changed to an eager welcoming smile and she blew a kiss from her prayer book, to him in return.

I, always ready to discover romance, asked, "Is that your sweetheart?"

"It is," he told me, and that they were going to be married in a fortnight. Less romantically he added, that on the island, when a girl married, she was expected to bring, as dowry, half a hundred pounds. I don't know where she got it.

We had lunch at the one hotel which was bare and clean. They gave us good grilled herrings which reminded me of the "Potatoes and Point" of my Connemara childhood.

With evening the light changed and the islands were barbaric and cold. The little houses looked now as though they were tied down to the earth, to keep them from flying away in the winter storms. We went back across the bay to Spiddal in moonlight. The sea was calm and the Clare hills and the Galway coast, deep blue against the sky. The little foam of surf at the prow of our boat, glowed with what appeared to be brilliant balls of fire. Illuminated porpoises leaped out of the water and played a game with us, swimming safely backwards and forwards, outside the wash of the boat and in front of it; and—most lovely of all—there was a shoal of herrings, some miles in length, spreading over a wide surface of the water, making an effect of the most intricate fireworks.

The next day, going to the station, we drove into Galway on an outside car in torrents of rain, Gerald and I on one side, Betty and Horace on the other. It was ten miles or more to Galway from Spiddal, on an indifferent road then. The good road that was won later from the County Council, by Lord Morris' son, Lord Killanin, was known as Killanin's Avenue, before Spiddal and its owner shared the fate of many other Irish houses and their owners—burning and exile—in 1922-23.

Betty writes in 1895:

"I think it has been good for Gerald to pay these unofficial visits (to the Dufferins, Lansdownes, Smith-Barrys, Kenmares, Dunravens, De Vescis, etc.). They cannot help seeing his good qualities when they talk to him, and the ladies so admire his looks." They had been visiting the Lansdownes at Derreen in Kerry, the softest, most magical and coloured county in Ireland.

"Wild and romantic," Betty writes of Derreen, "the ideal spot in the south—astonishing richness of vegetation and mountain and sea and river, with palms growing among the oak trees. The people too are endlessly fascinating. One gets to love Ireland as one does a person! It is different from everything else in the world, the only English-speaking country where there is no 'middle class,' perhaps one of its greatest charms."

Frank Mathew has described the peace of Kerry as being "the first peace that is so akin to the last peace . . ." Derreen certainly was very relaxing. I remember, when I was staying there, Lady Lansdowne taking me to see a little cottage at the mouth of the Shannon, where she said she could lie

238

fallow and recuperate between years of work. None of these people stayed long enough for the inertia of the country to overcome them.

Horace formed a Recess Committee in 1896. So-called because it sat during the Parliamentary Recess, with the object of discovering how, without political change, Ireland could be provided with a Department of Agriculture and Industries suited to the needs of the country. I would say that the nearest approach to union with the North that there has been in my time, came, when Horace persuaded the best men of North and South to join his Recess Committee.

The Nationalist Party was then split. Redmond, who was leading the Parnellites, became a member of the Recess Committee. But the official Irish Party would have nothing to do with it. John Dillon said that it was a "red herring across the path of Home Rule"; an effort to kill Home Rule by kindness. It was easier of course to attack Horace Plunkett, an Irishman, than Gerald Balfour, who was an English official. So Horace was attacked.

However, the Committee weathered the storms that any committee trying to do anything in Ireland must face. The Department of Agriculture was the result.

One of my memories of those years is of a big party at Adare, with the Cadogans and Balfours as guests.

The fiery Bishop of Limerick, Dr. O'Dwyer, had been having some controversy with the Chief Secretary and he took the occasion of Gerald's visit to Adare, which was in his diocese, to write him a somewhat insulting letter. Gerald did not mind. But Dunraven came to me and said, "I think you should go in and talk to your Bishop."

I went. And, of course, found the Bishop, so fiery on paper, charming and gentle to meet.

I said to him, "My lord, are you mad to write in such a way to a man who has it in his power to give you so much of what you want for your people?"

"Ah," he agreed. "You're right, my lady, you're right!

If we were to put all the letters we write under our pillows till the morning and then read them again, the half of them would never be posted!"

On April 15th, 1897, Betty writes to Arthur Balfour:

"DEAREST ARTHUR,—I was so depressed at the reception of Gerald's Bill (Dept. of Agriculture and Industry) on Monday that I imagined Plunkett and Co. were dissatisfied. I suppose they are, so far as the amount of the grant is concerned, but I was pleased to get this from Plunkett this morning: 'After the Chief Secretary's speech last night I feel less of a rebel. While he is so friendly I can endure the Treasury and some if not all of its works. Any speech on dry economics will be criticised when it stands between the House and holidays . . .'"

CHAPTER NINETEEN

I MUST have lived a very varied life at this time. We hunted hard in winter (however faint my heart still remained and was to remain!). There were Horace's schemes which we were beginning to try out at Killeen, although Fingall continued in his disbelief. There were our travels through the country, organising the movement. Horace was in Parliament, which kept him in London a good deal so that there was more for us to do at home. I went to the Viceregal Lodge frequently. In January, 1898, Betty Balfour records that "the Lord Lieutenant is huffy, because he thinks he is not sufficiently consulted by the Chief Secretary." Gerald Balfour was in the Cabinet and the Lord Lieutenant was not. Chief Secretaries were usually in the Cabinet and there were rarely two Irish ministers, so there was often some slight friction between the Lord-Lieutenant and the Chief Secretary. Lord Wellesley, the Viceroy after the Union, had settled any possible doubt in his day, by saying, "I *am* the Irish Government!"

Betty and I both went those days and listened to A.E., installed now in Lincoln Place, editing the *Irish Homestead*. He was still under thirty then, but he was one of the people who did not change much with the years, having the young heart that never grows old. He used to look at one with such gentle eyes, and he was always human and tolerant; so tolerant for other people's ways of thought and living, however far apart those were from his own. If—as someone has said—a man is not human in the true sense of the word unless he fits into humanity, A. E. was the most human person who ever lived. I have this letter of his, written to Horace in 1899, which tells how he came to be brought into the movement:

"23. 7. 99.
"IRISH AGRICULTURAL ORGANISATION SOCIETY, LTD.
"22 LINCOLN PLACE,
"DUBLIN.

"MY DEAR MR. PLUNKETT,—I regret to say that the organising pamphlet is still in MSS. It needs to be touched up in reference to Creameries. Anderson returns to-morrow from the South. He must have had a most exhausting week. He has a wonderful way with the farmers and the sight of his bright kindly face is one of the greatest aids to the movement, I think. I think your article is excellent. Your economics are the only economics I understand and which ever interested me. A really philosophical something lives in them and I find them the best material solution of problems which had to be solved for Ireland before the transcendental idea which people of the class of Yeats and myself hope for, could take any deep root. In our philosophy, the fundamental idea is the spiritual unity of humanity; and your co-operative movement which is teaching the value of unity to Irishmen in their daily lives, is giving to our intellectual successors and to all idealists, their best illustration and argument. For this object lesson, though its first most necessary application is to material ends, must inevitably react on the mind of co-operators and promote a corresponding desire for a greater nearness to the human hearts in those about them. It is on this basis I am content to work, without even hinting at my own peculiar ideas, for I think that if there is any truth in them they will naturally flourish in the societies we are starting.

"Thanks for Lady Betty's note. She is very kind indeed and is heaping coals of fire on my head. I could not give up one of my evenings to see her tableaux, but people like her will understand how avaricious enthusiasts get over their time.

"Yours ever sincerely,
"G. W. RUSSELL."

In another letter, to Betty, he is giving her assistance in her tableaux.

GEORGE RUSSELL ("A.E.")

STOWLANGTOFT—1896.

(Back row, L. to R.) Ghillie, Lord Londonderry, Douglas Haig, Seymour Fortescue, Lord Enniskillen, Lord Chesham, Col. "Bully" Oliphant, Willie Jameson.

(Front, seated, L. to R.) Lady Fingall, Mrs. Willie Jameson, H.R.H. Prince of Wales, Mrs. Dick Cunningham, Lady Hesketh.

"I had made some sketches of Angel, Demon, Oonah and Ailen, but now that I have a list of tableaux scenes I will try to make some sketches of them. Meanwhile I send you four drawings made last night. I doubt them being much use as I have no knowledge of these matters."

Often during those years I would rush in to A.E.'s office, full of fury and indignation against John Dillon or some other enemy of our schemes. And his smile would be like a benediction, and his voice, cool flowing waters on my heated fires, quenching them.

Those earlier years he was in Lincoln Place. Later, in the room at the top of the fine Georgian house in Merrion Square which Horace's friends had presented to him. There, in the intervals of editing the *Irish Homestead*, A.E. painted the walls for his own pleasure. He made lovely magic forests, with fairy princesses moving through them, to an unknown and unimaginable distance. When he was bored, he painted them out and painted the walls afresh. Sometimes I talked to him of fairies. I had not been sure that I had ever been near any or felt their presence since my childhood in Connemara.

"Come with me to Rosses Point." He said, as though he were chanting a poem. And I was sure, hearing him, that I would find the fairies if I went with him to Rosses Point. But I never went. And I only saw the fairies in that room where it was easy to believe in them. The windows looked out across the grey roofs to the Dublin mountains which, wherever one goes in Dublin, are always in sight, as they are in my view now, from the windows of my flat where I sit telling this story.

Sidney Sime stood in that room once and looked round him at the walls and said, "Good Heavens! Is this the room in which potatoes and pigs are grown!"

I may not have seen the fairies, but I have seen or felt the presence of ghosts, elsewhere than at Killeen. One of those days Betty and I drove out to Howth Castle, which the Ashbournes had rented from Lord Howth. When we arrived, we found Lady Ashbourne in the hall, with a footman standing beside her, holding a plate of butter on a lordly dish, while she applied the butter to the bridge of her nose! She told us that she had heard our carriage coming, and had run upstairs to tidy herself. Leading to her room there was a short flight of steps and as she went up she saw a lady standing at the top. She had only time to notice that the figure wore curious, old-fashioned grey clothes, when it suddenly disappeared down an old stone staircase which led to a dungeon. In her alarm Lady Ashbourne had fallen and hurt her nose. The story was that a duel had been fought on that staircase for the sake of a lady, in which one of the duellists had been killed.

I had seen that Grey Lady too, when I stayed at Howth earlier. I had been awakened in the early morning by some-one standing in the half-light at the end of my bed. I thought it was my maid who was sleeping in an adjoining room, and was irritated by her stupidity in calling me so early. While I struggled between sleeping and waking, to tell her what I thought of her, she turned away and went through a door that I knew led down the stone steps to the dungeon. "Silly fool!" I thought. "She will fall." I tried to call out to her, and at that moment I heard a movement and a loud snore from the next room where my maid was fast asleep.

To my mind Howth is the most interesting house in Ireland. For one thing it was never spoilt in the terrible period of Victorianism, when so many other Irish lords had gone mad over bricks and mortar and ruined their castles.

The tradition of Queen Granuaile was kept fresh then as now, by the extra place that is always set at the Howth table. That place is for the Queen of the West, who was described by Sir Henry Sidney, the Lord Deputy, busy suppressing the native Irish, as, "a most famous feminine sea captain," and by Sir Richard Bingham, the Governor of Connaught, as, "nurse of all the rebellions in the province for forty years." She married first, an Irish O'Flaherty, and secondly, a Burke. In her prime she went from her fortress near Renvyle, to visit her sister Queen—Elizabeth, in London, and, returning, landed on the Point of Howth and knocked at the door of the Castle asking for hospitality for the night. The steward, seeing a rather wild and dishevelled party of travellers, closed the door. Granuaile returned to the beach, full of fury, and found there the young heir of Howth playing with his nurse. She kidnapped him and carried him off to her Western fortress where she held him hostage until the ransom that she demanded was paid. That ransom was that for ever after an extra place should be set for her at the table at Howth Castle and the door of the Castle left open. I saw the place set so yesterday. It is laid for lunch and dinner, Granuaile evidently not being expected to breakfast or tea! The door remained open until the recent Troubles, when it had to be closed and has so remained.

Gormanston, another old castle in Meath, also has a strange tradition. A fox surmounts the family crest and it is said that whenever a Lord Gormanston is about to die, living foxes surround the Castle. The grandfather of the present Lord Gormanston was taken suddenly ill and had to be rushed to Dublin for an immediate operation. The next morning, at Gormanston, a small page boy rushed into the cook and said, "Oh, ma'am, the Hounds are surrounding the castle. There must be going to be a Meet!"

The cook looked out of the window. "They are not hounds, they are foxes."

Very shortly afterwards the news came that Lord Gormanston was dead.

Fingall was hunting in the neighbourhood that day and never found a fox. An old countryman told him, "My lord, you may go home. Every fox in Meath is at Gormanston."

Digressions again.

Our second son and youngest child, was born at the Chief Secretary's Lodge, and called after Gerald Balfour. Betty and Gerald had lent the house to us more than one summer when they were away at Whittingehame. It was wonderful —and so good for the children—to get from the lifelessness of Meath in summer, to the Park and the open spaces of the

245

Fifteen Acres with the wind and air over them and nothing between you and the mountains. Some English paper published a good story that Gerald had let the house to us, and I was greatly upset. Gerald smiled characteristically: "If they did not say that, they would say something else."

So he and Betty went off and we were left to our delightful temporary residence. Dr. Gibbons, as I could not be under him this time, had insisted on my having an English nurse, not believing in the efficiency of Irish ones. When I told Lady Cadogan that Mrs. Greene was coming to me, she held up her hands in horror. "My dear, we are all in terror of her! She hardly goes to any one except Royalty."

However, Gerald, who frequently upset our calculations, took it into his head to arrive before his time. They wanted to put him into an incubator, but I refused to have him brought up as a chicken! And a charming Irish nurse who was called in pulled him through the early days on Sherry whey. The grand lady from London arrived, to find the footman holding the baby while the nurse was taking a bicycle ride in the Park. There was never the right cover to any dish for my trays and Gerald smelt like a Dublin cabman.

I told her at once there was to be no nonsense, and that Irish servants much preferred holding the baby to doing their own work. Having put all her signed photographs of Royalty round her room, much to the joy of our servants, who took turns to view them, she settled down admirably to Irish life. She too went bicycling in the Park while someone else minded me and the baby. She wrote to us afterwards that she had never enjoyed any time more in her life!

We were in London for the Queen's Diamond Jubilee Procession and saw it from the Baroness Burdett-Coutts' house. I thought it looked like a wonderful circus as it went by. There was every colour in the world in it. I remember the Queen's cream-grey horses, and "Bob's" little figure. But the finest men in the whole procession were the Dublin Metropolitan Police. In the evening we all went out to see the illuminations.

The crowds were immense and in St. James's Street I got swept away from my party. I do not know what would have happened to me, but for a big policeman who appeared miraculously beside me. "Keep your hands down by your side," he said. "If you put them up, your arms will be broken."

The crowd was swaying and I was very frightened. I felt so small. "They will trample on me," I said.

"We will go with them," he answered.

He guided me and we went like swimmers in a current, making our way steadily to the edge of it and so to shore. We reached one of the side streets.

"Turn up here," my rescuer said, "and you will be out of the crowd." We were out of it.

I made my way back to the Baroness' house where I found Fingall, in much alarm, not knowing what had happened to me.

From London I went with Mrs. Willie Jameson to Schwalbach to take the sulphur baths—a delightful German place where you had all your meals out of doors among the flowers and the fountains. Although we were supposed to be doing the cure, the food was delicious. In those days it was chiefly for women and very few men came there, but after the War a great many came out for the cure. It was very good for your inside, no doubt, but bad for your clothes as they got saturated with sulphur. To wash off this sulphur we went for a weekly bath to Schlangenbad, a lovely little village in the heart of the mountains, to which, incidentally, came many of the naughty ladies of Paris to improve their complexions. The water was glutinous, almost like oil. And the baths were of marble, sunk into the ground. You walked down into them, feeling like one of the Romans of old.

When anybody wanted to pay you a compliment, as a gallant friend of mind did, they offered you a rose bath. For this, the petals would have been picked from hundreds of roses and strewn on the top of the glutinous water. You lay in your bath with roses up to your chin and presently a tray was laid across the bath on which was placed a cup of delicious chocolate and *brioches* for your enjoyment.

I had had trouble with my eyes and went on to Wiesbaden to see the famous oculist, Pagenstecher. He was very rough in his examination, lifting up my eyelids and pulling out some of my eyelashes. He hurt me so much that I lost my temper and gave him a slap on the side of his face. He was horrified. Such a thing had never happened before in his Augen Klinik. He wrote me down in his appointment book as " the excitable little Irish lady."

In August, 1897, the Duke and Duchess of York paid their state visit and made a tour through Ireland. I was asked to meet them at Adare where I often stayed during those years. It was one of the meeting places of Irish life and culture and beautiful, with its ruins of two abbeys and the glorious Desmond Castle close by. The monks must have been attracted there by the lovely river which flows beside the house. It was full of excellent fish, as no doubt it had been when the monks caught their Friday dinner in it. The house had been built in comparatively recent times entirely by local labour and was not very comfortable. Most of the seats had been copied from Italian church pews. They were beautifully carved but extremely painful to sit on.

It was at an earlier party at Adare that I had heard my own name spoken as I came down to dinner. There was a screen between me and the hall and, behind it, an elderly colonel was advising a young subaltern:

"Don't be wasting your time on that little lady. You'll get nothing out of her. For one thing she is a Roman Catholic, and for another . . ."

I came round the screen hastily to the speaker's embarrassment and never heard what the other reason was!

For the Royal visit the party was a very small one. Gerald and Betty Balfour, Lord and Lady Castletown, Lord Roberts, Nigel Kingscote; Derek Keppel and Lady Eva Dugdale were in attendance. They went shooting every day and for the first time I saw what a good shot our future King was.

248

I had brought two coats and skirts back from my German visit, one green and the other Parma violet colour, in a light and very bright tweed. I wore them at Adare and they were much admired by the Duchess of York.

"Of course, Lady Fingall, these are Irish?" she said.

I felt terribly ashamed and stuttered evasively, "Oh, Ma'am, I always try to wear Irish Industries."

Then the Duchess and all the ladies of the party asked me to get them similar tweed. Nemesis! I wrote at once to every tweed manufacturer in Ireland to see if they could produce the stuff. Luckily there were hems to my skirts for me to cut patterns from. But, by the time I had done, there was not much hem left! The material was an unusual light hopsack. None of the manufacturers could produce it. But Mother Morrogh Bernard at Foxford saved the situation. Wonderful woman! She had it specially made for me and delivered within a fortnight. She asked then if this new Foxford line might be called Fingall tweed. Of course I was much honoured. And Fingall Tweed is still one of the products of Foxford.

From Adare the Royal party went up to the Abercorns at Barons Court. I had also been invited and I asked humbly if I might travel with them. We went the first part of the journey, up the Shannon, on one of the new steamers. It should have been a beautiful journey in full summer—through Lough Derg, with the green land of Tipperary on one side and the wild heather-clad Galway hills the other. I only remember that it was wet and bitterly cold, and, sitting on deck we played the old-fashioned game of "Slap hands" to keep ourselves warm. We got into the train at Athlone and found a delicious lunch prepared for us. But we had hardly got our teeth into the first cutlet before the train stopped at a station and His Royal Highness was told that he had to receive an address. This recurred several times and Lady Eva, the other ladies and I, fought for the ribbons from the bouquets that were handed in.

When we got to Barons Court we found that our luggage

had been lost. And there we were, in our travelling clothes, with nothing to change into. We arrived late and a crowd of lovely women were sitting in the hall, grandly dressed, with tiaras, waiting for us. I was very conscious of my own dishevelled appearance, with my hair hanging in streaks under my little sailor hat; and I so admired the neatness of the Duchess of York, whose tidy fringe of hair seemed quite undisturbed by the journey. We had to dine as we were, and the luggage arrived late that night.

The next day my hostess asked me to show His Royal Highness the garden. She said, "If you see the head gardener, do make yourself known to him. He was at Killeen when he was a little boy."

We found the head gardener—very grand he was in his tall hat—and I stopped and spoke to him, telling him who I was.

He was delighted to meet me, and we shook hands warmly. Then he clapped the Duke of York on the back, saying:

"And is this your guid man?"

I explained hastily: "No, no. This is the Duke of York."

The Duke laughed and said, "Yes, I *am* her guid man."

"Be careful, Sir," I warned him. "Remember we are in the North, and under Scottish law, if you say that before witnesses, we shall be morganatically married!"

We returned to lunch and our "morganatic marriage" made a very good joke for the party. I said to the Duke, "Now, Sir, you will have to look after my boy."

He answered: "I will, if you put him in the Navy."

The Duke was very domesticated, and talked a lot about his children, to whom he was a most devoted father.

Many years later Killeen went up for the Navy and was spun for his eyes.

I happened to be sitting, just afterwards, next to the Prince of Wales, as he now was, during a shooting party at Elveden, and I reminded him of his promise and told him that my son had just been "spun" for the Navy.

He asked, "What for?"

I said: "Sir, I am afraid for something that even you cannot overcome. He has very bad astigmatism."

"Ah," he agreed. He could do nothing. "The Navy must have eyes."

.   .   .   .

Horace wrote to Betty Balfour in July, 1899, from Brighton, where I imagine, as usual, he had gone to recuperate.

". . . I have been in correspondence with Lucy, who wants my nephew to contribute to *Punch*. Burnand wrote to him, saying that that letter to Maimie shows genius and that he does not believe any young Guardsman wrote it. The sentence about ' Vulchers liking soldiers because they are often kind to them' is, says Lucy, worthy of Kipling. The boy undoubtedly inherits a little of his father's brilliant imagination, and I shall try to get him to do a little literary work. (This refers to the present Lord Dunsany, E.M.F.) . . . I hope some day he will get to know your brother. . . .

Anderson turned up last night and all to-day he and I have been building Co-operative castles in this bracing air. . . ."

In the autumn of 1899 came the South African War. I remember this and one of our friends coming to say good-bye, young men we had hunted with and danced with. "What shall I bring you back?" one of them asked, who was not to return. They went gallantly as to a picnic. I remember them going away, which is what those left behind always remember of War. My friends who went out were nearly all killed. Those who were not ambushed by the Boers, died of dysentery, enteric and malaria. So many of them died before they saw a Boer at all. We had not dreamed in those days of how wonderful the medical organisation and the food supply should be in the Great War, 1914-18. The papers came in with reports of defeat after defeat, and apparently no victory on our side. This, for a great Empire fighting a small

251

and primitive people, was a terrible humiliation. Fingall went out with the Yeomanry, and was on the ill-fated Beira expedition with Charrington.

I was in London when the papers came out with: "The Earl of Fingall's horse shot under him." And it was some time before I could get any definite news that he was safe. But the pony had been shot, and Fingall would not leave the wounded animal. He stayed with it and dragged it back to camp when night fell to make cover. He brought the pony —a Texan—back to Killeen after the war. That pony had a mouth like a steam engine and was no pleasure to ride, so he was put out on grass and ran wild in the fields until he died after a happy old age.

From Bellair, where some of this book was written, we visited two charming elderly ladies whose brother had been on the Charrington expedition with Fingall. They remembered, too, how many had died of dysentery, enteric and malaria in that war before they heard a shot fired. They spoke of an occasion which I had quite forgotten, when they had seen me present medals to the Irish Yeomanry in Dublin at the end of the war and: "Indeed, you have not changed much, my dear," one of them said.

The Queen came to Ireland in 1900. She came in her own yacht, which was commanded by Count von Leinigen. There was some difficulty in bringing the yacht alongside the pier at Kingstown, and a voice from the crowd was heard: "Come down out of that, Lanigan, and let ould Tiphook bring her in!" Tiphook being the Irish pilot. But Count von Leinigen negotiated it safely.

The Queen stayed at the Viceregal Lodge, which the Cadogans vacated for her, moving themselves into the Castle. As she drove through the town in state, an old woman was heard exclaiming: "Sure, she is only an old body like ourselves!" I went out to the Viceregal Lodge to be presented to her, and kissed the plump hand of a very old lady. She brought her little donkeys and drove them about the grounds of the Viceregal Lodge. Her visit was really a gesture of

252

gratitude for the bravery of the Irish soldiers in the South African War. She had not liked the Irish, and she made that gesture only just in time.

I remember the sorrow for the old Queen when she died a few months later, a feeling, too, that with her death a chapter had ended. For many years of her reign there had been a clear sky; or, the clouds in it were so small and so distant in that time when countries were much farther away from each other than they are now, in these days of aeroplanes and wireless, that it would have been easy to have been unaware of them. An era had ended with the South African War and the old Queen's death, which was hastened by it.

But I think, too, even with the sorrow, there was the relief that always comes with the end of anything, especially anything that has lasted a long time. For so many years the Queen had been old and sad. Now there would obviously be a much more lively Court. The Court in those days ruled social life. And as Prince of Wales, King Edward VII. had already brought the American element into English Society which would certainly help to enliven the new Court.

Soon after the end of the war, Fingall and I and our small daughter went on a yachting cruise with the Dalziels. Sir Davidson Dalziel, as he then was, had bought the *Clementina* from the King of the Belgians. She was very luxurious and rather florid as to decoration. I was told to make up a party for the cruise. Besides ourselves and our host and hostess, there were Lord Forrester and his daughter, Horace Plunkett, and George Dalziel. We crossed to Ostend in bad weather. Mary Forrester was as poor a sailor as I was, and we were very glad to go ashore at Ostend. There she and I decided to see Bruges with its wonderful Van Eycks and Memlings, and to rejoin the yacht at Antwerp. From Antwerp we went to Amsterdam and Rotterdam and saw the Dutch Galleries. I think Mary Forrester and I were the only members of the party who enjoyed the pictures. The only pictures that impressed Horace were Rembrandt's "Night Watch," and—for quite a different reason—Paul Potter's "Bull." He thought

253

that magnificent, and it sent his mind off at once on the question of improving the bulls of Ireland!

After that we went up the Kiel Canal. I had been promised a visit to Russia, and we had planned to go to Moscow, but at Kiel we were told that it was useless trying to get through, because the trains from St. Petersburg were being derailed by the great heat. The feeling at Kiel was very anti-British and pro-Boer, and the papers were full of unflattering pictures of Queen Victoria and unpleasant references to her. We changed plans then and went across the North Sea to Sweden and Norway.

I am reminded by the story of Horace and Paul Potter's "Bull," of another occasion when we all went to stay with the Blumenthals in Switzerland. (We had met the famous composer and his wife in London, where they had a very interesting circle.) There was a party arranged to ascend the Rochers de Naye, above Montreux, one early morning in time to see the sun rise. We went up while it was still dark, in a little funicular railway, and in the cold dawn we all sat shivering, wrapped in blankets, waiting for the sun. When at last it rose in all its glory over the mountains and the glistening snow, I turned to Horace: "Oh, look!"

Horace's eyes were fixed on some little black objects wandering over the bare lower mountain slopes.

"Yes," he said slowly, "I wonder that we never thought of goats for the Congested Districts."

If he brought no memories of sunsets back from Switzerland, he did import more and better goats. Of course they, accustomed to sparse living on the Swiss mountains and fending for themselves, were the very things to supply nourishing milk to mothers and children in the poor Irish districts. So Horace's goats were let loose in Ireland, where there were enough goats already. These were livelier and better goats and even more destructive. They ate everything before them—hedges, gardens, barks of trees and the clothes when they were hung out to dry. They climbed up on the tops of cottages and ate thatch, on occasion! They leaped out of hedges as we rode by, terrifying the horses and upsetting the motors!

So we worked for Ireland those days!

While Horace was Vice-President of the Department, we tried out his schemes at Killeen. We did everything that the Department advised. They had discovered that in ancient days the Boyne valley had been an orchard country and that the apples of it had made good cider—known as Boyne Cider. "The Bottle of the Boyne!" said Father Finlay, making speeches about this new dream.

Perhaps the climate had been different then. Fingall gave up his best horse paddock to make an orchard. Over at Dunsany, too, they planted apple trees. The Mowbrays and Stourtons followed suit loyally. But we never toasted each other—or Ireland—in the Bottle of the Boyne! We sprayed and pruned and did all that we were told. But pests came and American blight and the early frosts in May, and our apples were poor return for the rich grazing we had sacrificed. When they were plentiful there was no sale for them and we fed them to the pigs; and my apple-fed pigs made a small fortune in the War! In due course the trees were cut down for firewood.

"Wibberleyisms," we called these schemes, from Wibberley, one of Horace's friends, who was responsible for most of them.

One of his ideas was to make Ireland a milk farm. He tried that out in Meath, where the grass was so rich that the cows turned to fat instead of milk, as the corn we grew shot up high, sprouted a small head, and then lay down flat under the wind and rain. Meanwhile I turned half my garden into a tobacco field, and the smell of it was beautiful on a summer evening, and I believe the tobacco we grew was likely to kill any one who smoked it undiluted!

Old Larry, the gardener, looked across the pale scented blossoms, gloomily. "Worse than a nursery of childer," he said, "and more trouble." When he gave notice, I gave up the tobacco instead and kept him.

Now our orchards have gone back to grass, and Oliver

255

puts his horses in the paddocks where his father put his. And our schemes have a dream-like quality when I look back on them.

Not long after my son and daughter-in-law had come to live there, a neighbour in Meath gave a lift to an old woman on the road, and they drove past Killeen.

"That's a fine castle," my friend said. "And how do they like the young Lady Fingall?"

"She's a nice quiet lady," the old woman answered, "a nice quiet lady." And she looked back and remembered. "But th' ould one——" She made an expressive gesture. There had evidently been no peace with "th' ould one," who was far from quiet! "She was always pestering us to have gardens and hens . . . *and* ducks . . . and she had us *desthroyed* with goats!"

So our great efforts and thirty years of work are remembered by those who endured them!!

CHAPTER TWENTY

I HAVE various memories of those years; often without any connecting link. I went to Newmarket for the first time with the Londonderrys. We stayed with Mr. and Lady Isabella Larnach at Llandwades House, which they had just built.

There used to be very few women at Newmarket in those days, when each had to come with some member of the Jockey Club. Many of them came from the neighbourhood, riding. Probably the Newmarket enclosure represented then the most exclusive society in England.

The King was there that day. At the side of the Stand there was a special bench, which was sacred to him and to a few very important ladies who were his friends. It was called the "holy of holies!" In my ignorance I only saw a very ordinary seat, and being tired, sat down, finding it pleasant to rest. Presently the Duchess of Devonshire swept up, very magnificent.

"Do come and sit down here!" I invited her politely, drawing my skirts aside.

She glared at me and sat down at the other end of the bench. When I looked up, I saw that every one was laughing, including the King. Presently Lady Londonderry arrived.

"Come away, my dear. That is no place for you!" And she explained the sanctity of the bench. I went back to Llandwades miserable, wept all night and said that I would never go to Newmarket again.

I was told: "But you were the success of the day. Every one was laughing."

I was persuaded to go again the next day, and when I arrived, the King was charming to me. I said: "Sir, how could I know?"

"Certainly not," he said. "And you *shall* sit on the bench." And he put me there beside him.

The Duchess was so furious that she never forgave me, and I was not asked to her famous Fancy. Dress Ball at Devonshire House.

That autumn I went to stay with the Jamesons at Stowlangtoft, in Suffolk, where they had some of the best partridge shooting in England. King Edward used to invite himself there for shooting twice a year or so, when he was Prince of Wales, and later when he was King. He liked the informality of the parties at Stowlangtoft, and it was very easy and simple meeting him there.

The parties were generally quite small. They might include the Londonderrys, Lord Enniskillen, Percy Chubb and Percy La Touche—the "two old men," as the King called them; Sir Seymour Fortescue, Dorrien Smith, and often, of course, Douglas Haig. Flora Hesketh would probably be one of the ladies and Mrs. Keppel another. These are just a few, I remember. Of course there were other guests on many different occasions.

The King had a great affection for Mrs. Willie Jameson. And the house was very warm and comfortable, the parties intimate and friendly and very unroyal.

One day, I remember our host fussing to get the guns out of the tent after lunch, while the King and Dorrien Smith, who was called the "King of the Scilly Isles," delayed, talking. Willie put his head into the tent and called:

"Come on, you two Kings!"

I saw rather an angry light in the King's eye for a moment, then he laughed and all was well.

The lunches for those shooting parties were ridiculously luxurious. A tent would be erected where the morning's shoot was likely to leave off, and then a wonderful lunch prepared by a staff of servants. There might be hot-pot, Irish stew, curry, *pâte de foie gras*, *en croute*, and other delicious food.

Edward VII. was never a very keen shot. He did not care enough about it. He used to ride a pony to the drives. Once I remember him complaining of the Londonderry brothers with half-humorous indignation: "What with Bertie, who

258

wipes your eye, and Londonderry, whose dog takes your bird, it is no use shooting in that company."

Sir Pertab Singh, who had been a great friend of Douglas Haig's out in India, was a guest, I remember, at Stowlangtoft. He had a simple and childlike character. We used to get him to take his turban off, unwind the many yards of it, and put it on again, to show us how it was done. One day I said to him: "Why have you no jewels, Highness?"

He said: "My wife, she wants jewels. I say, 'I have no jewels.' What for you want jewels!"

Later he invited me to go and stay with him for the Durbar. "And you will be as my sister and my cousin and my aunt," he promised me. But in spite of this delightful prospect, I had to refuse the invitation, as I found that it would cost too much!

He was a great polo player, and his team nearly always won in India. There were so many polo accidents at one time that Lord Roberts began to get alarmed.

"Lord Roberts does not like these accidents," said Sir Pertab Singh, having received a cup from the Field Marshal. "But after all a man must die!"

It was only at Stowlangtoft that I ever talked to the King at all intimately, until the occasion of his very last visit to the Iveaghs at Elveden, of which I shall tell later. One day, when we were out shooting in that Suffolk country, he showed me a little silver medal of the Blessed Virgin, which he wore on his watch-chain. He said that it had been given to him by a lady whom he had greatly loved. He spoke with deep feeling. I thought for a long time that it must have been some foreign Princess—Italian, perhaps—evidently a Catholic. But afterwards I was told that there was a very beautiful Catholic lady in London, who was a great friend of the King's. They said that she was more lovely than any of the famous beauties of the time, but that she was never in the limelight. She was said to be very devout.

She lived quietly in Queensbury Place, and some old Irish ladies, friends of mine, whose house was opposite hers, used to be much interested to see the King's brougham frequently outside her door.

When he showed me the medal, I said to him: "Oh, Sir. You should not wear a medal like that on your watch-chain! I will give you a chain for it to wear round your neck." I gave him a thin platinum chain, but I never knew whether he wore it or not. When he died, there were rumours that he had died a Catholic, and I often wondered if the little chain and medal had been found round his neck. The lady he had spoken of with so much feeling, afterwards went into a Convent, I believe.

I only looked into this English world and out again. I belonged to Ireland, and always returned there to my real life and background.

Lord Wolseley had been Commander-in-Chief in Ireland from 1890 to 1895. He and Lady Wolseley were the best hosts I have ever known, and at the Royal Hospital they always made you feel that you were the one person in the world they really wanted to see. I think he was *the* greatest soldier we ever had, but he was unlucky.

I remember a lunch party later at his house in Grosvenor Gardens, when I sat between him and Sir Herbert Tree and they were discussing the theory of luck. Lord Wolseley said that luck was the greatest factor in life, and that if your star was in the ascendant you could do nothing wrong. But when you were out of luck you could do nothing right. He instanced Napoleon, who always followed his star, which only failed him when he went to Moscow; and then, although he had planned everything carefully, the weather turned against him; snow came earlier than usual, and the expedition was a disastrous failure.

Sir Herbert Tree, on the contrary, said that it was in your own hands, and that you made your own luck or otherwise.

I joined in: "It was a jolly lucky day for you, anyhow, when you found Dorothea Baird to play Trilby!"

Lord Roberts followed Lord Wolseley as Commander-in-Chief. We all adored "Bobs."

He used to hunt, and after a day's hunting would be welcomed home by Lady Roberts and enfolded in her large embrace, being quite lost in it, for she was as ample as he was small. She evidently thought his hunting as dangerous as his campaigns, and always expected to see him brought back on a stretcher!

He came to Killeen several times for hunting. And there was a night when my dinner-table had suddenly to be rearranged. I had lost my head for a moment over the always difficult job. Lord Roberts came to my rescue, standing at the end of the table as though he were arranging armies on a battlefield.

"Put that man there and that lady there."

He had it in order in a minute.

His antipathy for cats is well known. Another night at Killeen, as he came in to dinner he turned pale and said: "There is a cat in the room."

"No, Lord Roberts," I assured him. "There is no cat."

"I am quite sure there is," he insisted.

Unbelieving, but to please him, we searched, and found behind a screen, a tiny kitten, strayed in from Fingall's "Cattery."

This "Cattery" was Fingall's special hobby. I believe that it started originally with a family of kittens found in my best hat, which Fingall rescued on their way to be drowned! He kept them in one of the old towers next door to his study, where they increased and multiplied. Luckily there was a passage through a wall six feet thick, from the study to the tower. But the barred tower window was always open to all the cats of the neighbourhood, who treated it as a Rowton House. At one time there were at least sixty cats in residence, and Fingall looked after them himself, and knew all their pedigrees and characters! The room was beautifully arranged for them, with benches, sand on the floor, and straw. He brought them food at regular intervals. No one else dared to approach them, as they were perfectly savage.

261

During those years I frequently stayed with the Guinnesses at 80 Stephen's Green. They were great friends of ours, and I think we were in a sort of way connected, as a McGuinness of Iveagh had, many years ago, married a Plunkett and is in the Family Tree.

One night, soon after the South African War, I was staying with them, and at dinner sat beside Count Paul Metternich, the German Ambassador in London. He was tall and handsome in a typical German way, with hair *en brosse*. Remembering our then recent experiences at Kiel, I said to him: "Count Metternich, why do you Germans hate the English so much?"

"We do not hate the English," he answered. "But we hate the British younger son; for wherever we try to plant our flag, we find that he is there before us."

Then he went on to speak with real understanding and appreciation, of the English country houses from which those younger sons went out to plant the English flag in the far corners of the earth. He had looked at such houses, with their gardens and lawns and fields about them, and the village at their gates and the village cricket field and all the rest. And he understood fully the influence of that background and the memories which the Younger Son carried with him, when he went out to plant the Flag in the far corners of the earth.

The next day I was asked to take Count Metternich out to Kilruddery. We drove on an outside car, and I taught him how to sit on it. As we drove through the Wicklow country under the two blue Sugar Loaf Mountains, and turned and looked back to Bray Head and the Irish Sea, shining in the summer light, my companion said slowly: "I don't wonder that you Irish love your country. It is so beautiful."

There was another occasion when I drove with Lord Iveagh on his coach on the outskirts of London and again Count Metternich was of the party. It was summer and occasionally we passed a green field where white-clad boys were playing cricket. "Ah!" said the German Ambassador. "That is what makes English character. The game in which they all play together for the spirit of the team." We talked of it then, that cricket field which is so much the centre and symbol of English life. It stands for something very good and typical of the people who play it. You must not loose your emotions at cricket, and you must play absolutely fair. I am always moved and touched when I go to Lords for the Eton and Harrow match and see the old men who played there themselves as boys, watching their grandsons play now.

Somewhere about this time, Hugh Lane appeared on the scene, young and full of enthusiasm. He was a nephew of Lady Gregory, whose house at Coole was for so many years a centre of Irish culture; and, being poor and having a flair for pictures and furniture, he had taken it, when little more than a boy, to London, where he worked for Colnaghi.

Now he was back in Dublin, busy with his plans for a Gallery of Modern Art. He was living in lodgings and practically starving himself so that he might buy pictures. I came to know him, and used to ask him down to Killeen to feed him. He repaid my hospitality fully.

Killeen had not been changed essentially since I came to it on my marriage, and it was still the house of which Bernard Holland had said, standing in the hall and staring about him: "Good Heavens, what a house for *you* to live in!"

My sisters-in-law had now married and I had a free hand, so Hugh Lane and I got to work on Killeen together. I do not know how many week-ends we worked. He was indefatigable. He would arrange a room a dozen times and rearrange it, before he was satisfied. I enjoyed it immensely. Gerald said later: "Mother, if you ever go to prison, I know you will make your cell pretty. And—you will make friends with the rats!"

We collected our treasures and discovered many new ones. The ebony furniture which had come back from Portugal with the wife of the 4th Earl. One cabinet was lined with tortoiseshell and had secret drawers and beautifully carved ivory figures inside. We found, in a garret, two Chinese chests on their original stands, and a forgotten spinet in the Servants' Hall. Other treasures we pulled out together, were some Louis Seize and Empire Consols, beautiful Queen Anne bedspreads, and Chippendale furniture which Henrietta Maria Wollascott had brought with her from Woolhampton Court.

Hugh Lane used to chuckle with joy when he found each new treasure. He loved beautiful things—old things especially —and would fall down and worship a picture or a piece of china.

Fingall looked on patiently while we worked. Like George II., he distrusted "Boetry and Bainting" in a man. He was so polite to Hugh Lane, of whom he had remarked to me: "He is a good fellow. It is a pity he is like that."

With his usual tolerance he let us have our way, only stipulating that we must go no farther than the corridor leading to his study. Hugh Lane drew a picture of Fingall standing at the study door with drawn sword, and called it, "The Earl's Last Stand."

He gave me some rules for furnishing and decorating, while we rummaged and searched and found treasures, and arranged them together.

He said that the lovely walls of Killeen should never have paint or paper on them. Castle walls should be left as much like stone as possible. It was permissible to hang tapestry against them or arras of brocade or velvet, and he admired the hand-printed papers in the bedrooms—some of the earliest ever made. He said also that there should be no flower-beds near the Castle. They would be out of keeping with a fighting castle. Trees and shrubs, one might have. And he allowed me the water-garden at a little distance, which was really a continuation of the Moat.

He said, going back to furnishing: "Anything beautiful will go together—particularly anything Chinese."

The best things at Killeen were the Oriental china and some very good carpets and rugs. The only tapestry we had, hung in one of the best bedrooms, to hide an ugly wall cup-board. But I had some old brocade, and he made me send it to Hatfield of Charlotte Street in London—who had done Windsor Castle—to be made into a screen. He examined the pictures that we had called the "Toasted Ancestors," since they had been damaged in the fire. "They are not pictures, but they will make good furniture," he said, and took them over to London to be restored, dismissing my suggested artist in Dublin: "I would not trust *him* with a tea-tray."

The pictures in the drawing-room had not been touched by the fire, so we had a good background to start with. The walls of that room and of the hall were painted a soft stone colour. The drawing-room was octagonal with three long windows at the end and an alcove. A beautiful room to arrange. Hugh Lane put a bust of Erin that he got from Charles Gatty, in a place of honour—quite in keeping with our lives. He got Hicks, the famous Dublin cabinet-maker, down, to put delicate little shelves in the alcove. We filled these with *famille rose* and *famille verte* china. On either side we put tall alabaster vases which looked lovely when I had filled them with flowers from my garden. We found two deep blue Oriental jars to stand on the Chinese chest.

Then we discovered many old fans, and miniatures, which I took to Mr. Hatfield to have framed, and we decorated one corner of the room with them. Another corner with relics and holy pictures.

We brought down the books which had been in a small room at the top of the house and turned the big room next the drawing-room into a library. Hicks made for it some beautiful bookcases of old mahogany, to Hugh Lane's design. It is interesting to note that those bookcases, which cost eight hundred to a thousand pounds then, could not now be made for double the money. The books had also been brought over by Henrietta Maria Wollascott. They were not interest-ing, being mostly religious and medical, but some of the bindings were beautiful and decorative.

Sometimes Hugh Lane even exhausted me. He had been

working himself all the week, and then he came down and worked us all the week-end. The servants forgave him, even the sin of breaking the Sabbath, because he was so attractive and charming that he would whistle the birds from the trees. I have a memory of Russell, the carpenter, sweating under his orders. But Russell would have shed his blood for the family, much less his perspiration! And Curtin the perfect butler, helping to drag furniture about, although he had never been engaged for that! In the hall we put oak furniture with blue china against it. For light there was a lovely hanging candelabrum from the ceiling, and two boys' figures holding up branches of candles. When we had a party, a footman would light the candles while we were at dinner, and the effect was beautiful when we came out.

We were pleased with our work when it was done. Many years later, Lord Wimborne, during his Viceroyalty, stood still, entering the drawing-room at Killeen for the first time: "What a beautiful room!" And other people had said it, too.

Of course Hugh Lane made me jolly well work for him in return for all the work he had done for me. I had to give parties for his Gallery, and collect people and money to help him. There was a possibility of Lord Iveagh giving him his wished-for Gallery in Stephen's Green. But when we thought we had persuaded Lord Iveagh, someone told him that the Lord Mayor and Corporation would have control of the Gallery, and it was never given. Then there was Lutyens' beautiful idea of one built on a bridge over the Liffey, as they build in Italy. But that came to nothing. And now Hugh Lane's collection—minus the thirty-nine pictures of the famous Lane bequest, which are held in London—is in the Modern Art Gallery at Charlemont House, Dublin.

In those days he was always trying to get people to be painted for his Gallery. His idea was that we should pay fifty pounds to be painted—say by de Lazlo—and then we should give the picture to the Gallery. It was settled that I should be painted in white muslin and a blue sash. Hugh

Lane, having arranged this, looked at me and said: "You will be very difficult to paint. It would have to be done quickly. There is so little to get hold of. It is like a light in a window and the light goes out."

I remembered that Dunraven had christened me "The Elusive Lady," and we might, I thought, call the picture that.

But when I went to London and was having a very gay time, I could not face getting up in the morning and putting on a muslin frock and driving in a hansom out to a suburb. It was all too chilly a prospect, and I chucked my appointment.

Mr. de Lazlo said to me the other day: "To think that I could have painted you for fifty pounds. What would it be worth now?" But that would not have been much use to me, hanging in a cold Gallery!

Then there was an idea of Gerald Festus Kelly. I liked his "Lady in Black" and thought it would be warmer than white muslin! Lane said: "You have chosen the best of the lot." But Gerald Festus Kelly had just gone to Paris, and that never came off.

Hugh Lane was merciless when he wanted anything, and always got what he wanted. I remember an auction in Dublin in an old house in Stephen's Green next door to the Iveaghs'—a house which had a strange history. An old Miss Magan had just died, who many years earlier had been a Dublin beauty. The story was that she had been engaged to a young man with whom she was very much in love. On the day of the wedding he failed to appear. The house was shut up for many years and the lady lived as a recluse in her country house in Meath. When she was dying she asked to be buried in her bridal dress. After the funeral they opened the Stephen's Green house, and, it was said, found the wedding breakfast still spread for the guests who had not come thirty years earlier.

Some beautiful old printed linen was sold at Miss Magan's auction. I thought of the long windows at Killeen, and bought it all. Then in came Hugh Lane, late. "You must let me have it. You *must*!" In the end he got nearly all of it!

But another time he was beaten. Naylor, an antique dealer on the quay, who was one of my friends, had a lovely Chinese screen that had belonged to Henry Grattan and had come from Tinahinch.

Mrs. Keith, a charming and clever neighbour of Horace's, who was helping to furnish his house, Kilteragh, then just built, came with me to see the screen, and between us we persuaded Naylor to let us have it for about one hundred pounds. The deal was clinched by Naylor—who was slightly intoxicated—putting an arm round each of our necks and saying, "I am giving you a present, but *anny*thing for the ladies—*anny*thing for the ladies!"

At this moment Hugh Lane dashed in, saw the screen and said, "I must have that screen."

Naylor said: "The ladies are before you."

"I have not bought it," I declared meanly. "Mrs. Keith has."

I knew that *I* could never stand up to Hugh Lane. She was firm, and Horace got the screen.

The last time I ever saw Hugh Lane was on a February day during the War, in his beautiful Chelsea house on the river. I believe the house had been a bishop's palace. It had a paved garden at the back and was full of lovely pictures and furniture. Almost immediately after that he sailed for America, having first made the famous codicil to his will, leaving the pictures he had willed to the London National Gallery, in a pique, back to the country that he loved. But unfortunately he failed to have it witnessed, and on his return journey he went down in the *Lusitania*. So the pictures are still held in London, and an empty room awaits the Lane collection in Dublin at Charlemont House.

When we had finished with the house at Killeen, Sir Frederick Moore, who was then head of the Botanic Gardens in Glasnevin, and an old friend of mine, helped me with the garden. He said: "If you will give up your strawberries and asparagus, I will make you the most lovely border in Ireland."

The garden was a very big one, with walls within walls. Instead of square corners, these were rounded, with many old fruit trees espaliered against them. The effect was like a bower, and although for many years the trees had borne no fruit to speak of, I would not have them cut down. Another grey mellowed wall cut the garden in half. It made a background for our border on one side, with gnarled apple trees on the other. We made it twenty feet wide each side. It was planned for a succession of colour and was at its loveliest in August, just about Horse Show time. We had another border of many flowering shrubs. And I made for my own pleasure, beds of heliotrope, the one flower that Horace ever noticed. Once walking across St. James's Park with Karl Walter, he stood still to look at and smell a bed of it: "Whenever I see that, I feel that she is near!"

Later, when cultivation began to be expensive, I turned half the garden—where we had once grown tobacco—into an orchard, and planted daffodils and tulips under the trees, where they still remain. The daffodils were brave and lovely dancing in a March wind and later, the tulips glimmered beautifully under the apple blossom in the dusk of an April or May evening.

CHAPTER TWENTY-ONE

WHEN the Balfours left Ireland, George Wyndham succeeded Gerald as Chief Secretary. And I was handed on to him and his charming wife, Lady Grosvenor, by Gerald and Betty as the "*amie de la maison*," someone who would be able to tell them about things and people in Dublin.

Gerald had gone away, keeping his heart whole, only leaving Ireland the results of his work for her. Betty had fallen in love with the country and the people. But George Wyndham came to Ireland in love with her already, and the reckless generosity of a man in that state, was increased in his case by his own nature. He was in love with so many things: with his lovely wife, with friendship (like Montaigne), with Ireland and with England, with life itself. He came to Ireland full of enthusiasms, dreams and plans. He would settle the Irish Question first by settling the Land Question. Before he left he would pull off what he called his "grand slam." There were to be three tricks in it: his Land Act (which he achieved), a University Act, and finally Devolution, which would be a form of Home Rule.

He came as the great-grandson of Lord Edward Fitzgerald, as conscious of that heritage as was the country that welcomed him, seeing Lord Edward in him. His first pilgimage, immediately after his arrival, was to the old church in Thomas Street which holds Lord Edward's tomb.

His mother, Mrs. Percy Wyndham, Lord Edward's granddaughter, whom he adored, as Lord Edward had adored his mother, had brought up all her children to that tradition. Someone asked George once if he felt anything passing Leinster House. He said: "I never pass it without a feeling of deep emotion." Again he said once that he felt "every minute that he was not in Ireland, wasted." He had much in common with his ancestor, besides a physical resemblance. If Gerald Balfour looked like Sir Galahad, George Wyndham should

270

THE RIGHT HON. GEORGE WYNDHAM.

ELVEDEN—DECEMBER, 1902.

(Back, L. to R.) Duke of Roxburghe, Marquis de Soveral, Duke of Montrose, Lady Iveagh, H.M. King of Portugal, Lady Mary Grosvenor, Lord Suffield, Lord Savile, Sir Arthur Davidson, Count d'Arnoso.

(Middle, seated, L. to R.) Lady Evelyn Guinness, Lady Lilian Wemyss, Countess of Fingall, Duchess of Montrose, Lady Helen Vincent, Mrs. Hope Vere.

(Front, L. to R.) Rupert Guinness, Admiral Capello, Lord Iveagh, Seymour Fortescue, Commandant Pinto Basto.

have lived in the days of Roland. He was most romantic and beautiful to look at—already iron-grey although he was still quite young, with, in contrast, dark brows above deep blue eyes. I have often said that he could have been a Troubadour—that he, alone of the men I have known, could have looked the part.

He was vitally alive, and because he was one of the givers out of life, always giving, he gave his vitality wherever he went. When he came into a room, it was like an enlivening wind, a breath of mountain air. You would know that he was there, even without seeing him. George was full of fire and enthusiasm, without fear. That living of every minute of his life at high pitch, I believe now, was one of the signs that he was to die young. He would never be at his second best. Flatness was intolerable to such a nature as his. Other men I have known—Arthur Balfour, Gerald, Horace Plunkett —would submit to be bored, even dull at times, but George Wyndham must always be at the peak, and so one remembers him.

He had, like all the Wyndhams, a genius for friendship. When I went to stay with him and Sibell Grosvenor at Saighton, he always met me at the gate as he met all his guests—not waiting for them to come to the door—and he would start at once to talk about Ireland. I must have brought to him, to some extent, the country that he loved. But he was a wonderful welcomer, and a welcome is as precious a thing as love or friendship. It is of the spirit and not to be made with hands. It is there or not there, and you could never imagine it, or light its fire in the cold, empty place where it had not been.

In those days when George was Irish Chief Secretary, I received one of the greatest compliments that I have ever had. Someone said to me:

"We knew that you had come into the room, because we saw George Wyndham's face light up." That "lighting up" was just his friendship, his welcome and pleasure in a friend's coming.

He gave out so much that he must have lived to exhaustion

point. Although his political work came first, he was no one-idea'd man, and he spent himself in a hundred ways. He had a fine literary gift and taste in literature. He was a scholar. He had the great family love that is revealed in the Fitzgerald letters and which was repeated in their descendants.

At the Chief Secretary's Lodge he often called me out to walk with him and listen to one of his speeches for the House of Commons. I used to say that he tried them on me, as representing the meanest intelligence, and that if I understood, that proved that any one would! We used to walk round the path above the sunk wall which circles the grounds of the Lodge, George Wyndham declaiming, and I listening, even sometimes daring to criticise. He used his hands beautifully when he was speaking, in a French way—a heritage no doubt from his French ancestors. Irish, French and Scottish blood mingled in him, each bringing their gifts.

Once I was staying at the Lodge for a Ball. It was June, and when I went to my room, the Ball being over, it was already an early summer morning. I was in my ball dress and just about to take it off and go to bed for an hour or so, when something hit against the window—a pebble, followed by another. I looked out. George Wyndham stood on the path below. "Be a sport," he said, "and come for a ride."

I flung off my evening dress quickly and got into a riding skirt. It took a little time, and George Wyndham had saddled the horses and was waiting with them when I joined him outside. We mounted and rode down the avenue and out into the Park, where the dew was still grey on the grass and the distant mountains quite asleep. We turned right outside the gate, circled the wall and so on to the Fifteen Acres, where we let the horses go. (Or—my horse went, and I had to give him his way as usual.) It was a magic ride. We crossed the immense space of the Fifteen Acres, ours entirely that summer morning, and came to the little scattered forest of twisted trees at the other side. They were black in the very early sunlight. One or two pale deer fled before us, into them. We crossed the road and, on grass again, cantered and galloped.

Suddenly into the exquisite world which was ours alone there came another sound—the galloping of horses pursuing us. They were heavy-hoofed in comparison with ours, or so it seemed to me. That sound following us was a sinister one in the now sunlit Park. We fled before it, but it gained on us steadily, and was always there. I did not dare to look back, and became terrified, remembering a May evening in this Park, not so many years earlier. It seemed that for quite a long time we rode in this way—only ten minutes probably. At last from sheer exhaustion I pulled my horse to a trot and looked over my shoulder. Two enormous mounted policemen and their horses were black between us and the sunlight. They were the Chief Secretary's Guard, whom he had forgotten, and who had got wind of our ride and were desperately pursuing their charge.

I may have suggested that George Wyndham liked every one. He did not. But Sibell—who was so lovely and kind, especially if you were in trouble—made up for that. She was very High Church, and made a tiny chapel at the Chief Secretary's Lodge with a lamp always lighted, where there used to be prayers, and she and George always liked their guests to go to them.

Sibell liked every one in the world, I think, and sometimes when she took your hand in that soft warm clasp of hers one felt that she did not know whose hand it was.

George was so full of schemes and enthusiasms that he could not keep them to himself. It was not in such a nature as his to be wise and secretive. He would be too trusting, and I think there was too much of the sun in his eyes for him to be a true judge of character. I used to fight him over this and say that some of his friends would let him down one day. He was, like many men, however great, susceptible to flattery, although it did not affect his friendship for me that I never flattered him.

I was at a party in London once, to which he came on, after making a speech in the House. A lady rushed forward to tell him how wonderful his speech had been, and how wonderful *he* was. He turned to me with a rather shy smile: "That is not what my little Irish friend tells me," he said to the flatterer.

Well, I believe the Japanese have a School of Flattery. And men may always be deceived by it—although they would be so angry if one told them so. Women are less simple. They have only to look in their mirrors to know the truth.

I remember George Wyndham hunting with the Meaths, looking wonderful in his red coat. Too young and too handsome, some people said, to believe in as a statesman. Galloping across country, he could get away and forget everything and become a boy as young as his own son. At Saighton he might throw off Ireland, the burden of her at least, and there, I suppose, the magic of Dark Rosaleen would be made bluer and mistier by the little distance.

Saighton was an old house with battlemented walls, which made a lovely background for Sibell's tall flower borders, and there was a monastic feeling in George's turret room. It was lined with beautiful books and had deep seats in the windows which looked over the Cheshire country to the spires of Chester Cathedral. George used to recite poetry in that room and read Shakespeare aloud to us in his beautiful voice. I could listen to him for hours. Sometimes Charles Gatty, who was often there, would play for us. He could get more Wagner out of a piano than any one else I know.

From Saighton we went, only just across the fields, to the Westminsters at Eaton—a hideous house. The former Duke of Westminster, who had built it, had admired St. Pancras Railway Station and sent for the architect who had designed that, and had it copied. I stayed there once, and it took a quarter of an hour to get from my bedroom to the drawing-room, down endless long passages that bore a distinct resemblance to station corridors.

George was always talking of his dreams—at Saighton, leaning his arms on the window-sill in that turret room—or at the Chief Secretary's Lodge with its view of the Irish hills. He had a great admiration for the religious orders who

274

worked among the poor in Ireland. And he loved many of the Western priests as they loved him.

A visit to Foxford moved him deeply. Charlotte Dease remembers being one of the party that went with him on that occasion from Clonalis, where they were all staying with the O'Conor Don. She drove on an outside car, with George the other side, he leaning across the "well," talking, until it was time to prepare his speech. "Now I must think of my speech," he said, and was silent, composing it while they drove.

At Foxford, as usual, Mother Morrogh Bernard hid herself, and a charming and very pretty nun, who was the secretary, received the party. An introduction was made.

"The Chief Secretary of Ireland—the Secretary of Foxford."

And the charming nun took the Chief Secretary over the mills and showed him everything.

Charles Gatty tells in *Recognita*, his book about George Wyndham, how affected George was by that visit. "He poured out his soul to me about it. 'And what do you think they have put up over the altar in the chapel?' he said. '*Mitis sum et humilis corde.*'"

Charles Gatty adds: "After all, the clang and din of well-advertised philanthropy, it was a joy to peep into a quiet five-mile circuit of social, educational, agricultural and industrial restoration brought about by the Sisters of Charity, and over all, the Divine Inspiration—'*Mitis sum et humilis corde.*'

During George's Chief Secretaryship, Winston Churchill came to Dublin and lectured on his War experiences and his escape from Pretoria. He stayed with George and Sibell. His lecture to the Dublin audience was vivid and good, but he forgot to mention the Irish regiments or the great deeds they had done. When he sat down the audience was strangely silent, and one could feel the flatness in the air. Then some one—I think Judge Fitzgibbon—got up to propose a vote of thanks, and laid stress on the gallant doings of the Irish soldiers. He was received with immense applause. At supper

275

later, Winston Churchill said to me that he had been a little disappointed in his reception.

I said, "Had you no female relative to tell you that you must first make friends with your audience? You forgot to mention the Irish regiments."

"What a fool I was!" he exclaimed.

In the dead of night he woke up his host to tell him what a mistake he had made.

About this time, too, a German Fleet under the command of Prince Henry of Prussia came to Ireland and went round all the ports, to the horror of Lord Cadogan. We visited the Fleet in Kingstown Harbour and were entertained to tea on the Flagship. It seemed to me that the ships were much less well polished and tidy than ours, and I noticed that some of the sailors looked in a very unfriendly way at their officers.

These were such packed years that I wonder sometimes how we fitted it all in. I went to London occasionally and stayed with the Jamesons, whose house in Princes Gate was always home to me. Then I would see George Wyndham and Sibell at 35 Park Lane, when they were over from Ireland.

(I passed the house the other day in a bus and could almost have sworn that I saw George at the window. It was an autumn day and the leaves on the plane tree before the house were yellow. The whole looked a little unreal, like a house painted in a picture of another time. That house, lying a little back from the road behind a wide path and trees, had always a withdrawn look as though it stood apart from the other houses. The plane tree was still in front of the house, and it seemed to me that only the number was changed. Then the bus carried me on.)

During one of my London visits of this time I was asked to lunch there, and George told me that I was to meet someone about whom he would like my opinion. I was a little early, and Sibell received me in the drawing-room with its rounded windows, looking across Park Lane to the Park. Presently George came in with his usual warm welcome, followed by Lord Lansdowne and an ugly little man, rather

276

like a Chinese idol. I was introduced to Sir Anthony Mac-Donnell, recently Lieutenant-Governor of the United Provinces and Oudh. We went into lunch, during which the Irish question was the sole subject of conversation. I knew that Sir David Harrel was retiring, and decided in my own mind that this must be the new Under Secretary.

I crossed that night to Ireland and broke my journey at the Viceregal Lodge. George Wyndham had not given me any instructions to keep silent, so at lunch the following day I said pleasantly to Lord Cadogan: "I think I have met the new Under Secretary."

"Oh, indeed," he said. "Have you? And who is he?"

"Sir Anthony MacDonnell."

"Indeed. It is the first *I* have heard of it."

The Lord Lieutenant was evidently much annoyed. He wrote to George Wyndham that it was very strange to receive his first information about the new Under Secretary from Lady Fingall.

I was in disgrace for a time.

"But," I defended myself, "you never told me to keep it a secret." And soon I was forgiven.

"Anthony Pat," as we called him, was George Wyndham's big mistake. George thought he had got a tool, but I told him: "You have got a tiger. You will never be able to chew that man. He will chew you."

I have always had an instinct for people. Women have instinct, where men have reason, but instinct is far the most useful gift. I was told the other day that King Edward asked Sir Anthony MacDonnell, who had had a far greater position, of course, in India, as a personal favour, to take the Irish Under Secretaryship. I do not know if that is true. But of course Anthony Pat remained, always, a great old Irishman.

Lord Cadogan, who was not a young man and was rather tired, resigned the Viceroyalty in August, 1902; and the Dudleys came. They were both young, extraordinarily good looking, rich, enthusiastic, charming. She had the beauty of an Eastern queen—more like Esther than Rachel—and was tremendously in love with her husband. Her one dream was to make his Irish Viceroyalty a triumphant success. He was the spoilt child of fortune. His father had been the richest man in England, and his mother one of the beautiful Moncrieffs. Still he remained amazingly unspoilt. Walter Callan, who was his secretary for many years, in Ireland and afterwards in Australia, remembers how, amidst all distractions, his attention could always be caught by anything that promised to be of use to Ireland, especially to the poor in the West. Lord Dudley came to Ireland a Conservative and Unionist, but left, convinced that some form of self-government by Irishmen, according to Irish ideas, was the only solution of the Irish problem.

The new Lord Lieutenant and his Consort made the usual State entry, with escorts of troops and enormous cheering crowds. Lord Dudley was much moved by this reception and stirred to new resolutions about what he would do for the country and the people. After being sworn in, he slipped away from the luncheon party at the Viceregal Lodge to walk alone through the gardens and shrubberies, thinking about Ireland and how he could serve her. He was deep in thought, walking between the thick laurels, when he heard stealthy footsteps behind him. They awakened him rudely from his dreams, and reminded him of the stories he had heard of the darker side of Ireland. He turned, but the laurels hid whoever it was that followed him. He quickened his pace and the footsteps quickened theirs, just as the galloping horses had pursued George Wyndham and myself on our lovely morning ride. In a clear space, at last, he turned, prepared to grapple with assailants, but saw instead the two special detectives whose duty it was to follow him everywhere. The reminder of that necessity, or supposed necessity, was for the moment, a cold douche on his spirits and heart.

Walter Callan told me this story. We talked about the brilliance and extravagance of the Dudley Season. In their first year in Ireland the Dudleys had spent £80,000. Their salary was £20,000. The Viceroy's heart was nearly broken by the efforts of some of his staff to get the expenditure down to £50,000. Economy was anathema to him. He could never say No to any appeal, but some of the expenditure was the princely extravagance of a very rich man who refused to count the cost. Walter Callan remembers some amusing items of it. There were thirty-two black horses hired from Dolland of London. About four of them were used regularly, but the rest were used only twice a year—at the Horse Show and Punchestown. But all thirty-two were kept and exercised and paid for, all the year round. It was with the greatest difficulty that "His Ex." could be got to modify this arrangement.

When Fingall was Master of the Horse, in the last months of the Dudley Viceroyalty, new liveries were due for the coachmen, grooms and outriders. Fingall pointed out that it was not worth while wasting money on these, for a month or two. Lord Dudley said: "I will have no damned economy, my lord!"

And the liveries were ordered!

Lord Dudley patronised a famous Hungarian barber in London, known as "Charles the Barber." When His Excellency wanted his hair cut he would say: "Telegraph to Charles to come across." Charles would arrive, say, on Tuesday. Walter Callan would go in to Lord Dudley with important letters, and when they were dealt with, would say: "When will you see Charles?"

"Oh, I can't now—I am going to golf at Portmarnock."

Again in the evening, when the files were being dealt with:

"Charles is still here, sir."

"Oh, I'll see him to-morrow. I am going to play Bridge now."

So it might go on for two or three days. In fact the story went that once Charles travelled back to London with Lord Dudley, the latter's hair being still uncut. In the end the Lord Lieutenant's hair-cut might well cost him £20!

Lord Dudley was the first Lord Lieutenant to use a motorcar. Walter Callan recalls his own first experience of motoring when he was working with Horace. They came

279

down to lunch at Killeen, having left Dublin at 11.15 and arrived at 1.15—twenty miles—and were received by us, he says, like Scott flying from Baghdad!

Lord Dudley used to drive pretty often down to Portmarnock to play golf. It was nine miles or so from the Viceregal Lodge. One day his Secretary was rung up by the Inspector General of the Police. "Would you ask His Excellency to drive a little more slowly, as his bodyguard find it hard to keep up with him?"

The Lord Lieutenant was filled with remorse when he realised that his guard had only push-bikes; and some motorcycles were provided.

All this time George Wyndham was busy on his great Land Act. He had introduced his first measure in 1902. His big bill was to be "the Bill of the Session," and he introduced and passed it in 1903. There had been a conference between the representatives of the Land Owners' Convention and representatives of the tenants. The first were prepared to sell, only if they could get a good price. The tenants were prepared to buy, if they could get the land cheap. The crux of the situation was that neither the very rich landlords nor the very poor wanted to sell, for quite opposing reasons. The rich did not need the money, and the poor had their estates fully mortgaged, and so would get nothing on a sale. The solution of the problem was found in a proposed bonus to the landlords, to induce them to sell. The bonus was, however, to cost the Treasury twelve million pounds, and Ritchie, the economic Chancellor of the Exchequer, did not see why such a free gift to the landlords of Ireland should be made by the people of England.

George Wyndham said: "It is to develop a backward part of the Imperial Estate." But the Treasury would not see it that way, and appeared to be obdurate. Ritchie, bent on safeguarding the national purse, would not give George Wyndham one million, much less twelve.

Wyndham said to him: "Unless you do, Land Purchase won't go in Ireland, and you will have further trouble." And then he suggested: "Come and see the country for yourself."

The Chancellor agreed to do this. Then George Wyndham went to the Dudleys and said: "Ritchie is coming to Ireland. I shan't be here. You must arrange it all."

It was just at this time that I first met the Dudleys at Adare. I shall always remember a night when I listened in the Oak Gallery above the hall to Lady Dunraven and her daughters playing, she at the piano, the girls, Rachel and Eileen, the violin and 'cello. And then Mr. Plumstead, the Adare organist, sat down at the organ, and Lady Dudley, with her lovely voice, sang from the organ loft: "Oh, for the Wings of a Dove!"

Miss Devereux remembers a night at Adare when some one played "The Wearing of the Green" in the hall, and the guests all sang it, and I, listening in the shadows of the gallery, ran forward into the light as the song ended, and clapped my hands. That was my rebel Irish blood stirred by the song. She remembers, too, she says, listening with the other ladies' maids in the gallery when Lady Dunraven played the harp in that hall.

From Adare, a little later, I went to stay with the Dudleys at Rockingham in Roscommon, which they had taken from the King-Harmans—a lovely place, with its lakes and islands and old ruins that had once been the stronghold of the MacDermots. Adeline, Duchess of Bedford, and myself were, I think, besides Lady Dudley, the only women. Horace Plunkett, Sir David Harrel, Lionel Earle and a couple of A.D.C.s made up the men of the party. We were to be joined by the Chancellor of the Exchequer, Mr. Ritchie, who was coming to pay a visit to the Congested Districts, and Rachel Dudley had determined to let him see the very worst aspect of Irish poverty.

He arrived at Kingstown by the afternoon boat and was asked: "Would you like to see a little of Dublin?" He said that he would, and he was driven slowly through the slums, the fashionable quarters being carefully avoided. This occupied the time until his train left for the West. He was

281

put into the train in the dusk, and when he arrived at the end of his journey, driven out through the dark country to Rockingham. The next day Lady Dudley took him out motoring. Again the route was carefully chosen, through what George Wyndham called "the agricultural slums of Ireland." The chauffeur had orders to drive slowly past the poorest cottages, where the parish priest had seen to it that the most miserable looking children were on show. If, by chance, a fairly prosperous cottage had to be passed, the car went at full speed, and Lady Dudley, putting out all her charms, distracted the Chancellor's attention. The programme was repeated daily during his visit. Sometimes he passed the same place a second time without recognising it.

At the end of that visit to Roscommon, Mr. Ritchie was taken back to the Viceregal Lodge, and from there to the boat. Returning to London, he declared: "My God! I did not know that in Western Europe such a country existed! The only two decent houses in it are the Viceregal Lodge and Rockingham. All the others are slums and broken-down cottages."

He was shocked also by the appalling roads over which he had been mercilessly bumped!

George Wyndham got his twelve millions. And it was certainly a jolly bonus for the broken-down landlords, and for the spendthrifts, who were relieved of their mortgaged estates and made a free gift as well, for the bonus went to the tenant for life.

Shortly after the passing of his Land Act, George Wyndham was taking a holiday at Monte Carlo. Wandering into the gaming rooms, he saw the Marquis of ——, hitherto an impoverished Irish peer, the centre of a group of gamers. Lord —— had had a big estate in Ireland, but never a penny in his pocket. As George Wyndham passed by, Lord ——, pointing to the pile of notes and counters before him, called out gaily: "George! George! The Bonus!"

Perhaps no Vicereine loved Ireland more than Lady Dudley. She left a great work behind her for the people, in the Dudley Nurses, which she established. They were distributed in the poorest parts of Ireland, where there had previously been no nursing service—only the handyman and handywoman of my childhood. What their coming must have meant to the sick and suffering people! She also took a tremendous interest in all our industries and in the School of Art Needlework, which Lady Mayo was running. I have over my bed now, a charming picture worked at the School to Lady Dudley's design. In the middle is a beautiful Virgin and Child, on each side white lilies, and underneath, these lines:

> "Let there be many windows in your soul,
>   That all the glory of the Universe may beautify it
> Tear away the blinds of superstition:
> Let the Light pour through Fair Windows,
> Broad as Truth itself, and High as God."

After the Dudleys left Ireland they still kept a fishing lodge on the West coast, to which she returned years later for spiritual peace and rest after the great strain of her War work. It was there, alas, that, bathing in Inver Lake when she was not strong enough, she was drowned.

In the spring of 1903 the Big Wind had come. It tore across Ireland from west to east like a tornado. Even the walls of Killeen—six foot thick, some of them—rocked. The children were in the nursery at the top of the house, and when the storm was at its height, I went up and brought them and their nurse down to the Oak Hall. The sleepy children thought it great fun, stumbling down the stairs, dragging their pillows and blankets. We lit a fire in the hall and stretched our mattresses on the floor. We could hear the wind howling through the shutters. Towards morning the exhausted children fell asleep, but I could not sleep, being too thin to enjoy the hardness of the parquet floor through a mattress! An early housemaid opened the door into the hall and saw what she took to be a row of dead bodies lying in the firelight. She gave a yell and fell down the back stairs and hurt herself, fortunately not seriously.

In the daylight we surveyed the damage. I had been certain that the old window in the Abbey would be down, but it was not. Trees had fallen in all directions. Although I felt sad about them, I knew that, like most Irish houses, Killeen had far too many trees close to it. We could not get to the station for days. Fingall went to the village, jumping his horse over the trees that lay across the road. No vehicle could pass until they were cleared away.

That summer King Edward and Queen Alexandra paid their Coronation visit to Ireland, and were given a wonderful reception. King Edward was the true diplomatist who takes advantage of luck and is given it. Someone said then: "Hasn't he the luck of the world!" For—though no one would have wished it so—the King's yacht, with the accompanying fleet, arrived in Kingstown Harbour simultaneously with the news of Pope Leo XIII.'s death. It was a unique opportunity for a gesture. The flag of the King's yacht was flown at half-mast. A telegram of sympathy was sent to Cardinal Logue, a Royal theatre visit countermanded. The next day there was a Levée at the Castle and in a sudden hush of excitement Archbishop Walsh made his entrance. No one had known until then whether he would come or not.

I have no recollection of the Drawing Room, but I do remember driving across country in a gig with Fingall to Celbridge Abbey, to consult Sir Gerald Dease as to what we, as Catholics, should do on such an occasion. I imagine that, having no suitable mourning clothes, I could not attend the Drawing Room, but I did go to the Park Races—in hastily collected black clothes, Miss Devereux tells me. The King was greatly pleased with his reception at the Races, and in great good humour, and the Queen, as always, charming and beautiful to all of us. She often did not hear what one said, but she smiled with that quick bright smile of the deaf, and then one did not want any words. They went on to the North, then did a tour of the West and South, including the Congested

Districts, finishing up at Queenstown, where the Royal yacht awaited them. Horace Plunkett and Sir Henry Robinson went with them; and in Connemara, the King's motor-car broke down. Horace Plunkett and Sir Henry Robinson had gone on ahead. When the King did not arrive, they returned in Horace's car and found that "all the King's horses and all the King's men" could not make the Royal car go. So John Brown, Horace's wonderful chauffeur, set to work. He was a genius with cars, and in a short time put the King's car right, and they were able to proceed.

At the end of this tour the King dubbed Horace, Knight of the Victorian Order. I always say that John Brown should have got that knighthood. It was quite unfitting for Horace, but paid him out for the derision he had cast on other knights, calling Dublin, "the City of Dreadful (K)nights."

My children used to say to him: "Uncle Horace, if you are ever made a peer, we think you should be called Lord Butterscotch." This was a reference to his creamery butter and the number of Scotchmen he had in the Department. But Horace remained K.C.V.O. and never became Lord Butterscotch.

That autumn we had an Irish section at a big English Exhibition. I was helping at it and had gone over, taking appropriately, a suit of Irish tweed to wear. It was bright emerald green. On my arrival I heard of the death of Fingall's Uncle George, who had supported Parnell's opponent in Meath and when he was defeated had never set foot in Ireland again.

There was I, with my green tweed suit and nothing else to wear. But Uncle George had led such a retired life for so many years that I hoped perhaps his death would pass almost unnoticed for a day or two, until I could get some black clothes.

However, I was busy at my stall, when the King, who was visiting the Exhibition and going round the stalls, stopped before me.

"How do you do, Lady Fingall?"

"How do you do, Sir," I said, curtseying, and aware at once that his eyes were on my green tweed.

"I was very sorry," he went on, "to read of the death of your uncle, George Plunkett."

I was fairly taken by surprise. How had the King noticed the death of an old Irish gentleman, living a retired life in London?

"Oh, yes, Sir," I said, more than ever conscious of my green tweed. "But how did Your Majesty know?"

"Ah!" the King said. "His brother, Sir Francis, is a great friend of mine, and one of my best Ambassadors. He does not talk too much, and always does the right thing by instinct."

I remembered that definition of the King's, of a good Ambassador. The incident proves the amazing memory to which Royalties are trained. King Edward was particularly wonderful in that way.

He bought an Irish cigar from me then, made from my own tobacco grown at Killeen. I was attacked afterwards for selling him a cigar that might have blown his head off. But I expect he was wise enough not to smoke it.

Uncle Francis—the Ambassador of whom he spoke—was a most charming person, with really wonderful manners, and very good looking. He was, at that time, Ambassador in Vienna, where he was a great friend of the old Emperor's. Franz Josef came personally to condole with the Ambassador when Queen Victoria died—a rare honour. The Emperor also had his portrait specially painted for Uncle Francis, and we still have it at Killeen. King Edward knew him better than most of his Ambassadors, as he used to be on duty every summer when the King went to Marienbad.

King Edward also paid an official visit to Vienna while Uncle Francis was there; and a magnificent Royal lunch was given for the Emperor at the British Embassy.

One of the things I have always regretted is that we did not accept Uncle Francis' invitation to visit him at the Embassy, and so missed seeing and hearing the beauty and gaiety and music of that wonderful pre-War Vienna, now, alas, vanished for ever!

CHAPTER TWENTY-TWO

KING EDWARD and Queen Alexandra paid another visit to Ireland in 1904, staying at the Viceregal Lodge. It was before the new wing was added to it for the Royal visit of 1911, and there was only room for the King and Queen and their entourage, with Lord and Lady Dudley and their staff. I stayed with the Iveaghs at 80 Stephen's Green, where they had a large party.

The King went to Punchestown, and there was a special train to Naas for the Viceregal and Iveagh parties. At Naas the grand Viceregal carriages, with their black horses, and the Iveagh carriages met us. The Queen did not go to the Races the first day, and by some mistake I was pushed into the carriage in which she should have driven. All along the route there was tremendous ovation, cheering and demonstrations, and I, thinking that I might be taken for the Queen, bowed graciously right and left. I was thinking that it was great fun to be a Queen when, as we went through some little village, a man jumped on the footboard and shook something into my face. I got a terrible fright and sank back, refusing to be a Queen any longer!

There was a wonderful reception again, for the King, at Punchestown. It was such a beautiful background for the scene, the course framed in the mountains, the green turf, the gorse out, the silk of the riders' colours as they showed between the black moving mass of people. Then the great crowds cheering as the King's carriage arrived. He was much moved by his reception and, speaking to me about it, praised the good breeding of the Irish crowd that was content to cheer at a distance, without trying to press round on Royalty, as the people did elsewhere. He added: "I have never had a better reception anywhere."

It was that day that I walked across the course with Sir

Ernest Cassel, who was a fellow-guest at 80 Stephen's Green, to the Priests' Hill beside the Big Double. And as we waited for the race to come down the hill, he talked to me in his guttural German speech, which somehow seemed to convey an impression of deep feeling, of his great affection and admiration for the King.

During that Royal visit, Lord and Lady Iveagh gave an immense dinner party for the King and Queen and the Viceregal party. My maid tells me that there were fifty waiters hired for it besides the household staff, and I remember that we were so crowded at table, even in that big marble hall, that we could hardly move our arms, and my neighbour and I made an agreement with each other to eat alternate courses!

There was another occasion when I was staying with the Iveaghs in Stephen's Green and, my hostess being indisposed, did deputy hostess for her, and wore her wonderful pearls. I could not have imagined that pearls had such life and warmth and magic. I felt wrapped about in light—and as though, if I had had nothing else on, I should still have been clothed, wearing them. Then when the party was over I went with my host to lock them up in a safe in the cellar. Groping through the darkness with candles, I felt there was a good deal to be said for *not* owning priceless pearls!

I went backwards and forwards to England at this time, usually to stay with friends, sometimes now to Chelsea House, where the Cadogans were very kind about putting me up. They called me "the lodger," and I was never allowed a latch-key, lest I should lose it!

There was a kind hall-porter—whom I christened "Robin Redbreast," from his scarlet waistcoat—who sat in the hall in his hooded chair and always smilingly let me in at night. Lady Cadogan and I would go our different ways, she to her grand and royal parties, and I more among my sporting and political friends.

One night I did go with her to an important party at Dorchester House which the Whitelaw Reids had taken for the American Embassy. I had never changed the way of doing my hair, and still wore it divided simply in the middle, with a bun at the back and sometimes a flat band of diamonds round it. We arrived at Dorchester House, and at the foot of the stairs, as I was about to follow Lady Cadogan, I suddenly looked into the mirror and saw, among all the glittering tiaras on wonderfully puffed-out hair, a funny little sleek head. I stared at it for a minute, then recognised it for my own! In sudden stage fright I ran back, and was still in time to catch the slow horse carriage and drive back with it to Chelsea House. Robin Redbreast opened the door to me, and I scuttled up to bed!

I missed a very grand party, and, what was worse, when Lady Cadogan returned, she came to my room, thinking that I might be ill.

"What happened to you? I hunted for you everywhere."

I told her the truth and she laughed. The joke was all round London the next day. Several people asked me: "Have you seen yourself in the glass lately?"

I had sat before the mirror in those early years and wondered what others saw in me and where the charm was that they discovered. I saw—one's own face, framed as in a picture, may be as impersonal as one's own portrait on the wall—a small rather pale pink and white face; grey eyes with dark lashes, not very large; a mobile mouth, a straight little nose which was my best feature. Nothing in the whole of this, to compare with the beauties of my time.

But it is not beauty that makes success, even with men, although they may think that it is so. I think the chief reason for my success was that I liked every one and enjoyed everything so much. I loved life and do still. Which is why, but for the years, I should not know that I had grown old. And, of course, I could talk. Like all Irish people, I was a spendthrift with myself, giving out everything. I often envied the more stolid English who could sit in silence, taking in and not giving out and so hoarding their strength and vitality.

London then was a town of great houses and grand society. It was much smaller and more select. There were tremendous class distinctions and the barriers between the classes were rarely broken down. One world lived inside those barriers, in a cage—a gilded cage if you like—but still a cage.

Millicent, Duchess of Sutherland, was giving her wonderful parties at Stafford House. I think I recognised in *Cavalcade* that beautiful staircase, quite the loveliest staircase of any London house, and, at the head of it, the little fair-haired figure with its back to the stage—Millie Sutherland. The Duke was not always in his place beside her. He hated parties and at those wonderful ones, which his wife gave, used to wander round like a lost soul. One night when I had just seen Sir Frank Swettenham, a famous ex-Governor of Malay, come into the room, escorting a beautiful lady, I asked the Duke who the lady was. He stared at me:

"My dear lady! It's no use asking me. You must ask Millie. I don't know who *any one* is. Why, I hardly know who *you* are!"

I think it was at that party that I was discussing with Sir Frank Swettenham the emancipation of women, a question then stirring the air, and he said: "Lady Fingall, I believe a woman's greatest ambition would be to enter Heaven dragging Satan after her by the tail!"

The Duchess had started a Salon at her parties, where talented guests were supposed to do things—to sing or recite or dance. I remember her cousin, Lady Constance Richardson, dancing beautifully, with short skirts and bare feet and causing a great sensation in those days when legs were hardly ever mentioned or seen!

I was at one grand Ball at Stafford House where you could hardly count the Royalties. The beauty of the ladies and their jewels in that brilliant setting was a sight to remember. I saw the Crown Prince of Germany dancing with Lady Drogheda. And Alfonso of Spain was there, looking for his English bride. Someone pulled me into a corner: "There is going to be some fun. There are two ladies here, either of whom may be Queen of Spain. Princess Beatrice of Coburg or Princess Ena of Battenberg!"

Princess Ena was fair and golden haired, the perfect lovely English maiden. She was very simply dressed, I think, in something like white tulle and a blue sash. Princess Beatrice was much more dashing, vivid and dark with a Russian beauty. My impression is that she wore red. King Alfonso seemed to be paying equal attention to both ladies.

Princess Beatrice afterwards married Don Alfonso, a great airman, eldest son of the Infante Jaime, cousin of King Alfonso and heir to the throne before the King's sons were born. Following on his father's wings, Don Alfonso's eldest son has just been killed in the air, fighting in Spain.

I stayed at Inchmurray with Cissie Ashton, afterwards Lady Scarborough, for Cowes, and was on the *Britannia* when the Kaiser was a guest. He looked like a Viking, with his fiercely-turned-up moustache, in his German yachting cap. Our Prince George, with his charming face, looked like a boy beside him. The Kaiser had a great admiration for Lady Ormonde, who was also at Inchmurray, and thought her the perfect type of English beauty. She must have been a great contrast to the German women, and lovely she looked in her blue reefer coat and yachting cap. You wanted less to be a goddess than to be very neat, to look well in those. It was sad for me that I was such a bad sailor for I would have had lots of fun yachting if I could have enjoyed the sea.

Another visit was to the Norfolks at Arundel, where I slept in an enormous four-poster bed in which an Empress and a Queen had slept. The house had then been recently altered to bring it back to the mediæval period. The beautiful old mantelpieces had been taken away and, in their place were put fireplaces with huge open chimneys for wood fires, which smoked abominably, so that the tears ran down one's face while one was trying to dress. Because my chimney smoked less than the others, several ladies of the party came to dress in my room.

I was told that the house was haunted and it felt ghostly

—that feeling being increased by the stained-glass windows. My dressing-room had been an old powdering-closet. When I stood before the mirror, the light, coming through the window, made one side of my face blue and the other pink.

There was an Abbot among the guests—a picturesque figure in his habit, with his bare feet showing through his sandals. As he walked in to dinner with a very decolletée lady, Bernard Howard whispered in my ear with his stutter, "What an in-in-inspiration. One is b-b-bare above and the other b-b-b-bare below!"

One of many interests I had at this time, was helping people to buy old furniture and Dublin in those days was a treasure store. Hicks, the famous cabinet-maker, whom I have already mentioned, was a great friend of mine. He was a craftsman and an artist, descended from a family of craftsmen—Dublin has a great tradition of cabinet-making—and he would not make anything that did not satisfy his own high standard of art. His work and fame travelled, in his lifetime, far beyond Ireland. Some of his furniture is in Stockholm and more in America. King Edward was one of his patrons and several Lords Lieutenant and Chief Secretaries. He said of himself:

"Hicks will be a Chippendale one day. He may be greater than Chippendale."

Looking at a set of chairs in a country house the other day, that he had copied from the original Chippendale, which had been sent to London to be sold, I believed him.

The master craftsman had an untidy workshop in Pembroke Street, where many great people visited him. The Duke of Connaught, when Commander-in-Chief in Ireland, was one of his patrons and friends, and a great deal of Hicks' furniture went to Bagshot.

In appearance, Hicks was a little red-haired man, with a perpetual sniff and a drip at the end of his nose. One day the Duke of Connaught was going round his workshop, looking at things, when suddenly there was a crash and a beam fell from the roof, missing the Duke by an inch.

"What would you have done if I had been killed?" he asked Hicks.

"Annything," sniff. "Annything, Your Royal Highness, but face the Duchess!"

When Hicks' wife died he said to me: "What is the use of life, your Ladyship, when you have lost your companion?"

The Cadogans, during their time in Ireland, were furnishing Culford which they had added to considerably. They bought much of the furniture from Hicks, and I assisted them. After they left Ireland I was at Culford for the house-warming. (How fleeting is the grandeur of the house made with hands! Now this place which they built in their pride, has been turned into a school.)

There was a lunch party during that house-warming, to which the King came over from Moulton Paddocks with his host, Sir Ernest Cassel. I was put sitting between them, with Lady Cadogan on the other side of the King. We were handed first some sort of white fish and crayfish with it. The King said to me, "You must eat the two together."

As I was putting my fork into the crayfish, I heard awful noises from my Royal neighbour, who was spitting his crayfish on to his plate.

"Don't touch it!" said Sir Ernest.

I did not dare look at poor Lady Cadogan's face. It was a very bad start for a luncheon party and I got so confused, saying, "Yes, Sir," to the King one side, and "No, Sir Ernest," to the other, that in the end I did not know which was which.

After luncheon, Sir Rennell Rodd, who had been sitting opposite, came up to me in the drawing-room:

"Well, Lady Fingall," he said, "I saw you having a terrible time at lunch."

"Yes," I said. "It *was* terrible. And in the end I was so confused that I didn't know which was King and which was Cassel—and they are so alike!"

He then explained to me that the King was particularly nervous of fish, having had recently a bad experience of ptomaine poisoning.

293

While George Wyndham was Chief Secretary, Tom Kelly—a rich American and extreme Nationalist, but a great friend of George Wyndham's and of the Dunravens—came to Ireland, and we persuaded him to take Castletown, the most perfect Georgian house in the country, full of priceless and beautiful things. It had been built in the early eighteenth century by William Conolly, who was Speaker of the Irish House of Commons; and a later Conolly had married Lady Louisa Gordon-Lennox, sister of the then Duchess of Leinster, and of the enchanting Lady Sarah Napier, and aunt of Lord Edward Fitzgerald.

We made Tom Kelly give a big Ball and determined to bring back, as much as possible, the ancient grandeur of that house. It was lighted all through, for the occasion, with candles. Tom Kelly had brought some wonderful furniture of his own to add to the treasures that were already there.

The Chief Secretary's party stayed at Castletown for the ball—I remember fighting with George Wyndham for the bath the next morning—and every one came from Dublin and the country about, and even from the yachts anchored at Kingstown. It was a beautiful sight. I don't know what it cost, but *we* sent the invitations and Tom Kelly paid the bills! I had a vision as we went up to bed, of the lovely ladies of long ago in their stiff brocade dresses and powdered hair, climbing up that marble staircase with its wonderful brass railing, carrying silver candlesticks in their hands. Did they look over their shoulders and smile at us in the candle-light? Ah, well. Candlelight plays such tricks and gives you magic if you have vision to discover it. Now we press a button and there is electric light. Whenever I perform this miracle, making light by a touch of the hand, I feel like God!

But the silver candlesticks are gone, with the ladies who went up to bed one by one, as we used to go carrying them, a procession of starry lights, disturbing the shadows of an old country house.

"You should not," the proverb says wisely, "choose women or linen by candlelight."

But then there was no other light to choose us by, once daylight vanished. Which is, perhaps, why some of us were chosen!

It was during this time that I was staying at the Chief Secretary's Lodge just as George and Sibell were leaving for Saighton, and I suddenly became very ill in the night. The doctor was called in and said that I had appendicitis and must not be moved. Sibell, with her usual kindness, said that, of course, I must stay at the Lodge and if necessary be operated on there. This was very upsetting to the two secretaries, Mr. Hornibrook and Mr. Hanson—"Mr. Ho and Mr. Ha," as George called them—who were left behind to shut up the house. I overheard Mr. Hornibrook considering bitterly the question of the silver he should leave out for me and which of it would be good enough. And—"Do you think they will want the kitchen or the dining-room table?" he asked in a tone of the most profound gloom. Fortunately, in the end, I did not need either.

George Wyndham's brilliant Chief Secretaryship ended sadly. He had achieved two tricks of his Grand Slam—his Land Act and his University Bill—but the last trick, which was a measure of Home Rule, betrayed him. So Ireland proved as unlucky for him as for her other lovers.

I do not think that he ever recovered from that blow and the shattering of his dreams.

I saw him for the last time, in 1913 at the Park Lane house, just before he went to Paris. He looked very ill and broken. A little later I was going up the stairs at a crowded evening party, behind Lady Cunard. She turned and spoke to me:

"Do you know—our beautiful friend is dead?"

I asked, "Who?"

"George Wyndham," she answered. "He died in Paris yesterday."

I turned and went downstairs again, got my cloak and drove home.

CHAPTER TWENTY-THREE

I OFTEN stayed with the Iveaghs at Elveden and was there several times when the King came to shoot over those famous 17,000 acres.

The Maharajah Duleep Singh had been sent to England as a child after his father's revolt in the Punjab, and when he grew up a sporting estate in Suffolk—Elveden—was bought for him. The house was red brick outside, and inside the young Maharajah had made it more an Eastern than a Western house, with Indian carved screens and a white marble staircase under a ceiling which had a D.S. and a crown in gold in each corner. The picture by Winterhalter, which still hangs in the hall, shows Duleep Singh as a very beautiful young man. The original of the picture is at Windsor and the Queen had allowed Lord Iveagh to have a copy for Elveden.

The new owners had added a great deal to the house. They built the vast marble hall, supposed to be a copy of the Taj at Delhi. Each pillar in it is carved with a different design and there is a gallery above, at one end of which, Casano's band used to play in the evening during those visits. It had cost a fabulous sum to put that marble hall, on the design of one made for Indian suns, down amid the cold marshes of Suffolk. If Killeen was the coldest house in Ireland, the marble hall at Elveden must have been the coldest room in England!

We used to assemble there for tea after a shoot and we sat there in the evening. There was only one large fireplace and during the King's visits, when etiquette and courtesy had to be observed, a good many of us froze. My maid remembers looking down from the gallery above and seeing King Edward, "a big fat man shaking with laughter." I was sitting beside him, so perhaps I had succeeded in making him laugh with one of my Irish stories, although as a rule they did not appeal to him. I never found it easy to amuse him, although he was

296

always very nice to me: "Jolly little lady," he used to say, "jolly little lady," when he found my name on a list submitted to him for a party to meet him, and he never scratched me out.

"You Irish, you are always laughing!" he said once, seeing Londonderry and myself and Derry Rossmore enjoying a joke.

I replied, "Yes, Sir, except when we are weeping!"

Another time I remember making him laugh was one night when I danced a jig in that hall at Elveden. (I had learned to dance jigs in the Irish Renaissance, at Killeen, when I and the children and the governess had had an expert—the blacksmith from Dunshauglin—to instruct us.) Casano's band was playing in the gallery above. I called up to the bandmaster:

"Can you play ' The Rocky Road to Dublin' ?"

"Never heard of it," he said.

"Can you play it if I sing it?"

I hummed it and they got it quite well.

I had to take off my skirt and dance in my petticoats, the full elaborate petticoats of those days; and I must have a partner, so I seized hold of Sir Frank Lascelles, who was Ambassador to Berlin, and made him stand opposite me. Not knowing the steps of the jig, he could only shuffle his feet and move as I told him. The King laughed a lot but I think it was the spectacle of my partner that amused him most. Some of the servants were in the gallery watching and my maid remembers that Mr. Harris, the House Steward, came down to the Housekeeper's Room afterwards and told her: "Your lady has just been dancing an Irish jig for the King."

Mr. Harris was one of the great servants of those days— kings of their own kingdom. The affairs and management of a great house lay on their shoulders—a world, a little State of its own. Within the last few years, going to the American Embassy in London I was greeted warmly in the hall by the butler—my old friend, Mr. Harris.

297

"I remember well," he told me, "the night I saw your Ladyship dance a jig at Elveden before the King. And how is Miss Devereux? Please remember me to her." After a little talk he announced me, taking my name from the footman with a personal interest, as though I were someone much more important.

They forgot nothing, those great servants, and remembered everything. There were two Matthews—no relations—each great butlers. The Zetlands had one. Meeting him too, again, after years, he remembered. "It used to be a pleasure to find your Ladyship's little things." For I was always losing everything! And always getting someone else to find them for me!

I usually had the same room when I stayed at Elveden. It was next door to the King's suite and there was a double door between the rooms, which was concealed on his side by a large bookcase. I often overheard conversations in the next room, however hard I tried not to. I heard some State secrets in this way, which I will not betray, and once I said to Arthur Balfour: "You must be careful. I can hear everything you are saying to the King."

But I heard the King's voice even more clearly. There was a curious vibration in it, which I recognise now when I turn on my wireless, and the German voices push out the others.

There was always a man in red livery standing outside the King's sitting-room. Miss Devereux remembers that I had to pass him to get to my bathroom and that he would let her know when the way was clear. A King's Messenger went everywhere with the King, and I suppose there were detectives, but they were easily lost in that enormous place among so many servants. When the Queen came to stay, she brought with her a maid, a dresser, and a sergeant footman.

King Edward's little fox terrier, Cæsar, whom he loved, always accompanied his master. Cæsar would often come in with my breakfast and share it with me. Then later, when I met him downstairs with his Royal master, he would be unaware of me! No human being can cut one as successfully

298

as a dog. From Cæsar's expression when I spoke to him you would have thought that he and I had never met before, instead of having shared our breakfast that very morning!

I said once to the King:

"Your dog is a horrid little snob, Sir. He does not mind eating my breakfast, but he won't look at me when he is with Your Majesty."

The King laughed:

"I think most dogs are snobs," he said.

Another King who used to occupy that suite, was Carlos of Portugal. He discovered that I could hear through the door and used to call out to me in the morning:

"What are you eating?"

I would say generally: "Bacon and eggs, Sir."

We were great friends and I have the signed photograph that he gave me. He was a great gentleman and such a jolly fellow. I cannot imagine how any people had the heart to kill him. He was particularly kind to me because he was interested in the Lady Fingall who had gone to Portugal with Catherine of Braganza.

He was very fat, and, out shooting in the English winter weather, he used to take off his coat, having his shirt open at the neck.

I asked him once: "Won't you catch cold, Sir?"

He slapped his chest, "Ah! I am well covered here!" he said.

It was just before his assassination that he was at Elveden when I was there; and on that tragic day, when he fell across his Queen in the carriage, it was the thickness of his body, I believe, that saved her life. The bullets were lost in his flesh. Years later his poor Queen told me that if she had not had the power of prayer that day and during the days following, she would have gone mad.

I have some photographs of those shooting groups at Elveden. They show the clothes we wore then when we went out with the guns. Long skirts and capes and felt hats perched on top of our heads, and sometimes veils. I had a green scarf, my maid remembers, from some Irish industry, which the King admired.

I liked the country and the days in the open air and the lunch, but I always hated the killing of birds. People talk about the cruelty of bull fights! I think of those shoots—those driven birds—so many of them hit, to get away and die in slow agony. I did not mind the shots that brought them down dead. I remember Harry Stonor bringing them down plop, one after another. Once, one hit me like a catapult and knocked me off my shooting-stick.

As at Stowlangtoft, the King used to ride a pony to the shoots. And the ladies of the party went out in long brakes and joined the men for lunch. The lunch tent used to be put up in a different place for every shoot—wherever the morning's shoot was likely to break off. The tent had a boarded floor and real windows and was heated. Fantastic luxury! We sat down to a long table—sometimes there were forty people at it. The lunch was a long business often and no wonder, with such good food! And the men had shooters' appetites after the morning in the open air.

I remember sitting, at one of those lunches, beside the Portuguese Ambassador, the Marquis de Soveral, known as "the Blue Monkey." He was a great figure and favourite in English society then, being a tremendous friend both of King Edward and Queen Alexandra. I had met him years earlier, during my visit to Spain, where they had not been very nice to him, despising him as a "Portugee." He and I had always been friends and he remembered it afterwards and was always so pleasant to me when we met, now that he was much sought after. At whatever party I went to in those later days where he was, he would come forward with a bow and an extended hand. "This was my first English friend," he used to say.

On my way to Elveden one winter day for a shooting party I lunched with Lord Coventry in London before my train. It was at a very good restaurant where the head waiter was a friend of his. He offered us oysters, of which I was always a

SHOOTING PARTY, ELVEDEN—JANUARY, 1910.

Back row, L. to R.) Hon. Harry Stonor, Countess of Buchan, Marquis de Soveral, Marquis of Bristol, Countess of Arran, Lady Evelyn Guinness, Mrs. Ronald Greville, Harry Legge, Col. Sir Arthur Davidson, Count Mensdorf, Lord Churchill, Lord Farquhar.

Middle row, L. to R.) Mrs. George Keppel, Miss Jane Thorniwell, Lady Farquhar, Lady Iveagh, H.M. King Edward VII, Countess of Fingall, Marchioness of Lincolnshire, Mrs. Willie James.

Front row, seated, L. to R.) J. D. B. Whyte, Lord Iveagh, Marquis of Lincolnshire, Walter Guinness.

ELIZABETH, COUNTESS OF FINGALL.

little afraid. "But," said Lord Coventry, "you can trust our friend."

We ate the oysters. After lunch Lord Coventry saw me to the train. On the journey I felt rather ill and when I arrived, worse. However, I changed and got through dinner somehow, hardly noticing who my fellow guests were except that the Prince of Wales was there. I escaped as soon as possible and my maid put me to bed. I did not sleep, and as the night wore on, felt distinctly worse and worse. I could not get my maid at that hour of the night and I went out into the passage to see who my neighbours were, in case I should need help. Over one door was, "H.R.H. Prince of Wales." Well, even at the worst, I would not dare disturb that sleep! Opposite was "The Marquis de Villalobar." "If I don't get better, the Marquis is for it!" I thought.

I went back to my room and there remembered that I had a flask of brandy in my dressing-bag. It had been there untouched for years. I opened it and drank some. It tasted vile and I am sure it was bad. In a few minutes I was violently sick which probably saved my life.

I stayed in bed the next day and only went down at tea-time, in a becoming tea-gown. Sir Charles Cust came up to me when I appeared. "Hello, little lady! What have you been doing with yourself?"

I told him of my terrible experience and of how I had nearly wakened the Marquis. Instead of being sympathetic he stared at me and then roared with laughter and went across to tell the Prince of Wales the joke, which I couldn't see as one.

The Prince seemed as much amused as Sir Charles. They both came over to me and I said in rather hurt tones: "You are very unkind and don't seem to realise that I might have died!"

Sir Charles looked at me. "Do you know what would have happened if you had gone into that room?"

"Well," I said, "I suppose the Marquis would have gone for a doctor."

"No," he said, "you would have gone mad. You would have found his legs on the floor. Before he did anything, you would have had to put him into them. And he has no hair and only one hand."

I sat next to the Marquis at dinner that night. He was a small man with a beautiful voice. I marvelled at the dexterity with which he managed his one hand, so that one hardly noticed the absence of the other. I heard the whole story afterwards. How this heir to a great Spanish name and great estates had been born with no legs, and no hair, and only one hand. The tragedy was supposed to be the result of a curse on the family. An ordinary child would have been allowed to die at birth, but this one grew up and became one of Spain's greatest Ambassadors. He had artificial legs and wore a wig and his clothes were wonderfully made to conceal his deformities.

He used to come out with the shooting-party, but, of course, did not shoot, and he had to be lifted up into the brake. He walked as if on stilts. This was the man who was afterwards Ambassador in Brussels, and fought so hard to save the life of Edith Cavell.

I had a letter a couple of days later from Lord Coventry, saying: "I do hope you have not been as ill as I have been."

The Prince of Wales—King George afterwards—was a remarkably good shot. I was beside him at Elveden when he shot two birds coming up, and then, taking his second gun from the loader, two going back. To me this was the more wonderful as there is very little good shooting in Ireland. Shooting and fox-hunting do not go together. In my excitement afterwards, not remembering who I was with, I jumped up and slapped the Prince on the back, and we shook hands and danced round for joy.

Sir Charles Cust, who had been watching, said to me later: "Little lady, you must not do that!"

"But," I said, "he pulled the chair from under me yesterday, and anyway, I am not used to Royalties!"

"Well," Sir Charles said, "I have grown up on the steps of

302

the throne and I can tell you that there are three kinds of people in the world; blacks, whites and Royalties!"

Miss Devereux's memories of a house like Elveden are really more interesting than mine. It was a world of its own and a life now gone for ever. "The Iveaghs lived like royalty," she says, as she had said of the Londonderrys, "and they were very grand and very simple in their tastes."

Lady Iveagh had two personal maids and always put away her own clothes and jewellery. She remembers Lady Iveagh as "old and stately."

There were twenty or thirty housemaids, and, as at Mount Stewart, they seem to have been kept somewhat as novices in a convent, not being allowed to go out out alone, or to visit the neighbouring cottages. There was a Housekeeper—as the butlers were kings, they were queens, the housekeepers of those days, in their regal black or grey silk, with a tiny scrap of lace on their heads, crowning them. And the House Steward —Mr. Harris—and a Groom of the Chambers, besides the footmen. Each visiting lady's maid had her own room, with the number of her lady's room written over it. The ladies' maids dined in the Steward's Room with the Housekeeper and the Steward and the Groom of the Chambers and any others of similar rank. They were waited on by footmen. It was as grand downstairs as up—perhaps grander! After supper the maids retired with the Housekeeper to the Housekeeper's Room, where tea was served.

It was the Housekeeper's business to go round and see that all the rooms were ready and the Groom of the Chambers saw to the meals served in the rooms. Many of the ladies had their breakfast upstairs. The meat, of course, came from the Kitchens, but, everything else from the Still-Room, which was the charge of three special maids. My maid's description of it— with its many shelves and pots and jars, and her memory too, of the kitchen at Stowlangtoft, a large tiled place, with a huge open fire and a spit on which to hang great joints of roast beef, and a cupboard for heating plates, make pictures, such as I have seen of Dutch interiors.

She remembers passing the King's room at Elveden, and, seeing through the open door, the table laid for breakfast. "Simple enough for any lady or gentleman." One of the housemaids told her that she had never seen any one as tidy as King Edward.

At the dinner hour, the immense house, away from the staff quarters, would be drained of life and light, strangely quiet and empty, except for that one great flooded dining-room. Sometimes during that deserted hour Miss Devereux wandered about the house, looking at the pictures and tapestries. On one such night she stood beside a carved screen, which, to her Catholic mind, resembled a Confessional. So she was thinking, when someone spoke the thought beside her. She turned and saw the King's Messenger, "a much-travelled man," naturally.

"Are you Irish?" he asked, after that.

"I am," she answered proudly.

"I thought so. There was something about you. I have always liked Irish women."

He had been in Ireland with the King and had nothing but good to say of the country and the people. He had been in Russia also, and he produced some scandalous tales of Russian monks. Miss Devereux was able to assure him at once that the Russian monks had nothing to do with the Catholic Church.

The maids often looked down on us from the gallery, when we sat in the hall in the evening. Sometimes we danced while the band played for us, and Miss Devereux remembers seeing Queen Mary dance a little. Of course none of us could leave until the Queen retired.

I was at Elveden in January, 1910, when King Edward came for what was to be his last visit.

Among the guns I remember, besides the King: Harry Stonor, the Marquis de Soveral, Count Mensdorf, Lord Churchill, Lord Iveagh, the Duke of Wellington and Lord Suffield. And the ladies of the party were: Lady Iveagh, Lady Arran, Mrs. George Keppel, Lady Evelyn Guinness, Mrs. Willie James and myself.

The King was a sick man then, and I used to hear them giving him oxygen in the next room. He only went out for a little time each day with the guns.

I sat beside him at dinner the last night. I had been teased by some of the party for being a Suffragette. The King was very anti Woman Suffrage and he grumbled at me then.

"What do you want with votes? You women have quite enough power already! You can get all you want without the Vote."

"Some of us, Sir," I said.

Then he went on, "I want to speak to you after dinner."

(I must explain here that George Haig, brother of Mrs. Willie Jameson and of Douglas Haig, had died a few years earlier. After his death, his sister discovered—or believed so —that he could communicate with her and use her hand to write messages. These messages were sometimes very trivial. "Geordie" as we called him, had been in life a person who was always correcting us and telling us things, and he had not apparently changed this characteristic. From the other world he told me what I was to wear, where we should find pieces of furniture that had been lost, and how we should behave. He reproved a little friend of ours for her flirtations, telling her that her one of that moment was damaging the career of a public man. Flora Hesketh said in her drawl: "Well, Geordie was a bore when he was alive. But he is a much worse bore now he's dead!)"

After dinner that night, the King took me to a corner of the drawing-room. He looked very solemn and I wondered what was coming. "Lady Fingall," he said. "Your friend, Mrs. Jameson, has hurt me deeply." He spoke in a very husky voice. He had a bad throat then.

"Oh, Sir," I said, astonished. "Surely you know how devoted Mrs. Jameson is to Your Majesty. She would never think of hurting you willingly. What has she done?"

He said, "She knows how much I loved my sister, Alice, and she has written to me, giving a message, which she says is from her, sent through her brother, George."

"What was the message, Sir?" I asked.

He hesitated for a moment. Then he said: "It was, 'The time is short. You must prepare.'"

I was shocked.

"Oh, Your Majesty," I stammered, "if Mrs. Jameson wrote that, she must have felt it to be her duty. But—did she give you any proof that it was from Princess Alice?"

"Yes," he said huskily. "She said that I was to remember a day when we were on Ben Nevis together and found white heather and divided it."

I said, "But, Sir, how could Mrs. Jameson or her brother have known that?"

He only repeated that he had been very much hurt and that I must write to Mrs. Jameson and tell her so.

I said, "Sir, I could not do that." And our conversation ended.

Afterwards the party chaffed me. Someone said, "You were catching it hot about the Suffrage!"

"Yes," I said, "I was. The King hates Suffragettes." The party broke up next day. The King went to Biarritz soon after. I never saw him again. In May he died.

CHAPTER TWENTY-FOUR

HORACE writes to Betty Balfour from Killeen in September, 1905:

"Next to Gerald, Walter Long was unquestionably the best man to send as Chief Secretary. He is not intellectual surely . . . but simple, direct and absolutely honest and disinterested. I never could understand how Long ever got into the Cabinet. I know now . . . The only pity is that he is regarded as a concession to the Ulster bigots and he does not seem to hold them in proper disrespect. I hope to know more of him soon, as I have some views upon the administration of the land purchase and redistribution powers of the Estates Commissioners and Congested Districts Board which I want to discuss with him.

"Sir Anthony will, I think, get strong again, but the wound is not healed enough for him to get away from the Phœnix Park which is not the place for an official invalid. He ought never to have been appointed but I should be sorry to see him go against his will . . ."

When Walter Long followed George Wyndham as Chief Secretary, I was passed on again to him and Lady Doreen, as the social guide, to tell them who people were. Anthony MacDonnell remained firmly at the Under Secretary's Lodge, since the Under Secretaryship was a non-political appointment; and things were naturally difficult between him and the die-hard Chief Secretary.

Indeed Walter Long had hardly seen his co-adjutor, who was laid up at the Under Secretary's Lodge during the first days after his arrival, until one day I said, "Let us walk across and call on Anthony Pat. And don't talk to him about Ireland. Ask him to tell you about India."

We went. I waited downstairs with Lady MacDonnell

and Annie, while Walter Long went up to see the invalid. I had to wait longer than I expected. As we walked back he said, "You were right. We talked about India and I found him amazingly interesting. And—what a strong man!"

Walter Long had been told, among other things, that he must make friends with an Irish Unionist landlord, Mr. Bagwell of Tipperary. Mr. Bagwell was asked accordingly to a small dinner party—of just the family and myself. The evening was a great success and Walter Long saw his guest off in the hall, in admirable good humour. Next morning we were going hunting and our post was handed to us as we were getting into the brake at the door. I was reading mine when Walter Long thrust a letter at me, rather abruptly:

"Do you know anything about this?"

I read the letter. It was from Mr. Bagwell, to the effect that he had frequently dined at the Chief Secretary's Lodge and been treated as a gentleman by gentlemen; and he did not know the meaning of this unseemly joke. I looked at Walter Long, bewildered. He handed me a parcel which had come with the letter. It contained two of his own silver spoons which, apparently, Mr. Bagwell had found in his coat-tail pocket when he undressed at the Kildare Street Club. Plainly Walter Long suspected me.

"I wish I had thought of it," I said.

No one ever knew who the perpetrator was, though I suspected one of the younger members of the family.

The Dudleys' brilliant and extravagant Viceroyalty ended with the return of the Liberal Government in 1905. But, so much had Lord Dudley come to love Ireland, that he came back a year later to serve as Chairman of the Congested Districts Commission. This entailed travelling about the country, staying at very indifferent hotels, listening to endless evidence, very different from the manner in which he had lived and travelled, as Lord Lieutenant; but it was a labour of love.

When the plan was in the air, he wrote to Walter Callan who was to serve him again as Secretary:

"7 CARLTON GARDENS,
"29th June, 1906.

"MY DEAR PATSY,—I am delighted to hear that you will act as Secretary to the Commission. It will be a difficult job but it would be splendid to be able to help those poor people in the West.

"I don't quite know when I shall be able to get to Ireland. I am in Bryce's hands and he still seems to hesitate about the personnel of his Commission. The first sitting, at any rate, I should imagine, will be in London, so my journey may be delayed on that account. But I am longing to cross. I never knew how fond I had become of Ireland until I found I had no particular reason for going there any more. Even the old Liffey will smell good in my nostrils.

"Yours ever,

"D."

Horace Plunkett had been defeated for South Dublin in 1900. He was not trusted as a Unionist, being suspected of leanings towards Home Rule, and was to share the fate of all men who try to walk in the middle of the road.

Once I was asked to try to persuade my cousin, Edward Martyn, to leave the Kildare Street Club, where he was very unpopular, as a Catholic and one of the few men of his class to become a Nationalist.

I said to him, "Edward, how can you stay in a Club where you are so unpopular?"

"My dear Daisy," he said, "it suits me. I like the food, and anyhow I am not half as unpopular as Horace Plunkett."

I came in for some backwash of this unpopularity and was called "the Sinn Fein Countess."

Some years earlier Horace had written to Betty Balfour from the Kildare Street Club where he was recovering from a bad attack of influenza:

"The hall porter at this club says there never was such a strange lot of callers! Outside my political adviser, hardly a friend of my youth and few of my class!"

309

After South Dublin, I did my best to stop Horace going up
for Galway. I knew his sweet reasonableness would have no
effect on my Western country people, against that virulent
demagogue, John Dillon. Betty Balfour writes to Arthur
Balfour on November 13th, 1901, from Whittingehame:

"MY DEAR ARTHUR,—The post that brought me your
letter brought me one from Gerald, taking identically your
view of the folly of his standing for such a place (i.e., Horace
standing for Galway). This being so, would it not be the best
thing to stop him even now? I should at any rate like him to
know your view and Gerald's. I have another letter from
Plunkett to-day in which he says:

"'Dillon is attacking me so savagely that I think I must
have a chance in Galway.' (This very characteristic of H.P.'s
optimism and goes for nothing.) 'I go there to-morrow to
reconnoitre the position and shall know better then. . . . He
(Lord Morris and Killanin) ran as a Home Ruler who would
call himself a Unionist as long as the Government behaved
themselves. I have to run as a Unionist and a member of the
Government. They are going to fight me on the Financial
Relations and the Boer War chiefly, I gather. If I discuss the
latter, it will do no good to any one but will destroy my
chances. If I refuse to discuss it, the Ardilaunites will say I am
trimming. Possibly I shall canvass and not speak, as all the
speaking is out of doors. I must try hard to win as it would
be a triumph for practical politics; while a bad defeat would
put great heart into Dillon in Ireland and Redmond in
America. Besides bigotry is more rampant in the North than
I ever knew it—Arnold Foster, whose rasping intolerance of
Roman Catholicism ought to ingratiate him with the Orange-
men, had his platform stormed by them in West Belfast the
other day, because he didn't quite approve of the phraseology
of the King's Oath!'

"All this is interesting but depressing both as to Galway
and the North of Ireland.—Yours affect'ly,

"BETTY B."

Horace would not listen to any advice and stood for Galway and was, of course, defeated.

After that he went out of politics and settled down to work for Ireland in Ireland. His defeat and subsequent dismissal from the Department, proved to be the greatest luck for his own work, for he was now free to devote all his time, energy and money to the I.A.O.S., which was really the child of his heart. His friends were so indignant at his treatment that they joined together and bought the beautiful house in Merrion Square which they presented to him for his work, and which was called Plunkett House. It was to become a centre to which, for many years, every one of distinction visiting Ireland made their way.

In January 1903, Horace writes to Betty Balfour, from the *Celtic*, on his way back from America:

"John Dillon and his wife, Bourke Cochran, and the great 'bloodless' surgeon, Dr. Lorenz of Vienna, sit at table with me—a strange mixture of prominent humanity. The surgeon speaks very bad English, but is a really great man. A wealthy pork packer in Chicago gave him £6000 to operate on a cripple son. He straightened the distorted limb, pocketed his fee, and then toured the States, giving gratuitous clinics and explaining his methods to hundreds of doctors. The humanity aforementioned have just been drinking tea together. The doctor says he told the pork packer he was not a rich man, but far happier than a millionaire. 'I can travel. I enjoy art and music. My work is a pleasure. Your wealth enslaves you. It has destroyed every pleasure but that of making more—if that is a pleasure.' He has been the chief topic in the American papers for several weeks and his striking portrait is known to every newspaper reader in the Union. Bourke Cochran grew eloquent upon the honour done in the twentieth century to a man who saved life, equal to the honour which other centuries have reserved for those who destroyed it. . . . I hoped that I might have some influence on his (John Dillon's) narrow mind. But I cannot get near him. He is a curious psychological study. He does not trust himself enough to unbend. He might risk his consistency to which he is enslaved and perhaps his reputation for omniscience. I have talked a good deal to him and while I have kept off most controversial ground, if he continues to denounce me as a sordid salary hunter, I shall think him intentionally untruthful . . . .

"In America I had mixed luck—on the whole, good. Firstly three weeks devoted to business, putting my affairs into much better shape. I have a large private income at home which a neglected business in the States has constantly drained. I have stopped the drain and after this year, if I have no bad luck, I shall have enough to be really useful to my poorer Irish fellow workers. . . ."

"Yes, I read *The Virginian*. The scene was my old range and I knew some of the characters. I never met the Virginian or anything *quite* like him. But his qualities were typical, though no cowboy ever had them all. The spirit of the range was well—very well—portrayed!"

During those years 1905 to 1907, we were busy with the building and furnishing of Kilteragh. Horace had taken a little house at Foxrock, outside Dublin, called The Barn—a low wooden bungalow. There was one long sitting-room with a big fireplace and Horace entertained in this pleasant wooden room. Wherever he was, he always had guests. When he had unexpected people to dinner and there was not enough to eat, Curtin, the butler, would be sent off to Jim Power, a neighbour, at Leopardstown Park, to borrow a leg of mutton. We had lent Curtin to Horace and he had never given him back. So we let him keep him, at great sacrifice to ourselves! He was the perfect butler, courteous and interested in every one, but so perfect that he had ceased to have any identity or mind of his own. He was responsible for a phrase Horace had invented and often used—"the Curtin mind"—by which he meant a mind that was a blank! Curtin had one failing, not uncommon in butlers, but Fingall always tolerant, said that you could not blame him overmuch for that, since it was a butler's duty to taste the wine! Once, at Kilteragh, during a Horse Show party, Curtin got very drunk. Great popping of corks could be heard in the dining-room from behind the scenes; but no wine appeared for the guests. I remember Lord Coventry sitting chuckling in his place. Horace did not drink anything himself, so did not discover the absence of wine until somebody told him. The next day he upbraided Curtin, whose excuse was, that his son had failed in an examination. "What would it have been," Horace asked, "if you had had to celebrate a victory?"

Jim Power always produced the leg of mutton, as he produced anything you asked for. "All done by kindness," was his motto. Jim Power was almost more of an institution than a person. He was the moving spirit at one time of the R.D.S., as of many other things in Ireland. A great organiser. If you wanted an industry started or a philanthropical society, you went to Jim Power. Or if you wanted your drains done you sent for Jim Power. He was always busy with somebody else's business, and always in the most extravagant way. He did the Kilteragh drains for Horace. They cost as much as the house and were like catacombs. He also altered ours at Killeen and they were on the same extravagant scale.

It was at The Barn that Horace thought of building a house for himself in the country between the Dublin Mountains and the Irish Sea, a house that should be planned to catch the sun in every room. Caroe, the Swedish architect, came to build the house and Horace lived at The Barn while it was being built, according to his ideas. When it was done—a house in the shape of a fan—the front of it had a blank look, like the windows of Danesfield in my childhood. Only the staircase windows, bathrooms and pantries looked that way, which was North. All the living and bedrooms on the other three sides, opened their windows to the sun, east, south or west, during some time of the day. There was a stoep facing South, built on the model of the one Horace had seen at Cecil Rhodes' house, Groote Schuur. Horace had given up politics, having never been a politician, but he knew too that some form of government by Irishmen for Irishmen was inevitable, and his dream was that the new Irish Constitution should be signed on that stoep. He built the house for his friends and for Ireland. For as long as it stood, it was to be at the service of both.

He had his own shelter on the roof, with a bed in it, where he slept, summer or winter, and which, by some mechanical device, he could turn from his bed towards the sun and against the wind. It was so cold when you visited him there, that you had to sit wrapped up in a blanket while you talked to him. Dr. Bernard, the Archbishop of Dublin, came down from such a visit, shivering : " No one but Horace Plunkett could stand such a place," he said. "I am like my ancestors and prefer a good old frowst, the windows shut, and a four-poster bed!"

From the roof Horace could see Dublin Bay with the mountains encircling it, the gleaming waters of the Irish Sea, across which so many of his guests came. Kilteragh was to be, as he had planned, a centre of Irish life. Every one interesting or interested, who visited Ireland, was entertained there, and it was near enough to Dublin for people to come out for lunch or tea or supper on Sunday. Men and women of the most directly opposed views, who probably never foregathered elsewhere, talked to each other in those rooms.

Horace's English guests would be met at Kingstown by John Brown with the motor, arriving at Kilteragh, if they had travelled by night, in time for breakfast. How good those arrivals at Kilteragh were! I had many and many of them. I can hardly believe now, when I come to Kingstown Pier, that I am not going to see John Brown, ready to take me to Kilteragh. I always broke my journey there on my return from London to Killeen. There would be a lovely early morning drive across the country to the foot of the Three-Rock Mountain, with my thoughts full of things to tell Horace—the people I had met and what they had said. As the car turned in at the gate, Horace would be on the steps.

He was always up to meet his guests with his delightful smile and handshake. Like George Wyndham, he was such a good welcomer. After a hot bath you would go down to the dining-room, where a beaming Curtin would have breakfast ready, and Horace would start you and hear your news. Then— Ireland claimed him again! You had thought only for a moment that he had belonged to you; but Ireland was a formidable rival, and she won, as she has always won. Horace was back at work. (He would have breakfasted early, on tea made on milk, and toast which he always prepared for himself. His own food was uncomfortable and strange—slops, fruits and nuts, while he gave his guests the best of fare.) And you were eating your breakfast alone, under A.E.'s pale magic shores and blue-green seas painted in a fresco on the wall. With only his dim sea fairies for company!

Caroe, when he had built the house, wanted to furnish it with cold modern furniture, but I would have none of that. So Lady Mayo, Miss Minnie Fitzgerald, Mrs. Keith and I undertook to find old furniture which would be much more beautiful to our minds, and much cheaper. We haunted auctions and sales at old houses, and of course enjoyed ourselves greatly. There were lots of good bargains to be found in those days—a treasure buried by junk in some half ruined old house. Horace's study he was allowed to furnish himself. (Horace's Last Stand!) As a result it was the only ugly room in the house.

The owner of Kilteragh cared not at all for beautiful things, but he consented to have his house made beautiful so that it might please his guests. I found him a treasure of a head housemaid—Margaret—small, with an upturned nose and sharp voice, who kept the house like a new pin, and even Curtin in order. She used to come and unpack for me and give me her opinion of my fellow-guests—an opinion worth having—before I went down to meet them.

The best known and remembered room in Kilteragh was the drawing-room, which ran the whole width of the house. It had a wide bow-window at one end, looking towards the sea, and another framing the Three Rock Mountain. There was a big open fireplace, set in with Caroe's beautiful brick-work, round which all manner of people stood and sat during the years 1907-1923, talking—nearly always about Ireland. The Grattan screen which we had held against Hugh Lane, and another of Chinese lacquer, shut in a comfortable corner about the fire. And there were seats in every window, which were lovely to sit in in summer.

Although he had a very good library, Horace read very little, and Omar Khayyám was still the only poet he really liked. I never remember him sitting down to read, and if he was not dictating or writing, he would be running round the golf course that he had made for himself in the grounds, with some unfortunate person like myself trying to keep up with him. He collected people as others collect pictures or china or silver, and when we had furnished the rooms, he put his collection into them. Sir Patrick Hannon said to me the other day that Kilteragh was a Museum of People.

Like Fingall, Horace did not know one tune from another, except " The Swanee River," but some of his guests were musical, and Caroe had built a hall that had wonderful acoustic properties. Mrs. Keith and I bought a grand piano that should be worthy of the hall, even if it was wasted on Horace. It was a lovely place to play and sing in and to listen in. There were no carpets or curtains to spoil the sound.

Soon after Kilteragh was opened, Lord Shaftesbury came and sang there, appropriate Irish and Scottish songs—" Maire, My Girl," " Annie Laurie," " The Mountains of Mourne," and I remember him singing " Emer's Farewell," to the heart-breaking and disturbing beauty of the Londonderry Air, which, played by a street musician in a grey London street, will make an Irish heart stand still, and then send it travelling, poor troubled heart, across the Irish Sea.

Lord Shaftesbury sang old English songs, too, with equal feeling. But it is by the others that I remember him. And there was an appropriateness about that Ulster music which he brought to the Kilteragh hall in those days when we

316

dreamed dreams, and one of them was of the new Irish constitution for all Ireland that should be signed on the verandah at Kilteragh.

On his mother's side, Lord Shaftesbury's Irish blood came from Ulster. He had married Constance Grosvenor, Sibell Grosvenor's daughter, and George Wyndham's step-daughter, and he was one of those who had fallen under the spell of Dark Rosaleen and given some of his heart to her. He had worked on the Congested Districts Board, and had come to love the poor people of the West, during that work.

I go through the Kilteragh Visitors' Book, which is a catalogue of Horace's Collection (of People). The first guest on July 11th, 1907, is Emily Lawless. I made a note about her, supplementing my earlier description: "A Jane Austen woman. You looked at her in vain to see any spark of the fire in her books."

Sir Nugent Everard came the same month. He was a great follower of Horace's and the first man to try growing tobacco, which he did at his place, Randalstown, in Meath. He practically ruined himself over it. Fingall and I are also in that party.

Then: R. A. Anderson, Horace's great disciple, who so often cleared the way before him, and has written an excellent account of his work in: "With Horace Plunkett in Ireland."

The Balfours—Gerald and Betty and their children. These are all on the first page. Jim Power is at the foot of it.

The situation of the house was symbolic, lying as it did between the mountains and the sea. It might have been a gateway to Ireland. But the mountains above held their secret, never to be divulged. So many of those who came were trying to discover that secret. And the mountains still hold it.

Lord Coventry came often. For nearly every Horse Show he was at Kilteragh or at Killeen. And sometimes he paused on his way to Mullingar or some other big Fair where he would be buying cattle, moving through the Fair with other farmers, talking their language and happy with them. He was a great old lover of Ireland.

The visitors to Kilteragh only wrote their names once in the book, so that it is hard to reconstruct the parties. I can only take here and there a memory, a picture, remembered for no reason except the whimsicality of one's mind, which records some things and forgets others equally important, as I open the book at random, taking here and there a name. It is characteristic of it that the first page contains the signature of a Conservative Chief Secretary, and the last page but one, the signature of the rebel leader, Michael Collins.

I open the Book of Memory in the same random way. Here are some of those that I remember at Kilteragh:

Lord Grey, the ex-Governor of Canada, who was such a charming friend and very much interested in Ireland. His daughter wrote of him after his death: "He was always lighting fires in cold rooms." And one can not say more or less of him than that beautiful epitaph.

Augustine Birrell. He is in the library, giving us his wonderful talk. A rare visit to Ireland, perhaps, during his Chief Secretaryship. He was usually in England in those years, making epigrams about Ireland.

George Bernard Shaw and Mrs. Shaw came often. I described Shaw to someone as being: "Rather like a child with a new frock which he is so anxious to show off, but with a heart of gold." That is how I saw him then.

Mrs. Shaw was an old friend of mine. I had taken her to Balls in Dublin before she married G. B. S. She was always kind and calm and full of humour, a delightful companion, and I preferred her companionship to that of her more brilliant husband.

From Kilteragh, I drove with George Bernard Shaw one day to Powerscourt. We stood on the terrace looking about us. Before us was a group of Scotch firs, their pink bark showing through the blue-green fronds; above, towered the bright blue Sugar Loaf, which, when I stayed at Powerscourt, seemed to be so much in my window and so overpowering, that I often longed to push it away. It has that effect in the country about it. I have seen the peak above a low garden wall, as though it had come there to make a background for a flower border.

We had gone first over the house, which is rather grandiose with its marble pillars and statues. When we came on to the terrace and stood looking at that view, which the Empress Eugénie, visiting Powerscourt, had said reminded her of Versailles, G. B. S., the Socialist, exclaimed: "There is something to be said for stipending some of the old families to live in their houses, just to show the newer generation how they lived in those days!"

We could not have foreseen then, the long trail of ruined houses that should lift their blackened walls against the Irish countryside in our time!

Again, at Kilteragh, Oliver St. John Gogarty and G. B. S. were both guests, Dr. Gogarty keeping the air electric with his wit as usual. Shaw, that day, told us of his early life in Dublin and said that he took to writing as an alternative to the only other job open to him—that of collecting someone else's rents. He said that he was determined never to have to look after property, but now found that his plays had given him a property to administer, beside which the most encumbered estate in Ireland would be a plaything!

There was another day when Yeats was at lunch and talked of his early days in London and of his work with W. E. Henley.

Presently Jim Power brought over the lovely Mary Anderson to open a bazaar for us, and she came to Kilteragh. I was to see her later again in her beautiful Broadway home in the very heart of England.

Henry Wolff, the great authority on co-operative banks, used to be there a good deal. And Sir Charles Gavan-Duffy came, one of our rebels, now turned ruler.

Shan Bullock, the writer, came often. He was a great friend of Horace's. And Horace wrote an introduction to his beautiful book, *After Sixty Years*.

319

He put some of his own feelings into that introduction. I know why he chose this particular and touching passage to quote from the Ulsterman's description of his boyhood beside Lough Erne: "It was always he, the barefooted, ragged Catholic, with his hair through his cap, and only a bit of oaten bread in his pocket, that I was drawn to for play or company. He was of another breed than ours, had softer ways and speech, better manners somehow, knew more about the country and its life and the things that mattered ; and supposing him to have a sister—generally he had five or six—there could be small question about it. Mary Roche, with her raven hair and wide soft eyes; Rose Healy, with her freckles and hair the colour of honey and the smile she had and the quiet chuckling laugh. . . ."

So Horace had felt, too—Ireland calling to him from outside the high walls and the thick walls of the Norman Castles!

Shan Bullock was a Civil Servant when we knew him—far from Lough Erne—and told me that he spent his working hours trying to dock wretched soldiers of their pay! He wrote many books. I have always thought his best: *The Squireen*, a terrible indictment of one aspect of Irish life, as *The Real Charlotte*, by Somerville and Ross, is of another.

Lord and Lady Bryce often came to visit Horace. I had not known them when he was Chief Secretary in Ireland, and it was not the thing to be friendly with a Liberal Chief Secretary! But when he returned from America after a brilliant career as British Ambassador, people were honoured to entertain him. And he was the best company in the world.

The Alfred Lyttletons were also friends of Horace's and his guests. She was a tremendous friend of Betty Balfour's, and I was to meet her later at Fisher's Hill.

Then there was a walk I took up the Dublin Mountains with Sir William Beach Thomas, a charming person, who talked just as he wrote. A country walk with him was like one of his lovely nature articles come to life.

Violet Martin of Ross, one of my childhood's friends, was

also often there. She was so alive. You could see the wit and fun bubbling up in her.

The Sidney Webbs came, and, true to their Socialism, would not change for dinner. They did a tour of Ireland, and Mrs. Webb came back to Kilteragh and reported: "They do not know the beginning of Socialism in this country. Every one of them is an individualist to his or her backbone."

It was quite true. There is no natural Communism in the Irish character. Naturally secretive, the people will hide even their pigs and hens from each other.

Many Americans came to Kilteragh. The Pages and Colonel House and Giffard Pinchot. The latter was a great friend of Horace's. He came on to Killeen and was delighted with what he called "the mediæval atmosphere," when we all danced a jig in the Oak Hall, coached by the champion dancer of the neighbourhood—the village blacksmith—and to the music supplied by a travelling fiddler.

James Byrne, who had helped Horace so much in America, and his beautiful wife, were of course guests on more than one occasion. They loved Ireland, and took Bally Donelan in Galway—once the home of Fanny Killeen—for a time. They had dreams then of settling in the country. That dream did not come true, but they frequently visited here. Mrs. Byrne was much interested in the literary movement, and used to go to Tulira, and to Lady Gregory's parties at Coole. She had a delightful story which lost nothing in her telling of it, of the Martyns' old butler, who at regular intervals was retired from service and pensioned off on account of his age, but as regularly returned to his post, until at last he was allowed to stay until he died!

George Adams, of course, was often there when he was working in the Department, and later when he visited us from Oxford, where he is now Warden of All Souls. "Our dear George Adams," Horace calls him in a letter to me.

Sir Malcolm Seton from the India Office and his charming wife, who came from the North and was one of our most ardent United Irishwomen, are others I remember.

We met Canon and Mrs. Hannay down at Westport, when we were doing some job there. He was writing—as George Birmingham—Irish stories in the vein of Somerville and Ross. They were pleasant companionable people, good company and great admirers of Horace's. I always thought her the cleverer of the two. When she died, one missed her humour in his work. I thought his *Wisdom of the Desert* the best thing that he ever wrote.

The atmosphere of Kilteragh was convivial and interesting. People always coming and going, good talk of affairs and work, and a background of great comfort.

General Smuts also came. I had ambled round a dance floor with him at the Chief Secretary's Lodge, in George Wyndham's day. I failed to discover the wonderful brain that lay behind that rather heavy exterior—the failure no doubt was my own fault.

I met Mrs. Stopford Green at Kilteragh, and again when I was down in the West of Ireland, which she was visiting also. With her was a dark bearded man with strange, fanatical eyes. They had been to some of the Western Islands, and he was terribly affected by the conditions in which the people there lived. The man was Sir Roger Casement. His name, too, is in the Kilteragh Book.

It was characteristic of Horace's capacity for forgiveness that George Moore should have been his guest, although he had written about Horace in his most unpleasant way. He was received and entertained so kindly, and then sent back to Dublin, with Susan Mitchell, in Horace's car. George Moore said to his companion as they drove away: "I really feel ashamed to accept so much kindness from Sir Horace after what I wrote about him." Then he added characteristically: "Still, I am glad that I wrote it."

Hearing that, I remembered that Edward Martyn had said of George Moore: "He is so clever that he makes even his caddishness amusing."

Sometimes the overflow parties from Kilteragh were sent on to us at Killeen. On such an occasion a little American

322

girl, who had lost the key of her suit-case, wrote on a post-card to her mother: "Last night I slept in the pyjamas of an Earless!"

Moritz Bonn came, and his wife and his sister. He was a close friend of Horace's for years, and one of the most brilliant men I have ever met. He used to say that he could not imagine any Irishman not being a Unionist or any Englishman not being a Home Ruler. Julie Bonn, his sister, had married Sartorio, the Italian landscape painter of the day, and they were very kind to me when I paid a visit to Rome during this time with the Herberts. The Sartorios used to give most interesting parties in their charming flat in an old Palace. I met D'Annunzio there, and we went to see a play of his, *L'Intruse*. It was weird, and acted so well that my hair stood on end.

There, too, we met Axel Munthe. Every one said: "You will fall for him at once. He will hypnotise you." He was supposed to have hypnotic power and to be adored by women, but he had no effect at all on me. I later met him at the house of my dear friend Mamie Crawshay in London, where one met everyone good and clever, who could be helped in any way. He had gone blind then, and it was her kind and generous nature to love most those who suffered. It seemed to me at this later meeting that he was much more gentle than when I had first met him; but, then, in the company of Mamie Crawshay everything that was best in one came out. She was the sweetest and at the same time the wittiest woman I ever met, and those two don't always go together. Her sister, Olive Guthrie, also a dear friend, I first remember as a rather wild, red-haired little girl at the Castle in Dublin, with her beautiful mother, Lady Constance Leslie. She was— and is—so gay and witty, too, and every one loved her. It was no wonder that the rich, handsome young Banker, Murray Guthrie, fell in love with her. I next saw her after her marriage to him, receiving at the head of the grand staircase at Stratford House, with wonderful emeralds on her white neck and in her flaming hair. But to her friends, still the sweet and loving little Olive they had always known.

That visit to Rome was very pleasant, and a break in our Irish life which tended to absorb us. Mrs. Herbert had her own circle which opened to me also. Horace joined us there on one of his journeys back from America. He was interested in the Agricultural works in Rome and liked the Campagna; but he was bored when I took him to see pictures and such things. The galleries were very cold and tiring, and I soon got what the Americans call "gallery ache."

Cardinal Merry del Val arranged an Audience with Pope Pius X. for Mrs. Herbert, Poppy and myself, and we were presented to His Holiness by the Cardinal. The whole neighbourhood about Killeen had thrust on me bundles of rosary beads and scapulars, begging me to get them blessed by the Pope. As we waited in an ante-room, I heard a loud trumpeting in the next room. Then the door opened and His Holiness came in, dressed in white, with a large bandana handkerchief in his hand with which he had been violently blowing his nose. I was so impressed by the benign beauty of his face, that in my emotion I dropped all the rosaries, scapulars, etc., on the floor. Whereupon, with absolute humility and simplicity, the Pope stooped, about to pick them up, and our heads might have knocked together if the Cardinal had not intervened! His Holiness said a few words to us in Italian which I could not understand. The Cardinal translated for us. The Pope was telling us how much he loved the Irish people.

We were also taken to see his sisters, two dear old peasant women who lived in an apartment near the Vatican. They were very simple and holy like the Pope, but as they spoke Venetian patois, we could only smile at each other.

We also met in Rome, Boni, the great Venetian who excavated the Forum. He allowed us to come and see a tomb which he had just opened. It might have been that of a princess or a very simple woman—a touching little skeleton, with a curious small bit of tatting and her bird and water beside her. I said to Boni: "If you ever come to Ireland, come and see us, and we will show you *our* prehistoric remains."

324

Our conversation was difficult, as he, being a Venetian, spoke bad Italian and worse English.

We were somewhat disconcerted when, sure enough, he did appear in Ireland not long after! I planted him first on Horace at Kilteragh, and we took him about—among other places, to New Grange, which was on the estate of my brother-in-law, Robert Gradwell of Dowth Hall, in Meath. He was thrilled with the prehistoric underground dwelling there, beneath a Rath. We had to crawl on hands and knees, with lighted candles, into the interior, where there was a chamber cut out of solid rock, with spirals and hieroglyphics on the walls. A hollow stone in the middle of the chamber might have been sacrificial. Boni said that the hieroglyphics were like some that he had discovered in the Forum. He was so excited over them, that when he crawled out he rolled over and over on the grass, like a dog, saying: "Bella! Bella!"

We felt very proud! He could give us no date for New Grange. It had been only opened up comparatively recently then by Dr. Coffey.

But Boni told us that he found the Irish Round Towers very similar to those in Southern Italy, built by the Phœnicians. Both had evidently been built for safety, and for giving warning of an advancing enemy, whose approach could be seen from that height, many miles away. Our Round Towers were nearly always built near a church—to protect the village, I suppose, of which the church would have been the centre.

Boni went all round Ireland with introductions from Horace. He was also greatly interested in phrenology, and used to stop the car, when he passed a country school, and rush in and feel the children's heads. Naturally they thought that he was mad. He told us that he had never felt heads that gave better promise than those of the Irish schoolchildren; and that if nothing unforeseen happened, theirs would be the most wonderful generation. I often remembered that afterwards, when the War came and the Irish Troubles. He went to see the Rock of Cashel, and was immensely impressed, as was old Lady Howard of Glossop, the great traveller, who had seen the Seven Wonders of the World and came to Ireland in her eightieth year for one reason only—to see the Rock! I took her. We started early in the morning, and she came back in the evening to Kilteragh, and said: "I consider that it ought to be the Eighth Wonder of the World!"

All those years the real spirit of Kilteragh was Ireland. And when these guests and many others had come and gone, we settled down to our own work. They were only shadows across the picture, and the real heart of the picture was Ireland—the I.A.O.S., the *Irish Homestead*, the Co-operative Banks, the *Irish Statesman*, the Dominion League later.

George Adams has given me two vivid little pictures of Horace at this time. Sir Kenneth Leys told him of a night when he was at Kilteragh and H. A. L. and Mrs. Fisher were fellow-guests. They were sitting in Horace's study one night after dinner. The host had dozed for a little, as he often did. Suddenly he woke up and, standing by the fireplace, he talked for ten minutes of what his dreams were for the country. "It was like a flame," George Adams said.

Before Kilteragh was built, and while it was a-building, Horace used to come frequently to Killeen—at one time nearly every week-end—bringing with him some of what the children called, "Uncle Horace's Wise Men."

Fingall would receive the "Wise Men" patiently, only saying to me alone: "My lady, you must take them off my hands!" On Sunday, after Mass, he would give his guests breakfast courteously and then leave them in the library with their papers and books, and retire to the study and his map of Meath, over which he would sit for the morning, planning his Meets for the week.

I used to run from one room to another, trying to be in two places at once. I would think with Fingall about coverts that should be drawn and new grass and the one-horse men who must get their turn. And then back to the library, where the "Wise Men" were deep in consultation.

After lunch Fingall would have his parade of horses, and there would be the endless discussion of hocks and spavins

326

and splints. Occasionally Horace came out, to be obviously bored. We used to sit under the eaves, shivering on our shooting-sticks. Sometimes neighbours came, and we would all discuss each horse solemnly and seriously, as though it were the one important thing in the world.

I am asked: "Do you think he is lame from the hock or from the shoulder?"

I reply despairingly: "From both!"

Meanwhile Horace's car, still a novelty, is at the door to take us on some Co-operative expedition, and I leave the parade, perhaps to go to tea with Sir Nugent Everard at Randalstown and discuss tobacco growing.

George Adams remembers his first visit to Killeen, when he motored down with Horace on a winter evening. It had been cold driving in an open car—even at twelve miles an hour!—and Horace always felt the cold. They were shown into the hall, where there was a huge fire, and Horace went straight to it, holding out his chilly hands to the blaze. Then Fingall came, welcoming them. He took in the picture of Horace at the fire, looking tired and cold:

"Well, Horace," he said. "Driving another nail into your coffin?"

The next day, George Adams remembers, he somehow escaped the stern taskmaster, and spent the morning with his host, going round the fields, looking at the cottages, considering what could be done for the people, and talking about them. His companion was very much touched by Fingall's feeling for his people, and never forgot that walk with him.

Horace was coming and going constantly between America and Ireland in these years. He was also much in London, where he had a flat in Mount Street and occasionally entertained there delightfully. He wrote frequently, but he was as bad a letter writer as Douglas Haig.

Douglas wrote about manœuvres and Horace wrote about Co-operation, with only here and there a personal word to light the serious way. Presently he took to typing, and then his letters were duller than ever. I have often said that the typewriter killed letter writing, for before that invention, reading a letter written in a difficult hand, there would always be an undecipherable word or two that might mean anything. And a woman looking at such a word might use her imagination to persuade herself that it is the word she seeks: something personal about her. I used to pore over Horace's letters, searching between the Co-operation and politics for the occasional personal word—as I sought in Douglas', between the manœuvres he was doing with the French Army!

Karl Walter and his wife were other good friends of Horace's. It was he who told me the touching little story—of Horace standing still in St. James's Park as they walked together across it, to look at and smell the beds of heliotrope—the only flower he ever stopped to look at or smell!

Lately at Droitwich I talked with Geoffrey Drage, who had worked and travelled with Horace through Ireland, and he wrote to me afterwards some of his memories: one of: "a meeting in County Mayo, at the time of considerable unrest, which consisted of course almost entirely of Home Rulers and Roman Catholics and which was held in the house of the Roman Catholic Priest with the Protestant Clergyman in the Chair; when we two, both of us Unionist Members of Parliament and both ' black Protestants,' got a unanimous vote for our Resolution."

The odd part of his wonderful success was that he was a very poor speaker; and I remember Members crowding into the House of Commons to hear him and finding it difficult to follow the drift of his argument. Neither was he an original thinker. He was a follower of Molière's maxim: ' *Je prends mon bien partout ou je le trouve.* . . . .'

". . . There was a time when Plunkett had almost the reputation and influence of Mr. Parnell with his countrymen, but that was of course before the publication of his unfortunate book, by which he alienated the Roman Catholic Hierarchy through deprecating the large sums of money spent in building churches, while there were, as he thought, other equally worthy—if not worthier—objects. . . .

He never wavered in his allegiance to you, or as far as I know in his recognition of what Gerald and Lady Betty Balfour did for him. The end, with the denigration of his work and the destruction of his house by the Sinn Feiners and his self-imposed exile in England, was nothing less than a tragedy."

The book to which Geoffrey Drage refers, is *Ireland in the New Century*, a great deal of which was written at Killeen. As usual, Horace wrote and rewrote until he had taken all the life out of it. Maimie, watching him at work one day, said: "Uncle Horace, do you think that any one will ever *read* that book?"

Unfortunately they did, and it did him more harm than anything else he could have done.

His reference to church building and to the control of the clergy over schools, antagonised to some extent the greatest power in Ireland.

One Bishop who had never read the book, described it as an "ignorant little almanack," and the "Skibbereen Eagle" had its eye on him! I disagreed with him about the church building. For, I said, the poor people had so little beauty and colour in their own lives. And the churches, with their brilliant, often crudely coloured Stations and Saints, and the vestments and flowers and incense, supplied all their need of colour and beauty. Whatever we might feel, the churches were beautiful for the majority of the people for whom they were built. And that Refuge, with all that it means to the Faith of the Irish poor, gave them what they wanted, and made their hard lives bearable.

CHAPTER TWENTY-FIVE

In May, 1910, I took the girls to a finishing school in Brussels, and spent a few days there. When I came down in the morning on the day of my departure, the porter greeted me with:

"Madame, je regrette que votre Roi est mort!"

I said: "Mais, quel Roi?"

"Votre Roi, Edouard."

They had the news in Brussels before it had reached many people in London.

I had known, of course, that the King had not been well, but the news came with the shock that Death always brings, even when it strikes a humbler head and not one likely to affect world destinies by its fall. My thoughts flew back to that last party at Elveden and to the strange message that Mrs. Willie Jameson had sent from Princess Alice: "The time is short. You must prepare."

I had been going back to London that evening, but I had to stay and buy black clothes for the girls, and leave early the following morning. I had a return first-class ticket, and when I had paid for my daughters' mourning outfit and my hotel bill I had one shilling left! Fingall had always warned me that I did not take enough money travelling, and would be caught some day. I was caught now. We had a very bad passage, and I was terribly sick. At Dover I spent my one and only shilling on a telegram, engaging myself a cabin for that night, on the Irish Mail. In the train going up from Dover they brought round tea, which I looked at longingly, but had to refuse. A nice American man in the carriage said:

"Ma'am, are you not going to have some tea after that crossing?"

I said: "I'd love to, but I can't afford it."

"Allow me?" he said kindly. And I most gratefully

330

accepted. He told me that he had travelled all over the world and had never had such a crossing.

There was a pall over London. Every one was in black (they had had one day in which to get it) and with long faces. The feeling was almost more tragic than it had been after the Queen's death. There was a more personal feeling for the Queen; but her death was expected, and she had been old for a long time. Edward was a comparatively young man, and tremendously alive, and such a strong power with foreign countries. His friendliness and *savoir faire* had made him a wonderful diplomat. There was a feeling of foreboding in the air those days after his death, although there was no talk of war then, a feeling too of the ending of a chapter—a chapter that had held peace, and such a peaceful England.

Arriving in London, I drove straight to Princes Gate for a hasty meal. The gloom was in my face, and Willie Jameson, welcoming me himself, promptly ordered a bottle of his best champagne. I went on to Ireland, but could not sleep in the train or on the boat. Willie Jameson said afterwards: " I should never have given you champagne when you were tired—old brandy, of course, would have been the thing."

I stayed in Ireland, but Fingall went over for the funeral, and saw it pass from the windows of Brooks's Club. He was much affected by the sight of the King's charger and his little dog—my old friend, Cæsar—led behind the coffin.

At first London, after that, plunged into mourning. All parties were cancelled, and it looked like ruin for a good many tradesmen who had invested in the coming Season. Then it was made known that the new King and Queen wished the mourning to be modified, so that some financial loss should be avoided. Ascot was held as usual, although every one wore black. That was the famous "Black Ascot" of 1910. I went to it, and was very proud when Lord Coventry took me up to the Jockey Club Stand. From there I looked down on the enclosure. The women were wearing very wide hats that year with long tight skirts. Seen from above, against the green turf, they looked like nothing so much as an immense flight of crows that had just settled! But when you came close to them, never in their lives had the beautiful women looked more lovely. I remember Lady Westmorland and the Duchess of Sutherland, their fair loveliness enhanced by the frame of black, and the Princess (Daisy) Pless, and Leila Milbanke, a dark-eyed beauty.

Going to Ascot in those days, the poor long-suffering men had to carry our cloaks on the walk from the station, which was sometimes very hot. I wonder if they would do it now! I remember, too, the fight for the mirror afterwards in the ladies' cloakroom. It was all still very exclusive. I used to say that I met my real friends—horsey men and vets, often from Ireland—in the Paddock.

I was beside Lady Londonderry on the Jockey Club Stand, watching a race in which a horse of hers was running. She had her glasses up: "I am afraid he can't do it," she said, so calmly. "No. . . . He is losing. He can't do it."

On my other side an American lady, also with a horse running, began to scream so that I thought she must be ill.

"What is the matter with her?" I whispered to Theresa.

She gave the lady one glance. "Oh, my dear, pay no attention. She cannot control herself."

My next memory is of the Coronation. Fingall, discovering that his coronet and his Coronation robes had disappeared —and that replacing them would be enormously expensive— was only too glad of the excuse to avoid the Coronation and to stay at Killeen. So I went over, and Lady Huntingdon and I went to the Coronation together. We were seeing the last great pageant of pre-War England, although we had no idea of that. I remember the State carriages of many peers and peeresses rumbling through the London streets towards Westminster, that morning. Lady Huntingdon's grand carriage swayed greatly on its springs, the movement making her fall asleep—we had been up since six o'clock—and made me feel rather sick. It was strange to be wearing full Court dress at that hour of the morning, and it stirred a memory of going to one of the old Queen's Courts, also in the morning, a long time ago.

Lady Huntingdon wore a magnificent tiara, and I remember straightening it for her when we got to the Abbey, after the swaying of the carriage which had set it awry. I wore only a flat band of diamonds, deciding that the real coronet would look much better without any other ornament, as indeed it did. We wore our trains as cloaks and carried our coronets on our knees. Some wise people hid little packets of sandwiches and even tiny discreet flasks inside their coronets, to sustain themselves during the long hours.

I remember the arrival at the Abbey and being helped down the steps of the carriage by a gorgeous footman, and our trains being straightened out for us. It was all very impressive and awe-inspiring, and it was encouraging to see the kind and friendly faces of Sir Douglas Dawson and Colonel George Crichton, ready to conduct us to our seats in the North Transept. The chairs we sat on—nicely shaped and fine mahogany chairs—were afterwards presented to us, with our names on the back of each. I am sitting on mine now as I tell this!

I recognised many people I knew and had seen in such different settings. Just below us sat Lady Winchester, whom I had known as the lovely "Tossie" Garnett, hunting in Meath many years earlier. She looked just as lovely and just as neat in her Coronation robes and jewels as when I had seen her at the top of the Hunt, galloping over the Irish fields and taking the great fences of Meath. Her second husband, whom she had married when he was Henry Paulet, succeeded to the première Marquisate on the death of his brother in the South African War. He is hereditary Bearer of the Cap of Maintenance among other things. I saw, too, Evelyn Downshire, looking beautiful, with an enormous tiara. And May Limerick, like a dark Irish rose, with her wonderful eyes. And Priscilla Annesley of the perfect profile. And another familiar figure was Lord Mowbray and Stourton, descended from King Harold, and looking a real Saxon noble.

333

Little memories of the Procession and the Ceremony come back to me. The Procession of the Royal Guests was of many colours and from all nations. It was headed by the Crown Prince and Princess of Germany, and towards the end of it after a small pale Prince of China, walked two dark figures, making one think of something out of the *Arabian Nights* They were the Prince of Ethiopia, Dejasmatch Kassa, and his attendant.

I remember the little Prince of Wales, destined to be a crownless King for such a brief reign as Edward VIII., and his brother, whom we knew then as Prince Albert—now King George VI.—following him into the Royal box. I saw Lord Curzon carrying the Standard of India and looking most "superior." And the Heralds with their tabards of the Royal Standards, making me think irresistibly of Court Playing Cards come to life! The moving colour of the procession, with always the crimson predominating in it, was beautiful against that dim grey background of the Abbey. And the ceremonial, full of tradition and poetry. The offering of the Sword—"With this Sword do Justice"—like a William Morris poem. The Golden Spurs, the Ivory Rod with the Dove, the Sceptre with the Cross. The Crowning with the Crown of Edward the Confessor. I saw Lord Kitchener carrying the Third Sword or Pointed Sword of Temporal Justice, in the Procession of the King's Regalia. And our friend "Bobs," looking so small beside him in figure, but very big in everything else, carrying the Pointed Sword of Spiritual Justice. The handsome Lord Shrewsbury, Theresa Londonderry's brother, with his White Wand as Lord High Steward of Ireland. Sir Neville Wilkinson, a superb figure with his height and extraordinary good looks. In another world he was to be famous as the owner of Titania's Palace, and a tireless worker for the better treatment of children.

I remember the great guns of the Tower firing salutes after the King's Crowning, and the shouting of the people: "God save the King." And, earlier, the Westminster School-boys roaring themselves hoarse in the ancient privilege:

> "Vivat Regina Maria!
> Vivat. Vivat. Vivat."

The little Prince of Wales looked so nervous when he came after the Archbishop of Canterbury, to do Homage to his father, kneeling before him and taking off his coronet as he pronounced the words for himself and the other Princes. Then, when he rose and touched the King's Crown and kissed his left cheek, it seemed to me that his hand trembled and for a moment the Crown shook. I thought it might fall. What an omen it would have been if it had! But it steadied again. None of us could have foreseen then the happenings that were to prevent St. Edward's Crown being laid, at the next Coronation, on the head of that little Prince—crowning him as Edward the Eighth of England.

I saw the four Duchesses—of Hamilton, of Montrose, of Portland, of Sutherland—lifting the Canopy of Cloth of Gold over the Queen for her Anointing, as four Earls and Knights of the Garter had held the King's Canopy: "Tall and most divinely fair," the Duchesses were.

The Queen looked wonderful. One might have had a vision of what her reign was to be and how she should be the King's strength and comfort through the years that were to come.

When the Archbishop laid the Crown with its shining Star of the Koh-i-noor and the other stars, catching all the light, on the Queen's head, the Princesses and the Countesses put on their coronets. I can hear now the little rustle all about me in the North Transept as we crowned ourselves with the Queen. It was moving. I felt that we almost shared with her, at that moment, the great duties and responsibilities laid on her with that Crown. We wore our coronets until we left the Abbey. And it was most romantic and thrilling, I found, to feel a Queen, even for a few minutes.

Fortunately one cannot see into the future.

Looking at the proud figure of Lord Kitchener, one could not have foreseen the *Hampshire*. Nor did any of us know what the next four years held. Those lovely and gracious ladies about me in the North Transept. The Ladies in the Queen's Procession. Many of them are grey-haired now like myself. And how many were to have their world broken to pieces within a few years by the War! While some of the proud titles were to become extinct, with their heirs dead on the battlefield.

That Coronation of 1911, with its Royal Guests from Germany and Austria and Spain, has a dream-like quality to me when I look back on it. As well it might have. That world came to an end in August, 1914.

The King and Queen paid their Coronation visit to Ireland a month or so later in that wonderful summer of 1911. They held a Court in Dublin at which Maimie was presented. We were staying in the Castle for the Court, but, as accommodation was limited, we were put into the State Steward's House across the Yard, where I had once lived. Our Meath neighbour, Lord Conyngham, was lodged in the same house. After the Court, having returned and dismissed our maid, we had undressed, and were just getting into bed when there was a knock at the door.

I went to it. "Who is there?"

"Victor—Victor Conyngham."

I opened the door. There was Lord Conyngham, in a dressing-gown with military boots showing under it.

"An awful thing has happened," he explained. "I can't get my valet. He is not in the house. And I can't get out of my boots. If I go to bed in them they will say in the morning that I was drunk. What am I to do?"

I said: "Well, Maimie and I will do our best!"

We did. We each of us tugged at one leg, and after a long struggle we got the boots off!

We did not know those years, that we were riding gaily across the coloured country that was our life, towards a ditch which should engulf many of us; and that those who crossed it would find themselves in another world—a world from which there should be no return ever to life as it had been.

We rode gaily. The speed of life was quickening and not yet breathless enough to have become exhausting. Motors still travelled at round about twenty miles an hour. We still paid visits that lasted a week, so that we knew our fellow-guests by the time we parted, and had time to unpack and settle into the life of the house before we had to pack again and go. With the present-day week-end visit, or its equivalent of mid-week days, one has hardly arrived before one is off again. There is only Saturday evening to take a look at the party, Sunday evening to talk to someone, and often, a fellow-guest with whom you were obviously intended to become friends, arrives the night before you leave.

We dressed fantastically those days: for the morning; for riding; for playing croquet or tennis, in long full skirts; for shooting, for tea, for dinner. Our frocks were voluminous and our luggage, of course, absurd. There were any number of buttons and hooks to do up the back. And when Maimie and I went visiting together in those immediately pre-War days, we had to take a maid each, or we should never have been down to anything in time. Maimie dressed for breakfast, then for shooting, then for tea, then for dinner. I had breakfast in my room, so escaped one dressing.

Once at Elveden, Lady Iveagh came to me for sympathy after the arrival of Lord and Lady Howe to stay: "My dear, I do think it is too much when *two* people bring five servants!" They had brought a valet, a maid, a secretary, a footman and a pony-boy!

We stayed several times with the Rothschilds at Tring. Lord Rothschild had always been a friend of mine. And the Leo Rothschilds were very kind, asking Maimie to hunt from their place, Ascott, close by.

For one visit we arrived at the station by a rather late train. Thinking that we would be late for dinner, I hurried Maimie to the carriage, leaving our maid to look after the luggage. "Come on as quickly as you can," I told her.

There was, of course, an omnibus for the maids and luggage. We drove away and when we arrived were met by our host and hostess. But after their greeting: "What have you done with Haldane?" they asked.

We looked at each other in horror. "I am afraid," I said guiltily, "we must have left him with the luggage."

Presently Lord Haldane did arrive, having travelled in the luggage cart. Fortunately he was very forgiving!

Tring was very magnificent. In the morning my maid brought the breakfast menu, for me to make my choice from it. I looked at it. There seemed to be at least a dozen breakfast dishes and several different kinds of tea, with Chinese and Indian names.

I tried to choose and gave it up. "Oh, bacon and eggs," I said wearily, as usual.

She went away, and came back with a broad grin on her face: "My lady, that is the only thing you cannot get in *this* house!"

The furnishing was magnificent, too. Lord Rothschild would receive his guests in the hall and then lead them through an enormous glass partition, curtained with heavy red velvet, into the drawing-room—a panelled room with a white ceiling all lit by invisible electric light, a new idea in those days. The furniture in that room was rather heavy. Four great cabinets, splendidly carved, stood up against the walls. The side cupboards were filled with richly bound books, the middle pieces held rare and beautiful crystal ornaments and gold work which caught the light.

They had a barbaric custom at Tring. The gentlemen never joined the ladies in the drawing-room after dinner. Instead, the ladies were taken into the smoking-room at about ten o'clock, and there we sat, ignored by the men and boring them by our presence, until nearly twelve. It seemed like an Eastern custom and made us feel that the great Jew Lord looked upon our sex as the inferior one!

Lord Rothschild was rather fond of me, and we used to take walks together, while the others went hunting.

There were beautiful gardens at Tring and wonderful hot-houses, full of flowers all the year round. It was of a Miss

Rothschild that a jealous French lady, also a gardener, had said: "*Madamoiselle a, au moins, cinquante jardiniers pour faire les toilette des roses!*"

At Tring, there was one house filled entirely with old-fashioned moss roses. They smelt deliciously. As we walked through, one of them touched my face. I picked it.

"I suppose you don't mind?" I said laughing, to my host.

To my surprise, he said: "No use asking now. You have taken it."

I was hurt and angry and threw the sweet rose away and walked back to the house.

At dinner that night, Lord Rothschild said to the company: "Lady Fingall likes to take things, rather than have them given to her."

I was a little chilly to him for the remaining day of my visit; but as we left, an enormous bunch of moss roses was thrown into my carriage. A charming *amende*.

I must acknowledge that I have always been a flower thief. If I ever get to Heaven, I shall steal St. Joseph's lilies if he does not hold on to them! Once I was at Kenry, Lord Dunraven's house on Kingston Hill. It had woods about it and lovely gardens, with huge beds of lily-of-the-valley. Walking among them with my host, I stopped to pick, then went on picking as fast as I could, while he was talking. I filled my hands with the white delicate flowers, only wishing that my hands were larger. In a sudden silence I glanced up. My host was looking down at me quizzically.

"My dear lady," he said. "Why not take a scythe to it?"

Once I asked Lord Rothschild's advice about how I could help a rather unlucky friend of mine. He said surprisingly: "Lady Fingall, never have anything to say to unlucky people. You can do them no good, and they may do you harm."

I said: "Isn't that a hard theory with which to go through life, Lord Rothschild?"

He stuck to it. But though he may have avoided unlucky people—or said that he did—his charity was boundless.

We often went, of course, to stay with the Coventrys at

Croome, their lovely house in Worcestershire. It was the very heart of England, that orchard country. In the autumn the air smelt of apples and in the spring of blossom. It was the right background for Lord Coventry, and there he looked like a happy farmer in his tweed coat and gaiters. I used to go about with him into the old farmhouses, that were as beautiful in their own way as Croome. Black beamed on white, with tightly packed gardens about them, and always the fruit trees. They had the sweet feeling of peace and tradition, and the Spirit of the Place which is one of the loveliest things of the English country. The people who received us in the low-ceilinged rooms were charming. Lord Coventry knew everybody and treated them all as friends.

Croome itself had a peaceful, restrained beauty. "Capability Brown" is supposed to have built the house and designed the gardens and plantations, but later, one of the brothers Adam came and lived there for three or four years. He altered some of Brown's work and almost certainly made the lovely dining-room with its exquisite garlands and flowers on pale green walls; although there was a theory that this may have been done by Chippendale, one of whose beautiful mirrors is over the chimney-piece.

In the drawing-room there hang two beautiful Gainsboroughs—George III. and Queen Charlotte, who had visited Croome. He, a fine figure of a man, and she, rather pale and faded, with tall white feathers in her hair. They paid their visit in 1788 to the 6th Earl of Coventry, whose portrait by Ramsay in the library is, I think, the finest picture in the house. When the King was leaving, he asked his host if he had any request to make of him. Lord Coventry replied:

"Your Majesty, I would be very grateful if you would make my friend, Lygon, a peer."

His friend and neighbour, Lygon of Madresfield, was accordingly made Lord Beauchamp.

From Croome we went to lunch at Madresfield. I had stayed there, having known Lady Beauchamp as Lettice Grosvenor, when her mother Sibell, and her stepfather,

George Wyndham, were at the Chief Secretary's Lodge. At lunch I sat beside Lord Beauchamp and was given some Worcestershire cider. I thought it delicious and asked for more. Towards the end of lunch I saw Lord Beauchamp looking at me rather curiously, and when the time came to leave the table I found that I could not move my legs.

I said: "Something awful has happened to me, Lord Beauchamp. I think I must be paralysed."

He laughed: "It is not as serious as that—only—*we* drink that cider in wine glasses."

I had to be assisted into the drawing-room, where I sat in solitary state. It was the only occasion in my life on which I have been intoxicated.

Lord Coventry was a great friend of the monks at Evesham and often used to go and see them. I sometimes thought that Lady Coventry suspected me of trying to convert him. Quite mistakenly. He was far too good to be converted to anything! But her fears may have been increased by this friendship of his. Since his youth at Holland House, where he had met a good many Catholic ecclesiastics, he had always had a great admiration and feeling for the Catholic Church.

One afternoon we went to tea with Mr. and Mrs. Baldwin. I was considering starting pig farming at Killeen, and Mr. Baldwin was an expert on the subject of pigs. We discussed middle-white versus big-white pigs for most of the afternoon. I had no idea then that I was talking pigs with the future Prime Minister of England.

Lord Coventry was very witty. I remember him saying in his dry way of a trainer who had suddenly taken to wearing spectacles: "Well, my lady, now that he is wearing blinkers, let us hope that he will run straight."

When he was eighty years old himself he went to see his old friend Lord Halsbury, and wrote to me: "I have just been to see Lord Halsbury—eighty-three, with all his faculties—very encouraging!"

Sometimes our visits to Croome were for Cheltenham Races. The Coventrys had their own box at the end of the

341

Stand, from which we could see the saddling and the start and watch the race, without leaving the comfort of a delightful room. From that box, a few years ago, I saw Killeen win the National Hunt Steeplechase on Sir Lindsay.

That was soon after he had succeeded his father; and an old man, who had been steadily backing Lord Killeen, came a long way to Cheltenham specially to back him for this race. Before it started, he was heard saying: "Isn't it too bad! I came to back Killeen, and they have put some damned fellow called Fingall, up!"

I hope someone enlightened him, so that he won his money on the "damned fellow Fingall" after all!

I was at Newmarket in 1923 for the great race for the Cambridgeshire, between the French horse, Epinard, and Lord Coventry's mare, Verdict.

Lord Coventry was very fond of the people about us in Meath and they of him. He had said to me before that race: "My lady, I have a great fancy for Verdict."

I told the local doctor, the policeman, the postman and the carpenter. The latter was a great gambler. The news spread, and at last the whole of Killeen and Dunsany were on Verdict, to a man and woman.

I saw the two horses going out. When I saw the French horse, my heart went down into the Newmarket shoes that Coventry had given me! Epinard was a great upstanding dark chestnut, and, though she was over sixteen hands, Verdict looked small beside him, and Lord Coventry always spoke of her as the "little mare." She was not even in the Book. I could not see her having a chance against the great French horse. And I thought of all the fortunes of Killeen and Dunsany on her. Still Lord Coventry said: "I have great confidence in Verdict."

Epinard showed the way at the beginning. But, as they came up the hill, the French horse was looking hot, and the mare came creeping, creeping up to him, caught him and passed him. Verdict won by an eyelash!

Lord Coventry was so popular that the whole course

broke into loud cheers. It was like the enthusiasm in Spain for a popular bull fighter. Even the bookies yelled as loudly as any one for Coventry's success. The King went up and shook him by the hand: "Coventry, I would far rather that you had won, than that I had won myself!"

There was never such an ovation at Newmarket and never so popular a win. I saw one old man with the tears running down his face. When I got to Lord Coventry, I just took his hand and held it. He had eyes like an old dog.

There was great rejoicing in Meath, not only over the spoils but for Lord Coventry's sake. The spoils, however, were considerable. The doctor alone had won £75.

Lord Coventry wrote to Horace on November 10th, 1923.

> "CROOME COURT,
>> "SEVERN STOKE,
>>> "WORCESTERSHIRE.

"MY DEAR PLUNKETT,—Many thanks for your kind congratulations, and I am glad to know you are back in London again—*Verdict*, excellently trained and ridden, ran as straight as a die under punishment, and defeated the beautiful horse *Epinard*—never before beaten—handsomely.

"The French are good sportsmen, and two friends from Paris, who had come to see their champion win, were the first to congratulate me! It was a wild scene, and I haven't recovered yet from the congratulations kindly given.

>> "Yours very truly,
>>> "COVENTRY."

I backed Verdict again a year later and I have Lord Coventry's letter to me about the race.

"As I told you I hoped to do, I put your £1 on Verdict both ways and tho' she ran a good race, she could not cope with Twelve Pointer, and I enclose cheque £5, 10s. I didn't go to see her run for I am a dreadful cripple from rheumatism, and shall soon have to join the Bath-chair brigade!

" I hope you are keeping well. Things are famous politically, and I expect I shall have to go up for the meeting of Parliament.

" We are leaving our trainer to decide whether Verdict runs in the Liverpool Cup on Friday but if Twelve Pointer goes we shall have no chance, for he escapes full penalty, but I hear he may not run.

" Yours very truly,

" COVENTRY."

On December 26, 1924, he writes:

" CROOME COURT,
" SEVERN STOKE,
" WORCESTERSHIRE.

" MY DEAR LADY FINGALL,—How very nice of you to remember an old and devoted friend, and the calendar will always be on my table—I have meant to look for some little remembrance to send to you, but I have not been able to get to London, and at Cheltenham the show in the shops was, this year, unattractive!

" I hope you are all well—we could not race at Cheltenham to-day but the frost is going rapidly. It is a sad time, old servants and pensioners succumbing to the weather! I had hoped to see Lady Mary at Cheltenham Races to-day, but they are put off!

" With the best of good wishes for the New Year. Believe me,
" Always yours truly,

" COVENTRY."

" I have an earlier letter of his, written to me on January 2nd, 1920, after Horace Plunkett's death had been announced and the report contradicted.

" 2nd Jan. 1920.

" CROOME COURT,
" SEVERN STOKE,
" WORCESTERSHIRE.

" MY DEAR LADY FINGALL,—I was beginning my letter of thanks to you for your kind wishes for the New Year in a very

344

different way. But, thank God, there is no longer any occasion for anxiety. On the 9th December I walked from the Carlton Club to Bond Street where I had to attend a lecture about Spitzbergen, with Horace Plunkett, and thought him looking well and in excellent spirits, but he had engagements which prevented him coming inside which I was sorry for, because I should like him to have seen the marble which pleased me very much, and I am half-inclined—if I can find any money— to put a small amount in the Exploration Company. But it *would* be a dreary region, for the ice only begins to disappear in the first week in July and forms again in the first week in October! And there are three months of complete darkness! With all the very best wishes for the New Year.

" Yours very truly,

" COVENTRY."

Lord Coventry died in 1930, leaving the world the poorer for the passing of a great gentleman.

CHAPTER TWENTY-SIX

Not long after Horace had been given Plunkett House, there was a gathering of his workers there. The I.A.O.S. had promulgated their famous slogan, "Better farming, better business, better living," and, at this meeting, it was A.E. who pointed across the room to some of us women: "This is where you come in. We can do the better farming and the better business, but you must do the better living." Then started the United Irishwomen. And the United Irishwomen were always United and we never had a quarrel.

After a great deal of work, and with financial help from Horace and from the Carnegie Trust, for our organising, we succeeded in forming about fifty societies through the country.

Besides our practical doctrine of "Better living," or included in it, was an aim at establishing social life in the rural districts, the dullness of which had sent the young flying to America. We had dancing classes and choral societies, and organised outdoor games, Hurling for the boys, Camogie— the feminine and milder form of the same dangerous game!— for the girls. Our fame spread and from England came people anxious to see what we were doing. They went back and started the Women's Institutes, an exact copy of what we were trying to do in Ireland. With help from the British Government, very soon almost every parish in England had their Women's Institute.

We flourished, with the inevitable ups and downs, enthusiasms and disheartenment of any such movement, until the "Troubles" after the War. Then, when five little girls knitting together might be considered a seditious meeting, we almost ceased to exist. But we have come to life again. And we only need more support and more branches and more enthusiastic workers.

On August 23, 1911, Horace writes from The Hermitage,

Bletchingley, Surrey, to me in Ireland and in the thick of Horse Show festivities.

"I suppose the Horse Show is as ever or more so. Still I wish I were there. One sees lots of friends and need not look at the horses. . . .

"Tell Maimie I am not going to read *The Times* any more! It describes her in embroidered white muslin (a dream, I'm sure), but says nothing about the hat."

Lord Kitchener had come over to stay with the Iveaghs at Farmleigh for that Horse Show. He was busy then, furnishing his house, Broome, and I was told off to take him round the Dublin antique shops and look for things he wanted, and help him to buy them cheaper than he would have got them.

I saw Lord Kitchener closer now than I had seen him at the Coronation two months earlier, carrying the Third Sword —The Pointed Sword of Temporal Justice. And I found him a dour, wooden-faced man with a decided cast in his eye and very dull company. He had, however, a delightful A.D.C., Captain Fitzgerald, who used to accompany us on our shopping expeditions. As a reward for my work I had the honour of arriving at the Horse Show one day with the Field-Marshal. I did feel rather proud when every one cheered as we walked through the Jumping Enclosure and up to the Stand.

Lord Kitchener's house, Broome, was of course, in Kent, and quite near Oxenhoath, the lovely place belonging to my brother-in-law, Sir William Geary. One day when we had been shopping, I said, "Next time I am staying with my sister Lady Geary at Oxenhoath, I would like to come over and see Broome and your interesting things. I can look at them even if you are not there."

"Oh, no," he said, with surprising firmness. "No one is ever allowed in, if I am not at home."

"Now," I said mischievously, "I know that what I have been told is true—that when you went to foreign palaces, you pinched anything you took a fancy to!"

That was a very gay Horse Show Week, with Balls every

night. Kitchener, who was the Lion among the visitors, refused to go to Balls to the disappointment of the Dublin hostesses. He would not even accept an invitation sent to him by Lady Paget, wife of the Commander-in-Chief, for the Ball she was giving at the Royal Hospital. However, Lady Paget persisted and begged me to try to persuade the iron Field-Marshal to come. Up to the very last minute he was adamant, and it looked as if I had failed.

"All right," I said, "I won't help you any more to find your antiques." At this he gave in. And I arrived at the Royal Hospital triumphantly, leading the unwilling Lion, who made a most imposing figure in his uniform. Someone who was present, reported:

"For a time Lord Kitchener stood at the top of the hall beside his hostess, but Lady Fingall was not yet satisfied. She had to persuade the soldier to dance in the State Quadrille, and she succeeded."

I did succeed, and made him dance with me! We must have been the funniest sight. My large partner had to be dragged round, and he looked like a great dog, on his hind legs.

Kitchener never liked or trusted the Irish and I always believe that but for him, Ireland would have been whole-heartedly in the War, and that there would have been no rebellion. When John Redmond made his famous offer at the outbreak of War, Kitchener refused to take the Irish on their own terms—that they should fight together, in an Irish Brigade, under their own flag. Geraldine Mayo's School of Art had been busy embroidering that flag, but alas! it was returned to us. Questions were asked in the House about that incredibly stupid and hurtful gesture. The enthusiasm was allowed to cool. The Irish were distrusted and knew it. They distrusted in their turn. There was no Irish Brigade; although thousands of Irishmen joined the Irish regiments, while their brothers, who might have gone with them, joined the Volunteers, to fight eventually against England in 1916 and the troubled years that followed. And John Redmond, who had trusted those who would not trust him, was broken by it.

When Kitchener went down on the *Hampshire*, two fine men went with him. His A.D.C., Fitzgerald and Hugh O'Byrne of the Diplomatic Service, who, they said, if he had lived, would have been, in time, one of our best Ambassadors.

Hugh O'Byrne was a great friend of ours and used to stay with us at Killeen, where I remember him suffering so much from asthma, that sometimes he had to sit up by a fire all night in an arm-chair. I have one amusing and frivolous memory, connected with him. While he was at the Embassy in Paris, Miss Minnie Fitzgerald, who was a connection of his, and I, went there for a few days. I wrote to him beforehand and said that we expected to be entertained and taken out every night. On the morning of our arrival we went out early, and like most women, made straight for the *Rayon des Jupons* in the *Galeries Lafayette*! Who should we see there already, but Hugh O'Byrne, sitting patiently amongst the most lovely petticoats!

"What on earth are you doing here?" I asked.

"Waiting for you," he said. "All the ladies, visiting Paris, always come straight here. So I knew I should find you!"

He had already been to our hotel and being told that we had gone out, guessed where we might be, and followed us. Those were the days of lovely petticoats, rustling silks and taffetas, flounced, laced and beribboned. And the *Rayon des Jupons* had an enchanting selection of them for our patient friend to sit among, while he waited!

He did not take us out every night, alas! We had not let him know in time, of our visit, and he was already booked up. He told us that, unlike London, where hostesses were often thrown over by their guests at the last moment, in Paris, which was a much smaller Society, a Diplomatist could not break his engagements. There was a Freemasonry of hostesses, and they stood by each other, so that a man doing such a thing would not be asked again.

There was a question of our selling Killeen at one time. We had been offered a big price for it by a returned Irish-

349

American who had gone to America as a poor emigrant and made an immense fortune. He had the romantic desire to possess an ancient and inconvenient Irish Castle.

Fingall thought that we should consider the offer. If he had foreseen the future, no doubt he would have been sure of the wisdom of selling, then. While we discussed it he suggested that Oliver should be consulted. He was then about fifteen and home from Downside for the holidays. I went to him and told him of the Irish-American's offer, expecting him to be altogether against the idea.

He said at once: "Oh, yes. Let's sell it."

I was horrified. "Oliver," I protested, "you can't sell a place where your ancestors are buried and which has been in your family for eight hundred years, as you would a Waterbury watch or a pound of tea!"

This made him thoughtful.

"Oh," he said slowly. "Have we had it all that time, Mother?"

"Yes," I told him. "Nearly eight hundred years."

"Well," he said. "Surely if we have had it all that time, it's somebody else's turn now!"

I have many gay memories of those years immediately before the War. Maimie and I went visiting. We stayed with the Downshires at Easthampstead for Ascot. There Lord Downshire kept a private Fire Brigade and whenever there was a fire in the district he would be called out, and would go off immediately to deal with it. He used to have a rehearsal every Sunday for his guests, some of whom found this rather a bore.

During that Ascot Week, we went to the Races every day, and, as always happened, I was asked to the Royal Box the day I was wearing my least smart frock! One was never asked on the day one had expected and for which one had saved one's loveliest dress. We came back from the Races to change into riding habits and go for an evening ride in the Forest, which was lovely. Or sometimes we went on the river.

At the end of the week there was Ascot Sunday, when

350

every one made for the river. The Downshires had a big launch to take the whole party and we went down to Clievden, having lunch on board. This expedition, which should have been so delightful, was a doubtful joy to me, as, even the swell on the locks made me feel slightly ill and I had to retire downstairs.

They always had an Ascot Ball at Easthampstead to which all the neighbouring hosts and hostesses brought their parties. There was a beautiful ballroom. The first time I saw it, it was lit entirely by candles—and lovely it was. Later, when electric light came in—I have an idea that Easthampstead was one of the first country houses to install it—the effect was much less beautiful. The gardens also were lit up for the dancers to walk in or sit out in between the flowers on a summer night.

Such house parties laid a heavy responsibility on hosts and hostesses, as their guests often brought wonderful jewels. Once at Easthampstead I was not sleeping well, and I heard a tramp, tramp, on the gravel outside. I began to think that it was a burglar and got up and looked out of the window. I saw a respectable looking man disappearing round the corner of the house. Presently he came back the other way, walking with no sign of secrecy, now and again looking up at the windows. I decided that he had a right to be there and when I asked about him in the morning, I was told that he was the night watchman.

In the winter of 1913 we took a house in London. We found a most charming one in Egerton Gardens, for which such a modest rent was asked that Fingall said there must certainly be something wrong with the drains! We had them thoroughly examined, however, and no fault could be found. So we took the house and brought over some of our servants and moved in. The house belonged to a diplomat who was abroad, and the Dowager Lady Kenmare, who had a beautiful taste in decoration, had had it some time before us, and had left signs of her tenancy.

There was a Chinese sitting-room at the back of the house,

351

which was set apart for me, and what the girls called "Mother's *beaux*." I felt something strange about that room from the first; a sensation when I was there alone, that someone else was in the room with me. So persistent was that feeling that I could never settle down to read or write there, peacefully. Presently someone told me that the house was haunted, although not by an evil ghost, and when we were giving it up, I discovered why we had got it so cheap. We had taken on one maid with it, and, making arrangements for our departure, I asked her if she would stay on for a few days after we and our servants had left, to hand over to the agent.

"My lady," she said, "I would not stay a night alone in this house for a fortune!"

So it was true! Later, I heard more. The immediately previous tenants had been a young officer of the Guards and his mother. Each of them had seen, several times, in my sitting-room, an old gentleman in a snuff-coloured coat, sitting by the fire. Neither had said anything to the other, until one day they were both in the room together, and each saw him and betrayed the fact by their expressions. "So you see him, too?" the mother said.

"Yes, I have always seen him. But I did not know that you did."

The house had been built on the site of a cottage, in which an old gentleman, who had been a great philanthropist, had lived in a previous century, and for some reason, he had haunted the place ever since. However, apart from my feeling about that room, the ghost did not trouble us much.

That winter Maimie hunted with the Whaddon Chase and the Rothschilds' Staghounds. She used to stay sometimes with the Rothschilds at Tring, or again with the Leo Rothschilds at Ascott.

I suppose that following Season of 1914 was the gayest and most magnificent that London has ever seen. To me there was something terrible about it. I felt it at the time. The wild extravagance, the entertaining, the money spending.

352

There were two or three parties every night and invitations were sent, through mutual friends, to absolute strangers. Just cards with a scribbled word, conveying somebody's compliments.

We lived in a small house and only gave tea parties, or had a few people to a quiet lunch or dinner. Yet we had invitations for several Balls every night. It was quite common for people to go to two or three, one after another, leaving a party which they found dull for better amusement elsewhere. I felt like a parasite, especially, when, as sometimes happened, I had not the remotest idea who the people were, from whom I was accepting hospitality which I could never hope to return. But I went as a dutiful mother, with my daughters, and shook hands with people I had never seen before, and ate their wonderful food, in their own houses, or at the Ritz, and sat on the bench with other dowagers, watching my daughters dance.

Maimie met plenty of young men hunting, and my girls were well supplied with partners. But the manners of the young men were as bad then, as they are now. There was one great Ball given at the Ritz at an enormous cost in order to launch a débutante daughter. All the young men accepted their invitations and went. At another dance a few nights later, the hostess of that Ball said to us piteously:

"Do get Maimie to introduce some of her young men to Evelyn. She has not danced yet to-night."

I looked round, "But, my dear. All these young men were at Evelyn's Ball!"

"Yes," she said. "But they do not remember her."

Again I was dragged by a party of young people, girls and men, to a Ball in Grosvenor Gardens. We had already been to others, and, when we arrived, it was discovered that the party was over and the hostess gone up to bed. The young men, not at all daunted, started up the band again, ordered some supper, and prepared to enjoy themselves. We went home, sick and ashamed.

Then a very old friend of mine gave a Ball at her house

in Hill Street, and, the same night, some very rich German Jews had one at the Ritz. All Maimie's friends and partners were going to the latter, so she must go to it too, or she would get no dancing. And I must go also. My old friend never quite forgave me. She said that when she gave her next Ball, she would put up a sign-post with a finger pointing, "This way to the Christian Ball!"

Well, we danced on the edge of an abyss. And a good many of the young people who danced so madly that Season were to be swallowed up by it. Those who reached the other side were to be many years wiser and older.

One day that summer we were having a small lunch party. Among our guests were Mr. and Mrs. H. G. Wells. As we drank our coffee, I heard a carriage drive up to the door and presently, a knock, and the footman opening it with something of a stir which reached the dining-room. Asking my guests to excuse me, I went out to the hall, to find Theresa Londonderry, resplendent, filling it.

"Who have you got in there?" she asked.

"Horace Plunkett and a few others—H. G. Wells."

"The writer? I'll come in." She came in, swept to a place beside Wells, and sat down. "Mr. Wells, I am so glad to meet you." They talked for a while and presently I heard her say in her clear voice:

"Mr. Wells, who do you think is going to govern England?"

H. G. Wells looked out of the window. In the street a coster was just passing with his barrow. Wells pointed at him with his finger.

"That," he said, in his high, squeaky voice. "*That* is going to govern England."

At one time I had been very much interested in Theosophy and used to attend Theosophical lectures at a friend's house. Although I expect I had not been able to keep my mind on the lectures or the subject for long! That summer Lady Churchill asked me if she might bring Mrs. Besant to tea, and would I get a few people to meet her? I said yes. (Now that I think of it, I believe I hardly ever say No. It is not a word with which I am at all familiar!) So I collected a few friends, all followers of Theosophy.

Early on the morning of my tea party, the telephone bell rang beside my bed:

I answered: "Who is there?"

It was my Theosophic friend. "Would you like Mrs. Besant to bring the Messiah?"

"Bring *who*?" I said.

"The Messiah," she repeated.

I held on to the telephone for a moment. Then I said rather faintly, "Oh, certainly. What would he eat?"

"Oh! He loves cakes."

I rushed to Maimie and said, "The Messiah is coming to tea. We must make sure that none of the holy men from the Oratory are allowed in this afternoon, or we shall be excommunicated!"

So careful orders were given, in case an Oratorian should choose that one particular afternoon to pay a call.

In due course the guests arrived. Mrs. Besant had a wonderful way of speaking, a commanding and imposing manner, and a head like a man's. I should not like to have seen too much of her, or she might have hypnotised me.

The Messiah, Krisnamurti, was a charming Indian boy— very high caste, I should say, slender, with dark, melancholy eyes. He certainly liked cakes!

That night we all went on to Mrs. Besant's lecture at the Queen's Hall. One of the party travelled with Mrs. Besant and the Messiah in the bus. The bus was crowded and Mrs. Besant turned to a woman and said:

"Won't you give your seat to the Messiah?"

"Certainly not," said the woman. "And if he *were* the Messiah, he would not take it!"

I have never seen the Queen's Hall so crowded as it was that night. Mrs. Besant stood on the platform, dressed in white, like a priestess. The people were so closely packed that a sixpence could hardly have fallen between them.

355

We had a ridiculous little dog with us in London, originally bought by Gerald at the Dogs' Home. He had christened him —most unsuitably—"Larkin," after the Irish Labour Leader, the stormy petrel of those days. Our Larkin was a meek little old Yorkshire terrier with soft hair covering his eyes. He had, obviously, once been an old lady's pet.

One day he disappeared and Gerald rushed up and down the Brompton Road, looking for him, in vain. In the evening came a telephone message, via Brooks's Club, from a lady living close to us in Egerton Gardens, to say that she would be most grateful if the Earl of Fingall would kindly remove his dog from her larder, where he was sitting on a ham, and growling at any one who approached! The only address on his collar was "Earl of Fingall. Brooks's Club."

We used to be at home on Sunday afternoons, and we were frequently astonished at the number of distinguished people who thought it worth while to come to our house. Our old friends, of course, came, and many Irish people: Bernard Holland, Sir Henry Primrose, who had been Gladstone's secretary, the Bernard Shaws, Edmund Gosse, Lord Grey, Lord Milner, and some of his "young men." Other friends of this time were the Merry del Vals, so good looking and charming. His family was of Irish descent and he was also particularly interested in Ireland.

Naturally the subject most talked of at those Sunday afternoon parties was the Irish situation. People would come fresh from Ireland, with the latest news. Sometimes T. P. O'Connor came, and, less often, John Redmond—in June preoccupied with the Buckingham Palace Conference. The Ulster Volunteers were drilling and had armed to resist Home Rule. (There had been the Curragh incident in March, the Larne Gun Running in April, with not a policeman or a soldier interfering.) The South had followed suit under their flag. All over Ireland now, men were drilling out on the hills under cover of the darkness. Ships carrying consignments of arms were slipping into lonely harbours where a party of men were waiting to unload and disappear with the arms—many of them

356

obsolete—before the police could come on the scene. A story was told of Shane Leslie, up in the North, going out secretly at night at Glasslough, on his way to drill with the National Volunteers. And in the hall, meeting another furtive figure—his father—going to drill with the Ulster Volunteers! They might reasonably have "paired" and gone back to bed!

We were surprised at the number of distinguished foreigners who came to see us, those Sundays. Maimie and I wondered whether they were her friends or mine. There was a German Baron whom we had met with the Rothschilds at Tring. He had told us that he was studying banking in London and had asked if he might come to see us. And a Count Luschka, a charming and good-looking Austrian, whom we met at parties also—his dancing was wonderful. He had a beautiful aunt who accompanied him; and like all the others, he too seemed deeply interested in Ireland.

Then, rather to our astonishment, Prince and Princess Lichnowsky, the German Ambassador and his wife, arrived one day. He was very good looking, tall, with great distinction, rather English in appearance, charming and gentle. He was deeply attached to England and his great desire was to keep peace between her and his own country. Princess Lichnowsky was tall too, fair and of rather ample build; a beautiful, temperamental creature. She adored cats and used to have three or four great furry creatures sleeping on her bed.

The Lichnowskys gave wonderful parties that summer at the German Embassy, where they had a row of enormous footmen in gorgeous livery lining the hall and stairs. These fierce-looking people used to terrify me. Once I told a friend that I was afraid to pass them alone, and asked him to come down and see me out.

Like every one else at our Sunday afternoon parties, the Lichnowskys used to talk of Ireland. I remember him one day sitting in a corner with John Redmond.

All the time, through that incredible summer, there was an ominous feeling. I was fey, perhaps, to be aware of it. If I felt omens and portents, I thought that they were for the Irish trouble that was coming. We were all waiting for that. No wonder that so many distinguished Germans had found our little London house and our Irish parties interesting!

In June there was the Sarajevo murder, a happening that did not seem very close to us. The failure of the Buckingham Palace Conference, which sat for three days, appeared closer and more important. And following it, came from Ireland, the story of how a yacht had slipped into Howth Harbour on a summer Sunday—with two ladies, Mrs. Erskine Childers and Mary Spring Rice, looking charming in yachting clothes on deck—a yacht, that hid beneath its shining decks a cargo of rifles; of how a party of Volunteers had marched out to unload them in full daylight; and, how (since this was not the North) the military were ordered out to intercept them, as they had not been ordered out at Larne!

The two parties met on the Malahide Road, and, while the leaders parleyed, the Volunteers, halted behind their officers, seem just to have melted away with their rifles before any one was aware of it, jumping over the hedges and being lost in the open country, leaving the English on the road. This was in the true tradition of Irish guerilla warfare, the red-shanks taking to the fields, as the Irish have always done, while the English stayed on the roads, as long as there were any, and tried to conduct, from them, their campaign in this wild country!

We heard how, on the way back to barracks, the military were stoned by the Dublin crowd, and the rearguard lost its head and fired, killing an old woman, a man and a boy on Bachelor's Walk, and injuring several more. Those three deaths in Ireland, and the assassination of the Austrian Archduke, lit a torch that set fire to Europe. Our eyes had been turned West to Ireland those last days of that incredible Season of 1914, when we were all riding madly towards the gulf, and had nearly reached it. From another quarter, as a thunderbolt, came the War.

CHAPTER TWENTY-SEVEN

ONE of the saddest men in London those days, was Count Mensdorf, the Austrian Ambassador, whom we had known in happier times at Elveden and in Ireland, where, when he stayed with the Iveaghs, and we were also guests, Maimie and I used to take him to Mass. Somebody met him the day War was declared, walking towards the river with an air of most profound melancholy. He said that he felt almost like making a hole in the Thames.

The Lichnowskys too, left London, heartbroken; he, having striven up to the very last minute for peace between the two countries that he loved.

The other day at Torosay, Lord Tyrrell talked to me about the outbreak of War when he had been secretary to Sir Edward Grey. He told me how the notes were prepared for that famous speech of the Foreign Secretary's, made on Monday, August 3rd, 1914, in the House of Commons. No more momentous speech had ever had to be made by a Foreign Secretary. It must convince and form the opinion, not only of the English people, but of the whole Empire.

Sir Edward Grey had only brief time on that Sunday in which to prepare his speech. He did not do it in his office. Instead, he and his secretary went to the Zoo, which was quiet on Sunday, when only the Fellows and their friends have the right of private entry. And, in the Bird House, among the birds that he loved, the famous speech was prepared, which declared our support of France and Russia and Belgium and justified it.

He delivered the speech in the House of Commons that Monday afternoon, and so great an impression did it make, that a Radical and Labour anti-War Meeting, arranged for the following evening in Trafalgar Square, was called off.

But Sir Edward Grey was back in the Foreign Office the

359

same night and saw from his window the lamps being lit in St. James's Park.

"The lights are going out all over Europe," he said. "We shall not see them lit again in our life-time."

That saying of his is now as famous as his speech. He spoke the truth, alas, for all of us.

We returned to Killeen. In Ireland we had forgotten Bachelor's Walk, and remembered only Redmond's dramatic offer of his Irish Volunteers. The Irish leader, being a gentleman, put his cards on the table and did not try to bargain with England in her hour of need.

In spite of Kitchener's fatal mistake in refusing the Irish Brigade, the Irish regiments formed new battalions, asked for recruits and got them. The 10th Division emptied Dublin of young men and was cut to pieces on the grim rocks of Suvla Bay in 1915. But that is history. My War story concerns only my personal memories.

Fingall was busy with recruiting. A remarkable organiser, Captain R. C. Kelly, had been sent over from the War Office to take charge of this department. He and his clever wife, who writes as Joan Sutherland, became friends of ours during their time in Ireland, when they lived in the Master of the Horse's House in the Lower Castle Yard.

It was difficult to get about from Killeen, with limited motor service, so we took a Dublin house in Elgin Road, and Fingall and Captain Kelly went by train each day to various recruiting headquarters. From Elgin Road it was easy, too, to get to Kilteragh, more than ever a centre of interest those days.

We were all busy and thinking of nothing but the War. Remembering the work of those years, I think that one could not ever exaggerate the greatness of English women during the War. Great ladies sold their jewels, gave up their houses for hospitals, and worked, themselves, often in the humblest capacity, night and day. What a contrast to that Season of 1914!

Millicent, Duchess of Sutherland, was running a hospital

in France, and the Stafford House parties belonged to another age. The Duchess of Westminster had her hospital at Le Touquet. Lady Dudley had another. Lady Ridley ran her hospital for officers in Carlton House Terrace; Lady Northcliffe one for the Ranks in Wellington Place. Lady Carnarvon found her vocation during the War, as many another woman found hers. Nearly all the nurses in her admirably run hospital in Bryanston Square were Irish, because she had discovered that Irishwomen made wonderful nurses.

These are just a few that I knew.

At Victoria, May Limerick, looking like a picture of Erin, with her dark hair and great Irish eyes and delicious brogue, was running a Canteen for soldiers on their way to the Front. When Irish soldiers came through, she accentuated her brogue for them, so that they took away the sound of Ireland in their ears. And when they came back on leave, that Irish voice greeted them. Again, it seemed a long time ago since she used to ask, before a Dublin Castle party: "D'ye think, should I wear me tiara?"

Mary Greer and Ethel Mulock were running Sir Ernest Cassel's magnificent Convalescent Home down on the Coast, about which ridiculous spy stories were spread. Olive Guthrie and Lady Fitzgerald had Ciro's as a club for soldiers. I don't think any man coming back to London in those days from the War, ever lacked a warm welcome.

Then there were the brave women at home, knitting endless socks and mufflers and sleeping helmets, which were often to be used for polishing lorries and guns. And those depots where the pathetic little parcels of the poor were received, which represented so much love and sacrifice. And all the women in the hospitals and in munition factories and on the land, hoeing turnips or driving cattle. I remember the courage of the mourning women who never wore black. There was one—I had last seen her in such a different world, at the Coronation—who lost two sons and never missed a day of her hospital work.

Early during the War, the famous Mademoiselle D'Esterre

came to Dublin. She held her classes in London at that time for poetry and elocution; and many of the younger M.P.'s, learning to make speeches, passed through her hands. Maimie had attended some of her classes, and so I had come to know her.

When we women had to take on our shoulders a great deal of the public work that men had done previously, taking the Chair at Committees, addressing meetings and so on, I thought Mademoiselle D'Esterre's visit to Dublin was a great chance for us to learn how to do these things properly. So I got a class together and Mademoiselle D'Esterre undertook to teach us as much as she could.

She was a very alarming person, and often so rude that some of our class left early in high dudgeon. After being one of her pupils, I never again felt frightened making a speech, for she was far more terrifying than any audience you could ever face.

Here are some of her instructions to her pupils that I remember:

(1) "Never apologise as being unused to public speaking. They will see that at once.
(2) "If ever you should make a point, sit down immediately, for you may never make another.
(3) "When you are speaking, make a picture for yourself. For instance, think of a garden and make the flowers your points; walk down the path, taking a flower here and there, each as a point. Never turn back. If you miss the delphiniums, go on to the hollyhocks, or from the hollyhocks to the phlox and so on. Always talk to the end of the room and never look at the people beneath you."

She used to call upon each of us in turn to get up and speak for five minutes on any subject that she decreed. I needed that vision of a garden one day when she pointed to me: "Speak for five minutes on Bimetallism."

362

I had not the remotest idea what Bimetallism was; nor have I now! But up I stood. I walked down the path at Killeen between my lovely borders. I saw the peonies, the white feathery spiraea, the delphiniums, and beyond, the unchanging security of the mellowed grey wall.

"This subject," I said, "is one of extreme difficulty and has puzzled some of the greatest brains of the world. In fact it is almost impossible to realise its difficulty and importance. We are still very much in the dark as to its real significance . . ."

And so I meandered for some time along that garden path, until I had a sudden brain wave. "Thou shalt not crucify humanity upon a Cross of Gold!" I quoted triumphantly, not even knowing where the quotation came from, and, so sat down.

Mademoiselle D'Esterre could only laugh for a minute or two. Then she said:

"For absolute rubbish, Lady Fingall's speech takes the cake," and, turning to me, "you get the prize!"

I went home with my book of poetry—the third prize I had won in my life, two of them equally undeserved.

When we learnt how to take the Chair, she declared:

"Lady Talbot de Malahide takes the Chair better than any of you, and says less."

Presently I was made Chairman in Ireland of the Central Committee for Women's Employment, which was started by Sir Matthew Nathan when he was Under Secretary. Among others whom I remember working hard and well on that Committee, were: Lady Arnott, Mrs. St. Lawrence, Mrs. Noel Guinness, Lady Talbot de Malahide, Mrs. Macken, Miss O'Reilly, and Mrs. MacDermott; and we had a wonderful secretary, Mrs. Hill Tickell.

The Committee worked in a room in Mount Street, which was damp, and caused the arthritis which afterwards crippled me. I was walking across Merrion Square one day, on my way to our Committee, when I felt the first spasm of pain. It was so fierce that I clutched the railing beside me, and held on to it in agony. A drunken man reeling across the road, called

363

out in the friendliest way and with deep sympathy: "And is that the way with you too?"

It was the way with me, alas! Although not what he thought!

Presently Maimie was nursing at the Royal Herbert Hospital at Woolwich, known popularly as "the Royal 'Erb," and Killeen was in France.

When he was leaving Sandhurst and trying to decide what regiment to apply for first, Sir Bryan Mahon wanted him to join the 8th Hussars, in which his grandfather had fought in the Crimea. Desmond Fitzgerald and George Morris both wanted him to join their regiment, the Irish Guards. But Douglas Haig was for his own regiment, the 17th Lancers, which had just come back from India. Douglas gained the day, and Killeen joined the 17th Lancers. Lucky he was too, for the 8th Hussars suffered terribly, and the Irish Guards were nearly wiped out.

Meanwhile Gerald, who was always a wizard with motors, gave a false age and joined the Mechanical Transport as a private. He went over to England and got lost; and I had to go over and find him, with the Irish Sea full of submarines.

During the crossing I went on the Bridge with the Captain, and he showed me, not very far off, a little dark object in the sea. "That is a periscope," he said.

I felt strangely unfrightened, watching it.

Gerald remained driving in the M.T. for a little time after the War, and drove for Lord French when he was Viceroy. He had the most amusing experiences when he had his meals in the Servants' Hall at the Viceregal Lodge and elsewhere, and listened to the gossip about the great, upstairs. One day he drove a high Staff Officer across the Park, to the Chief Secretary's Lodge. The officer talked to him pleasantly.

"Are you Irish?"

"I am," said Gerald in a brogue that did credit to his very early training and nursing—the footman and the Sherry whey!

"Where were you born?"

364

"Not far from here," said Gerald, driving in at the Chief Secretary's Gate.

I was in London when Killeen was wounded, fortunately not seriously. But I was afraid that he would be sent to a hospital in Leeds or Manchester or somewhere, whereas, if he was sent to London I could see him easily, and we had so many friends there. Someone said to me, "General —— at the War Office arranges these things. You probably know him. He hunted in Meath long ago."

So I went boldly to the War Office and asked for General —— and sent in my card. I was told that he would see me and I waited for a long time in a crowded room, full of grief-stricken women, also waiting. At last my turn came and I was shown into a room where a man with red tabs and a General's badges sat at a table, writing. He looked up at me with nice doggy eyes. I did remember him then, out hunting in Meath, and dancing with him in Dublin once or twice in that vanished world when Fingall had been Master of the Meath, and I, a faint-hearted Mistress, making myself pleasant to new-comers in the hunting field.

"Oh, General ——" I said diffidently, "I wonder if you remember me . . . ?"

He looked at me severely.

"Remember you? You were my dream for three years! What can I do for you, now?"

I mentioned three hospitals to which I would like Killeen sent, in the order of my preference. Lady Carnarvon's first, then two others.

The doggy-eyed man made a note on the table before him.

"I am very glad to be able to do something for you. But you can see how busy I am." With that I was outside the door.

But when Killeen woke up on the hospital ship coming from France, he found a large card with: "Lady Carnarvon's Hospital," written on it, across his chest.

While he was in hospital and Maimie at the Royal 'Erb, I was a good deal in London, at my usual home in Princes Gate with the Jamesons. It was there that Douglas made his dramatic appearance which I have described earlier in this book. Horace was a great deal in America, trying, with his friend, Colonel House, to bring America into the War; while his other friend, Moritz Bonn, was using all his brilliant gifts of propaganda to keep America out, and help the German cause. He is now, like many others who served the Fatherland, in exile, because of his race.

I used to go to some of the wonderfully interesting week-end parties which the Pagets had at Warren House, on Kingston Hill, during the War years. It was a charming long low house and there was a beautiful Chinese garden which Sir Arthur Paget had made. Through it, you walked to the green stretch of Coombe golf links on which a good many statesmen and soldiers snatched an hour of recreation during those years. I remember—among others there—Arthur Balfour and Sir John Cowans, and Constance, Duchess of Westminster, back from her hospital in France; Walter Page, the American Ambassador—a friend of Horace's too—one of the ugliest and most attractive men I ever met. And the Duchess of Marlborough, so lovely with her large eyes and long neck and her charming voice with only the faintest American intonation. Horace would come with Colonel House, when they were both in London.

Colonel House was then the power behind Wilson and they say that Wilson broke away from him at Versailles and that if he had not done so, but had listened to House, European history would have been different. Colonel House was a gentle, clean-shaven man, with wonderfully quick and intelligent eyes. When he said anything you knew that he meant something. He talked to you in such a quiet gentle voice and always as if you were the one person in the world he wanted to talk to. He had a wonderful power of influencing people and imposing his personality on them. The true cosmopolitan —he was at home anywhere in the world and, wherever he went, he would always find the most interesting person there.

In those days when he was the great man behind the

Throne, people used to whisper his name, "House." Deliberately, perhaps, he made himself seem a smaller man than he was. He was an Internationalist and he worked for the peace of the world. After Versailles he continued to work for it. He was always interested in Ireland and used to come with his beautiful wife to Kilteragh.

At some party (I cannot remember where) I sat beside the gloomiest American I had ever met. It was just at the end of the War and this man had been feeding the starving people in the Balkans. He saw no hope anywhere for any country. He was very anti-English and prophesied the complete downfall of England. A melancholy dinner it was, and sent me home miserable and sleepless.

The next day, lunching at Minnie Paget's, I sat beside Walter Page and told him of my depressing dinner the night before, with his pessimistic countryman.

I said, "I can't remember his name. I think it has something to do with a sweeper."

"Hoover," the Ambassador said. "Don't worry. He has been going through Hell, feeding starving people all over Europe since the War began, and his nerves have all gone to pieces."

Again I was lunching with the Pagets, and was called away in the middle of lunch to the telephone.

I went with my heart in my mouth, as one always answered a sudden call or opened a telegram in those days.

"Who is speaking?" I asked.

"Mabel Fowler," the answer came. "I could not wait to tell you that Killeen and Bob (her son) have both got the M.C.!"

Killeen apparently had fought a rearguard action and extricated his men from a tight place, without loss. When I asked him later what a rearguard action meant exactly, he said, "Oh, just running away backwards and not getting caught!"

Another of those War days, I lunched with the Northcliffes in St. James's Place. J. L. Garvin was also a guest, and we talked about nothing but the War.

A politician was discussed and someone said to Lord Northcliffe:

"I thought he was a friend of yours?"

He struck the table with his fist, making all the glasses ring: "I have no friends in this War. Only England. And nothing but to win it!"

Then he talked about France and his great admiration for the bourgeois and peasant women of France. He spoke of how the indemnity to Germany was paid after 1870, from the stockings of the peasant women—those hard-earned, hard-saved little fortunes, wrung from the earth, and brought out to clear French earth of the enemy. We talked of that great central plain of France which I had seen, driving as a child from the Pyrennees to Brittany, in a *diligence*. I remember still, those women, bent double, working in the fields.

During the War, my mother was living in a Convent at Brompton Square. It was always a peaceful interlude going to see her. She had a quality of rest within her, added to the tranquillity of the Convent, into which one slipped from the sad War-time London.

Sometimes as I went in, I would meet some tall young soldier coming away. Mother was one of those people who would always have visitors without any effort on her part, having that rare quality of real sympathy, which made people come to tell her things, knowing that their concerns touched her heart as deeply as did her own. She was a wonderful listener, and while someone else talked of their affairs, her grey-blue eyes would light up with laughter or fill with sympathy.

Several young soldiers used to go to see her. One of the Comyns, I remember among them, a grandson of her old friend of Danesfield days—later to be killed, alas! Maimie said once, "You know, Mother, Granny has far more followers than *we* have!"

My mother had lived in this Convent practically since my father had died. Shortly after his death we had all had a very strange experience. My sister, Lady Geary, at Oxenhoath, in

368

Kent, I, at Killeen, and my mother, in London, all heard, at intervals during the day and night, a certain knock which my father had always used, and called "the family knock." It was terribly distressing and we could not sleep, listening for it. The knock continued to come: at Oxenhoath, at Killeen and in the London Convent.

My mother consulted a priest, who said that if my father could not rest, there must be something that he wanted done. Shortly after, the thing was made clear that he wished put right. I was able to do my share of it and I never heard the knock again, but it continued at Oxenhoath and at the Convent, so loud that every one heard it.

Not long before my mother died, I went to see her one day and met an Irish friend in the passage outside her door. She said:

"Your mother has a visitor, so I only just looked in and came away."

"Oh!" I said. "Do you know who the visitor is?"

"No, I just saw an old gentleman with a long beard, sitting on the sofa beside her."

I laughed. "Well, I must see who Mother's new admirer is!"

I paused at the door. There was no one there except my mother. I went in.

"Miss O'Donnell said you had a visitor, Mother. An old gentleman with a long beard. What have you done with him?"

"Oh!" my mother said softly. "Did she see him, then? You know I can't see him, but I know that he is there."

CHAPTER TWENTY-EIGHT

MEANWHILE, in Ireland, the division between the constitutional Nationalists and the Sinn Feiners had widened. Redmond's Volunteers had sent their young men to France and to Gallipoli. The Republican Volunteers were drilling by night on the hillsides. Presently in London, when I went there, people were saying to me: "What is this Rebellion that Sir Matthew Nathan is always talking about? Is it nonsense?"

"It isn't nonsense," I said. "Unfortunately Sir Matthew is right. And presently you will know."

Sir Matthew had become a great friend of ours. We often stayed with him at the Under Secretary's Lodge, and he with us at Killeen. He foretold the Rebellion of 1916. But no one in England would listen to him, not even Birrell, the Chief Secretary.

We still had our Dublin house in Elgin Road, and, during the spring of that year Sir Matthew often came to dine with us. One night in April we had a small dinner party. There were present, Lady Edina Ainsworth, Lord Basil Blackwood—who was afterwards killed in the War—he was then private secretary to Lord Wimborne, John Healy, editor of the *Irish Times*, and Sir Matthew Nathan. Towards the end of dinner there was a knock at the door and the parlourmaid ushered in a young naval officer. He had an air of haste and excitement.

"Is Sir Matthew Nathan here?"

Sir Matthew answered: "Yes, I am Sir Matthew Nathan."

The sailor looked at him. "But how am I to know that you are Sir Matthew Nathan?"

Fingall spoke: "I am Lord Fingall, and I can assure you that this is Sir Matthew Nathan, the Under Secretary."

The young man looked from one to another.

"But how am I to know that you are Lord Fingall?"

Mr. Healy stepped in: "I am John Healy, Editor of the *Irish Times*, and I can assure you that you are speaking to Lord Fingall and to Sir Matthew Nathan."

But we were dealing with the cautious Service. In the end the young man said: "I am afraid I shall be obliged to ask you to come back with me to the Under Secretary's Lodge, to see if your own servants will recognise you before I can give you some important papers."

Sir Matthew went away with him and we were left speculating—the wild terrified speculations of those War years. What had happened? I thought: had the Fleet been sunk, or some such disaster?

When I went to bed, I could not go to sleep. Presently I said: "I am going to ring up Sir Matthew."

Fingall said: "You can't, at this hour. You must wait until morning."

I said: "I am going to." And I did. I got the Under Secretary's Lodge, and Sir Matthew came to the phone. I said to him:

"I can't go to sleep, thinking that something awful must have happened. Just say whether it is something terrible or not."

Sir Matthew's voice, calm as always, came through the telephone: "On the contrary, the tidings that the young man had to bring were *most* satisfactory."

I went back to bed, greatly relieved.

We were at Kilteragh for Easter. On Easter Sunday, Sir Matthew and his sister-in-law, Mrs. Nathan, came to lunch. He told us what the tidings were that the naval officer had brought: the news of the landing and capture of Sir Roger Casement on the coast of Kerry.

Sir Matthew had spent that morning at the Viceregal Lodge with Lord Wimborne, and he assured us that with Casement's arrest and the cancelling of the next day's Volunteer Parade by John MacNeill, all immediate danger had been averted. We could go to Fairyhouse Races on Easter Monday

371

as we had planned. But he counted without Connolly and some of the other leaders.

Fingall took Captain and Mrs. Kelly to the Races next day. I stayed at Kilteragh. I had planned to take Mrs. Nathan to the Abbey Theatre that night, and during the morning I rang up the Under Secretary's Lodge but could not get any answer. Then I tried Sir Matthew's office at the Castle.

"I want to speak to Sir Matthew Nathan."

"You can't." The voice was that of the old man who looked after the Under Secretary's telephone.

"Why not?"

"There is a rebellion on! Can't you hear the shooting? They have just shot a policeman at the gate."

I rushed to the window. Outside, in the peaceful spring sunlight, Horace and one of his male guests were playing "old man's golf."

"Horace!" I shouted out of the window. "There is a Rebellion on in Dublin!"

He turned and looked at me.

"What nonsense! Someone is pulling your leg."

"But they say so at the Castle—Sir Matthew's office."

"Well," he said. "Ring up the Kildare Street Club." And went back to his golf.

I rang up the Club and spoke for Sir Horace Plunkett. Was there a Rebellion on in Dublin?

"Never heard a word of it," said the porter.

A few minutes later the telephone rang.

"Tell Sir Horace that there *is* a Rebellion. They have taken the General Post Office and shot a policeman."

Meanwhile Fingall and the Kellys were at Fairyhouse, where the Races were run to the accompaniment of rumours. The enclosure, of course, was full of khaki-clad soldiers from Dublin and the Curragh. Someone arrived on the Course with a bullet hole in his car. People left early, as the rumours gathered. The Rebels had seized Dublin; they held the roads. The soldiers had to get back to the Curragh and their barracks in Dublin, somehow. Fingall's party was joined by several

372

young officers who were friends. Luckily he had Horace's big car. In it they left Fairyhouse and went to Dunboyne Castle, where they found the Morrogh Ryans, knowing no more than they did.

The soldiers rang up their Barracks and asked their Commanding Officer for orders. The C.O. did not speak himself, but a message came: "Stay where you are until further instructions."

So they waited during the long afternoon and evening. Mrs. Kelly wanted to get back to a young baby. But no one knew what was happening on the Dublin road. Mrs. Morrogh Ryan ransacked the house for a meal for her uninvited guests. If the rumours were true, it looked as if food was going to be scarce and precious for a time.

The April dusk came. Again a young officer rang up his Barracks and asked for orders. They came: "Stay where you are until further instructions."

When it was dark someone—not a soldier—went out and walked through the shrubbery. There was a scurrying and rustling in the darkness of the laurels. He came in thoughtfully: "The house is surrounded." But they had let him pass. They must be waiting for something.

A puzzled soldier rang up his Barracks again. "Stay there until we send for you," the answer came.

It was Fingall, at last, who made a move. It was now or never to get to Dublin, if there was to be a siege; and there were back roads through the mountains which could not all be held, unless the whole country had risen. The quietness of Meath, of the village at the gates, forbade the idea of that.

The soldiers were so glad to act and put an end to this waiting. It was soon after ten o'clock when the house was ransacked for mufti—Fingall and Captain Kelly were also in uniform. The men of the party changed into some semblance of civilian clothes, threw their caps and uniforms into the bottom of the motor-car, then got in and drove away. Those who stayed at the door, to see them go, were not at all sure that they would ever see any of them again.

That was about 10.30 at night. At eleven o'clock, reinforcements joined those waiting about the house, with orders to capture—or kill—the little British party. But that we did not learn until long afterwards, or that the voice that answered the telephone repeatedly on that afternoon: "Stay where you are until further orders," came from the Dublin Telephone Exchange, which was held by the Rebels.

Fingall and his party got through safely, having taken a circuitous route through the mountains. They dropped the Kellys at the back door of the Castle—strangely enough, that was possible. They were to be prisoners there, with Sir Matthew Nathan as fellow-prisoner, for the next week. The soldiers reached their Barracks, and Fingall returned to Kilteragh, where we had been having an anxious time. I was soon able to ring up our parlourmaid, Ellen, at Elgin Road, and she told me that all was well, that a priest and a parson, held up on their way from the boat, had asked for lodging and been given it.

"They are getting on beautifully together, and are both busy burying their dead," she told me.

Close by, there was that terrible ambush, when the soldiers marching from Kingstown, not knowing what foreign country they were in—and some believing that they were in France or Belgium, amazed to find the people speaking English—had been surprised from a corner house commanding the road and the two forks into which it divided at that point. The poor bewildered soldiers were received sometimes with bullets and sometimes with offers of food; the latter they were afraid to accept, lest the food might be poisoned. In the Churchyard opposite our house, a large ditch was dug as a hastily improvised grave. Strange sights and happenings for the respectable Dublin suburbs!

To Kilteragh came rumours and news. Constance Markievicz, dressed in a green uniform, was commanding the Rebels in the College of Surgeons. Dublin was in danger of food shortage. Horace at once saw the necessity for a Food Committee! So he and his nephew, Tommy Ponsonby,

374

Sir Henry Robinson and Mr. Leonard, started one. Horace, to my terror, got out his car and motored into the Castle each day for his Committee. For greater safety he used to drive very fast. One day, when he and Tommy Ponsonby were going at full speed through Merrion Square, a party of British soldiers at the corner of Westland Row called on them to halt. Horace thought that they would recognise his party as friends, and did not stop. A number of shots rang out and the car was hit. Horace stopped then. But the firing continued for a second or two. One bullet went through the windscreen, another through Horace's coat, and Tommy was shot in the back, rather seriously. Having reassured the soldiers as to his identity, Horace drove his wounded nephew hastily to hospital, and went on to the Castle and his Committee.

Meanwhile, at Kilteragh, we had improvised beds for people who were landing at Kingstown and could not get through. Horace used to go down to meet the boat and see what he could do for his friends and sometimes for strangers. Presently we wanted clean clothes, and Horace drove me into Elgin Road to get them, at breakneck speed. I shall never forget the terror of that journey.

It was all over in a week or so. The end of the Rebellion left the greater part of the country still unstirred; and once again England blundered. Sir John Maxwell had been sent over as Commander-in-Chief—a soldier used to dealing with such situations, according to his ideas, in Egypt and India. The Rebels were tried by court-martial with scrupulous justice, each case given full trial on its merits, although there was no plea for the prisoner and no doubt ever of the verdict. Then there were the slow executions. So many each morning. Sixteen in all. A small number in men's minds in that time of war, with daily casualties of thousands. But death in action is another matter. To the Irish people, being told of these executions in barrack yards, it was, as someone wrote: " As hough they watched a stream of blood coming from beneath ʾsed door."

We were back in Elgin Road, and General Blackader, who was President of the Courts-Martial, used to dine with us sometimes. He was a charming, sympathetic person, half French, very emotional, and terribly affected by the work he had to do. He came to dinner one night greatly depressed. I asked him:

"What is the matter?"

He answered: "I have just done one of the hardest tasks I have ever had to do. I have had to condemn to death one of the finest characters I have ever come across. There must be something very wrong in the state of things that makes a man like that a Rebel. I don't wonder that his pupils adored him!"

The man he had condemned was Patrick Pearse. He also tried Constance Markievicz. She was condemned to death, but reprieved because of her sex, sentenced to penal servitude for life and afterwards released. My thoughts went back to the lovely girl who had delighted parties at Adare and at the Castle.

The Chief Secretary had come to Dublin on a Destroyer on Easter Monday night. He drove through a fusillade of shots to the Viceregal Lodge, where he stayed until the Rebellion was over. He then returned to London, resigned his office, and insisted that Sir Matthew Nathan should resign with him, although it was quite an unusual procedure, for the Under Secretary's office is permanent and non-political. Sir Matthew was broken-hearted, but never wavered in his loyalty to his Chief. Ireland had won some of his heart, as he showed in a letter he wrote me after he left:

"I suppose I have not forfeited all right to take interest in Ireland, and I want to hear your Irish opinion of what has been happening, and of the future.

". . . Have you seen A. E. lately? Ought not the people who can influence thought in Ireland to initiate a movement for combining the two ideas of maintaining the British connection and developing the national individuality of

376

Ireland? It has been one of the Government's mistakes to treat the latter purpose as essentially antagonistic to the former, with the result that they have made it so. . . ."

. . . .

His Chief, Birrell, will be better remembered, I think, by his Birrellisms than by what he did for Ireland.

Horace writes to me in 1916:

"Give my love to Mrs. Willie and tell her how I rejoice in Douglas's growing fame. How splendidly he has won it by the hard and faithful study in years of peace, really requiring more qualities than being at one's best when the opportunities come. The faith that good honest work is never wasted, is what I most admired in Douglas, in days long before the War, when he showed what he was. Let me know *what time* (Irish) the car is to be at the boat when you fix the day."

The following year he writes to Betty Balfour from the Plunkett House, Dublin, just after his return from America:

"I left the United States on 1st May, having left the Chicago hospital a few days earlier than I was advised, in order to meet Arthur in Washington. I wanted to see him on a few points and to arrange an interview with a few sane and influential Irish-Americans. To-day I have a letter from Shane Leslie, Winston Churchill's first cousin, of whom you may know, telling me that the interview took place after I had left, and did great good. Leslie is now living in New York and working upon the Irish-American situation with a view to preventing mischief from the German-Irish combination.

"I was too ill to do much while in America, but I kept up my correspondence with the people out there I went out to see and was more or less in touch with American sentiment. If you remember the memorandum I wrote for Arthur in

377

February, 1916, and which he circulated among the Cabinet, you will count me a good prophet. I said that if the Americans came into the War—which I had always insisted they must—they would, contrary to the general impression, render invaluable service and be a decisive factor in bringing war to an end, and I gave my reasons for my belief. I read this document with a good deal of pleasure now. If the Americans had not come in, the outlook, with Russia in its present condition, would be, to say the least, gloomy. Personally I am convinced that, if our publicity work had been as good as it was bad, we should have had this invaluable assistance nearly two years ago. It would have been immensely more effective before Rumania's blunder and the development of submarines: it would have ended the war long ago.

"I rushed home when I could have been of use in America in connection with the food supply—for the farmers there listen to me much more readily than they do in Ireland—but I felt I was bound to come and struggle again in the Irish bog as soon as I was fit for work.

"I think the Convention will come off and that something will come out of it, but until we know the composition of the body, the chairman and the secretary, I shall not prophesy. The handling of the Irish question since the war started has been more stupid than ever before, and as a consequence the country is terribly out of hand. Far the most numerous and the most influential political section is that which is vaguely called Sinn Fein, but it is rather a sentiment than a party. There is no clear policy and no leader, little organisation. If a real leader appeared it might lead to some settlement.

"I suppose Arthur will be home soon. His mission is certainly the biggest success of his public life. . . ."

The Irish Convention sat in Trinity College in 1917 and 1918, under Horace's chairmanship, to search for a solution of this eternal Irish problem.

In November, 1917, while the Convention was sitting, I

THE RIGHT HON. SIR HORACE PLUNKETT.

LORD KILLEEN

being led in by Major-General Sir Robert Hutchison (now Lord Hutchison of Montrose) after winning
a race at Cologne during the British Occupation.

met Lord Londonderry as we were leaving the Theatre Royal. His letter, written to me the same night, will indicate our conversation. Bryan Mahon complained to me afterwards that I kept his guests out of bed writing letters to me!

"THE ROYAL HOSPITAL,
"DUBLIN.
"26th Nov., 1917.

"DEAR LADY FINGALL,—I was not in a position to answer your indictment on Saturday, as the passage of the Theatre Royal was hardly the ideal background, so I refrained to even controvert anything you said, and I should be inclined to continue this attitude of indifference to most people, but your views and beliefs naturally affect me.

"There is a certain amount of difficulty in arguing this matter with you, because I am unwilling to say anything to even cause a ripple in a delightful acquaintance, so if you will bear with me for a moment and accept everything that I say in the spirit that it is meant, I will just touch on one or two of the invectives which you hurled at my head.

"Do you really think that the dramatic situation of recanting principles is likely to appeal to me? There would be nothing easier than to rise in the Convention and by means of a few phrases to gain thunderous applause from a number of very ignorant men. Suppose I had reason to suddenly change my views, what purpose would I serve? Because if that is what you intended to suggest, please let me say at once that if the principles which I hold are so flimsy that Sinn Fein pressure can completely change them, those amongst whom I live are of totally different material. And, after all, what is the gist of your argument, that we are so stupid or so avaricious that we will not subscribe to the Sinn Fein programme? Let me say that there is no difference between the loyal Nationalist programme and the Sinn Fein programme, the distinction lies in the attitudes of these two sections towards the Empire as explained by their leaders. Redmond, so far as he expresses a definite view at all, claims

379

that the feelings of benevolence which he undoubtedly entertains towards England and the Empire will ensure that separation will not be the result of the policy. Sinn Fein frankly states that the policy is intended to lead to complete separation.

"My views are contained in a few sentences. I am absolutely convinced of one thing, and that is that, so long as the British Empire exists, Ireland must remain politically within the circle of the United Kingdom; and whatever path is chosen, long or short, or through whatever intermediary stages, man in his wisdom or his folly may ordain she shall pass, that Ireland will be politically governed in exactly the same manner as England or Scotland or Wales. My plan is a Federal one with which I need not weary you now.

"The demand to which you and others with varying degrees of invective ask me to agree, is to give powers to Ireland—in a word, 'to keep her quiet'—powers which a Federal Government are bound to take away. I feel I can imagine the quality of your vituperation when this moment arrives, and what is the alternative, if these powers (chiefly Fiscal powers) lately ceded to stave off a threatened catastrophe are not returned by Ireland to a British Government with willingness and enthusiasm? How does a Government representing forty millions deal with four million recalcitrants? Are you prepared in the hope of soothing present-day aggravations and irritations to sow the seed of an infinitely more bitter struggle than you could possibly have now? If I was entirely lacking in principle, which I hope I am not, I could propose two courses which might serve the needs of the moment. One would be to surrender to all Sinn Fein demands, knowing that this step would entail a bloody revolution at the end of two years. This surrender might just serve the purpose of temporarily strengthening the position of the Empire, in that this tiresome problem would be in abeyance while patriots were fashioning a machine of Irish Government. It would not gain one single additional recruit for the Army, so with surrender even this advantage would not be gained. But this position of admitted independence cannot stand under a Federal system, and even suppose no Federal scheme immediately follows the war, do you imagine that an Irish Government, no matter how it is composed, is unlikely to avail itself of the power of blackmail resident in an independent Irish Parliament to extract from Great Britain concessions which Great Britain may not wish to make, and in fact may not be able to make?

"I am not thinking of the moment in my work in the Convention. I am thinking of the future and the road along which lies the solution of the problem. You and your southern Compatriots are idealists; you have always thought that the acquisition of what was in your minds at the moment meant satisfaction and living subsequently and forever in peace, goodwill and happiness. Your friends have averred this during every great Irish controversy, and the only result is that differences are more acute now than they have ever been before, and the demands formulated more exorbitant and more impossible.

"The second course I might pursue were I still totally lacking in principle is to back the Separatists' demands. This would result in Great Britain applying Coercion forthwith to the whole of Ireland and perhaps Conscription as well. If the law was administered with even-handed justice, I have very little doubt that, with probably far less difficulty than I anticipate, you would again see after a lapse of time an era of peace and prosperity which followed on a period of Irish history as dark and as menacing as the present one, and which came to an end when your friends allied themselves with the forces of combined Radicalism and Socialism in 1910, although these political tenets were wholly repugnant to their views and beliefs.

"There is no truth nor object in denying that Ireland prosper under the Union. There is Belfast, a mor industrial success, and there is agriculture in Ireland, manifestly in a prosperous condition, ar that had Irish Nationalists flung themselves local patriotic endeavour instead of always standing aloof and encouraging agitation and the hopeless pursuit of romantic and sentimental ideals, you would see a very different state of affairs in the political life of the country. There is no limit of local self-government which the evolution of modern government may not reach and to this movement I am a willing subscriber, but I repeat that this must limit Irish aspirations so long as the British Empire exists, and if it does not exist, God help Ireland.

"I will say this, that if I contemplate you seriously—and I need hardly say that I do—I feel indignant when you upbraid me, in no measured terms, either, for presenting an obstacle to a policy to which enlightened opinion in the Empire certainly and in other countries, with the exception, doubtless, of Germany, will be opposed, and I say this because the suggestion of Ireland as a separate national and political and fiscal unit has never received support in the Colonies, and must present a strategic danger which Great Britain could, under no circumstances, admit.

"I will say at once that, while I am willing to proceed on the lines of Federation, I am convinced that it is folly to choose this moment to establish so far-reaching a change; and as far as I can judge the only reason you desire a change which you never have defined, if I may say so, is because Sinn Fein will in your opinion break out in open revolt. Do you imagine you are going to restore Redmond? Never have I had an illusion so shattered as regards Redmond: an Irish leader with the gift of superb eloquence, but without a plan of any kind—and this is your prospective Prime Minister!

"I venture to apologise for writing you so long a letter. If I had not been so presumptuous as to entertain feelings for you stronger than those of a mere acquaintance, I should have felt inclined at the Theatre Royal to have retorted in the style of a 'tu quoque' couched in courteous terms, and also, if I had taken sufficient interest, to have written you a letter which would have contained the bitter and acute side of the controversy. I have not done so, so I will make two requests of you.

"The first is not to attack me again, and the second is not to quote me as saying that Ulster was the cause of the war. This I repudiate absolutely. One of the many causes controllable by human agency was the criminal folly of the Irish-Radical-Socialist alliance, which reduced our Army, wrecked our Constitution, and for wholly immoral reasons unconnected with the real issue, endeavoured to force on a free community a measure of Home Rule which, mark you, is now repudiated by every one.

"Believe me.

"Yours sincerely,
"LONDONDERRY."

I wrote to Lord Londonderry on November 28th, 1917:

"21 FITZWILLIAM PLACE,
"DUBLIN.

"MY DEAR LORD LONDONDERRY,—First, I must thank you most sincerely for taking my somewhat vitriolic outburst so kindly, and letting me have such a clear and frank explanation of your point of view on this ever-puzzling I.Q. As to your question whether I think ' the dramatic situation of recanting principles' is likely to appeal to you, I never dreamt of your posing in any way, or doing anything whatsoever in which you did not believe, nor did I for a moment suggest that you could be affected by any pressure from Sinn Fein. What I had thought was that with the change going on in every one's views owing to the different conditions now existing all over the world, *you* might enlarge the outlook of the Ulster attitude that does not seem to recognise that a change is inevitable. That was what I meant in saying I wanted you to *lead* instead of following—I have *not* accused Ulster of stupidity, but I do maintain that her material interests take the first place in her heart. I never gathered there was any idea of complete separation between England and Ireland in the programme of the Nationalist Party or in that of the large majority of Sinn Feiners, and I absolutely agree with you that it would be fatal to both countries.

"As to your suggestion that I am asking you to give power to Ireland merely to ' keep her quiet,' I would remind you of that big bribe, the Wyndham Act, which doubtless kept her quiet for a while, yet in spite of it all she still demands not further bribes, but liberty to govern herself; this is a lesson which ' he who runs may read,' and I, like you, am thinking of the future.

"What you said to me at dinner as to your ideas on Federalism has immensely interested me, for I believe, too, *that* to be the final solution of all our problems. Did you ever bring forward a scheme? Can it not be advocated now? Dunraven, we know, is a keen Federalist; so was Lord Grey and many others I have met. Mr. Bernard Shaw told me he would willingly stump the country preaching Federalism if he could get any one to help him.

"I don't think I quoted you as saying Ulster was the *cause* of the War, but we both seemed to agree at that dinner that the situation in Ireland (i.e., the arming of Ulster) was a big factor in bringing it to a head.

"I feel this is a most inadequate answer to your splendid and well-reasoned letter; but, good as I may be with my tongue, I am no use with my pen.

"When we meet again, which I hope will be very soon, you may feel quite safe from any further ' attack.'

"Please believe me when I say it was my deep interest and belief in you which made me speak as I did.
> "Ever yours most sincerely,
> "E. M. FINGALL."

Alas, the Convention went the way of all other hopes for Ireland.

The War dragged on through the spring and summer of 1918 and into the autumn. Within a month of the Armistice, the U-boats caught the Irish Mail and the *Leinster* on her morning passage to Holyhead was torpedoed and sunk, in full daylight within sight of Kingstown Harbour. Ex-King Manoel of Portugal was one of those who had intended to travel on her. He had come to Ireland for a meeting of the Red Cross, of which he was a patron. He stayed at the Viceregal Lodge, and Lady Arnott gave a luncheon party at 12 Merrion Square for him to meet various Red Cross workers, including myself. King Manoel postponed his departure for a day in order to accept Lady Arnott's invitation. Otherwise he would have crossed on the *Leinster*.

We heard the news after lunch, and King Manoel exclaimed to his hostess: "Miladi, you have saved my life!" and kissed her hand.

CHAPTER TWENTY-NINE

I USED to think and say, during the War, that if ever that list of Dead and Wounded could cease, I would never mind anything or grumble at anything again. But when the Armistice came at last, we seemed drained of all feeling. And one felt nothing. We took up our lives again, or tried to take them up. The world we had known had vanished. We hunted again, but ghosts rode with us. We sat at table, and there were absent faces.

For us, I suppose, the Irish Troubles were a continuation of the War. Through that first year after the Armistice there was spasmodic raiding of the country houses for arms. A varied and quaint collection the results of those raids must have been, when the raiders examined them. An odd sword or two, a dead soldier's revolver, an ancient musket; strange antique firearms, that for years had decorated a country house hall.

They went to Carton one night and were very polite to the butler, who opened the door in answer to their knock. If his Lordship[1] was in bed, they said, they would not like him to be disturbed. And they took away, among other things, Desmond Fitzgerald's revolver, which had been sent back from France with his effects, and was a precious possession to those who loved him. Later—I believe—by the kind intervention of the last Governor General of Ireland, then a rebel leader, it was given back. Such things happened all through the country.

During a Horse Show party at Killeen, which included some young soldiers back from the War, a number of men came to the North Door and demanded to see "his Lordship." I insisted on going with him. When he opened the door I saw a group of figures against the night sky. The light

[1] Lord Frederick Fitzgerald.

streamed out on their blackened faces. Familiar voices asked Fingall for a subscription to the Irish Republican funds.

He said: "When the Irish Republic is the Government of the country, I will subscribe to it, not before."

"Thank you, me Lord, we know you will," they said politely, and the night swallowed them.

One Sunday they went to our neighbour, General Hammond, and took a sword. Fingall had walked over there for tea, and there was no one at Killeen that afternoon except the servants. This is Miss Devereux's story:

Towards evening she was in the garden, talking to the gardener, when she saw a young man approaching down the path. At first she thought that it was one of the postmaster's family bringing a telegram. Then she remembered that that could not be so on Sunday. The young man came up to her and said: without "Miss or Ma'am":

"We want you in the house."

Then she saw that he had a revolver in his hand.

The thought was in her mind, she said, to say to him: "Put up your revolver," but she did not say it. For a second they stood there, in a group of three, she and the gardener, who, she remembered afterwards "never opened his mouth with it all," and the young man with the revolver in his hand. And, about them, the peace of the garden.

At first, telling this story the other day, she could not remember what time of the year it was, but then remembered that it must have been autumn, and October, for there were apples on the trees (that I had planted, where once we had tried to grow tobacco), and as she went with the young man towards the house he put up his hand and picked an apple.

"Don't touch those apples," she said dauntlessly.

"We have a right to touch what we want," was the answer.

She went with him into the kitchen, where a group of men waited. They were all armed. One of them, apparently a leader, said:

"We want guns; and you have four hundred rounds of ammunition!"

387

Miss Devereux said: "I never saw a gun in Lord Fingall's hand in my life. Surely, when he did not handle guns, he would not have ammunition!"

They said that they must search the house, nevertheless.

"Are you not afraid of us?" the leader asked.

"Not a bit," said Kate. "I am never afraid of honest Irishmen. I hope you are that."

"Oh, we are," he answered.

Two of them went upstairs with her. The rest were told to stay below. All the time, she said afterwards, she was thinking of his Lordship over at General Hammond's, and how he might return across the quiet fields at any moment, with no idea of what was happening at Killeen. And she was thinking hard how she could get rid of the raiders before he came back. She showed them, with secret pride, his simple room. She could see that they were surprised by the bareness of it. And then Killeen's and Gerald's, just the same. From one of the boys' rooms they took an electric flash-lamp. Miss Devereux told the man as he took it that that was not worth stealing.

"We are supposed to get equipment," he replied.

They asked for the Strong Room.

"A queer thing," the leader said, "if there is no Strong Room."

"What do you mean by a Strong Room?" she asked cunningly.

"A place where ammunition and guns are stored."

Miss Devereux declared positively and truthfully that there was no such place at Killeen.

They went downstairs and back to the kitchen, where the kettles were steaming, ready to make the servants' tea. The raiders hesitated and looked longingly at the tea-cups. Then the leader asked if they could have some tea. They hadn't had a bit to eat all day, he said. They were given tea and bread and butter, for which they said, "Thank you," very politely.

Miss Devereux stayed in the kitchen while they were

388

having it, feeling that she must not let them out of her sight, lest one of those revolvers should go off and hurt someone. Then she had a thought, and, going just outside the door, called softly to one of the maids: "Delia. Come here." She meant to send her out to intercept his lordship, and tell him to keep away until the raiders were gone (advice that he would hardly be likely to follow!). She probably knew that, but at least he could be warned of the visitors his house was entertaining that afternoon.

The raiders heard her low consultation with the maid, and took sudden fright. They went out in a great hurry, but still had time to turn back at the door and say thank you again, for the tea. Miss Devereux watched them go across the fields in the evening light, scattering as they went. She said to herself:

"They are no strangers here."

For obviously they knew all the paths and the short cuts.

Presently Fingall came back, having just missed them. He said of the guns that they had not found: "They might have killed themselves with them—but not the men they meant to kill."

From now on we were to live in an atmosphere of such happenings. Knocks coming to the doors of country houses— those doors that had so often stayed open all night. Men outside demanding arms in the name of the Irish Republic. During those years they closed the door at Howth Castle, which had remained open through the centuries, for Granuaile. Strange that another Granuaile—Ireland (for they used that cipher name for her in other Rebellions) should have closed that door! In due course the arms—or some of them—were used. We were peaceful enough in our corner of the world, although we never knew when that peace would be disturbed.

Horace went to America in the winter of 1919—to Battle Creek, alas, for an operation.

He wrote to me on December 29th, 1919, from 290 Park Avenue, New York.

"I dined with the Byrnes after a long conference with Colonel House. . . . The Houses asked me to dinner to meet Lord Grey on January 1st, but I thought it better to think of nothing but getting fit. . . .

"I know little yet of the state of feeling in America. First impressions are, if not disgusting, disquieting. Everybody seems discontented and reckless. The new rich and the new poor are grinding and being ground by the working masses, and these are ugly and angry in their attitude to society. House was very depressed and depressing. Poor man, he had the bitterest disappointment of anybody at Paris, and he shares the unpopularity of his master who has cast him and every other man he ought to cherish. He has refused huge offers for books and articles—an example to our Viceroy. He could write one of the most interesting books of modern times. . . ."

On January 1st, 1920, the day on which Horace was asked to dine with Lord Grey, the report reached us of his death.

We were sitting round the fire in the library at Killeen— Fingall, his cousin, Frank Anderton and I—when a telegram came from Plunkett House. I felt stunned for a moment, but strangely dulled. I said: "I don't believe it; but if it is true, I am almost glad, as he will be out of pain at last." We went up to Plunkett House, where R. A. Anderson had had a notice posted, saying that credence was not yet given to the report. Almost at once came the contradiction, but first, Horace had had the unusual experience of reading his own wonderfully eulogistic obituary notices.

Betty Balfour had written to me on New Year's Day, 1920, from Whittingehame:

"Oh, Daisy, my dear, my dear!

"This is tragic news to greet the New Year. The loss of the best man Ireland ever had. . . . My heart is too full now to write more. His countrymen are sure to give him plenty of fine words now he is gone—but why did they not give him more loyalty and support when he was alive?—and *he* never turned against them or forsook them.

"He has earned his rest, and his 'Well done, Good and Faithful Servant,' if any man ever did; but I wish he could have seen his heart's desire first. . . ."

Horace's letter to R. A. Anderson explained what happened.

"The Battle Creek Sanitarium,
"Battle Creek,
"Michigan.
January 5, 1920.

"My dear R. A.,—I left New York on the evening of the 31st December, and arrived here on the 1st of January. I was suffering rather badly from insomnia, and when I had been examined here they put me to bed, where I still am, and subjected me to a regular course of treatment which is beginning to have its effect. An essential part of the treatment is seclusion from the outer world. Telegrams and cables kept coming about a report that I was dead. I do not think it was in the American papers, but was cabled over to England, probably by one of the reporters, whom I refused to see, out of spite. I was hiding from the press and was being pursued by a swarm of journalists. One of them may have thought that any one who did not seek publicity must be dead, and cabled accordingly. I know nothing more, but it is all very annoying. I probably should have known nothing about it till now, only that my London solicitors cabled the Sanitarium to know what they were going to do with my remains.

"I cannot tell you how sorry I am that my family and friends should have been the victims of such an outrage. The only consolation I have is that it is not likely to happen again in my case until the end comes. I must not write more now, as I am still resting in bed.

"Yours ever,
"Horace Plunkett."

His letter to me, after a brief reference to the false rumours, shows him back at work at once:

"Now that I am back here, I must do my best to get help for the Irish Dominion League and the *Irish Statesman*, and also try to save the worst Anglo-American situation I remember, by treating its cause—the Irish factor."

At the end of the letter he says:
"The League and the *Statesman* are the one hope of Irish peace."

Fingall paid a rare visit to London in the summer of 1920, and wrote his impressions to me of post-War London:

"London is hot and dusty, but not excessively so. Taxis in plenty, fares quite reasonable and every one quite civil. (Taxi drivers in particular; but I've only had two.) Many new faces in the Lords, and many of them unattractive. The attendants somewhat aged, but really everything practically just the appearance of July, 1914, when I last saw it. I walked across the Park two or three times on Monday and ran into quite the old crowd. . . . The little female attire I have seen in the streets is scanty, but reasonable and decent. . . . All those I've met, of course, asked after you . . . in particular Lord Zetland, who seemed very full of life and who was very nice to me. I told him I wished they would send him, a sensible man, back to us. . . ."

All through 1920 things in Ireland were getting steadily worse. There had been shootings of policemen, village bonfires night after night as the police barracks were burnt, tragic fires, involving sometimes loss of life among those burnt out and among the burners. Cars flew about under cover of the darkness, driven by armed men and loaded with petrol tins. Ireland was in the "news," and there were constant visitors from England studying the question. Many of them came to Kilteragh. George Adams used to bring over people from Oxford who were interested. Alexander Lindsay, now Master of Balliol, came, just as the burning of the police barracks had begun. He went over to look at one of those blackened ruins and, meeting the parish priest, asked him why the people had done this.

The P.P. replied: "Because the police had put barbed wire round the place, and that was very provocative."

Alexander Lindsay came back to Kilteragh, bewildered. He said he felt quite at a loss with a people who found defence provocative!

Another visitor was Sir William Robertson, who was with Horace on the Carnegie Trust, where there was great rivalry between them, Horace wanting to get money for Ireland and Robertson trying to keep it for Scotland. Driving in the neighbourhood, they passed St. John of God's, a large lunatic asylum. Sir William asked: "What is that?"

When told the purpose of the building, his comment was: "It is not nearly big enough."

Presently the British Government made one of the worst mistakes they had ever made, even in Ireland. Unable to combat the campaign of assassination with their ordinary forces, they decided to fight their opponents with their own weapons. If they could not find an assassin and get a jury to convict him and execute him, they would employ men who would take the law into their own hands, without trial. They increased the numbers of the R.I.C. with new recruits, many ex-soldiers fresh from the battlefields—and some ex-convicts fresh from gaol. The supply of dark green cloth being limited, these appeared half in their old khaki and half in R.I.C. uniform, and were christened after a famous old pack of Hounds, the "Black and Tans." In addition, a new force was formed, called the Auxiliaries. These were mostly ex-officers, many of them shell-shocked. They had little or no discipline, being all of equal rank. Some were Irishmen, wanting any job after the War, and little knowing what they were going to be asked to do. They were dropped down in barracks throughout the country, where they led as unsuitable a life as could be chosen for men still war-shattered. Their barracks were fortified with steel shutters and barbed-wire entanglements, as though they were in dug-outs in France. But here they lived in the midst of a populace where any man's hand or any woman's, might be against them. No social life was possible, and they spent their days in their fortified barracks, with occasional lorry drives at break-neck speed through the country, leaving terror and destruction behind them. They drank a great deal, and their usual raiding time was at night, when the villages trembled at the sound of their lorries coming through the dark and quiet country. As well they might tremble.

A policeman had been shot. It was the signal for a reprisal, and a reprisal meant the burning of a village. Very often the inhabitants had nothing to do with the first outrage, the perpetrators of which usually came from a distance. Then the neighbouring Big House might be burnt down, in turn, as a counter-reprisal. And so it went on, following the circle.

One of those days, as we drove to Dublin from Killeen, our car was pushed into the ditch by a lorry load of drunken Black and Tans. Filled with indignation, I drove straight to the Castle and demanded to see someone in authority. I was shown into Sir Matthew Nathan's old room. A tall pale man, whom I did not know, came to meet me. He was obviously a high official. He listened to my story and my denunciation of the Black and Tans and the policy of the Government in sending them to the country, with obvious feeling. When I had done, he said:

"Lady Fingall, undoubtedly things are being done in the King's name that cannot go on. But you must realise the life that these men live, in a country where every man and every woman is a potential enemy."

On October 20th Horace writes to me from Mount Street after he had spoken at a *Peace with Ireland* meeting.

"It was a bad speech, extraordinarily well received. Bad because it was a large (1500) audience, and the acoustic properties of the Hall were vile. If the distant audience didn't hear they made trouble. The effort to make them hear made it impossible to think, and I muddled my points. The report will look well if they take certain passages, bad if they take others. It was too logical to be free from the danger of having one side of the argument only reported. For instance, I condemned murder as much as Lloyd George, but denied that it was at the instance of the better Sinn Feiners—or of any but a murder gang. I then went for Lloyd George on his reprisals speech. No report will give both sides of that part.

"I have heard a good deal more of the political situation than I can send through the post. It is very, very dark. I don't know whether I can accomplish anything, though I think I may save the Co-operative movement from destruction."

I find that an impassioned correspondence was going on at this time between Betty Balfour and myself. She accepts my facts, but accuses me of only seeing one side, and sends me in return reports of outrages committed by the Irish side. But one of her letters says:

"Miss Somerville[1] is here, telling me terrible stories of the Black and Tans."

That winter Horace is in America again and in the Sanitarium at Battle Creek, from which he writes to me on Christmas Day, 1920:

"I am reading Margot's indiscretions. You would certainly be interested in them, and I shall bring them home. . . . She certainly had your genius for making friends with interesting people."

Presently travel was made difficult. Trees blocked the roads as they had blocked them after the Big Wind, trenches

---

[1] E. Œ. Somerville.

395

were dug every night, bridges blown up, and the first car going that way in the morning unwarned, would be wrecked. Trains carrying soldiers were held up when the railwaymen refused to work them. With bridges gone, some railways were not used for months, and the grass grew over them.

One of those nights Horace, driving home from Dublin, found a party of young men digging a trench outside his gate. They had just begun, and they made way for his car to pass. He said: "If you dig that trench across the road, you are going to block my way to Dublin!"

They agreed politely that they had not thought of that. They had been ordered to block the road against military lorries that might pass; but the trench would do just as well the other side of the Kilteragh gate, and so they moved their tools and began again, a few yards down the road.

In June, 1921, General Sir Robert Hutchison[1], who had been in Ireland during and after the 1916 Rebellion, and had become a friend of ours, wrote to me from the Rhine, where Killeen was now on the Staff of General Morland, Commander-in-Chief.

"GENERAL HEADQUARTERS,
"BRITISH ARMY OF THE RHINE.
"June, 26.

"MY DEAR LADY FINGALL,—I was delighted to hear from you. The boy's all right, and we will keep an eye on him!

"We (Chief and I) all went to Mayence on Wednesday and stayed with Degoutte, who commands the French. He lives in a lovely old palace which belonged to the Nassau family —no doubt Killeen will tell you all about it.

"I have passed the *Round Table* on to K. I quite agree with that able article on Ireland.

"More than a year ago I told L. G. my views on Ireland and also recommended a solution on the Dominion plan. I think in his heart he agreed, but his fellow Cabinet Ministers could not or would not move from force.

"Oh, the pity of it! Force will do no good. The English

[1] Now Lord Hutchison of Montrose.

396

are stupid people, and knock their heads against walls until either the head or the wall breaks; they do not realise that they are up against the Irish people. You cannot break a people. The end will be a settlement by negotiation. Why not now rather than later? An evil spirit exists in certain quarters in London, and until that is removed the bloody war will continue. I would not go to Ireland under present policy—that I have told them. The regular Army is being put in a false position, most unfair. So much do I feel about the whole thing that I am contemplating going into the political strife purely on the Irish question. I have been asked to do so, but I doubt whether I could exert any influence in the House, and perhaps I could do more as a soldier. Until I see clearly I won't move.

"I have just returned from a visit to Silesia, where we have another Irish situation. Germans—Ulster; Poles—the South and West of Ireland; but luckily, at present, no murders. I think the situation there will clear in a very short time, but it requires goodwill in Paris and London about all things.

"Herself sends her love to you and I my sympathy for your distracted country.

"Very sincerely yours,

"R. HUTCHISON."

That month things were at their very worst. One day came a letter to Horace from Mother Morrogh Bernard at Foxford, enclosing a report of atrocities committed there by the Crown forces. The note recorded the fact that Foxford had been one of the most peaceful towns in Ireland—no doubt largely owing to her influence, although she would not say that—and was practically the only place where the police continued to patrol without arms. Yet on the night of May 27th military had arrived from the neighbouring town of Swinford and rounded up a number of young men in the town. Some of these were taken to Swinford, stripped, their bodies painted by an officer, yellow, white and green—the Sinn Fein colours—and then they were thrown into the river.

Shots were fired at them whenever they lifted their heads above the water to breathe. After some time the soldiers left, and the victims were able to struggle to shore and reach a neighbour's house, where hot drinks and warm clothes no doubt saved their lives.

The officers responsible, meanwhile, returned to Foxford, and took out the remaining prisoners who had been left there, to the bridge over the Moy. Here these, too, were stripped and appallingly ill-treated, beaten and also painted green, white and yellow. In each case the religious emblems the men wore were torn from them and insulted. Then they were asked if they could swim, and on their saying that they could not, they were told, "that they were going to meet their God," and flung over the bridge, an eighteen-foot fall into the river. The depth of the water saved them, and they were able to creep under one of the arches of the bridge and hide while a searchlight was played on either side of it. Even after the searchlight had ceased and the soldiers had gone away, satisfied that their victims were dead, the wretched men were afraid to move. It was two hours before they dared leave the arch to which they had been clinging, and make their way to shore.

This is the briefest account of what had happened. The report of the old nun, who was truly the Mother of Foxford, was full of just horror and indignation. No charge had been brought against any of these boys, she recorded. And they had been lying in bed at the time when an attack had been made on Foxford Barracks the previous morning, presumably the excuse for the outrage. There had been no casualties in the attack.

Horace wrote to me in London:

"June 21, 1921.

"I suppose there is no objection to the typewriter when I work it myself.

"To-day I received from dear old Mother Bernard the enclosed report of happenings at Foxford. My first idea was

398

to write a furious letter to the press. I flew into Dublin to see Father Finlay, but he was not to be found. I then went to the Castle, where there was no one in authority except Cope, who, I had been told, was to be trusted. After a long consultation with him I got a promise that a thorough inquiry should be made immediately. On this understanding I agreed to suspend all action until I heard the result of the inquiry. The old lady had asked me to bring the matter before Lord Fitzalan, and I said I should ask you to do this. Even if you have seen him, I think you should see him again, as this is such a splendid opportunity for him to do a real service both to the Church and the poor of the country he has got to rule. . . ."

He added a note of the result of the inquiry:

"The atrocities reported by the nuns at Foxford, and made the subject of a special inquiry by the military authorities at the request of Sir Horace Plunkett addressed to Sir Nevil Macready, prove to have occurred substantially as stated by the Reverend Mother. The officer responsible is being severely dealt with. Sir Horace feels that his intervention in the case and Sir Nevil having dealt with it personally, renders it improper to make any propagandist use of the facts."

A Sister of Charity tells me that they remember at Foxford the great pride Mother Bernard felt when she heard that someone in a London drawing-room had spoken of "this little nun's audacity in defying the British Army," adding: "Who is this nun?" And I, being present, had stood up and answered:
"You need not query anything Mother Bernard says. If it comes from her, it is true, and her motives are unassailable."
Mother Bernard thought it very courageous of me to defend a friend where she had no friends. But that did not need much courage.
The great old nun herself was over eighty when she faced

the British Government and the Crown forces in defence of her people.

These things happened in beautiful summer weather. It was a wonderful and unforgettable summer, that of 1921. Such long evenings over the quiet country where there was Curfew now at eleven o'clock and motor Curfew at seven o'clock, so that the country seemed to belong to the sheep and lambs and birds, who were not bound by Curfew, and did not recognise it! But people are ill at night, and babies frequently choose to be born during those hours, knowing nothing of Curfew, either. The doctors drove in fear, and messages summoning them must be carried on foot by the poor, who have no telephones. And such messengers made terrifying journeys and were sometimes shot "by mistake."

Mails were raided and searched frequently—by the other side—and our letters might arrive with a Censor mark. Not the familiar Censor mark of the War days, but a blue pencil scrawl: "Passed by Censor, I.R.A." We poor moderates those days had a bad time, walking in the middle of the road and likely to get hit by the bullets from either side. More than ever at Kilteragh the sad Irish Question was discussed.

Gerald Heard, Horace's secretary since 1919, refers to those last years at Kilteragh as "the twilight." Lord Coventry had ceased to come over, as had a good many others. Those who came were serious and anxious, concerned with the Irish Question.

The Desmond MacCarthys—a charming and distinguished literary couple—came. He had Ireland in his mind and on his mind those days, being one of the people working in London for a settlement. And Aubrey Herbert had come earlier, I think, a knight as always, championing all oppressed people. Now, alas, he was going quite blind after his distinguished War service in which he had triumphed miraculously over that handicap. And J. M. N. Jefferies, the brilliant *Daily Mail* Correspondent, whom we called "the stormy petrel," because no peaceful happenings ever brought him to our Irish shore.

We used to go often to Kilteragh from Killeen for the week-end. Gerald Heard remembers that Fingall derived amusement on these visits, from weighing himself very carefully at his Club on Saturday before he went out to Kilteragh, and then again when he returned on Monday. He used to say that he could alter his weight by two or three pounds by taking every dish that was offered to him, and then sitting still and listening to the conversation. He always went off early to Mass on Sunday, and remarked once that in no circumstances would he miss that, because, whatever wise people might think of religion, he didn't know, but he knew that if he chose to leave the Church, he was quite free to do so. What he felt a gentleman was not free to do, was to belong to an organisation and break its rules.

Meanwhile that lovely spring and summer of 1921 progressed, and with the days the campaign of terror on both sides increased and lengthened.

There was a man named Michael Collins, of whom Scarlet Pimpernel stories were told. He had a price of some thousands of pounds on his head, and a description of him was posted in every police and military barracks in Ireland. Those searching for him were always entering a room by the door when he had just gone out of it by the window; and so on. He had even gone into Dublin Castle, they said, disguised as a man with a coal cart, delivering coal. He had been arrested in a hotel on suspicion and compared with his own photograph.

"You are like Collins. But you are not he." And he was allowed to go.

That summer King George went to Belfast, insisted on making his own speech and being backed by his Ministers. He appealed for peace in Ireland. There followed Lloyd George's letter to de Valera suggesting a conference. A Truce was called. And presently Michael Collins was one of those who went over to London to negotiate the Treaty.

CHAPTER THIRTY

THE Laverys' house in Cromwell Place was a meeting ground for Irish people in those days. I had known Lady Lavery since she first came to London after her marriage. She had Irish ancestry, Martyn blood from Connemara, and although she came from America, she always adored Ireland and took a deep interest in Irish affairs. Her house had come to be a centre of activity for a political group whose aim was real freedom for Ireland, by friendly treaty with England.

Hazel Lavery was beautiful, intelligent and a wonderful hostess; and for us who were her friends, London will never be the same without that warm welcome she had for us always: "When will you come to dinner or lunch? Whom would you like to meet?"

She mixed her guests with gallant audacity. Michael Collins used to stay at Cromwell Place when he went over during the negotiations that preceded the Treaty. He was devoted to Hazel—and no wonder. At her house he and Arthur Griffith met intimately men like Lord Birkenhead, Winston Churchill and Lord Londonderry, and were able to talk things over in a friendly way as they could have done nowhere else. I remember so many interesting lunches and dinners at that house, with usually some important significance behind them. Dinner was often in Sir John's studio upstairs, which made such a delightful background. And it might be said truly that the Irish Treaty was framed and almost signed at 5 Cromwell Place.

I have been told that there was even a day when Hazel sat down to lunch courageously between Lord French, the ex-Irish Viceroy, and Michael Collins. It was a very short time since Lord French had escaped an ambush at Ashtown cross-roads, by the hairbreadth chance of an Irish train being in advance of its time!

LADY LAVERY.

Michael Collins was what he looked—a big simple Irish-man—and remained so. One day he was at lunch at Cromwell Place, with Lord Birkenhead as another guest. Hazel had a small Peke who was pawing at Lord Birkenhead under the table. Hazel looked down and called the little dog. "Oh, I am sorry. I thought you were making advances," said Lord Birkenhead.

Up rose the big I.R.A. leader, towering over him in wrath:

"D'ye mean to insult her?"

Hazel threw oil on the troubled water quickly: "Lord Birkenhead was only joking."

"I don't understand such jokes," said Collins.

The Treaty was signed in December. The British troops left. The English flag was pulled down from its flag-post in Ireland after more than seven hundred years and the new Irish tri-colour, with the white of peace between the orange and green, run up instead. The British troops departed and the soldiers of the new Irish Army, in their dark green uni-form, took their place. And at Easter, 1922, the Republican Rory O'Conor held the Dublin Four Courts against the newly established Free State.

Tim Healy had been made first Governor General. About the same time the Irish stamps were issued—not beautiful—a white map of Ireland on a red ground and a green ground. And the map appeared quite empty, which fact some cynics soon discovered, christening the stamps "empty Ireland." But an old countrywoman, peering at them for the new King's head, exclaimed: "Sure, that's no more like Tim Healy than I am!"

Under his rule, the Viceregal Lodge was run with sim-plicity and dignity. He was a man of great taste, and collected Waterford glass before others knew its value. He had a wonderful collection on his dinner table. Also he collected Spanish gold plate, which should be even more rare and wonderful now.

One day I was lunching at the Viceregal Lodge and sitting

beside the Governor General. He asked me if I noticed any difference in the dining-room. I looked round and discovered that the two ugly black marble chimney-pieces that I had always known there had been replaced by two lovely Bossi ones. All the Lords Lieutenant had put up with those others, but Tim Healy could not bear to look at anything so ugly.

After many years of enmity—bitter on one side—John Dillon and Horace had come together in a mutual concern for the country they both loved.

Horace writes to John Dillon from Kilteragh on Good Friday, 1922:

"MY DEAR DILLON,—We have both been silent spectators of the amazing ups and downs—mostly downs—of our public life. I am absorbed in the activities which centre at Plunkett House. I think I should go mad if I were not. I often wonder what you are thinking. I know you have for long held that certain developments have to work themselves out before Ireland can begin to build the future for which, if only the destruction would stop in time, economic conditions seem favourable. Do you see any light?

"If you are in Dublin, would you care to lunch Sunday? I shall have Lady Gregory and Professor Henry, the arboriculturist, at the meal. As there is no post, will you phone if you get this?

"Yours sincerely,
"HORACE PLUNKETT."

On the 24th May he writes to me from London:

"I am utterly unable to understand the new 'pact.' It looks like a complete surrender by Collins and Griffiths to the de Valeraites. The Belfast situation contains material for the biggest kind of explosion, and British opinion may get roused if the Treaty is torn up and the missing officers are not accounted for. Still I don't think there is any danger of the

Black and Tan régime being restored. An economic blockade is a more serious possibility. This would mean unrestricted looting of the well-to-do."

The next day he writes again:

"The Irish news is getting steadily more alarming. I dread this drift to Civil War. I do not see the Irish papers, but the English papers suggest that they dare not tell the truth. The actual position seems to me to be this. The Free Staters could not preserve order or start any kind of government against armed opposition, nor could they come to any agreement with the Opposition except by throwing over the Treaty, which they seem to have done. And now Craig has given them the excuse they wanted for this, by declaring that the Northern Government would not take part in the Boundary Commission which is part of the Treaty. The total exclusion of the unarmed (or rather the disarmed) majority of the Irish people makes the situation wellnigh hopeless. This is the chief evil of the Lloyd George Irish policy. Lord, how plainly we foresaw it all, and how blind the 'Moderates' were to their vital interests!"[1]

I was staying in London in July, 1922, at Princes Gate, and in the middle of a big dinner on a Saturday night was taken suddenly ill. A doctor was sent for and diagnosed acute appendicitis. I was ordered to a nursing home at once, to be operated on the next morning, and was carried down to the waiting car by two of the dinner guests—Douglas Haig and the Duke of Leeds. In all my agony I could not help feeling that I was making a distinguished exit!

All the great surgeons were away for the week-end, and when I was brought down to the operating theatre in the morning I found, gazing down at me, three young men, who looked as if they had hardly left school.

"Which of you boys is going to cut me up?" I asked.

[1] This is a reference to the Convention.

The youngest looking one said, "I am."

I asked: "Have you ever done it before?"

He laughed: "I wish I could count the times."

"Well," I said. "Remember one thing: it takes a lot of chloroform to put me off. I lap it up."

As I was going round and round in space, the last words I heard were: "She does lap it up!"

On July 4th, Horace wrote from Kilteragh, to me in London:

"The isolation is more complete than in the Easter rising. No posts for anywhere but England and America, etc. And this only from Kingstown. I think Dublin will be evacuated by the Anti-Treaty forces, which will repair to the hills. How long it will take to end the tragedy, God knows. If you were well I should be glad you are not at Killeen. I have no reply to my wire to Fingall. If there was any probability of getting my car to him I would go and fetch him. All is quiet, I think, in Meath, but the surroundings of Dublin on the North side are very disturbed, and I should probably have the car taken before I got to Killeen.

"At this point I had to go into Dublin and to my great joy I find on my return your cheery, plucky wire. I hope it is *quite* true that you are going on so splendidly. You have suspected something wrong about your appendix for some time, and I trust you will now have great rejuvenance. Do send me a bulletin to-morrow. If you are still doing well I shall have no anxiety.

"In Dublin I gathered that the fight there may soon be over. . . .

"The I.A.O.S. is to get a substantial grant from the Provisional Government. If it gets one from the Northern Government I shall be able to save it. It will be impossible to have a meeting of the Committee on the 11th, I fear, as so many of the railways are broken up. But if things improve in the next few days I will decide upon a plan that will enable the work to go on."

I was ill for a long time after my operation, and life at Princes Gate with so many people coming and going was too much for me. I was glad to get back to the comparative quiet of Killeen, even in those troubled days.

Horace writes to John Dillon again on August 12th:

"I am in no heart to write now, but I may attempt one more volume on my Irish and American experiences with the main purpose of leaving behind me some ideas upon rural civilisation which others may have more success in applying to life than I have had. Politics, though little to my taste, cannot be avoided and there are two questions upon which I am anxious to know the truth because they affect my attitude to the Ulster difficulty as we have known it.

"In the settlement Redmond tried to bring off in 1916, though I dare say you never had any hope of it, I gained the impression that Lloyd George smoothed away the partition difficulty by letting Redmond believe that it was merely a temporary expedient and assuring Carson that it would be permanent. The other matter is more important and I think is of public record. I have always thought that Asquith's failure to call Carson's bluff in 1911 or 1912 (I forget which it was) one of the greatest political blunders in our times. If the Prime Minister of England had then said to the House of Commons and so to democracy and the world: ' Here is a Privy Councillor, who in a year or two may be Lord Chancellor of England, actually announcing that he will drill and arm a section of His Majesty's subjects to challenge the supremacy of Parliament if it dares to do what the Cabinet are asking it to do, etc.' I personally believe from remarks made to me by Sinclair and Andrews, Carson would not have had the support of " Big Business" in the North. Be this as it may, the excuse I have heard made over and over again for the Government of the day is that the Nationalist leaders advised against taking Carson seriously or at any rate doing anything which might make him a martyr. I should greatly like to know the truth on these two points and

I know none so likely to have the facts as yourself. Needless to say I should not quote you without your consent.

"I hope you are in good health. Any time you want a quiet afternoon where shooting is less frequent than in Dublin let me know and come. Of course we have no telephone."

John Dillon's answer to this was lost, with all Horace's other letters, in the destruction of Kilteragh.

Again he writes on August 14, 1922:

"My dear Dillon,—I have a Horse Show party from which I shall be glad to detach myself for a quiet talk. Thursday is the best day for me as the I.A.O.S. Committee meets Friday morning and may sit indefinitely. I cannot use my motor or keep it here. I have to warn my guests not to come by motor as the Republicans are in possession of this district. The 12.15 train is the best for lunch and I will expect you by it unless I hear to the contrary.

"No, I had not heard of Griffith's death. I too deplore it. He was not a gunman. The situation is greatly worsened by his passing.

"Yours sincerely,
"Horace Plunkett."

"Taxis are not taken—so far—from this house. I reopened to say that if you preferred Sunday you would meet Bernard Shaw. I don't know whether he attracts you ! Kindly wire if you make this change."

Arthur Griffith had died on August 12.

At the week-end I was one of that memorable party to which John Dillon had been invited. The Bernard Shaws were staying at Kilteragh. On Saturday morning Hazel Lavery telephoned to me from the Salthill Hotel, Monkstown, where she and Sir John were staying:

"Do you think Sir Horace would like me to bring Michael Collins over to supper to-night?"

Horace and the Bernard Shaws were much interested at

the idea of meeting the Rebel leader. And that evening they came, Sir John and Hazel, and Michael Collins, who wrote his name in the Visitors' Book in Irish: *Micéal O'Coleann.* Mr. W. T. Cosgrave was also of the party.

Collins was not at all an eloquent man, and my recollection of the dinner is that it was very quiet, and almost dull. The guests left early because Michael Collins said he had to be in Cork next day. A car with an escort followed them. I believe they went for a drive in the mountains and Collins left the Laverys back at their hotel at Salthill, saying: "I will be back in Dublin next week."

He *was* back the next week, to lie in state in the Chapel of the Sisters of Charity at St. Vincent's Hospital.

On Wednesday, August 23, we read the morning papers with horror. Later Mrs. Bernard Shaw and I were sitting together over the fire in the Kilteragh study, where Michael Collins had been with us such a short time ago. Suddenly the door opened and Hazel appeared, in deep mourning. She said:

"I knew it before I saw the papers. I had seen him in a dream, his face covered with blood."

Collins' party had been ambushed on the evening of August 22, just as the light was beginning to fail, near Macroom, in his own county of Cork.

He had said, "I don't suppose I will be ambushed in my own county." And on the Sunday evening on which he drove down from Dublin, he had laughed at the alarm of his town-bred driver, slowing up nervously at the sight of a little dark crowd at a cross-roads near Mallow. Did the driver not recognise the Cross-road dancing, familiar to a countryman?

Hazel and I went together to see him lying in state in that peaceful white Chapel of the nuns at St. Vincent's Hospital, with the tall candles burning at his feet and head. Four splendid young men, in the still unfamiliar green uniform, guarded him in his last sleep. Michael Collins lay in full uniform, and to him Death had given her full measure of beauty and dignity, increased by the effect of that white bandage round his head, which hid the wound made by the bullet that had killed him. His face had taken on an almost Napoleonic cast. I whispered a question to one of the young men, guarding him. Where had he been hit? Without speaking, the soldier touched the back of his own head. We said a prayer, and left him. That was the end of a paragraph of that chapter of Irish history, in the making of which he had played so large a part.

CHAPTER THIRTY-ONE

ON October 16, 1922, Horace writes again to John Dillon:

> "THE PLUNKETT HOUSE,
> "DUBLIN, Oct. 16, 1922.
>
> "MY DEAR DILLON,—As long ago as Sept. 20 I thanked you for a most interesting and kind letter you had written me on the 19th.
>
> "Looking over your letter again—and I shall read it and its contents probably many times—I find there is nothing particular to answer. But it will be very helpful to me if I write the book I feel I ought to write for the benefit of those who are working with me, and their successors, in the social and economic development which appears to me to be the best service for those of us who are either barred out of legislation and administration, or who have no taste for the political arena. I was very anxious to have accurate knowledge about the betrayal of the Parliamentary Party by the British Liberals. Once the Coalition was formed, one could expect nothing else. But I am bound to say the treatment of your Party in the years 1914 to 1916 is monumental in its perfidy. My experience of Labour people in England leads me to exonerate them. Indeed I think the whole blame should be placed on the shoulders of the Party leaders.
>
> "In regard to that article of mine on Foreign Affairs, I quite agree with you that the unity issue cannot be forced at this moment. At the same time, I see no prospect at all for peace in Ireland, or in either of the twenty-six or the six counties, until unity is either actually achieved or at least shows itself above the horizon. For this reason I think it well to bring moral pressure to bear upon those who are opposing unity, and to keep public opinion informed upon what I always call the 'dirty business of the clean-cut.'

"You may be interested to know that there is quite a chance of restarting the *Irish Statesman* under a three-year guarantee, which would ensure its being kept alive for that time. It would be bound to support the Treaty; its Charter would preclude excursions into Bolshevism, etc., but otherwise the Editor and a small Council of sound advisers would be absolutely free. I have a feeling that a paper which had a limited circulation, but which went to the important press of Britain, the United States, and the Dominions, and which explains the Irish situation with absolute candour, although, one would hope, with an understanding sympathy, might react upon whatever public opinion in Ireland moves the young men who have taken charge of our destinies.

"The last pronouncement of the Bishops of your Church appeared to me to be a remarkably fine and courageous document. I wish it could have come earlier. The next few days will be highly critical. I do not know what measures the Provisional Government have in contemplation, if there is not a pretty large surrender of arms, stolen property, etc., but it looks as if things could not drag on as they are going now.

"Yours sincerely,

"HORACE PLUNKETT."

That autumn and winter the Irregulars had started the campaign of burning country houses. It began as an organised plan directed against members of the new Irish Parliament, in an effort to force them to resign and make the Treaty unworkable. To be a member of the Senate meant that your house was automatically put on the Black List. As a result of this policy, the bad landlords who had remained aloof from Ireland and from the people, might go scot free. But those who had tried to serve the country, were, for this very service, put on the list of those to be destroyed. And, in the end, of course, the burning was not confined to Senators' houses. It became a bonfire for a generation that was having its full fling and escape from the dullness of Irish rural life. (Which

412

we had tried to alleviate, but they had found a better game than our Hurling and Camogie!) Motor-cars were free for the taking, petrol unlimited. Some made the most of this wild hour, before they went back to the hard work on the farm and the parental tyranny that existed to a peculiar degree in Irish country life.

Horace writes to me on November 27 of that year from Algeciras, where he and Lennox Robinson had gone to look for health and sun:

"The news of Childers' execution has come. I knew the man well and am quite sure of his absolute sincerity in his disastrous fanaticism. I doubt not he met his fate with fortitude and am sorry for him and those he leaves . . ."

On December 2 he writes to me again from Algeciras:

"Erskine Childers' execution was, I suppose, unavoidable. Had I been in the Government, I should have offered him his life if he would undertake to leave Ireland absolutely alone. He would probably have refused. . . . Beyond all question he was sincere in his insane hatred of Imperialism. But up to the time that we fell hopelessly apart, he was building up the case for his future action. His bravery, ability and industry were all of a very high order. If only he had taken a sound line he would have been by far the ablest man in Irish affairs. It is a tragedy if ever there was one."

On December 28th from the S.S. *Adriatic*:

"A very rough passage so far. I have not the facility of living in the past that you have, but I do it in a queer way. I bring up the memory of those far days when I travelled in small boats, and in such bad weather as this was miserable. We shan't be on land till the 2nd if this gale does not stop.

"Nobody interesting on board except (I suppose, for I have hardly spoken to her yet) Mrs. Clare Sheridan. She tells me

413

that her father Moreton Frewen is done for—won't live long. She talks of him as quite a good fellow and the best company she knows. The only other thing she told me, you no doubt know. She got into the Law Courts the last day before they were surrendered and burned. Rory O'Conor, she says, was much more intellectual than Mick Collins. The latter, however, had a 'splendid physique.' But he was wholly ignorant, and without any but military capacity of the guerilla kind. . . .

"I am devoutly wishing you the New Year your courage and unselfishness deserve."

Meanwhile, the country houses lit a chain of bonfires through the nights of late summer and autumn and winter and early spring. People who were wise, got their best treasures away to England. But that was not always possible, or they left it too late. And when the burning party came, often kind and helpful and sympathetic: "We can give you fifteen minutes and we'll help you. Will you hurry now!" it was impossible to remember what one most wanted to save. And often it was valueless things that were stacked on the lawn, to be examined when the cold day broke on the blackened walls and ashes, while the Romneys and the Chippendale furniture and Waterford glass, or old Irish silver, had perished!

Like the previous raiders, these spoke often with familiar voices and they knew their way about the house, and, if there was a bomb to be laid, where to lay it. If they did not know the house, perhaps somebody inside had told them. People whose families had lived in the country for three or four hundred years, realised suddenly that they were still strangers and that the mystery of it was not to be revealed to them—the secret lying as deep as the hidden valleys in the Irish hills, the barrier they had tried to break down standing as strong and immovable as those hills, brooding over an age-long wrong.

It was those who had tried to atone for that wrong and to break down that barrier, who did most of the paying.

414

That question of what should be saved. An Irish gentleman, if he were worthy of the name, thought first of the people in his house, then of his dogs and the horses in the stables, and the cattle in the yard if the fire should spread through the hay and corn. Ten minutes. A quarter of an hour. The pictures must go if the horses were to be saved.

Because Lord Mayo was a Senator, they came to burn Palmerstown, wearing, several of them, since it was a cold night, the woollen jerseys which Lady Mayo had just given them. There was time to save either her pearls in her bedroom, or her fowl in coops under the dining-room window, where they would, inevitably, be roasted alive. I think her pearls were not insured. She hesitated only a second. Saved the fowl, and the pearls went.

They came, one of those nights, to Castletown, which holds as many wonderful things as a Museum and a Picture Gallery. They brought fifty gallons of petrol to burn the house, with its wonderful hall and the staircase that I remembered—where I had had that vision of the ladies of another time going up to bed with their candlesticks—its Vandycks and Hogarths, and the portrait by Sir Joshua of Squire Tom Conolly, husband of Lady Louisa, who was sister to the Duchess of Leinster and aunt of Lord Edward Fitzgerald; the vases with the Eagle on them, given to a member of the family by Napoleon, and the countless other treasures. All these, and the great historical memories of Castletown, were to be laid on the smoking pyre of the new Ireland. Just before the petrol was thrown, a motor-cycle came up the long avenue in a great hurry. And a breathless young man, with some mysterious authority, rode into the middle of the group of burners, to say that on no account was the house to be touched that had been built with Irish money by William Conolly, who was Speaker of the Irish House of Commons two hundred years or so earlier. So the petrol was loaded up again and probably used elsewhere. But Castletown was saved and still stands, looking with its many windows (three hundred and sixty-five of them, I have been told) and its air of unassailable dignity and tradition, across its wide park to the Dublin and Wicklow mountains.

Horace was away a great deal during those years which Gerald Heard calls "the twilight." When he was at Kilteragh he was often not equal to entertaining. He began to feel the house too big for him in the changing post-war conditions and had thought of giving it to Ireland for some national purpose, and building himself a small bungalow in the grounds. He sailed to America that December, and was busy, as usual, trying to collect money for his Irish schemes, when Gerald Heard wrote to me from Kilteragh—where he was now living, with Murray the chauffeur as sole domestic staff, and Lennox Robinson, neighbour at the West lodge— on New Year's Day, 1923:

"MY DEAR LADY,—I was so rushed, sending off the household, that I find I have let your kind letter stand over unanswered for days. I sent you ' Babbit ' the day before yours came, and since then there has been nothing to report. Sir Horace could not get a letter through from Cobh as none of the liners could call there on account of this sun-spot weather.

"The only two items of news are, first, that Lennox's father died on Saturday and he has gone down this wild night by boat to West Cork. The old man was, however, eighty-four. The other thing is not so near but far more tragic. A man on the Plunkett House staff was, as you have probably seen, taken out and murdered in a lane by Milltown station. I knew all about him and he had been mixed up with a lot of trouble. It was a horrible business.

"Well, after Death and Murder, I lamely wish you well for the New Year. Please also convey my duty to the Earl. At least I may hope that you are now up and I trust that you are really getting ready for Cannes. The rain and cold have been severe lately.

"For myself I was never better, T.G. We are said to have—— (a famous I.R.A. Leader) from Kerry, with a column

416

of die-hards in the district, but so far I have had no visitors and very few others have even seen an irregular . . ."

A little more than a month later, Gerald Heard was to see the irregulars. He and the chauffeur were now sleeping at opposite ends of the house. Before going to bed on this particular night, he had drawn all the fuses of the downstairs lights, so as not to give any one who might break in a chance of seeing their way about. He had also locked up the house. He stayed up reading that night until after twelve o'clock. And he heard, at intervals, in the distance, several loud explosions, which, he learnt afterwards, were other prominent Senators' houses being blown up. It was one o'clock before they reached Kilteragh. A knocking came on the door and a challenge to those inside to open. They refused. Finally they broke in at the pantry, and Gerald Heard, with Murray, met them there. There were about twenty, all armed, and rather feebly masked. They argued for a little while— he says—after which, he and Murray were taken out under an armed guard, and kept standing by the garage until the mine that had been laid blew up. The raiders then left, apparently, and Gerald Heard and the chauffeur returned at once to the house, to find it heavily wrecked, all doors and windows gone, several of the floors blown through, and great extents of wall and ceiling brought down. The rest of the story is best told in his own words:

"That morning, as soon as the offices were open, I got into the Government Building, and asked for a guard. The Government was then hiding behind barbed wire and they refused to send any one. I next got a builder to come out and begin to board up some of the windows, for people were hanging about to loot the place, and already a respectable-looking woman had driven over in a pony trap and had begun to dig up the rose trees in the front beds. The builder, however, did not send any one till midday and the men would not stay when the light began to fail. The house was too wrecked for Murray

417

to stay in it, but my wing was not quite uninhabitable so I stayed there. At one, I heard steps outside and, looking out, could see a figure. On asking who he was, he came out into the light and was a Civic Guard. He said he would be on the spot all night. He cannot have been so, for within two hours the house was ablaze. It was noticed by the steward's son, for there was a very strong wind from the West and it carried the smoke —for the house was burning at its East end—into his window in the East lodge. They (the steward's son and Murray) ran along and warned me. I thought that it would only be possible to get out through the window, but on our getting to the stairs, they at the foot and I at the top, it was found still possible. The telephone exchange had been thoroughly wrecked for some months, so we could tell no one, and, of course, no neighbours would come near the place. We three tried to move what we could out of the Library, which was only then beginning to burn, and from the hall which was, when we began, only on fire on one side. We worked till dawn. By then the house was a shell and the larger pieces of furniture in the West wing were all out . . ."

This is Lennox Robinson's account of the burning:

"I was living at the time in one of Sir Horace's lodges, the one near the post office. On the first night, I was sitting up late, talking to a friend, and there was a knock on the door. It was Gerald Heard, who had come to tell me that men had forced an entrance into Kilteragh, had exploded land mines in the hall and in the study, had set fire to the house, and gone away. Mr. Heard had succeeded in putting out the fire. My friend and I went up to Kilteragh with him. The Great Hall—half hall, half sitting-room—was a dismal sight. The explosion had blown out every pane of glass, the electric light was extinct and the wind blew dismally through the dark room. It was a dry, cold, windy night. We smelt burning and found that a fused electric wire in a bedroom upstairs was starting a fire but it was a very small one and we easily quenched it. Mr. Heard was living alone in the house and I begged him to come back with me for the night, but he refused.

"I saw him next morning. We went into Dublin together, I to my work, he to try and get military protection for the house.

"I got back from Dublin about six o'clock and went to Kilteragh. I knocked and rang but could get no answer so went home and eventually to bed.

"About eight next morning I was awakened by knocking. I went down to find Mr. Heard in an exhausted state in the porch. He managed to tell me that the raiders had returned, got into the house while he slept and set fire to it. It was utterly burnt out.

"The flames had wakened the gardener, living in the other lodge and he had managed to rouse Mr. Heard and together they had saved a little of the furniture—but very little. I put Mr. Heard to bed—never a strong man, he was in a state of collapse—but he managed to remember Sir Horace's American address, and the code word he had made for use in such an eventuality. The word was 'Extinct,' and it was my melancholy task to cable it to Kilteragh's master.

"It was difficult that afternoon to guard the furniture that had been saved from looters. One respectable couple drove over in a trap and proceeded calmly to dig up plants and bulbs. They seemed quite surprised when they were forcibly restrained."

So that was the end of the house that Horace had built for Ireland, the meeting place of so many streams—often troubled waters—of Irish life. In the winter dawn Kilteragh stood in that country between the mountains and the sea, a shell, a symbolical shell perhaps. The flames, fanned by a West wind, coming from the mountains as the burners had come, had finished whatever the mine of the previous night had failed to achieve. That book-lined room where we had talked of Ireland, the dining-room, with its table of boundless hospitality, set beneath A.E.'s fairy sands and seas; the hall, where A.E.'s magic again had looked down on our musical evenings, and where Lord Shaftesbury had sung his Irish songs from the Ulster glens. The work of two nights had made an end of all these, and of our dreams that they had held. And in the grey winter dawn, only the blackened walls of Kilteragh showed coldly and desolately.

CHAPTER THIRTY-TWO

TIM HEALY told Horace afterwards that the house wrecker was a young man named Plunket who was then living up in the hills with a few followers, coming down at night to raid the suburbs and destroy the houses of prominent men. Healy told him also that this young man was later shot in a fight in the hills and killed. If this was true it would be in keeping with the strangeness of happenings in Ireland.

Horace wrote to me on the 17th February, from the *Cedric* which was bringing him back from America:

"I am off the Irish Coast and heavy hearted. I shall post this at Queenstown, although I have a feeling that unless some family necessity keeps you at Killeen, you will be awaiting me in London. You are always at hand when I am in trouble.

"I cabled to the I.A.O.S. for details of the destruction of Kilteragh, more particularly the safety of 'Martha' (my family's name for Mr. Heard—a real Martha in his care of Horace—which we had all adopted. E.M.F.), and the servants, after I heard the news from the Press.

"It merely told me that all are unhurt, but that the house was completely destroyed. So I do not know yet whether any of my priceless records and treasures were saved. I gather they are not, or I should certainly have been given this amount of comfort. Of course it means a terrible handicap of all that remains of my life's work. It is true I had almost decided to live in a smaller house in the grounds, if, as seemed likely, that course should be indicated by the state of the country. Martha and I had a plan for making the big house serve a really fine public purpose. I should have consulted you first. I meant to sell the greater part of the land and have a bungalow in the 'pleasaunce.' Even now the time may come for the latter part of the programme. But it would be horrible to gaze upon the ashes of my home and its contents—a hideous monument in such beautiful scenery.

"I have no plans except the *Irish Statesman* which I have developed in my own mind to a really great service to thought in and about Ireland. Of all those and other plottings and plannings, when the facts are known to me and your mind is revealed.

"I wish I knew your whole plans as far as they are made. Perhaps I shall, in less than forty-eight hours. I feel terribly the loss of that room of all rooms in my life—the Kilteragh study. It gave you a change from the unchanging atmosphere of the old Plunkett Castles."

He added a postscript:

"I am getting quick with the machine from practising on board. Now that I shall have so little clerical assistance in my homelessness it is a great gain to be able to write faster than with a pen, and more legibly."

The loss which Horace felt perhaps most, was that of his private papers. All his letters from famous men—Theodore Roosevelt, Colonel House, General Smuts, Cecil Rhodes, among many others—had perished, with such of mine as he had thought worth keeping.

I wanted Horace to stay in Ireland, to rebuild Kilteragh and remain in the Senate. Gerald Heard's influence was in favour of his going to England. And, of course, there was the question of his health. Dr. Scholl had said long ago at Nauheim, "What care I for his stomach with a heart like that!"

And now it was a broken heart.

Perhaps I was wrong. Perhaps his day in Ireland was over. Ireland has the cruelty of the very young to the old who have served her, when their day is past. It would have been worse perhaps for him to have stayed in Ireland and to have been out of the new Irish affairs.

On October 29, 1923, he wrote to me from London:

"You are giving me the best help over this Senate business. It was bad luck that it got into the papers before my letter of resignation which made a perfect case for the step. They will press me to reconsider, and all I shall say will be, that if later my health permits of the discharge of the duties and the country desires my presence on that august body, I can offer myself when a vacancy occurs."

Again he writes from Mount Street, on November 7, 1923:

"The vanmen are in the room, changing the nice dining-chairs you bought me long ago, for cheaper things. This flat will henceforth be but an occasional office."

He moved to England and established in London at 10 Doughty Street, the Plunkett Foundation, which was to supply information on Co-operation for inquirers from all over the world. And the dreams he had had for his own country went to the far ends of the earth where they were better appreciated. Lately George Adams gave three lectures to Chinese students at Nanking on Horace Plunkett's agricultural philosophy, and at Chee Loo in Shantung he was told: "We would like to have a photograph of Plunkett."

Horace took a furnished house at Weybridge, as a temporary residence while he searched for a permanent home. He wanted to be as near as possible to the top of St. George's Hill, where he would have that wonderful air and view.

When I was over, he and Gerald Heard were considering a house which I did not like. But I saw one next door which took my fancy immediately. I squeezed myself through an opening in the fence—being skinny I slipped through easily —and saw two young men sitting on the lawn. In my best manner I approached them and said: "Is this house to be let?"

They, for a moment, looked taken aback, and one of them said: "It is extraordinary! We were just speaking of putting it on the agent's books, as it is too far from our business in London."

I went over the house and discovered that it was almost the exact counterpart of Kilteragh, only on a much smaller scale. The same entrance hall, the same staircase, with a big window, the same library, only smaller, the same drawing-room going the width of the house, the dining-room with a long stoep off it, and a large balcony which would make an open-air sleeping place.

I went back and said to Horace: "I have found a house for you. I will look no further." He and Gerald Heard came in with me rather sheepishly, and went over the house. They saw others, but eventually my choice, The Crest House, was bought. Within its view was that unique institution, the Whiteley Village for old people, and on a sunny day you could see over London, with the Crystal Palace gleaming, and even to Windsor Castle.

Another strange thing was that the furniture which had been saved from Kilteragh fitted the new house as if it had been made for it.

By November Horace was moving in and writing to me:

"There is no doubt about the health and comfort of your choice. Till the furniture arrives from Ireland there will be no possibility of having guests, except the most familiar . . . I am lazily writing a good article for the *Irish Statesman* of November 24th. I think you will like it. All on Ireland's agricultural policy. . . ."

In April 1924 he wrote:

"When are you coming over, and when is Fingall coming to see if he likes The Crest House as well as Kilteragh? Alas, I don't, but it will be nearer to Brooks's."

In June of that year there is the earliest entry at the opposite end of the Kilteragh Visitors' Book—one of the things saved from the fire—which was now to hold The Crest House guests.

424

Colonel House and his wife are the first names written. Olive Guthrie and I were in the same party. Horace collected people at The Crest House as he had done at Kilteragh.

His old Irish friends came—among them, A.E. And the Laverys, and with them, Desmond Fitzgerald, a Minister in the new Irish Government. The Bernard Shaws and the Hannays. And George Moore. And Moritz Bonn, Horace's old pre-War friend, still a friend, although they had worked so hard against each other in America. And Kevin O'Higgins, the most brilliant man in the new Ireland, who might have done anything, if his career had not been cut short by an assassin's bullet, one Sunday morning as he walked to Mass. And Evelyn de Vesci came, as lovely, in her increasing age, as in her youth. And her daughter, Mary Herbert. And the Balfours, near neighbours at Fisher's Hill. Lord Passfield and Beatrice Webb, who refused to take her husband's title. Alice Holroyd Smyth and her lovely daughter Mary used to come too. And Colonel Chetwynd Stapylton and his niece Dorothy, who were a tremendous help to Horace in every way.

Some brilliant new friends—among them: Sir Arthur Lowes Dickinson, Julian Huxley, Naomi Mitchison.

But Irish people belong to Ireland and need their own background; and Horace must have been lonely often, looking from his windows at the lovely English countryside. Perhaps he would have been more lonely in the Ireland of those days. But The Crest House could never be Kilteragh. Nor could we ever recapture something that lay buried under those ruins and ashes.

CHAPTER THIRTY-THREE

HORACE's letters from The Crest House show where his heart still was. He wrote to me on December 21, 1923, as he was about to start for America:

"While the car is loading up for a sorrowful good-bye to the new home, a word of good-bye to you all. Tell them I shall be looking out over the waves to the other side of the island I still love, for the men and women who will ever please more than 'every prospect.'"

On 17th February, 1924, he writes to me from S.S. *Cedric*, on his way home:
"I am much better and think it is only a question of time and rest to get into health again. (He had been ill in the meantime.)
I shall never be able to work again as during the last thirty-five years, but I may be able to direct some useful work and help those I love for the remainder of my days—and after. I hope to see you soon."

On the 25th February, 1924, from The Crest House:

"I am distressed about the arthritis. I am afraid the Killeen air is not good for it. Why don't you and F. come and see whether the new Kilteragh is not a better change from the Valley of the Skane than the old?"

On February 27th, 1924, he writes to John Dillon.

"MY DEAR DILLON,—With my home and all its records of a life crazily devoted to Ireland an ash heap, I am struggling to get back some of my nervous energy. I still want to spend

426

most of my resources in helping to make things better where I belong. But I am warned to go slow for a time and have bought myself a house very inferior to Kilteragh, yet very healthy. I built Kilteragh as a meeting place for all genuinely interested in our country and if I achieved anything worth while, it was by assembling people there. My Visitors' Book was saved and it is a pleasure to look over the list of people who met there. I am always comparing my happier lot with that of those who lost their all in those terrible years. Do you see any light yet? Have you any hope? You probably never looked for gratitude in public life but you must have a good deal of satisfaction in your long work for the tenants. It is hard to explain everything that has happened, but if I can write the story of the last years of British rule, the part played in the tragedy by Lloyd George may appear in a new light. The loss of all my papers, including, by the way, a most illuminating letter you were good enough to write upon your and Redmond's negotiations with Kitchener and others, will make the task almost impossible. But publishers are pressing me and I may try to bring out some of the truth. I can't make myself more unpopular than I did with a book which I wrote twenty years ago!

"I hope the reduced strain has improved your health. I sometimes think nothing but health matters.

"Yours sincerely,

"HORACE PLUNKETT."

On March 15, 1924, he writes to John Dillon:

". . . I dare say Griffith denounced me as a British spy and a great many other things, but I have no recollection of it. Someone once told me that he said I was an honest man, but so, very often, are spies . . .

"You asked me in a former letter if I was ever going back to Ireland and I cannot yet answer that question. The doctor won't hear of me doing so for some time because I am still cursed with insomnia . . ."

427

On the 1st May, 1924, he writes to me at St. Marnock's, where I was staying with the Jamesons.

"St. Marnock's is worth many Punchestowns. My love to Mrs. Willie. Ask her if Geordie has any message for me in the new circumstances. He told me to stick to my Irish work and I hope he knows why I don't—at least not as I wish."

On July 10, 1924, he writes to John Dillon:

"Do you ever come this side? If you do I shall suggest your running down here for a little visit and talk.

"Do you see any light yet? I wish the Boundary question could be left alone for a while. Until we have got our house in order we can do nothing with that neighbour. With your experience you will hardly expect England to do anything."

On October 23, 1924 (his birthday), he writes to me from Mount Street:

"When you get this I shall have completed the three-score years and ten which I should not have seen but for your care at many a crisis in my health. Furthermore, but for you I don't know that I should have wished to live so long. May you follow this much of my example and add another ten or twenty years in your unselfish and joy-giving life, to my record."

On February 11, 1925, he writes to John Dillon, from Mount Nelson, Capetown:

"Hertzog charges me to thank you for so kindly thinking of him and to assure you of his high appreciation of the thought. He is a nice fellow and so are many of his Ministers. But they have problems as difficult as you to face. The people here are however less 'temperamental,' and the situation is not so immediately critical.

"The voyage did me good—lots of good. But I must get up country or at any rate away from Capetown if I am to get a rest and cure my lungs. The difficulty is that Parliament meets in a couple of days and they are after me about agricultural co-operation which is taken up by the Government here and is largely based on my writings. So you may imagine it is difficult to escape interviews, meetings, conferences, etc. I always try and do a turn for Ireland as you will see if you skim the enclosed cuttings."

On 20th January, 1926, Horace writes to me:

"No! I have not taken to Clairvoyants—I have only studied another case of automatic writing. It is a much more interesting one than Geordie's, which is rather childish, though not more so than Raymond's. I was told confidentially that my medium had done a good deal of talking with Michael Collins, the 'sitter' being a friend of hers and mine. That explains the knowledge of two things by the medium—the visit to Kilteragh just before the poor fellow was killed and the talk about defending Kilteragh. When I first saw the writing the probability seemed to be that Michael Collins alone could have concocted the message: with the facts now known the probability is far more in favour of the usual explanation, namely, that the medium, quite unconsciously, draws upon information she has, and very likely has forgotten, and also upon the thoughts passing through the minds of others present. That last is the strangest phenomena of the lot. I mean the extraordinary acute observation of muscular movements which accompany thought. Of course this would be no explanation, were it not for two considerations. (1) Many people can and do write automatically, things unknown to them, once known but long forgotten or known only to others present. (Some say others absent.) The other explanation—that dead people are directing the writing hand, is far more difficult."

The following are taken from Horace's last letters. Though there were many others, they are not of any public interest.

"August 12, 1930.

(This was written shortly after Fingall's death.)

"I particularly intended to tell you that dozens of people asked me in Dublin what your plans were, and there was sincere delight when I told them that you were going to make your headquarters there. . . .

"Don't think I am sermonising when I say that there is no real happiness for the old except in making others happy. This you have done all your life, and it is time that it should bring you some reward for all the sacrifices it has cost.

"The flat will, I feel sure, turn out to have been a wise choice. It is in the healthy part of Dublin because the prevailing winds tumble down on it which made Kilteragh such a Hygeia. It is modern in all essentials, You will be warm, airy and well lit. The little kitchen will supply all your needs quickly, and housekeeping can be done by phone. Every one worth knowing in Ireland comes to or passes through Dublin. Without troublesome planning, you can visit friends in other parts of Ireland and you can run across to England. Your English and American friends you will be able to see much more often and easily than at Killeen. All things considered I don't see how you could possibly have arranged more wisely for the years that remain.

"Lastly I hope to see more of you and perhaps to do more work with you as in the far-off days when you helped me with the Viceregal people and in a hundred other ways. You had a much larger part in the agricultural co-operative movement than you realise. *The Times* I gave you, shows how it is forging ahead over here. The future of the Irish Free State depends absolutely upon the rural community—upon the improvement of the farming industry, the economical disposal of its products and upon the reorganisation of social life among all classes in the country districts. Young people must do the hard work of the United Irishwomen. But you must guide it. No one else understands its importance as you do, nor grasps the necessity of getting people to understand that the rural problem has its three sides, expressed in the Irish formula, Better Farming, Better Business, Better Living; which has gone all over the English-speaking world. Team work between the three lots of people who are working along these three lines is absolutely essential. The Better Living is the crux. You know all its difficulties, and with patience and sticking to the fundamental principles which you can talk over with such ' wise men ' as Father Finlay and A.E., you can surmount them in time. You could not do this from Killeen; you can from Dublin.

"I am getting very old and may crack up at any time. But my heart is as young as ever and it is yours. I have only one piece of advice to give you. Try not to think bitterly of the people you will have to meet, if you can help it. Follow the advice you have always given me and don't say them . . .

"And so to bed."

"THE CREST HOUSE.

"26 May, 1931.

"What memories that look at the Letterfrack Hotel brings back! I am glad you went out to the Wild West whence you came into the less romantic world.

"I suppose you will soon be coming over here and I do hope I shall be in a cheerier mood than when you were last in this wretched substitute for Kilteragh."

"Aug. 4, 1931.

"You will be in the midst of the Horse Show activities. For a few days, nothing but horses will be given a thought. I still think, notwithstanding all the worries, the Free State is in happier case than the rest of the world."

"THE CREST HOUSE.
"December 12, 1931.

"I am glad you endured the trip to Ballyragget and paid that well-deserved visit to one of the best priests in Ireland. I shall do my best to see it (Ireland) once more in January—and repeat the message we have tried to hand down from the

431

best of our forbears. It is impossible to forecast the future of Ireland or any other country in such times; but the principles you have backed in your own tactful way for some forty years are sound and have borne fruit more abundantly than you imagine . . ."

I had recently gone down with our secretary, Miss Franks, to open the new United Irishwomen's Hall at Ballyragget. On that expedition we had passed the ruins of many beautiful country houses which not long before had been occupied, and the centre of life and good work for the people; now "the monuments of Irish Freedom"!

Again on December 18th, 1931, Horace writes:

"The weather has turned cold, and I am confined to my bedroom—chiefly to my bed. I had a heavy day yesterday on colliery business. I forget whether you saw anything of Shortt when he was Chief Secretary. He is my most helpful director, excepting the Managing Director. The job gives me an insight into the appalling state of this country's business situation. The Government boosting propaganda is—rightly, I dare say—so optimistic, that it is well to be connected with some important industry. As the company does most of its selling abroad, we are made to realise how universal the depression is. Then again I am deluged with American correspondence. The change in that situation is more recent and more drastic than in other countries. I don't pretend to understand currency questions; but it is clear that the United States and France, having all or nearly all the world's gold, puts them in an exceptional position to ruin or save other countries. The former has enormous supplies of other assets and the latter has a huge colonial Empire to develop. America has some ten millions going hungry, while France seems to me to be the only country with an outlet for surplus population in Northern Africa.

"I don't know whether these facts and thoughts interest you when you have so many troubles nearer home to occupy your mind."

432

On 26th February, 1932:

"My temperature was 101 in the night and 95 in the morning. Low vitality and difficult to write.

"Lady Mayo is as fine a woman as I know. I wish we saw more of her. How clearly she sees through the people to whom she has devoted her life—and how splendid her acceptance of the facts and her courage in facing them."

And on 17th March, 1932:

"This is the first St. Patrick's Day that I have not been sent a shamrock wherewith to flaunt ' England's cruel red.' Significant!

"I was glad Ruth Draper came to see you.

"Came to town yesterday to hear Gerald Heard deliver a brilliant address, nominally upon Prison Reform, but really upon our civilisation generally. To-day I had to meet Constance Pim, one of our early U.I.'s. The Foundation gave her many hints for her work among the Quakers in the Welsh coalfields.

"De Valera has given us no hint of his policy. Beyond the Oath and the filching of the Land Annuities, which he won't get away with, he seems to have none at all. My own opinion is that he will give the only rulers we have got, a rest, which they badly want.

"Lady Denman came to the Foundation to-day, while I was there. Do you know her? She seems to have lots of sense. She is President of the Women's Institutes.

"The I.A.O.S. is in a bad mess, and I must go over and try to help it when I feel fit for the job. . . .

"I go home in the morning, and may find a letter from you."

That was Horace's last letter, written, strangely enough, on St. Patrick's Day, and talking of coming to Ireland.

He died at 7.15 on the evening of the 26th March, 1932.

433

CHAPTER THIRTY-FOUR

THROUGH the autumn of 1922 and the winter and the following spring, we, in the country houses, had awaited our turn.

During the Troubles of 1921 I had taken the precious Charters of Reading Abbey that had been found in the Priest's Hiding Hole at Woolhampton Court, to London, and, with Lord Coventry's assistance, had sold them to the British Museum. The day we took them, we lunched first at the Carlton, and then, still economy-minded from the War, we proceeded to the Museum by bus, Lord Coventry carrying the Charters under his arm. We had to change buses, and as I nimbly leapt on to the second bus and it started, I looked round, to see Coventry flat on his back on the pavement with the Charters clasped to his breast. The conductor refused to let me jump out until the next stopping-place. When I got back, I found Coventry with a crowd round him, being dusted, but fortunately none the worse, and we continued our journey.

At the British Museum we saw Sir Henry Howarth, who was deeply interested in the Charters. We had not thought of selling them, and were prepared to give them, since in the Museum they would be in safe keeping and in their right place. Sir Henry told us that these were a portion of the great Charters of Reading Abbey, of which they filled a very important gap. He began to add, that he was afraid the funds at his disposal might not permit him to offer us the price that we might expect. I was just about to say that we had not meant to sell them, when Lord Coventry held up his hand:

"I am quite sure that Lord and Lady Fingall would be glad that the Museum should have the Charters, and would not ask more than the Trustees could afford to pay."

After some correspondence we received about £300 for the

434

manuscript, and from our visit to the Museum we went home in a taxi! It was a relief in the later days of the Burnings to know that the Charters were safe.

We did what we could in the way of preparation, lest the fiery torch that flew through the country those nights, striking here and there, with now apparently little reason, should reach us. I made an excuse of having the drawing-room repainted by a local artist, to move the best furniture and the pictures into the Chapel. That was over the kitchen and less likely, for every reason, to be burnt than the rest of the house. They would probably spare the Chapel, and in many cases the servants' quarters were not touched. I sacrificed my beautiful pale green walls in the drawing-room and let the local painter do his worst with them. He was slow over the work, which suited me, as the decorating was only a pretence. Meanwhile, the things we valued most were stacked up in the Chapel and remained there.

Our neighbour, Summerhill—with its memories of the Empress of Austria and her hunting days—had been burnt in the earlier Anglo-Irish troubles by the I.R.A. The owner had been corresponding with the military authorities, who proposed to quarter soldiers in the house. He wanted to live there himself, and said so. Eventually he succeeded in persuading the British authorities to leave him his house. But, of course, in those days letters were often read in the post and enough of his correspondence had been tapped to put the I.R.A. on their guard. Unfortunately the final letter had not reached them. Having carried his point, the owner of Summerhill was in Dublin, engaging servants, and on his way home, when the house was burnt early one morning—by local people, it was said. If he had arrived home a few hours earlier he could have saved it.

In the autumn of 1923, the Burners came to Lismullen, the other side of the Hill of Tara. Sir John Dillon and his wife and daughter were at dinner, when a party of young men in some sort of uniform knocked at the door. Sir John went out, and the leader said to him:

"Sir John, we are very sorry, but we have orders to burn your house."

"But what have I done?" he asked, being one of the best landlords and kindest men in the country.

"Nothing yourself, Sir John, but there was a man killed on the road above, and this is a ' reprisal.'"

No use for poor Sir John to expostulate. Orders were orders, and the I.R.A. ruthless. They said that they would help him to get out his pictures and any furniture he particularly valued; but they must be quick, for they were going on to Killeen Castle—"and *that* would take a bit of doing!"

They cut some of the pictures from the frames that they could not take from the walls and carried them out with the most valuable furniture and silver. Someone remembered the gloves with the pearl-sewn gauntlets, that King James had dropped at Lismullen three centuries earlier as he fled from the Battle of the Boyne. They were flung through a window on to the lawn, where they were found in the morning. There was so little time and the usual confusion and uncertainty about what to save.

Still Sir John, good friend and neighbour that he was, managed to find a scrap of paper and a pencil and to scribble a note. Then he thrust it into the hand of a small barefooted boy, the son of one of his men, telling him to run as fast as he could with it over the Hill of Tara to his Lordship at Killeen. The second time in the Plunkett history that a warning had been carried by such a messenger across the Hill of Tara.

That night Fingall and I were sitting in his study after dinner, I reading, he asleep as usual. The shutters were closed and the lamps lit. It was, I suppose, somewhere about ten o'clock.

Suddenly I heard a sound at the window, behind the heavy shutters. I looked up from my book and listened. It came again. Someone was knocking on the glass.

"Fingall," I called. "Fingall! Wake up! There is someone at the window!"

436

Fingall came awake, with difficulty at first. "What did you say?"

The tapping was repeated, with a sound of increased urgency. Fingall got up, lifted the heavy iron bar that kept the shutters in their place, and pulled them back. Outside, a small face was pressed on the pane. So clearly did I see the little face in that startled moment, that, like the click of a camera taking a photograph, my mind registered it, and I can see it now.

Fingall pulled up the window. The autumn wind blew in, and with it a scrap of paper thrust by a small hand. Then the bare-foot messenger disappeared like a fairy into the night.

Fingall opened the crumpled note and held it to the light, to read the faint pencilled writing:

"DEAR FINGALL. They are burning my house, and they say they are going on to you. I thought I had better let you know. JOHN DILLON."

We looked out of the window. There was nothing there. Fingall pulled it down and closed the shutters again.

He refused to believe that they would ever burn Killeen, and it would have been a big job, as they said, with some of the walls six feet thick and stone floors in the basement and halls. However, we went upstairs and I collected what was left of the family jewellery in my jewel-case, and some other personal valuables, which I tied up in a blanket. The silver closet was built into the walls of the study, with an iron door behind the wooden one, which would have taken many tons of dynamite to blow up. Then I put on a fur coat, because the night was turning chilly, and we went downstairs again, made up the fire in the study, and sat down to await our visitors. Fingall fell asleep again.

Sitting there, one had time for thinking, while one waited, coming back every now and then from one's thoughts to listen sharply. The wind blew at the old windows. Presently

437

perhaps the headlights of a car would flash through a chink in the shutters. Or would they drive without lights?

They would probably come to the courtyard outside, as the people had always come—to Fingall's study door. And what would there be to stop them, with no walls about Killeen and no gatehouse, and only the simplest of gates that were never shut except to keep the cattle in? And I remembered how glad I had always felt about that open gate of Killeen, through which the country and the people could come in, and that there was such a green peaceful stretch round the Castle, and no high walls and thick woods shutting us into our kingdom, as at so many other country houses, which kept Ireland and the Irish people outside. I heard Father Morrisey talking in this room, many years ago:

"Isn't it grand to think that any one who likes can come up to this Castle and never be refused admission, with the gate always open!"

So the gate would be open to-night, I thought, and nothing to stop or delay Them.

My thoughts went on. How Killeen would burn. Badly— that old Norman Castle of stone, that had been built as a Pale fortress. Then I remembered the big oak staircase: that would send up a glorious flame. And I remembered, too, how I had often thought that Killeen would make a lovely ruin. And I saw it now in my mind, with the light falling through its empty window spaces and its battlemented walls lifted gauntly against the sky.

But there would be plenty of time to wake the servants and get them out, if it should ever reach their quarters. And the stables were well away from the house. I thought of a lot of things that night, sitting there with my jewel-case on my knee. Of how we had talked Co-operation in the Library, and how I had run from that to Fingall, planning his Meets in this room, with a map of Meath before him; and then back again to the Library, to Horace and his "Wise Men." Of how Horace was going to save Ireland by better business, which should lead to better living. And of those nights when

438

he first talked in the old Library upstairs, and a scatter-brained girl came back from her scatter-brained thoughts to listen to him. And Fingall woke up and listened and was unbelieving.

"You should not give the Irish anything that they do not ask for."

That was what the English were always doing; and now they had given them what they had once asked for—too late— when they no longer wanted it, but something else, and we were paying for that. And Kilteragh was in ashes. And they were on their way to burn Killeen. . . . But Oliver had said: "If we have had it all that time, it's somebody else's turn now."

At such a moment Life, and the faces it has held, and the experiences of it, stand out with a strange clearness, like the sharpening of a hill or a tree against the sunset, before the darkness covers them. So, in those hours, I saw pictures of the life that Killeen had held. For the destruction of a house must end a life and a way of living. One may build again, but it will not be the same.

My first vision of Killeen the night of the Ball, when it was all lit up like a fairy castle. Our arrival from our honeymoon. Bringing Oliver back as a baby and his welcome from the people. Hunting days, starting from the stables. Hunting teas about the fire in the hall at the end of a day. Hugh Lane and myself refurnishing the house; the parades of horses in the yard, from which Horace and I often fled to the garden to talk about orchards and tobacco growing. The tobacco plant glimmering beautifully at evening and—oh! the scent of it! Old Larry glaring at it and threatening to give notice because it was worse to manage than "a nursery of childer." And then the border that Sir Frederick Moore and I had made, and the beds of heliotrope—the one flower that Horace noticed and which he would stop to look at if he saw it growing anywhere—as once in a London park, his thoughts going back to Killeen and my garden there: "Whenever I see that, I feel that she is near!" Our apple orchard, which

439

only provided wood for the War. The smell of that blossom had been lovely, too. A. E. and his fairies, and the number of times he had cooled my anger with the peaceful waters of his voice. And our journeys about the country—that visit to Aran with the Balfours and returning at evening across an enchanted sea. And George Wyndham's dreams. My last vision of him—another heart broken by Ireland.

I half dozed and came awake. The wind blew on the window, not as it had blown that night of the Big Wind when we had slept in the hall. I remembered many storms rattling against these great walls and through the windows, and how I had often said that when I came out of my bedroom door I never knew down which staircase I should be blown. When they had burnt Killeen, I thought, we would rebuild it with the compensation money. We should have a smaller comfortable house for two people growing old, and their children and their friends. I thought of my struggles to heat Killeen, and how all the roaring wood and turf fires could only warm corners of those great rooms. We should have a lower house, well-fitting windows, no draughts or ghosts, and the bathrooms that I had always dreamed of, with plenty of hot water. I kept myself warm through the cold hours of darkness with these comforting thoughts, while Fingall slept, and I stayed awake, waiting for the burning party.

We waited all night. But they never came. They burned a small place on the way and then, perhaps, had had enough of it, and Killeen certainly "would take a bit of doing." And perhaps they were weary.

For the cold dawn broke on Fingall and myself sitting shivering in the study, with the fire going to ashes, I in my fur coat with my jewel-case on my knees. With the coming of that early light creeping through the chinks of the shutters, my warm and pleasant dreams vanished. Presently we pulled the shutters back and the study was grey and chilly in the morning light.

"They won't come now." And we climbed stiffly and

440

wearily up the great staircase to bed. We had crossed another river with that night, one that many of our friends had not crossed; and we were left—survivors, as our house was a survivor—to face the new day, with whatever it might bring, and whatever altered life it might hold for us to live.

THE END

INDEX

444

447

460497030307
087 695 8633